THE NEW AMERICAN JUDAISM

THE NEW
AMERICAN
JUDAISM

How Jews Practice Their Religion Today

JACK WERTHEIMER

PRINCETON UNIVERSITY PRESS

Princeton and Oxford

Published by Princeton University Press, 41 William Street, Princeton, New Jersey 08540
In the United Kingdom: Princeton University Press, 6 Oxford Street, Woodstock,
Oxfordshire OX20 1TR

press.princeton.edu

Library of Congress Control Number: 2018937067
ISBN 978-0-691-18129-5

British Library Cataloging-in-Publication Data is available

Editorial: Fred Appel and Thalia Leaf
Production Editorial: Jenny Wolkowicki
Jacket image: Participants of the annual Burning Man Arts Festival gather in the Black Rock
    Desert at Camp Sukkat Shalom to celebrate Shabbat. Photo courtesy of Bradley Portnoy
Production: Jacqueline Poirier
Publicity: Tayler Lord
Copyeditor: Joseph Dahm

This book has been composed in Adobe Garamond and John Sans Pro

Printed on acid-free paper. ∞

Printed in the United States of America

1 3 5 7 9 10 8 6 4 2

TO JOSHUA CHANAN AND JUDY ZEVA

AND DANIEL MELECH

WITH MY LOVE

Contents

Acknowledgments

My family and friends have sustained me while I worked on this book, and none more so than my wife, Rebecca. Throughout our lives together, she has been a partner in all my undertakings. Her reactions and insights as we've talked about my research have both challenged and encouraged me. No less important, her enthusiasm during the course of this lengthy book project has been heartening.

Our sons Josh and Daniel and daughter-in-law Judy also lived with this project over an extended period. Their gentle teasing (and not so subtle eye rolling) when I trotted out some new findings and also their willingness to engage seriously with the subject matter helped turn this book into a bit of a family affair. It is to them that I dedicate this book, with love and the hope that through their own lives they will help write new chapters in the evolving story of American Judaism.

A number of individuals played special roles in nurturing my work, through both their engagement with the topic of this book and their confidence in me. Neal Kozodoy and Riv-Ellen Prell read the manuscript with care, offering valuable suggestions for improvement. Their interest in my work preceded this book by many years. As editor of *Commentary* and *Mosaic*, Neal initiated me into writing for nonacademic audiences and continually has challenged me to draw out the implications of my findings. Riv-Ellen and I have worked on a number of research projects over the years, all of which have been enriched by her thoughtful observations. For over twenty years, Steven M. Cohen has collaborated with me on articles and larger studies. His incisive and consistently constructive suggestions have improved much of what I have produced. For this study, he ran numerous tables based on data collected by the Pew Research Foundation and without fail made himself available to answer my questions.

Since my earliest days as a graduate student, I have gained much from the wisdom and challenging observations of Ismar Schorsch and Benjamin Gampel; the former began as my mentor and the latter as my classmate in graduate school. As I worked through the material presented in this book, both eagerly engaged with me about my findings and their significance. The warm friendships we have shared for nearly half a century have been extraordinary gifts.

Two influential students of contemporary Jewish life who are no longer alive took me under their wing early in my career: During the many long walks we took in Riverside Park in the nearly two decades prior to his settling in Haifa, Paul Ritterband taught me how to think sociologically about the Jews. Charles Liebman, through his trenchant writing on contemporary Jewish life, has been a role model in how to serve both as an analyst and advocate—and most important, in how to ask questions about matters large and small. I have missed their presence during the writing of this book.

My work has been nurtured in several important intellectual settings. During my years of working at the Jewish Theological Seminary and under the leadership of three distinguished chancellors—Gerson D. Cohen, Ismar Schorsch, and Arnie Eisen—a unique culture has thrived, one that balances the polarities of religious and academic imperatives. For a decade, I served as provost at JTS, which set back my publication schedule, but also gave me an unparalleled perch from which to observe Jewish life. During those years, I published articles of a controversial nature, but never once did anyone in the administration question my right to express myself freely and without constraint. It has been a privilege to work at an institution that so values freedom of inquiry and expression.

The AVI CHAI Foundation has served as a second home for nearly fifteen years. The support of Mem Bernstein and Arthur Fried, current and past chairmen, members of the Board of Trustees, and Yossi Prager, North American director, has provided me with multiple opportunities to engage in research about Jewish education. Thanks to the vision and largesse of the foundation's leadership, I was able to launch a series of team research projects. The lively conversations during those team efforts have been among the most stimulating and unforgettable experiences of my career. And then the chance to engage with the foundation's leadership and extraordinary staff around those research findings and their policy implications brought the work to a new level.

It was important for me, as a scholar housed at a Jewish institution, to broaden my horizons and learn from students of other American faith traditions. An invitation in 1995 to join the Congregational Studies Team, sponsored by the Lilly Endowment, provided just such an opportunity. It wasn't always easygoing: in the early years I struggled to make sense of the theological categories others took for granted, but it proved to be a great education. This book has benefited from the comparative perspectives I gleaned from our team meetings. More recently, I participated in a research project headed up by James Davison Hunter, which explored character education comparatively in a dozen different types of high schools. There too I learned much from James and my other colleagues.

For the purposes of this book, I embarked, beginning in 2014, on a systematic effort to interview rabbis of all movements and outlooks about their perceptions of how Jews in their orbit enact their religious lives. What I learned has been invaluable. I am indebted to them for their candor and insights. Listed by denominational affiliation and their location at the time they were interviewed, the roughly 160 rabbis are the following:

Conservative: Rabbis Rachel Ain (New York), Morris Allen (St. Paul, MN), Nina Bieber (Sherman Oaks, CA), Carolyn Braun (Portland, ME), Aaron Brusso (Westchester, NY), Richard Cameras (Los Angeles), Elliot Cosgrove (New York), Menachem Creditor (Berkeley, CA), Ed Farber (North Miami, FL), Ed Feinstein (Sherman Oaks, CA), Jeremy Fine (St. Paul, MN), Felipe Goodman (Las Vegas), Marvin Goodman (San Francisco), Corey Helfand (San Mateo, CA), Lauren Holtzblatt (Washington, DC), David Kalender (Fairfax, VA), Elana Kantor (Phoenix), David Seth Kirschner (Closter, NJ), Aaron Melman (Chicago), Daniel Nevins (JTS, New York), Hillel Norry (Atlanta), Paul Plotkin (Margate, FL), Josh Rabin (United Synagogue), Josh Ratner (MA), Harold Schulweis (Los Angeles), Michael Schwab (Chicago), Howard Shub (Palm Beach, FL), Michael Siegel (Chicago), David Singer (Dallas),

Josh Skoff (Cleveland), Gerald Skolnick (New York), David Small (Hartford, CT), Elie Spitz (Tustin, CA), Gil Steinlauf (Washington, DC), Gail Swedroe (Austin, TX), Gordon Tucker (Westchester, NY), Michael Wasserman (Phoenix), Steve Weiss (Cleveland), David Wolpe (Los Angeles), Elana Zelony (San Francisco).

Haredi: Rabbis Aaron Kotler (Lakewood, NJ), Shlomo Landau (New Jersey), David Niederman (Williamsburg, Brooklyn), Yisroel Rosenfeld and Yossi Rosenblum (Pittsburgh), Avi Shafran (Agudath Israel of America).

Modern/Open/Centrist Orthodox: Rabbis Daniel Alter (Denver), Saul Berman (New York), Avi Bossewitch (Miami), Yonatan Cohen (Berkeley), Jeffrey Fox (New York), Barry Freundel (Washington, DC), Efrem Goldberg (Boca Raton, FL), Yitz Greenberg (New York), Kenneth Hain (Long Island, NY), Yosef Kanefsky (Los Angeles), Dov Linzer (New York), Asher Lopatin (Chicago), Chaim Marder (White Plains, NY), Steven Pruzansky (Teaneck, NJ), Kalman Topp (Beverly Hills, CA), Mitchell Wohlberg (Baltimore), Daniel Yolkut (Pittsburgh), Alan J. Yuter (Baltimore); Maharat Ruth Balinsky (Washington, DC).

Orthodox Outreach: Efraim Buchwald (Jewish Outreach Institute, New York), Rabbis Steven Burg (Aish HaTorah), Raphael Butler (Afikim, New York), Yaacov Deyo (Aish, Los Angles), Zvi Drizin (Chabad, Dallas), Dovid Eliezrie (Chabad, Orange County, CA), Bentzi Epstein (Dallas Area Torah Association), Jon Erlbaum (Chevra, Philadelphia), Yossi Gordon (Chabad on Campus International), Eli Hirsch (Philadelphia), Zvi Holland (Phoenix Kollel), Moshe Kotlarsky (Lubavitch Headquarters, Crown Heights, Brooklyn), Chaim Levine (Aish, Seattle), Yitzchok Lowenbraun (Association of Jewish Outreach Professionals, New York), Zalman Marcus (Orange County, CA), Yaakov Meyer (Aish, Denver), Hirshy Minkowitz (Chabad Atlanta), Efraim Mintz (JLI, Crown Heights, Brooklyn), Zev Pomeranz (Aish, Denver), Pinny Rosenthal (Manhattan Jewish Experience, New York), Bentzy Schechter (Partners in Torah of Detroit), Menachem Schmidt (Chabad, Philadelphia), Eliezer Schneiderman (Chabad at the University of Delaware), Aaron Yehuda Schwab (Denver Kollel), Motti Seligson (Chabad Lubavitch Media Center, Crown Heights, Brooklyn), Aharon Wasserman (Denver Jewish Experience). Also Bassie Marcus (Orange County, CA), Baila Olidort (Chabad Lubavitch, New York), Jodi Samuels (Jewish International Connection, New York).

Reform: Rabbis Aaron Bisno (Pittsburgh), Joe Black (Denver), Richard Block (Cleveland), Herbert Bronstein (Chicago), Mitch Chefitz (Miami), Stanley Davids (Jerusalem), Lucy Dinner (Raleigh, NC), Dennis Eisner (San Mateo, CA), Meir Feldman (Great Neck, NY), Tara Feldman (Great Neck, NY), Daniel Freelander (Union for Reform Judaism, New York), Elyse Frishman (NJ), Wendi Geffen (Chicago), Laura Geller (Los Angeles), Arnie Gluck (NJ), Tom Heyn (Miami), Michael Holzman (VA), Walter Jacob (Pittsburgh), Samuel Karff (Houston), Steve Leder (Los Angeles), Robert Levine (New York), Cliff Librach (Danbury, CT), Seth Limmer (Chicago), Jill Maderer (Philadelphia), Steven Mason (Chicago), Mark Miller (Orange County, CA), Leon Morris (New York), Gary Pokras (Buffalo, NY), Peter Rubinstein (New York), Jeff Salkin (Hollywood, FL), Herman Schaalmann (Chicago), Amy Schwartzman (VA), Ronald Segel (Atlanta), David Spey (Fort Lauderdale, FL), Rick Steinberg (Irvine, CA), David Stern (Dallas), Lance Sussman (Philadelphia), Ron Symonds (Pittsburgh), Sarah Weissman (Los Gatos, CA), Elaine Zecher (Boston), Danny Zemel (Washington, DC), Marcie Zimmerman (Minneapolis).

Religious groupings outside the mainstream: Rabbis Dan Ain (Because Jewish), Sharon Anisfeld (Boston Hebrew College), Lester Bronstein (Reconstructionist, Westchester, NY), Chaim Seidler-Feller (Hillel, UCLA), Shai Held (Mechon Hadar, New York), Marc Margolius (Reconstructionist, New York), Rachel Nussbaum (Kavana, Seattle), Steve Sager (Cleveland Reconstructionist), Rebecca Sirbu (Rabbis without Borders, New York), Jonathan Slater (Institute for Jewish Spirituality, New York), Dan Smokler (National Hillel), Toba Spitzer (Reconstructionist, Boston), Ethan Tucker (Mechon Hadar, New York), Elyse Wechterman (Reconstructionist Rabbinical Association). And Louis Polisson (rabbinical student, JTS), Josh Warshawsky (rabbinical student at the Ziegler School, Los Angeles), Cyd Weissman (Reconstructionist Learning Networks, Philadelphia).

Sephardi Jews: Rabbis Elie Abadie (Manhattan), Joshua Bittan (Los Angeles), Yoself Bitton (Brooklyn), Daniel Bouskila (Los Angeles), Raymond Harari (Brooklyn), Ben Hassan (Seattle), Jeremy Rosen (Manhattan).

I have benefited too from conversations with academic colleagues and other observers of the Jewish religious scene. My thanks to them for graciously taking the time to inform my thinking and answer my questions: Professors Isa Aron (Hebrew Union College [HUC], Los Angeles), Michael Berenbaum (American Jewish University), Sylvia Barack Fishman (Brandeis University), Samuel Heilman (CUNY), William Helmreich (CUNY), Lawrence Hoffman (HUC New York), Ari Kelman (Stanford), Sara Lee (Rhea Hirsch School of Jewish Education, HUC, Los Angeles), Shaul Magid (Indiana University), Michael Meyer (HUC, Cincinnati), David N. Myers (UCLA), Bruce Phillips (HUC Los Angeles), Ron Wolfson (American Jewish University). Several keen observers and communal professionals offered gracious assistance: Dr. Alisa Rubin Kurshan (UJA-Federation of New York), Maya Bernstein (Upstart, Palo Alto, CA), Shawn Landress (Jumpstart, Los Angeles), and Alex Pomson (Rosov Consultants, Jerusalem). On *Reform Judaism:* President Emeritus David Ellenson (HUC), Professor Samuel Joseph (HUC Cincinnati). *Conservative Judaism:* Professor Elliot Dorff (American Jewish University), Rabbis Jerome Epstein (United Synagogue of Conservative Judaism), Joel Meyers (Rabbinical Assembly, New York), Elliot Schoenberg (Rabbinical Assembly). *Orthodoxy:* Blu Greenberg (New York), Elana Stein Hain (New York), Jay Lefkowitz (New York), David Pollock (JCRC New York), Ruthie Simon (Yeshivat Chovevei Torah), Drs. Steven Bayme and Lawrence Grossman (American Jewish Committee), Professors Michael Berger and Michael Broyde (Emory University), Rabbis Bob Kaplan (JCRC, New York), Mayer Waxman (Union of Orthodox Jewish Congregations of America), and Harvey Well (Associated Talmud Torahs, Chicago), Professors Alan Brill (Seton Hall University), Adam Ferziger (Bar Ilan University), Chaim I. Waxman (Rutgers University), Rabbis Steven Weil and Dan Hazony (Orthodox Union). *Reconstructionism:* Rabbi Richard Hirsh (Reconstructionist Rabbinical Association Philadelphia). *Sephardic Jews:* Mijal Bitton and Rahel Musleah (both of New York). *Trends in American re-

ligion: Former Presidents William McKinney (Pacific School of Religion) and Barbara G. Wheeler (Auburn Theological Seminary), Professors Nancy T. Ammerman (Boston University), David Campbell (Notre Dame), Jackson Carroll (Duke University), Chris Coble (Lilly Endowment), the late Carl Dudley (Hartford Seminary), Penny Edgell (University of Minnesota), the late Nancy Eisland (Emory University), Charles Glenn (Boston University), James Davison Hunter (University of Virginia), Gerardo Marti (Davidson College), and E. Stephen Warner (University of Illinois). And as the book manuscript was completed, anonymous readers offered insightful commentary of great value.

My interest in the condition of American Judaism has been long-standing, initially culminating in my book *A People Divided: Judaism in Contemporary America* (1993). After a hiatus of a dozen years, I resumed research on aspects of this broad topic and published a number of essays preparatory to working on this book.

My thanks to the editors of those publications for permission to draw upon material from those essays when writing this volume:

"All Quiet on the Religious Front? Jewish Unity, Denominationalism, and Post-Denominationalism in the United States." A report issued by the American Jewish Committee, May 2005.

"The American Synagogue: Recent Trends and Issues," *American Jewish Year Book*, 2005.

"The Perplexities of Conservative Judaism," *Commentary*, September 2007.

"What Does Reform Judaism Stand For?" *Commentary*, June 2008.

"The Outreach Revolution," *Commentary*, April 2013.

"What You Don't Know about the Ultra-Orthodox," *Commentary*, July–August 2014.

"Can Modern Orthodoxy Survive?," *Mosaic*, August 2014. https://mosaic magazine.com/essay/2014/08/can-modern-orthodoxy-survive/

A Note about Transliteration

There are a few standardized formats for transliterating Hebrew, Yiddish, and Aramaic words into English. This book intentionally does not utilize them. Much of the terminology about contemporary American Judaism has entered the English vocabulary in a simplified form. Terms such as "Hasid," "Haredi," and "Hanukkah," to cite common examples, all begin in Hebrew with the letter *chet* and are properly transliterated with an H underscored by a diacritical period or dash. But in news articles and other popular media, they are spelled simply with an H. Given the subject matter of this book, the simplest and most common forms of transliteration are employed, even though they do not adhere to a formal academic style.

INTRODUCTION

The twenty-first century, thus far, has not been an auspicious era for religion in America. After surveying the national scene in 2015, the Pew Research Center concluded that the American public is becoming less religious "at least by some key measures of what it means to be a religious person."[1] These measure include "the percentages who say they pray every day, attend religious services regularly and consider religion to be very important in their lives; [all] have ticked down by small but statistically significant margins" since 2007—and that followed several decades of decline on all these measures. Cumulatively by 2015, close to one-quarter of Americans claimed they were unaffiliated with any religion. The erosion of membership was especially sharp in the once-dominant liberal Protestant denominations.[2]

Religion, moreover, has fallen into no small amount of disrepute in recent decades. First came the widely broadcast scandals involving clerics of different faiths: not only were individual priests, ministers, and rabbis accused of dreadful crimes, their religious organizations temporized, when they did not engage in cover-ups. Then came the upsurge in religiously inspired violence around the globe, highlighted by terrorist attacks such as the murderous events of 9/11. No less damaging, the so-called culture wars pitting contemporary sensibilities against traditional religious teachings have perplexed, if not alienated, the faithful. To add insult to self-inflicted injury, outspoken atheists, particularly among the academic and intellectual elites, have taken to the media to pronounce religion passé and denounce believers as deluded.

To be sure, countervailing trends are also visible. Even though the mainline groups have been in freefall since the 1970s, Protestant denominations of a more conservative bent and the Catholic Church are holding stable. Some take heart from this, though one wonders whether to celebrate along with *Christianity Today* when it trumpets the good news with a headline reading "Evangelicals Stay Strong as Christianity Crumbles in America."[3] Megachurches continue to attract many hundreds if not thousands of worshippers to weekly services and other programs. And all kinds of independent churches, unaffiliated with any specific denomination, are springing up across the country, experimenting with new musical, choreographic, and artistic forms.

Even in this time of decline, a sizable number of Americans, it would seem, harbor a *wish* for stronger religious involvement that surfaces at times of stress. In the immediate aftermath of the 9/11 attacks on the United States, houses of worship registered a temporary uptick in attendance, though that fizzled out after a few months.[4] A hunger for religious connection was on display again when Pope Francis visited the United States in 2015, not only in the hearts of the faithful who thronged to his outdoor masses, but among even larger numbers of non-Catholics who attended to his words with great curiosity.[5] Religion is certainly not as marginal to society in the United States as it is in European countries, but neither is it as robust as it used to be nor can it count any longer on the kind of official imprimatur that President Dwight Eisenhower bestowed upon it in 1953 when he famously pronounced "our form of government has no sense unless it is founded in a deeply felt religious faith, and I don't care what it is."[6] Despite the evidence of continuing faithfulness in certain sectors of American society, then, it is hard to escape the conclusion that ours is an era of religious recession.

Not surprisingly, given this broader context, American Judaism too has suffered declining numbers of adherents and flagging observance—even as pockets of strength are evident.

Observers of the Jewish religious scene unsurprisingly are divided over which is more significant—plummeting rates of participation or higher levels of energy among those who are engaged. Some, in fact, reject the notion that American Judaism is in decline, but rather contend it is merely undergoing a transition: the Jewish religion is being transformed, not abandoned, they contend. Most heartening to such commentators is a new spirit of inclusiveness and innovation. Whereas synagogues in the recent past primarily attracted conventional family units, today they welcome all kinds of family configurations. And for those who prefer alternatives to synagogues, it is possible in most large and midsize Jewish communities to find options for congregating geared to millennials or baby boomers, singles and childless Jews or empty-nesters, and many other types of Jews meeting in unconventional settings.

Moreover, the extension of leadership opportunities to once marginalized populations is widely regarded as a boon to Judaism. Heterosexual men no longer monopolize positions of religious leadership. Now women and men—both "straight" and gay or lesbian—serve in the rabbinate and cantorate and in positions of educational and denominational leadership. It is assumed that their ascendance makes it possible for different sensibilities to be brought to bear on religious issues, which, in turn, opens new avenues for reinterpreting sacred texts. Even within the Orthodox world, the sector most committed to traditionalism, much rethinking about questions of gender and sexuality is evident—leading at times to changes in policy.

Also of note to those who see the glass as more than half full is an evident spirit of religious experimentation in all sectors of Judaism. Synagogues have been refashioning their religious services, paying a good deal of attention to the atmospherics and music at times of prayer. Building personal relationships in congregations, even in synagogues with membership in the thousands, is a high priority of clergy. And the mixing and matching of all kinds of spiritual practices with conventional prayer is ubiquitous. Textual study, long understood by rabbis as a religious act, is attracting new learners and benefitting from new technologies. All of these developments point to a nascent revival of Jewish religious life—or so some have argued.

And yet surveying the same scene, other commentators on the national scene find evidence of considerable weakness and vulnerability in Jewish religious life. Rates of intermarriage have spiraled upward, while declining percentages of intermarried Jews claim to be raising their children exclusively in the Jewish religion. Over two million individuals of Jewish parentage no longer identify as Jews, and many others who do claim to be Jewish eschew identification with the Jewish religion, choosing instead to define themselves in cultural or ethnic terms. And outside the Orthodox community, rates of childbearing are depressed relative to the recent past, leaving observers to wonder who will populate Jewish religious institutions in the future.[7]

Not a few commentators have linked these developments to declining participation in Jewish religious life. A Conservative rabbi of my acquaintance confides his fear that his bustling congregation, which hosts a day school enrolling hundreds of children, may be overwhelmed by a cultural "tsunami" primed to sweep away everything he has labored to accomplish. He is hardly the only rabbi to worry about building on quicksand. Analyses of recent survey data seem to buttress these anxious prognostications. They show that each of the religious movements in American Judaism has experienced dramatic changes in its fortunes, with the largest ones facing the likelihood of considerable membership losses in the years to come.

Depending on which sets of evidence they deem most compelling, observers set forth diametrically opposite prescriptions for what is needed to ensure a thriving religious life in the near future. Those who focus on the rich panoply of attractive options and the collapse of barriers to participation call for more of the same. They take heart from these developments and regard American Judaism as poised for renewal.[8] Simultaneously, there is no shortage of commentary explaining why each religious movement must change in order to survive, why synagogues are in desperate need of reinvention, and why Judaism itself must undergo "radical" revision or else continue to lose active participants.[9] Needless to say, some observers advocate for both prescriptions simultaneously.

Before rushing to celebrate the new era of Jewish religious diversity or launching far-reaching reforms to stave off further losses (or both alternatives), some stock taking is in order. What do we know about the lived Judaism of American Jews, the religion of ordinary Jews? What in Judaism resonates with individual Jews and their families? For those Jews who seek to participate in the religious sphere, what is on offer? And what is happening when Jews gather for public worship in congregations and unconventional religious settings?

The short answer to this last question is that a good deal is happening. Despite or perhaps because of the evident signs of decline, those Jews who *are* interested in religious life are actively rethinking how they pray, study, and express their Judaism, where they meet for religious congregating, what can inspire intensified religious participation, and how more Jews can discover transcendent meaning for their lives in Judaism. It's not that all this activity can mask or somehow make up for the erosion of religious life that has already taken place. At best, the many new initiatives are designed to stem the losses, and perhaps to win back some of those Jews who have ceased to be active practitioners of their religion. But the vitality and investment of energy are no less real or important than the evidence of decline.

This book takes it as a given that Jewish religious life in this country has endured a recession. Evidence of this decline has been widely reported in news articles about synagogues forced to close their doors or merge with other weakened congregations, the drop in membership within many congregations that continue to keep their doors open, declining numbers of synagogue members who attend with any frequency, and the dramatic increase in the proportion of Jews who do not identify with Judaism.

There is no shortage of efforts to explain these patterns: some have cited the role of capitalism,[10] and America's hyper-individualistic culture;[11] others have placed these developments into the context of a broader societal shift away from civic participation;[12] still others have highlighted the low levels of literacy about Judaism among wide swaths of American Jews;[13] and still others would cite the triumphalism of secularists, especially in the academy and elite cultural circles, who neither value religion nor claim to understand it.[14] The turn to postmodernism in the academy, moreover, has percolated down into other sectors of society; with its relativization of truth and insistence that all human endeavor is socially or subjectively constructed, postmodernism has further undermined religious truth claims.[15] Put succinctly, whereas mid-twentieth-century American culture strongly encouraged at least token religious participation, by the early twenty-first century the American culture with which most Jews identify is highly skeptical, if not dismissive, of such involvement.

All the more remarkable, then, are the countervailing trends: several million Jews still claim to be adherents of the Jewish religion, attend some kinds of religious services, continue to learn about their religious traditions, and invest themselves to an extent in the renewal of Judaism. Their experiences, their practices, their struggles with and for Judaism, and the efforts of their religious leaders to remix Judaism in order to entice them into vibrant settings for religious gathering are at the heart of the story this book tells.

It's a tale of surprising juxtapositions and contradictions. Even upon casual inspection, Jewish religious settings present some remarkable, if at times jarring, tableaux. Who would have imagined just a few years ago, for example, that in a number of Reform temples members are invited to prostrate themselves, with heads to the ground, during a portion of the Yom Kippur service they refer to as the "Great *Aleinu*"? In the recent past, strict rules of decorum in Reform synagogues curbed perambulation but instead confined congregants to fixed pews. Bowing to the ground was seen as a practice only hidebound Orthodox Jews perform on the High Holidays. Today, in many Reform temples, the emphasis has shifted to swaying, clapping, dancing, and movement. Describing her response to the Great *Aleinu* practice of her synagogue, one congregant enthused that it "has become possibly my favorite moment of the whole grand liturgical experience . . . , and I always wish I could pause time and just stay there, in that posture, in that relationship to God."[16] Were this practice unique, it would not warrant much attention, but across the spectrum of Jewish life, Jews are finding meaning in once rejected but now reappropriated religious traditions.

Turning our attention to a Conservative synagogue, we find the premier congregation of its denomination in Washington, DC, moving in a different direction. The synagogue sponsors a Jewish Mindfulness Center. Its menu of options includes meditation practices, healing services, yoga, Jewish mysticism classes, and immersion in the ritual bath (*Mikveh*). Though the last is a traditional practice usually associated with women's purification after their monthly menstruation period or a way for men to prepare themselves for the Sabbath and holidays, here the emphasis is on body image and is particularly addressed to teenage girls.[17] The panoply of practices offered by this Conservative synagogue—Eastern prayer devotions mixed with New Age and

Hasidic teachings plus contemporary self-help guidance—would have been inconceivable in synagogues of any denomination just a few decades ago, but now clergy in a range of settings are reconsidering how to infuse the experience of prayer with heightened intentionality.[18]

The texture of Orthodox congregational life is no less in flux. Torah study, always a feature of such synagogues, is now attracting far larger numbers of regular learners. Of particular note are the numerous men engaged in daily Talmud study. In Orthodox synagogues across the country, members gather daily to join with hundreds of thousands of mainly Jewish males around the world studying a daily page of Talmud prescribed in a synchronized curriculum—the *Daf Yomi*, or daily folio;[19] those who complete the cycle will cover the entire Babylonian Talmud in the course of some seven years and five months. These classes are supplemented by others focusing on different sacred texts, works of Jewish thought, and religious guides to self-improvement and other topics.[20] Despite the clear lines of gender differentiation in Orthodox synagogues, women are assuming new roles in these educational activities—both as learners and as teachers. In some congregations, women serve as clergy, offering classes and functioning as religious guides to male as well as female congregants. They also are studying Talmudic texts, long regarded as the province of males alone. None of these developments was conceivable just a few decades ago.

If we train our eyes only on conventional synagogues, we will overlook unexpected developments at the margins. Indeed, what characterizes the current religious environment is the declining influence of the major denominations and the rise of religious start-ups. Jewish religious life today, as distinct from the mid-twentieth century, is far more likely to feature synagogue hopping, enabling Jews of different backgrounds to study together in Orthodox outreach centers or self-styled pluralistic settings, and a relaxed approach to crossing denominational boundaries to attend a variety of religious services. Labels and neat categories are deemed artificial and therefore expendable, while a spirit of innovation and tinkering is stimulating the creation of hybrid forms of Jewish religious identification. Once dismissed as passing fads on the periphery of Jewish life, unconventional approaches to Judaism now are flourishing—and increasingly influencing the core.

Take, for example, the ease with which today's American Jews create their own do-it-yourself forms of Judaism. On the most basic level, this has led increasing numbers of Jews to eschew synagogues and rabbis in favor of ad hoc arrangements they make for themselves and their families. The Bar or Bat Mitzvah, to take a prominent example, came into vogue in the middle of the twentieth century as a very public embrace of Jewish responsibility by young Jews in the presence of an entire congregation; today many families have privatized the milestone, celebrating the event only amid family and friends and severing it from any communal connection. On another level, this DIY mentality has led to the easy merging of traditions and religious expressions drawn from multiple sources. If as a result of intermarriage family members stem from different backgrounds, holiday gatherings will mix and match prayers and rituals from different religions. The same is occurring at marriage ceremonies joining in matrimony a Jew and a Gentile.

Leaders are no less likely to favor hybrid approaches. As already noted, so-called New Age practices are combined with Hasidic Jewish meditation. Jewish clergy are also eagerly studying church practices to learn what is attractive to worshippers. And visits to megachurches have become de rigueur for synagogue renewal experts.[21]

Internally, there is also much cross-fertilization. The once sharp boundaries between Hasidic Jews and their arch-antagonists, the Mitnagdim, are rapidly collapsing in the so-called Ultra-Orthodox sector. (Emerging in the eighteenth century, these two sectors of Eastern European Jewish society were bitter foes; time and common enemies—such as secular and non-Orthodox Jews—have brought them closer together.) At the Lakewood Yeshiva, a bastion of Mitnagdic Judaism, young Hasidim and their erstwhile fierce opponents now study side by side, with some of the latter eagerly reading Hasidic texts, an act that had been anathema in the past. So too in the non-Orthodox sectors of American Judaism, the wisdom of Hasidism and the Mussar movement, a product of the Lithuanian Mitnagdim, is eagerly absorbed by Conservative and Reform Jews.[22] In some instances the direction of influence is reversed: Orthodox religious educators are adopting pedagogical methods developed by their Conservative and Reform counterparts. And though harder to prove, one suspects that feminist readings of Jewish texts pioneered by

non-Orthodox women have had an impact on the outlook of some Orthodox thinking.

The obverse of this boundary crossing is the spread of highly idiosyncratic approaches to Judaism. Cafeteria religion, picking and choosing only
those morsels of Judaism that seem personally appealing, is the new—and
perhaps only—norm among most Jews. This leads to odd juxtapositions:
a Conservative rabbi, for example, reports on a congregant who boasts of
never having missed a day when wrapping *tephilin* (phylacteries) is required,
but the same congregant also makes no bones of his utter scorn for the Jewish
dietary restrictions (the laws of *Kashrut*): to him they are too "ridiculous" to
observe. Religious skepticism has made such deep inroads that Conservative
rabbis have produced an official responsum weighing whether an openly
avowed atheist may serve as a prayer leader (*shaliach tzibbur*). (The responsum says no, but in practice it is ignored in many synagogues.) Reform rabbis, in turn, marvel at the willingness of congregants to abandon almost every
aspect of Jewish practice, but when it comes to death rituals, they demand
adherence to the gold standard of *traditional* ritual observance. With no
rhyme or reason, one Jewish ritual is observed punctiliously, while another is
dismissed with contempt. Picking and choosing is not a surreptitious exercise, but boldly announced.

The spirit of what the late social scientist Charles Liebman labeled "personalist" religion has triumphed. "My brother," reports an Orthodox rabbi,
"is a wonderful, socially conscious Jew . . . married to a non-Jewish woman.
He does holidays with us and calls me every week to wish me a *shabbat
shalom* [a good Sabbath]. This year he called and said, 'my wife and I have a
wedding on Saturday when it's Yom Kippur, so I am going to do my fasting
thing on Wednesday; that will be my Yom Kippur.'" As is the case in many
Jewish families today, one sibling may embrace a more traditional approach
to Judaism and another will observe the religion idiosyncratically or not at
all. And also in line with the new personalism, even the most sacred day of the
year is now subject to rescheduling if it doesn't fit one's busy schedule. Not
surprisingly, news reports are proliferating about families shifting the Passover Seder from its Hebrew calendar date to the weekend before or after,
whenever guests find it more convenient to gather.[23]

But the trend is not only toward radical innovation. Some Jewish adults are embracing traditional practices they had never seen enacted within their families while growing up; some are becoming *more* punctilious in observance. Individuals who had once been minimally connected Jews find their way to study halls where they stretch their minds to grasp the flow of Talmudic reasoning. A learning center in Chicago, for example, offers Talmud for adult beginners "from a Queer perspective."[24] Long abandoned religious practices, such as the immersion in a ritual bath (Mikveh), are attracting non-Orthodox Jews. And in synagogues where the early autumn holiday of Sukkot had barely registered a few decades ago, members vie to invite each other to their decorated booths. The new personalism can lead to the discovery of meaning in rituals once deemed arcane.

These seemingly anarchic developments are not occurring in a vacuum. Just as the spirit of experimentation has captured the imagination of some Jewish groups, the larger American scene is exploding with new forms of religious expression: churches no less than synagogues are paying more attention than ever before to the musical and choreographic dimensions of public worship;[25] independent churches, like their synagogue counterparts, are eschewing denominational affiliation so they can invent their own liturgical forms; growing numbers of Americans are floating between different houses of worship and unconventional settings of religious gathering; and the new vogue is *bricolage*, a term sociologist Robert Wuthnow appropriates to refer to the tinkering especially evident among millennials who "join together . . . seemingly inconsistent, disparate components."[26] Even as bar churches are springing up, rabbis are launching "Torah and Brew" conversations in local pubs.[27]

Broader patterns of disconnection also mirror what is happening in some sectors of the Jewish population. Just as there has been a spike in the population of "Nones" who identify with no Jewish religious outlook, increasing numbers of Americans call themselves nonbelievers or "Nones."[28] In Protestantism and Judaism, once leading religious denominations have fallen on hard times, even as formerly marginal ones are gaining adherents. Church attendance is down, and so are the numbers of regulars in synagogues. Patterns of Jewish religious life are being shaped in the larger spiritual marketplace of America—one that, as we have noted, is in a religious recession, even as experimentation and remixing are widespread.

Given all these contradictory developments, the task of describing and explaining the current Jewish religious scene has grown more complicated. In the past, the dominant mode of reporting on the condition of American Judaism concentrated sharply on denominational developments. In such a reading, the pronouncements of national leaders and the vitality of their movements are the stuff of high drama. Taking pride of place in recent accounts were the battles raging within denominations over the participation of women, LGBTQ individuals, and the Gentile spouses of Jews in Jewish religious settings. The ideological struggle of rabbis for the soul of their respective denominations is another dramatic story line: it seems that self-styled progressives are forever warring with self-styled traditionalists. And then there is the question of numbers: which movement is gaining or losing members?[29]

These themes are not irrelevant to the lives of average Jews. But even taken together they offer only a partial accounting of what is happening in American Jewish religious life. This point was driven home to me in a very personal way as I reflected in recent years on my own book-length contribution to the study of American Judaism. Roughly a quarter of a century ago, I wrote an analysis of "Judaism in Contemporary America."[30] *A People Divided*, as I titled my study, focused heavily, though not exclusively, on the changing policies and positions of the major Jewish religious movements, and how those shifts brought the movements into heightened conflict. With the passage of time, it has become clear to me that the much-publicized debates over denominational policies, though riveting to some, actually obscured far more important subterranean developments. If we shift our attention from the national organizations to local communities, a very different picture of American Judaism emerges.

To make sense of the current Jewish religious scene, I therefore resolved to attend in this book as much as possible to developments affecting the lives of ordinary Jews in their local communities rather than the preoccupations of the elites at a far geographic remove from the folk. But how does one learn about nonelites, those conventionally referred to in Jewish parlance as *amcha* (literally meaning God's people and figuratively a term for the Jewish folk)? Ideally, one would engage in ethnographic studies in multiple religious settings, observing how attendees participate and then interviewing them on what Jewish religious practices mean to them[31]—or, to use the language of sociologist Nancy Ammerman, one would listen to the "sacred stories" they tell to make sense of their religious lives.[32] Though a small number of such studies have appeared, there is little research to date on the religious lives of congregants as told in their own words, perhaps because of the practical challenges of finding the resources of time and money to engage in a wide-ranging ethnographic study encompassing Jews across the country.

I've embarked on a different course. Over a period of some years, I have conducted hour or longer interviews with over 160 rabbis of all types in every region of the country. Almost every interview focused on two key themes: the interviewees' perceptions of the religious lives of the Jews they encounter and the steps taken by clergy and laypeople to address the religious needs of those Jews. Quite a few of the conversations took surprising turns as my informants spoke openly about subjects close to their hearts. Some of the most illuminating insights emerged from conversations that veered off topic and wandered down unplanned byways. I am mindful, as were the rabbis who graciously took the time to speak with me, that these leaders are not omniscient. There are things about their congregants' religious lives they probably do not know. But what was more striking to me was the frankness of my interviewees about the congregants they do encounter, their struggles to strengthen the religious experiences of those congregants and their self-conscious awareness of their own limitations.

In choosing my interview subjects, I aimed for a cross-section of rabbis and other observers from different regions of the country, serving in urban and suburban settings, and of course in congregations of different denominations and also in nondenominational settings. My preference was to speak with rabbis who had at least a decade of experience since completing their rabbinical studies, but generally I did not include many who are within a decade of retirement. I came away from most interviews energized by the thoughtfulness and intentionality the rabbis bring to their work—and also their sobriety in grasping the nature of the challenges they face.

My sources of information were not limited to rabbis. I have spoken with several dozen knowledgeable observers of the American Jewish religious scene, in some cases for the purposes of eliciting information about specific developments, in others to hear perspectives about more open-ended questions. I also have personally attended several hundred synagogues over the years, as a visitor or guest speaker, and those visits provided me the opportunity to speak with ordinary Jews in different types of settings. Positioned as I am at a training institution for future Jewish leaders and educators, I have learned a good deal from my students about the communities they know.

Sprinkled throughout the coming pages are vignettes and perceptions drawn from these encounters. They are not, however, attributed to named individuals. Because I opted to conduct "on background" interviews with a promise of anonymity, I am asking readers to put a good deal of faith in my reliability in those sections of the book that draw upon unattributed statements. This is hardly an unknown research practice, although it may be a bit unusual in that my sources are knowledgeable observers who describe the activities of others, not only themselves.

Most of this study, though, is based on information readily available in the public domain—sermonic materials, news accounts, survey data, online articles, and various reports and scholarly books and essays. With the aid of Professor Steven M. Cohen, I have drawn extensively upon data collected by the Pew Research Foundation for its 2013 study of Jewish Americans. Though the published report of initial data has been widely cited, for the purposes of this study a good deal more data were run to get at specific questions of religious involvement. I have also tapped the rapidly expanding blogosphere for insight into how Jews of different outlooks think about religious issues. By meshing these easily verifiable and cited sources with findings from off-the-record interviews, I hope to present a rounded portrait of Jewish religious life unavailable through written sources alone.

This book scrutinizes Jewish religious life in today's America through three distinct lenses. Its opening section focuses on the lived religion of ordinary Jews. Here we encounter differences between the range of non-Orthodox Jews, including those who claim no religious identification but nonetheless participate in some activities. Another chapter examines the so-called Ultra-Orthodox (Haredi Jews), Modern Orthodox, and Sephardi Jews. (The latter are virtually invisible in almost all studies of American Jewish life.) Among the questions discussed are the following: What do Jews believe about God? How frequently do they participate in religious activities? Which religious rituals resonate the most? And which have been reinterpreted in recent years to strike contemporary chords? Care is taken to analyze how Jews of different denominations, genders, geographic regions, and age groups vary in their religious participation.

The second section looks at religious life through the lens of denominational life. Successive chapters on Reform, Conservative, and Orthodox Judaism delineate the strengths and weaknesses of each religious movement. The emphasis in these chapters is not on denominational pronouncements, but on internal tensions and the responsiveness of these movements to local congregations. The concluding chapter of this section examines why each of these movements has become a leaky vessel and what might be done to shore all of them up.

Religious renewal lies at the heart of the third, and final, section. Successive chapters address the three main arenas of religious renewal in our time—efforts to renew worship services in synagogues through innovative approaches to music, choreography, study, meditation, and individualized attention; the massive, and underreported, growth of Orthodox outreach efforts, which now touch the lives of several hundred thousand non-Orthodox Jews annually; and innovative programming geared toward Jewish millennials and those unaffiliated with the major movements.

My own posture in this volume also warrants comment. I am simultaneously an academic observer of American Jewish life and also a practicing adherent of Judaism. In the former capacity, I have endeavored to survey the entire scene and not limit my purview only to those expressions of Judaism I find personally congenial. But I also have written critically, asking hard questions about how well different groups have succeeded *according to their own standards*. No one group is idealized in this volume, and yet I hope no group will feel it has been treated unfairly. In writing critically, I have been influenced by my own understandings. It cannot be otherwise about a contemporary phenomenon: I am implicated in this story and am deeply concerned about its outcome. In writing this book, I have tried to find a sweet spot between a posture of Olympian detachment and one of subjective opinion.

Here, at the outset, it is necessary to address a number of definitional questions. To begin with, what do I mean when I refer to "Jewish religious life"? First, let's distinguish between religion and religiousness.[33] The former often entails a set of doctrines about correct belief and behaviors; the second is about the actual practices of religious people. The first is what the elites teach as the true requirements of the religion; the second is how ordinary Jews, often described by sociologists of religion as the folk, enact their religious lives. This book does not ignore religion. The middle section is all about the organized Jewish denominations and their changing views and policies. But the primary purpose of this volume is to examine the religious activities of ordinary Jews and identify what is being made available to those who seek religious involvement. Those themes are addressed in the first and third sections.

It should be clear from the foregoing that I understand the category of religion in a formal sense. Colloquially, one often hears people say that Israel is the religion of America's Jews because of the strong passions it arouses; or allegiance to one of the major political parties is the religion of large sectors of the population, as in the quip about Reform Judaism being "the Democratic Party with holidays thrown in."[34] No doubt, quite a few American Jews are more passionate about the welfare of Israel or the state of American politics than about the requirements of Judaism, however understood. But these commitments are not the subject of this volume. Instead, I adhere to the dictionary definition: "religion is an organized system of beliefs, ceremonies, and rules used to worship a god or a group of gods."[35] This, as we shall see, is a sufficiently complex topic.

For example, some of the categories routinely employed to study the religious lives of American Christians cannot be applied readily to their Jewish counterparts. Conventionally, the religious behavior of Americans is understood through the prism of belief and worship: Do you believe in God? What kind of God is that? What about angels and miracles? How often do you attend public worship services? These are obvious questions that apply to Jews no less than to Americans who identify with other religions. But for Jews, religious observances and ritual performance are far more important than matters of belief, and even prayer.

Rabbinic Judaism has long stressed the importance of all 613 commandments identified in the Torah by the rabbis, the long catalog of "dos and don'ts."[36] These range from Sabbath and holiday observance to dietary restrictions, from modest dress to purity laws, from publicly enacted ethical imperatives to private acts of kindness. Survey questionnaires usually ask about only a handful of these commandments: lighting candles as the Sabbath begins and partaking in a Passover Seder, fasting on Yom Kippur, desisting from handling money on the Sabbath, lighting candles to celebrate Hanukkah, and giving to charity. Critics are wont to dismiss these as "ghetto measures" of Judaism, claiming they are long outdated and too parochial. For many Jews they are not. Still, in an age of highly idiosyncratic religious practices, inquiring about the standard items alone may miss entirely what some Jews regard as their most important Jewish religious rituals—engaging in acts of *tikkun olam* (repairing the world) through good deeds, social justice work and advocacy, charitable giving, reading certain types of books or blogs, performing spiritual exercises, communing with nature, observing Jewish mourning rituals, to take a few examples. There is no commonly agreed upon list of required religious practices any longer. The first two chapters of this book will go beyond the standard measures, but given the idiosyncratic nature of religious living today, they can't possibly cover all forms of Judaism practiced by ordinary Jews.

A word in this connection about spiritual practices: A large sociological literature tries to distinguish between religion and spirituality, and tends to view them as antithetical, or at least as operating in very different spheres. The former is "organized, traditional and communal"; the latter is "unique to each person" and interior. Rich traditions of spiritual meditation exist within Jewish religious traditions, even if they have not been the dominant modes.[37] This study therefore does not dismiss the new Jewish spirituality as irrelevant, but to the contrary attends to some experimental efforts to connect ordinary Jews to the wellsprings of Jewish spirituality through meditation, the study of Hasidic and Mussar texts, and even Jewish mysticism. That said, as a study of *Jewish religious life* in America, this book does not examine spiritual practices with no discernible relationship to Judaism. No doubt, many Jews find it meaningful to commune with nature, derive uplift from viewing natural wonders, engage in Eastern meditation practices, or in other ways "do" spiritual things. There is no reason to doubt these are acts of spirituality, but there is no good reason to assume they necessarily are acts of Jewish religious activity, that they are connected to teachings and expectations of a religious system known as Judaism. Just because Jewish people engage in a practice does not mean their behavior is an expression of Jewish religious activity. (The same reasoning will be applied mutatis mutandis to reports of Jews engaged in social justice and political activism.)

It can be argued, of course, that a simpler method to gauge religious behavior would be to study the teachings of the various Jewish denominations.[38] Each of the movements offers a spectrum of approved practices and, to some extent, disapproved ones. The expectations of Orthodox or Conservative or Reform Judaism would establish parameters—the first committed to the broad range of observances, the third offering the greatest latitude, and the Conservative movement maintaining a middle ground. There may have been a time when this schematic approach would have worked because adherents strove to live within the approved range—although with only limited success. Under current circumstances, though, denominational positions offer little guidance: first, the intensely individualistic ethos of our times means that what the denominations suggest is just that—a suggestion; second, increasing numbers of Jews do not subscribe to any denominational identification; and third, the denominations themselves are no longer as clear about their expectations. Reform Judaism, for example, used to mean that the observance of Jewish dietary laws and head coverings for males in synagogue were forbidden. Now, both are optional. The Conservative movement, as we shall see, has a broad range of adherents, some of whom could fit fairly easily in the Orthodox camp and others in the Reform camp; its majority and minority opinions, moreover, leave a great deal of confusion as to preferred practices. And within Orthodoxy too there is a wide spectrum of observance and belief not necessarily consonant with the official ideologies of its institutions.

Because religious performance is so variable, we now face an additional challenge: where to look for it. Certainly, the home and places of worship are the most obvious sites. But religion may be found in the workplace or supermarket or on a sports field. Some scholars of religious life have gone so far as to claim it can be "hidden in plain sight."[39] The challenge is to learn more about what takes place in unconventional settings, as illustrated by the apocryphal story about a Jewish man who was running late for an important business appointment and frantically circling to find a place to park his car. "Please, God," he prayed, "if you help me find a spot I'll come to synagogue with greater regularity." Still circling, he added a second vow: "God, if You help me find a spot, I'll don *tephilin* [phylacteries] daily. God, you have to help me out." Just then a car pulled out of a parking spot. "Never mind, God," he blurted out, "I found one myself." Does this "prayer" rise to the level of a religious act? And if it does, how can we possibly know how frequently Jews offer such prayers? We cannot, and this book will not be able to document such private acts. But we ought to bear in mind the larger point: religious activity can occur in many settings, not just in houses of worship.[40]

Further complicating the task of studying religious life is the question of how narrowly to define Judaism. It's hardly a simple matter to disentangle the religious dimension of Jewish life from ethnic and cultural connections. To describe the Jews as adherents of a religion is to minimize, if not ignore, important aspects of Jewish identity—and to impose upon Jews a set of categories drawn from other cultures and religions. For much of their history, Jews did not have a word for their "religion," and, as Leora Batnitzky, a professor of Jewish thought, has contended, the characterization of Judaism as a religion is itself a modern invention. Moreover, as she aptly notes, it is a problematic conceit because it seeks to force Jewish life into the procrustean bed of Protestantism. The Protestant notion, she observes, "denotes a sphere of life separate and distant from others, and . . . is largely private not public, voluntary not compulsory."[41] For much of their history, the Jews have understood matters differently: religion was intertwined with folk culture;

Judaism required participation in public spheres; and there hardly was anything voluntary about it, for even Jews who trampled upon or ignored the sacred practices of the Jewish people were still regarded as Jews—including those who wanted no part of Jewish religious life.

In our time, applying the category of religion to Jews is even more problematic. What can be more "religious" than sermons and public references to God's will in houses of worship? And yet, anyone who attends synagogue services will note how little God is invoked in sermons or conversations, as distinct from prayers. In most places of Jewish gathering, explicit references to God's will—often described as "God talk"—are absent. This is true also in the private sphere: a friend described to me how his father managed to live as a fully observant Orthodox Jew yet never spoke about God in earshot of his son, and the latter confessed he had no idea what his father's theological beliefs were. This is hardly uncommon, largely because Judaism stresses ritual performance and deeds over belief. Rabbinic thinking appreciated that belief and religious fervor wax and wane over the life course—and perhaps even within a single day; punctilious observance of the *mitzvot* (commandments) therefore was seen by the rabbis as the necessary stable factor.

The Jewish religion, moreover, differs from Protestantism in its inseparable connection to a specific people. An old joke tells about Goldberg who attends synagogue to speak to God and about his neighbor Levine who comes there to speak to Goldberg. Both types of Jews can be found in almost every synagogue of any Jewish denomination. Being a Jew means to be tied to the fate of a particular people in all its habitations—and that too is deemed a religious imperative. To capture this aspect of Jewish identification, writers refer to "Jewish peoplehood," a neologism partially invented to capture a dimension of Jewishness without a parallel in Christianity.[42] (A Google search of the word "peoplehood" reveals that more than half the web page options refer to Jews.)

Why then write a book about Jewish religious life, rather than the totality of the contemporary Jewish experience? Why not cast a wide net to include the ties American Jews feel to one another and to Jews in other lands, notably the special bond with Israel? Why not refer to Jewish art, music, literature, dance, material culture, philanthropy, and politics, among other possible dimensions of American Jewish life? To ask the question is to answer it: the subject is too broad for a single volume.

But there also is a more substantive reason. Evidence is mounting of declining group solidarity within some sectors of the Jewish populace, a phenomenon also noted among other American ethnic groups. Already in 1985, the sociologist Richard Alba described "the twilight of ethnicity" among Italians whose ancestors arrived in the United States in the late nineteenth and early twentieth centuries.[43] Other social scientists like Herbert Gans have continued to trace the declining influence of ethnicity upon other populations far removed from their immigrant forebearers. Writing about "the ethnic structures and cultures" of today's fourth- and fifth-generation Americans, Gans found that "European ethnicity has virtually disappeared or at least is no longer visible."[44] To punctuate the point, he writes of "terminal ethnic identity" among "late generation ethnics."

Most American Jews trace their ancestry to immigrant ancestors who arrived during the period Gans describes, and there is little reason to believe Jews depart from the general pattern he observes. Peoplehood alone will not keep Jews engaged in Jewish life with any measure of intensity. Though I personally resonate strongly with the obligations and satisfactions that come with a strong connection to the Jewish people, ample evidence attests to the weakness of peoplehood *alone* as an instrument for the transmission of a strong Jewish identity from one generation to the next. Particularly in the absence of overt discriminatory anti-Semitism, families find it extremely difficult to transmit a strong Jewish identification to succeeding generations. Sacred religious practices, holidays, rituals, and commandments keep the Jewish people Jewish, a point noted already over a century ago by the Hebrew writer Asher Ginzberg when he famously observed, "more than Jews have kept the Sabbath, the Sabbath kept [guarded] the Jewish people."[45] And conversely, Jewish families without religion don't stay Jewish for very long.

This is not to suggest that religion is a magical amulet consistently able to protect American Jews from disappearing into the larger society. The numbers of Jews who choose to distance themselves from Jewish life despite their religious upbringing are hardly negligible. Religion is not a guaranteed antidote to assimilation. But it still is the strongest predictor of Jewish involvement. Judging from the evidence we currently have, Jewish religious identification and participation correlate strongly with all other forms of Jewishness. The more ritually observant Jews are and the more often they attend synagogue, the more likely they are to invest themselves and their financial resources in sustaining all forms of Jewish life.[46] And conversely, declining religious participation usually is associated with weakening peoplehood connections. Why, then, write a book about American Judaism? Because aside from anti-Semitic persecution, nothing is likely to play a larger role in determining the future of Jewish life in this country than the lived religion of ordinary Jews.

PART I

The Religious Lives of Ordinary American Jews

1

FINDING MEANING

THE IMPORTANCE OF BELIEF, BELONGING,

AND GOOD DEEDS

At a time when powerful social forces are eroding many aspects of American Jewish life, over four million adults by their own reckoning continue to identify with Judaism. To be sure, they vary considerably in their religious beliefs and practices. Some are minimalists, allowing religious activities into their lives only on rare and carefully circumscribed occasions; others are maximalists, regular participants in public worship who observe many traditional religious rituals and some new ones; and then there are those who fall somewhere in between—practicing some customs faithfully but ignoring many others.

Were we to rely solely on survey research about these Jews, the major emphasis would be on how little they believe and observe. Take the findings of the Pew Research Center for example. Here is a quick compendium:[1]

- "Jews exhibit lower levels of religious commitment than the U.S. general public, among whom 56% say religion is very important in their lives and an additional 23% say it is somewhat important." The comparative figures for Jews are 26 percent (very important) and 29 percent (somewhat important.)

- "Belief in God is much more common among the general public than among Jews. Even among Jews by religion, belief in God is less common than among members of other major U.S. religious groups."
- "Jews report attending religious services at much lower rates than do other religious groups. Six-in-ten Christians (62%) say they attend religious services at least once or twice a month (compared with 29% of Jews by religion)."
- A few traditional religious rituals are widely observed, such as attendance at a Passover Seder and fasting on Yom Kippur, but smaller percentages are performing these rituals than in the past.
- "Within all three denominational movements, most of the switching is in the direction of less traditional Judaism."

Aside from the unremitting negative news of these findings, it is striking how little survey data tell us about the texture of American Jewish religious life. And how can it be otherwise given the omnibus approach of survey research about Jews? Most such studies collect data on demography and also seek information about a range of additional themes—connections to the Jewish people, philanthropy, volunteering, cultural pursuits, both positive and negative interactions with non-Jews, and attitudes regarding American and Israeli policies, among other topics. Understandably, with such a broad purview, it's impossible for surveys to probe more deeply about religious beliefs and practices among American Jews.

As a consequence, we are left with many questions begging to be answered. The Pew study, for example, found smaller proportions of Jews, as compared to other Americans, who are convinced about the existence of God. The obvious question is, why is that so? And though there probably are a range of possible reasons, there is yet another question to be posed: Why do Jews who are either atheists or agnostics participate in some synagogue worship services? Synagogue attendance rates also are a bit of a mystery: Why do fewer than 10 percent of Reform Jews who pay membership dues to synagogues and 21 percent of those affiliated with a Conservative congregation attend services weekly, yet the rest continue to pay dues to support congregations they rarely, if ever, attend?[2] As to religious practices, surveys generally inquire about the observance of a handful of rituals. What do we know about how the rest of Judaism's "613 commandments" are observed?[3] Why are some rituals observed fairly widely and yet others seem to be falling by the wayside? And, most difficult to answer, what does the observance of religious rituals mean to average Jews?

As I address these questions, I distinguish between Jews who identify with the range of religiously liberal movements—Reform, Reconstructionist, Renewal, Conservative Judaism and also the so-called "Nones" who do not identify as Jewish by religion—and Orthodox Jews. The lines of division, as we shall see, are not necessarily as sharply etched as some would imagine, but Orthodox Jews are on the whole considerably different in their patterns of Jewish religious participation. Accordingly, this chapter and the next will focus on the non-Orthodox population, and then chapter 3 will examine the Orthodox.

God and Ultimate Questions

To gather information on the texture of Jewish religious life that surveys cannot capture, I interviewed close observers of Jewish religious behavior—rabbis and others who come into contact with many "ordinary" Jews—to reflect on which aspects of Judaism seem to resonate with non-Orthodox Jews today and which do not. As an icebreaker, I opened most interviews with the same query: What kinds of religious questions are you asked? In most cases, non-Orthodox rabbis responded that their congregants are more likely to pose questions about Israel and the Middle East or personal matters than specifically religious issues. Conservative rabbis noted inquiries they receive about the proper observance of certain holidays, especially Passover with its very complicated rules about foodstuffs that may not be brought into a Jewish house during the weeklong holiday. Both Conservative and Reform rabbis reported receiving many "What does Judaism say about . . . ?" kinds of questions—for example, about the immortality of the soul, when life begins, and how the universe was created. Most commonly, rabbis field questions from people facing life crises—how to cope when a marriage comes to an end, a child is in trouble, criminal charges are filed, or agonizing end-of-life medical decisions must be made. Often, rabbis say, congregants are less interested in answers than in being reassured that they are doing the right thing. Younger congregants often ask for advice on how to explain illness and death to their children, or how to pass along Jewish traditions to the next generation.

Many rabbis also report they receive quasi-theological questions from congregants at times of travail: Why does God allow good people to suffer? What does Judaism have to say about the afterlife? And how am I to believe when facing either my own or a loved one's terminal illness? These, of course, are among the most fundamental of all existential questions. But what is clear from the rabbis' responses is how questions about God arise for most synagogue-affiliated Jews primarily in the face of life-altering circumstances. Here lies a paradox: When we consider how central public worship is to the mission of synagogues, why do questions of belief arise so infrequently? After all, worship services are replete with references to God, whether the prayers express thanksgiving, petition, exaltation, or pleas for forgiveness. In most non-Orthodox synagogues (and many Orthodox ones too),[4] though, there is little discussion *about* God.[5]

That said, rabbis are well aware their congregants struggle to believe in a God Who hears and answers prayers and is actively involved in the fate of individual humans. To be sure, rabbis in non-Orthodox settings say some of their congregants hold fairly traditional theological beliefs, often reporting to their rabbis on material they have read on websites of various Orthodox outreach organizations. At the other end of the spectrum, rabbis report about congregants who seek spiritual uplift unconnected to God, perhaps some sense of oneness with nature or something transcendent. And then in the middle are those congregants who would rather not give the matter too much thought or struggle to imagine a deity unlike what they learned about in religious school.

When asked, Reform rabbis are the most direct about the problem God poses for many of their congregants. A Silicon Valley rabbi quotes an oft-voiced plea she hears: "I am a rational person and God does not make sense to me. Don't talk to me about that." Younger members especially are unlikely to find meaning in talk about God, she notes. This rabbi traces her congregants' skepticism to their surroundings, a high-tech environment that attracts many people with an advanced education and a scientific bent. Yet the same issues preoccupy Reform congregants in other regions of the country. The rabbi of a Mid-Atlantic congregation recalled her amazement upon hearing her synagogue president describe herself as an openly avowed atheist. The same rabbi asked members to jot down their concept of God during an adult education class. Many were inarticulate, and a surprising number confided their lack of belief. In still another region of the country, the rabbi of a Midwestern congregation flatly states: "God is very distracting to most Reform Jews. . . . Most people are not certain about their relationship to God or Judaism."

It's not only references to the Deity but also the language of prayers that creates what one Reform rabbi candidly describes as a "roadblock." For one thing, most Reform congregants and quite a few Conservative ones cannot read the Hebrew words of prayer, let alone understand what they mean. Hence the new Reform prayer book, *Mishkan Tefilla*, has been published in an edition including transliterations of every prayer. Quite a few Reform temples compile their own liturgical compendia, heavily laced with transliterations, to help congregants pronounce the words in Hebrew—or keep them to a minimum. For their part, Conservative rabbis report a significant decline over time in their congregants' ability to decode the Hebrew and to make sense of the worship service. A West Coast Conservative rabbi contrasts his current congregants with those of twenty years ago: in the past "there still were reflexive Jews who knew how to *daven* [pray], but they're dying out. The current population does not have the vocabulary or Hebrew and holiday literacy." As a consequence, worship services seem inscrutable, and certainly alien, to high percentages of those who do attend often, let alone to the infrequent attenders.

And then there are questions of meaning. When an individual engages in public worship just a few days each year, what sense does the entire exercise make? Public prayer is a discipline, requiring training and practice; it does not work as a sometime thing. One can imagine how awkward an infrequent worshipper might feel mouthing unfamiliar words. Worse still, often the English translations fail to mediate the dissonance between traditional Jewish theology and what the average synagogue-attender personally believes. At a time when a therapeutic worldview pervades every aspect of their lives, what are synagogue-goers to make of a liturgy that refers explicitly to sin, a category that is anathema to the mental health profession? Or for that matter, as a Reform rabbi observed, "People don't know how to deal with the prayers claiming that 'God alone is our help.' And what about physicians? People wonder whether they have to believe that." Some Bnai Mitzvah families, he reports, "ask for God-lite service" in order to sidestep the implications of many awkward prayers. But the more effort goes into eliminating dissonant concepts, the more confusion people feel about the purpose of the enterprise. Reporting on an odd conversation, a Reform rabbi describes the perplexity expressed by a congregant who asked him whether it is wrong of her to feel during prayer that she is speaking to God. "Is that contrary to Judaism because Reform de-emphasizes the supernatural?" she asked.

The candor of Reform rabbis about their congregants' struggle with belief in God should not lead us to conclude that such skepticism resides only within the laity of that denomination. Conservative rabbis apparently encounter less pushback in public discussions about God—or perhaps they speak less about God—but they too report about private conversations in which congregants wrestle with the traditional conception of an omnipotent God Who intervenes in earthly matters and hears, let alone responds to, prayers. "I told a congregant struggling with the traditional concept of God that I also don't believe in that kind of God," reports a Conservative rabbi on the East Coast. A West Coast Conservative rabbi describes the beliefs of his younger congregants as follows: "The God they are not interested in is a personal God who intervenes in history and commands in discrete language. That kind of God keeps them away. Young people feel they have a soul even if they don't believe in God." Rabbi Gil Steinlauf, the former senior rabbi of a large Conservative congregation in Washington, DC, addressed the issue head-on in a High Holiday sermon he titled, "Why Jews Should NOT Believe in God." The point of his address was not to pitch atheism, but to move his congregants away from the question of what they believe to how they might live as Jews.[6]

What these comments suggest is that today's non-Orthodox rabbis are acutely aware of serious doubts their congregants harbor about the traditional conception of God—and are willing to speak to the issue. Rather than ignore this reality, rabbis are addressing it directly in public, making the case that you don't have to be a believer to come to synagogue. Gil Steinlauf, for example, continued his sermon as follows:

> There are so many Jewish people who tell me, "I just don't believe in God." They try to conjure up an image of God as depicted in our prayers and in the Torah, and in good faith, they just can't buy it. What these good and well-meaning people may not realize is that these images and concepts of God in our Torah and prayers are actually more like vessels or tools that exist as a place holder, as a container to hold our experience of life that is unnamable.

Speaking for quite a few of her colleagues, a Reform rabbi reported: "We give permission to people who come here *not* to believe in God." A male colleague of hers noted his preference to frame conversations with skeptical congregants by asking, "Which God don't you believe in? Turns out, the skeptics discover, that other congregants don't believe in that God either."

None of this is to suggest that most Jews are atheists or agnostics. The Pew data indicate this is not the case. But it is to observe that questions about belief are handled in a far more open and less dogmatic way than one might imagine; and though it cannot be proved because we lack the comparative data, the difficulties of believing in God, let alone varied conceptions of God, probably are more frankly discussed now than in the past. This may reflect the rabbis' own theological struggles. In all likelihood, the more important reason is that rabbis have heard enough from their congregants to know they are addressing Jews whose beliefs run the gamut from traditional conceptions of God to agnosticism or atheism, and therefore references to the Deity may elicit considerable discomfort.[7]

To test the waters, a few of the rabbis I interviewed referred to their own efforts at administering informal questions to adult and teen congregants, asking them to characterize their conception of God. The results suggested a fair amount of confusion, embarrassment, and inarticulateness, even as some held fast to traditional beliefs. A more ambitious survey undertaken by one Reform rabbi was sent out the day after Yom Kippur a few years ago and was answered by 40 percent of the congregants.[8] Consistent with national surveys of Jews, the majority of congregants (60 percent) affirmed their belief in God. But the survey also elicited diverse views on the nature of this God. Fewer than half (45 percent) found evidence of God's work in the universe. When asked about their agreement with a traditional conception of a God Who "rewards good people and punishes bad people," 74 percent rejected that concept and only 40 percent believed in an all-powerful deity. "And is God just?" the survey asked. Although 26 percent said yes, 30 percent indicated they do not believe God is just and 43 percent were not sure. Perhaps most telling of what impedes their belief in such a deity, "two hundred congregants expressed concerns about justice, such as: 'God, why do bad things happen to good people?'"

What, then, did the congregants affirm about God? They associated God with the capacity *of humans* to do good, to help the sick and needy, and to offer hope; these resonated as Godly attributes. "Most of my congregants do not construe God as a celestial figure Who acts in this world. For them," the rabbi concluded based on his survey. "God is a presence or power. For them, God is not so much 'above' us in heaven as God is 'beside' us or 'within' us. Most believe that God 'acts' when we act with God's attributes, such as love, kindness, and justice."

Of course it can be said that a survey of a single Reform congregation may not be generalizable to other synagogues in that movement, let alone to Jews attending a different kind of synagogue or none. But coupled with reports by numerous non-Orthodox rabbis about how many of their congregants struggle with or are repelled by traditional conceptions of God, the so-called "God survey" adds one further piece of evidence that theological skepticism is a factor of some importance among synagogue members. And even those who claim to be believers are far from uniform in their conceptions of God.

Praying and Congregating

With all this skepticism and discomfort with traditional theological formulations—and in the absence of a strong communal culture encouraging participation—it is not surprising that regular, once a week or more, attendance at prayer services is limited to minorities in the non-Orthodox sector. Over 40 percent of American Jews claim to attend synagogue never or seldom, and even among the narrower population of Jews who identify as Jewish by religion, nearly one-third rarely if ever attend services. What's more, fully 65 percent of Jews who are members of Reform temples attend only a few times a year, such as for High Holidays; among members of Conservative synagogues, the few-day-a-year Jews number nearly 43 percent.[9] Rabbis also report that when the infrequent attenders do set foot in the synagogue, they are more likely than in the past to stay for only a short while. *Yizkor* services on Yom Kippur, a time when the deceased are remembered, attract the largest crowds in Reform and Conservative synagogues. Once that prayer has been said, synagogue sanctuaries tend to empty until the concluding *Neila* service. Conservative rabbis also note the significant drop off in attendance on the second day of Rosh Hashanah compared to the first day; Reform temples, if they offer such services at all on the second day of the Jewish New Year, experience an even more precipitous decline. And when the three festivals—Passover, Shavuot, and Sukkot—fall on weekdays (i.e., workdays), attendance in most Conservative synagogues tends to be sparse; Reform temples barely muster any attendees.

The obvious question is, why don't more synagogue members attend? It's a question that has prompted much hand-wringing in leadership circles, and not a little finger-pointing by critics of synagogue life, with boring synagogue services and poor rabbinic leadership serving as the standard, if simplistic, answers. No doubt at times there is a measure of truth to such complaints. But there are a host of reasons why Jews absent themselves from public worship, which may have little to do with the inadequacies of the congregations. Those who are skeptical of the religious enterprise are unlikely to attend unless they are subjected to family or communal pressure. And then there are others who protect their leisure time zealously. Why spend precious hours in the synagogue at services when recreational, shopping, and cultural opportunities beckon? For another, synagogues are intimidating environments for those unfamiliar with their rituals and liturgies. Adults who are highly competent in their professional and social lives find it off-putting to enter a space where they lack rudimentary skills, and therefore feel incompetent. "When I give a class on how to lift the Torah and dress it, how to light a Hanukkah Menorah, or make a Seder, people do not come," lamented a Reform rabbi. "It's not because they know; they're embarrassed that they don't know or maybe don't care." Whether it's indifference or the greater attractiveness of other options is not easy to determine, but non-Orthodox synagogues thus far have not found a way to draw the majority of their members to worship services with any frequency.

Perhaps the more important question to ask, then, is this: Why do those who do attend services with some regularity bother to come? In the perception of rabbis, the motivation often is social: people who attend with some regularity enjoy connecting with other Jews. Weekly services offer the opportunity to see friends and make new ones. Not surprisingly, the staff of congregations work hard to link members to like-minded individuals. They establish "communities of practice" among their congregants so that small groups form around shared interests, hobbies, and common stages of the life cycle. Synagogues like churches serve as places of gathering, often less so for worship than for social interactions.

This is especially the case in areas lacking dense Jewish population centers. A Conservative rabbi put it this way about his congregants: "Community matters to people in the Midwest. Here demographic realities have replaced ethnicity: people are lonely as Jews, so they find ways to connect." Much the same has been noted by rabbis in the South and also in suburbs lacking a strong Jewish infrastructure.

We should note how much this quest for Jewish companionship puts paid to the prevailing belief about today's American Jews, especially millennials. In our time, we are repeatedly told by observers that most Jews feel very comfortable among their Gentile friends and no longer seek a Jewish social group. They resist parochialism, abhor tribalism, and yearn for connections to all kinds of people. If they enter a Jewish setting they prefer to bring their non-Jewish friends along. Therefore, the conventional wisdom states, the old associationalism—the aspiration to join in order to make and see friends—characteristic of mid-twentieth-century Jewish behavior is now passé. Perhaps such is the case for Jews who absent themselves from synagogues. But it is not true of those who do attend with some regularity.

The quest for companionship, however, is not the only attraction. At least in the perception of rabbis, the desire to be part of a community is a second, albeit related, lure. Those who join want to belong to something larger than themselves, preferably to a congregation with some cachet. They take pride in their congregation—its history and traditions, contributions to the betterment of society, and caring efforts on behalf of its members.[10] As a Conservative rabbi of a large West Coast congregation put it after describing most of his members as nonbelievers, "They seek a personal narrative that's bigger than them." And many members of synagogues, it would seem, regard their association with a prestigious synagogue as elevating. If nothing else, it gives them a sense of belonging, and thereby an anchor, if not an identity.

In both Conservative and Reform synagogues, a concerted effort by the leadership is attracting people to engagement with mutual aid, or to use the Hebrew word, *Hesed*.[11] In a Conservative synagogue on the East Coast, the rabbi notes how much interest members express in getting involved by participating in groups that organize a *shiva* (a period of mourning for relatives of the recently deceased), *bikur holim* (visiting the sick) societies, committees to aid newlyweds and young families and those delivering Passover goods. Other Hesed committees raise money for school supplies, help at a shelter for the homeless, or collect clothing for Israeli soldiers. They also raise funds for nonsectarian causes such as relief for Haitians, refuges from war zones, and the like.

It would be misleading, though, to suggest that these activities bring large proportions of members into the synagogue precincts. A significant number of congregants in non-Orthodox synagogues continue to behave as so-called "three-day-a-year Jews" who attend on High Holidays and the occasional Bar/Bat Mitzvah, but rarely set foot in the synagogue sanctuary otherwise. In the perception of rabbis, these Jews appear lost and confused in the worship precinct, often displaying no sense of proper synagogue decorum: they may use their smartphones during services to send text messages or photograph the proceedings, and may not open a prayer book.

Why, then, do they attend at all? Perhaps, suggested one Reform rabbi, they come on the High Holidays because on some instinctual level they still relate to the traditional Jewish belief that on the Days of Awe one's fate is sealed. Like so much else that brings in the infrequent worshippers, the High Holidays are connected to the life cycle: in this case, to the awareness of human fragility. "Why else," he mused, "would they spend such energy on ensuring they have tickets? Why else would they still wish to be present?" Two additional reasons were cited by rabbis to explain the lure of the High Holidays: one is that infrequent attendees still want to derive some uplift, if not from the prayers then from the sermon. And the second is that attendance connects individuals to their families. Being in synagogue a few days a year, often sitting in the same pew as their forebearers, provides some congregants with a sense of continuity; they are partaking of an experience stretching back into the history of their family and also linking their children to previous generations of their immediate family.

Several of these motivations seem to come together during a new High Holiday ritual that has been adopted by a number of non-Orthodox synagogues. It is customary during the closing service on the Day of Atonement for the ark housing the Torah scrolls to remain open and, as a sign of respect for the Torah, congregants stand for the hour-long *Neila* service. In recent years, some Conservative synagogues, and perhaps others too, have invited attendees to stand directly before the ark for a moment of private prayer or reflection. Hundreds of people line up and snake their way through the sanctuary for the opportunity to stand with their loved ones before the Torah scrolls. It is unknowable what is going through their minds, how they formulate and express their private meditation, or what they believe about God. But what is beyond doubt is that hundreds of Jews in some synagogues—including those who attend regularly and others who come only infrequently—when offered the opportunity will patiently stand in line to have a few moments to express what is in their hearts, their deepest hopes and fears, at the most solemn moment on the Jewish calendar.

Frequent Attenders

As only a minority of members attend services frequently, it stands to reason that the regulars tend to fall into a limited number of categories: Among younger Jews in attendance are parents who try to model religious participation for their children. Empty-nesters who attend regularly tend to be people who were taken as children to the synagogue by their parents and developed the lifelong habit of participating in prayer services.[12] Converts to Judaism constitute a growing population among regulars: their early life experiences attending church week in, week out seems to translate into steadfast synagogue attendance. In many congregations there is a small core of members who were inspired by their Jewish educational experiences, a personal connection to the clergy, or some serendipitous inspiration to take on regular prayer attendance as a discipline. And then, not to be overlooked are those participants who find meaning, if not solace, in the rhythm of the prayers, the opportunity to sit quietly with their own thoughts and reflect upon the past week, and the chance to engage in some personal prayer and meditation. We have no way to know how many attend synagogue for these private reasons, but they most assuredly are among the regulars.

It is hardly a secret that many families with younger children attend services and sometimes become actively involved in other ways because the synagogue, as one rabbi put it, "holds them hostage" by making attendance mandatory during the year leading up to a Bar or Bat Mitzvah. They too can be found among the regulars, but only for a very brief time. Of late, this too is becoming a more difficult sell to many families who opt to mark their child's milestone in a private setting, rather than a synagogue. (Some demur, telling their clergy, as one rabbi reported, "We don't need community rabbi; we have community in our kids' dance class.") And once their youngest child has been called to the Torah for the first time, many families drop their synagogue membership—not infrequently the day after the Bar or Bat Mitzvah party.

It would be hard to overestimate the centrality of the Bar and Bat Mitzvah production in Conservative and Reform synagogues. Conservative synagogues struggle to recognize the coming-of-age ritual without permitting that ceremony to monopolize the entire Sabbath morning service. In most Reform temples, the Saturday morning service is attended almost exclusively by the family and friends of the Bar or Bat Mitzvah.[13] The consequences of this development have been profound for Reform temples. As one Chicago-based rabbi describes it: "Because the B'nai Mitzvah service is really focused on the child, with our kids leading almost the entire service, the only people who come are . . . invited guests. In reality, the service would be boring [to an outsider]; it wouldn't be fulfilling to me as a worshipper. And the people who are there are the unaffiliated, disenfranchised, shut down population. I sometimes feel like the Statue of Liberty: 'Give me your tired . . . your huddled masses yearning to breathe free.'"[14]

People, of course, come to synagogue not solely to engage in public worship. For some, the lure is an opportunity to study. Classes are available in most synagogues on a variety of Jewish topics, many having little to do with Judaism. There are reading clubs for discussing recent publications, classes on archaeology of the Bible, self-help classes on improving one's relationship with a spouse or child. Reform congregations offer Sabbath morning classes on the Torah portion of the week that tend to attract a highly committed core. Sometimes congregants are augmented by non-Jewish clergy from neighboring churches and academics from nearby institutions of higher learning who are attracted by the open-minded ways in which the study of the Bible is conducted. Most do not stay to hear the Torah chanted, but are there for the intellectual stimulation.

And then there are those who come to the synagogue to engage in some kind of social action program to benefit nonsectarian causes. Non-Orthodox synagogues, particularly Reform temples, have packaged themselves as places where Jews gather to venture forth into the wider society as volunteers. Not atypically, a Reform rabbi reports that "40 to 50 percent of my congregants are involved in social action. They volunteer, tutor, do voter rights registration, visit the sick, plant trees to green the earth. . . . Their connection to Judaism comes after their social justice involvement. I name for people what they are already doing and connect [them] to Jewish values." When controversial public policy questions are being considered, some congregations swing into action.[15] A Conservative rabbi reports that when same-sex marriage was on the ballot in his state, "This galvanized the Jewish community more than anything else. The last year and a half has been taken up by social justice work far more than *Halacha* [Jewish law]."

Indeed, the role assumed by a good many rabbis in our time is to sanctify the preexisting social and ideological commitments of their congregants by figuratively blessing them as somehow Jewish in inspiration. For congregants this system offers validation of what they wish to do in any event. And for rabbis, it offers a potential way to link otherwise unengaged congregants to something Jewish. If only Jews would understand how much they are motivated by profound Jewish values, the thinking goes, somehow their connections to Judaism will become stronger. Undoubtedly some individuals have experienced such religious growth while engaged in social justice work. A fair number of Conservative and Reform rabbis, though, express uncertainty about what this arrangement is accomplishing. Off the record, some will speak of how social justice work is often a way to "avoid waging the battles the synagogue cannot win"—that is, the campaign to deepen their congregants' involvement with prayer, observance, and other aspects of Jewish religious commitment. Or as a Reform rabbi, without a trace of irony, put it about her congregation: "We have a strong social justice message here. People love it. It's so nonthreatening."

Golden Rule Jews

We come here to the core religious imperative embraced by the large majority of non-Orthodox Jews. When their neighbors enact it, they are called "Golden Rule" Christians.[16] Among Jews, it may be linked to a variation of the same trope uttered by Hillel, the first-century sage, who encapsulated the teachings of Judaism in a pithy phrase: "what is hateful to you, do not do to your neighbor."[17]

There is no shortage of explications in blogs and articles of how ordinary contemporary American Jews understand their religion as fundamentally an imperative "to be a good person." Here is a characteristic example: "I'm not invested in who my God is or how (s)he is different from yours. I'm not invested in rules and scriptures and commandments. My religion is pretty much to be a good person, to treat people with compassion and respect, and to act in ways that are honorable and will not make me regret my behavior the next day."[18] What is articulated here is a complete rejection of the notion that to be Jewish involves the acceptance of some externally imposed commandments. The conception of Judaism as a package of expectations, let alone of divine commandments, seems to be alien to the current worldview. Rather, internally generated rights and wrongs are all that matter.

The momentousness of this shift in outlook was discussed by Charles Liebman, the distinguished observer of American Jewish life. In the recent past, he wrote, "People might disagree about [the religion's] specific contents while agreeing that Judaism referred to the norms, values and beliefs that characterized the Jewish religion. There were those who argued that Judaism was basically a culture rather than a religion and some even argued that the term civilization was more suitable. But at its core, Judaism . . . referred to . . . the relationship between the Jewish people and God. These norms, values and beliefs existed independently of how individual Jews behaved or what individual Jews believed. In other words, there was a structure or an essence called Judaism and the behavior or beliefs of individual Jews could be measured by the extent to which they conformed to or deviated from the norms and beliefs of Judaism."[19]

The shift described here is not from a population of Jews that once was highly observant to one that observes little of Judaism today. There never was a golden era of widespread religious observance in American Jewish history. And the purpose of raising this issue is not to wax nostalgic for some idyllic past when religious piety was the norm among Jews. Rather, what Liebman observes is how the ideal has disappeared. With the exception of some, but certainly not all, elites in the non-Orthodox sectors, the understanding of Judaism as a normative structure with clear dos and don'ts has fallen by the wayside.

What has replaced the normative conception is a kind of "Golden Rule" Judaism. Note the emphasis in the quote above about the importance of being "a good person." Jewish texts, of course, have a great deal to say about how the Jew is to live as a good person, how one's behavior ought to imitate God's perfection, and which actions are either prescribed or proscribed. In the current environment, those understandings of how a Jew ought to be a good person have been replaced with a more subjective, self-invented, improvisational approach, one highly influenced by the culture of America's elites. The large majority of non-Orthodox Jews have internalized a very contemporary set of values and ways of thinking about ethical decision making indistinguishable from those of their non-Jewish peers.

They have been encouraged in this direction by religious leaders who invented a new commandment during the 1980s—the injunction to engage in tikkun olam, repairing the world. Though virtually unknown a few decades ago, tikkun olam is now invoked across the Jewish religious spectrum, including by some Orthodox rabbis, and has gained such widespread currency that it has been cited by American political leaders of other faiths. To be sure, the rabbis of the Talmud already wrote about an obligation to care for the welfare of the city in which one lives. What they meant by that in practice is debatable, but they surely did not conceive of that responsibility with the kind of elasticity it has taken on today. "By the mid-1980s," writes Jonathan Krasner in his clear-eyed history of this term, "rabbis, educators, communal workers, activists and others were invoking *tikkun olam* as a value concept in support of a variety of humanistic and distinctly Jewish causes, ranging from environmentalism and nuclear non-proliferation to Palestinian-Israeli reconciliation and unrestricted Soviet Jewish emigration."[20] Whatever action a Jew undertakes in a well-meaning way has come to be seen as an act of tikkun olam.

Indeed, at any gathering of Jewish donors, one is likely to hear support for nonsectarian causes described as motivated by a Jewish religious imperative. Regardless of how remote the cause is to anything improving Jewish life, the rationale of tikkun olam is ready to hand. One donor may describe his interest in cleaning up the lakes and rivers of America as his Jewish cause, while another speaks of her interest in saving the whales. A good many Jews are convinced that mobilizing support for a political candidate who espouses the correct point of view is an act of tikkun olam. The term itself is sufficiently flexible to justify virtually any altruistic activity. Strikingly, it also serves as a religious justification for whatever causes are close to the heart of a do-gooder.

How did this new religious understanding come about? During the last quarter of the twentieth century, it became clear to observers of Jewish life how few American Jews were committed to religious imperatives. Rather than resist those trends in the non-Orthodox sector, a growing chorus of voices made the case in public for tikkun olam as an ersatz form of Judaism. A commitment to economic and social justice, one prominent writer influential in the Reform movement argued, could "serve as our preeminent motive, the path through which our past is vindicated, our present warranted and our future affirmed."[21] In other words, for Jews with little connection to Judaism, social justice would serve as a surrogate religion. Judging from oft-heard laments by numerous rabbis, emphatically including Reform rabbis whose movement unabashedly portrays tikkun olam as authentic Judaism, the promoters of this ideology have triumphed. Large sectors of the non-Orthodox population have embraced a Golden Rule religion rationalized through repeated invocations of tikkun olam. Alas, it has not brought large numbers of members into synagogues, nor has it translated into other forms of religious participation for the large majority of congregants. Note the rueful admission of a Conservative rabbi about his social action activists: "People who do this have virtually no other involvement with the synagogue."

The small proportion of members attending religious services in non-Orthodox synagogues provides quantifiable evidence of just how little has been gained by religious institutions as they've promoted the mantra of tikkun olam. The damage, though, is also qualitative: a rich, complex, and at times contradictory religious system has been reduced to a set of vague slogans—"Justice, justice, shall you pursue," "Made in God's image," "Love the stranger," and "Repair the world."[22] These may be the tropes favored by Golden Rule Jews, but they offer little religious depth or guidance.

2

A JUDAISM FOR PEAK MOMENTS

HOW NON-ORTHODOX JEWS PRACTICE

Beyond embracing a Jewish version of the Golden Rule as a religious imperative, non-Orthodox Jews continue to observe some specific religious rituals, even as they eschew many others. For individuals, this selectivity undoubtedly is often shaped by idiosyncratic needs or interests. But broader patterns are also at work.[1] Understanding why particular observances are retained across a wider swath of the population and once abandoned ones have been reappropriated offers important clues about what Judaism means to different sectors of the non-Orthodox population.

Rituals Retained, Abandoned, and Reappropriated

Child-centered rituals are among the more widely practiced observances. There is nothing especially new about this. Sociologists writing in the early 1960s already identified the rituals most likely to be retained as those with a pediatric dimension.[2] Survey research indicates that attendance at a Seder on Passover and lighting Hanukkah candles rank highest among rituals observed by non-Orthodox Jews, and both are child-centered. The former is specifically directed to children, for the Haggadah aims to explain to them the significance of the exodus from Egypt; and the latter involves gift-giving especially to children. It appears though that the percentage of Jews who partake of these customs has declined, perhaps because fewer non-Orthodox Jews have children at home.[3]

By providing an outlet for children to enjoy holidays in an exuberant fashion, some synagogues have succeeded in attracting a large turnout of parents who accompany their offspring to Purim festivities—either at the reading of the Scroll of Esther or simply at a holiday carnival. Simchat Torah partying is another attraction, as it gives children a chance to sing and dance in the synagogue in celebration of the cycle of completing and then beginning again the reading of the Torah. With the encouragement of their rabbis and the help of how-to classes offered by congregations, building and decorating a Sukkah has become a more popular home ritual among Conservative Jews, and to a far lesser extent Reform Jews.

A few Jewish holidays continue to be a time of family gatherings. The Seder and break-fast after Yom Kippur particularly are times for family togetherness. As one Reform rabbi put it, "The Seder has become a *shehecheyanu* time [an opportunity for thanksgiving that we are all still here and together], not one when we engage the Haggadah." With such a strong focus on family gathering, the connection of these holidays to the calendar of the Jewish people is attenuated. Little wonder, then, that some are rescheduling their get-togethers for the convenience of guests. Weekend evenings are much more suitable for accommodating out-of-towners than weekdays, and so growing numbers of families ignore when the rest of the Jewish people are celebrating the holiday and instead hold their Seder to suit the convenience of their guests. The goal is to "celebrate on the weekend whenever family can get together," a Reform rabbi reports, an unsurprising turn given the shift in focus from a holiday marking the liberation of a particular people to a holiday where family togetherness is front and center.

For a smaller but appreciable number of families, the Sabbath too is a time of gathering. Both Conservative and Reform rabbis estimate that a considerable proportion of congregants with children living at home or in fairly close proximity have some kind of Sabbath meal on Friday nights. If the Pew data are to be believed, these rabbis are exaggerating. Ninety percent of Orthodox Jews claim to light Friday night candles versus 34 percent of Conservative Jews, 10 percent of Reform Jews, and 9 percent of nondenominational ones.[4]

Congregations encourage families to welcome the Sabbath at home by offering model Friday night dinners to teach parents how to perform the proper rituals. For those Jews who do not have family living nearby, such as empty-nesters, both Reform and Conservative congregations are apt to offer a once-a-month Friday night dinner in the synagogue. Without minimizing these efforts, we should note how these dinners contribute to the erosion of home-based family meals on Shabbat. With both parents working outside the home and children who are overprogrammed, decreasing numbers of Jews make the time to dine together at home.

In addition to favoring family-oriented religious practices, non-Orthodox Jews tend to embrace rituals that can be translated into universal or American terms. Passover offers the quintessential opportunity for transforming a holiday marking the exodus of the Israelites from Egypt into a celebration of any form of freedom, whether the American civil rights movement, prison reform, union activism, or women's and gay liberation.[5]

With the rise of environmental concerns, Tu Bishvat—the New Year of Trees—has morphed into an Earth Day in liberal circles. Virtually ignored for much of Jewish history except in the most symbolic of ways,[6] the holiday took on a strong Zionist coloration in the middle decades of the twentieth century when the agricultural focus of Tu Bishvat was linked to plants grown in the land of Israel.[7] By the last quarter of the century, though, the association with Israel waned and was replaced with all manner of environmental concerns. The holiday has been linked in synagogue programs with "opposition to fracking, the importance of eating locally grown foods, reducing one's carbon footprint, and exploring why Jews should be vegans (or at least vegetarians)." In short order, the New Year for Trees has been redefined, Tevi Troy has noted, as a time to "indoctrinate children in environmental activism while cementing the Jewish community's ties to environmental causes."[8]

To a more limited yet still significant extent, the opportunity to engage in communal social gathering around holidays has attracted Jews of all backgrounds, especially those who are younger adults. Simchat Torah, when the cycle of reading the Torah is completed and then begun again, has become an occasion for celebration in very public ways. On the evening of the holiday in communities across the nation, neighboring synagogues of different denominations have merged their celebrations, often with the assistance of local authorities who close off streets to clear a path for the revelry, singing, dancing, and socializing.[9] A parallel development has been the emergence of all-night gatherings on Shavuot, a time traditionally set aside for Torah study. Neighboring congregations merge their study sessions. More ambitiously, in San Francisco a wide-scale festival known as Dawn has been held, also directed largely to young adults. Its organizers describe it "as a modern twist on this ancient Jewish holiday: Instead of staying up all night and studying Torah, the young adult Jewish community created Dawn to celebrate late into the night with off-beat religious discussions, multi-media art installations, dancing and musical performances." Though both holidays are integral to the traditional Jewish calendar, they have taken on new meaning and form in recent decades. We may speculate whether this is because they offer young people an opportunity to gather socially or serve as occasions for spontaneity and celebration or provide ways of accessing the Torah in a light-hearted, experimental fashion. Regardless of attendees' motivations, organizers have succeeded in translating these holidays into appealing happenings attracting large numbers of participants.[10]

The Life Cycle Connection

Life cycle milestones with personal and family connotations continue to be celebrated by a good many non-Orthodox Jews, albeit with some modifications of traditional forms in response to changing sensibilities. Chief among these are egalitarian concerns. To match the parties and ceremonies connected with a boy's birth, a Shalom Bat or Simchat Bat ceremony has become popular as a means to welcome the birth of girls with an appropriate religious ceremony. It remains noteworthy that the birth of a child continues to resonate as tangible evidence not only of generational continuity, but also of Jewish religious continuity. Whether for a male or a female child, prayers are uttered, the child is given a Jewish name, and a festive meal is consumed.[11]

As related by rabbis, it appears that circumcision is still widely practiced by Jewish families. Growing numbers of families opt to have their sons circumcised in a hospital by a physician without benefit of clergy and liturgy, and not on the child's eighth day. The tradition of naming a male baby at a bris has fallen by the wayside in many families, and if done at all occurs months after the circumcision in a synagogue ceremony on a Sabbath morning. Moreover, with sky-high intermarriage rates, the bris is no longer to be taken for granted, as either a surgical act or a ritual one.

Though numbers are impossible to come by, there appears to be a small but growing movement to reject the *brit milah* (bris) or covenantal circumcision on the grounds that it is a form of child abuse since an eight-day-old baby cannot give consent to the removal of a part of his body.[12] The fact that boys have a special ceremony marking their bodies for life while girls have no analogous ritual is also unacceptable to some egalitarians. And it appears that in some intermarried families one parent or the other cannot abide such an act.[13] What was taken for granted by Jews over the course of three millennia is now labeled by some as barbaric, cruel, and inhumane—precisely the charges hurled at Jews by anti-Semitic polemicists over two millennia. But now the harshest critics are coming from within the Jewish population.

Many who reject the physical act of the bris still hold a symbolic ceremony involving washing the baby's feet or anointing it; and most involve a baby-naming opportunity. One particularly noteworthy custom some promoters of an alternative bris have put forward involves the cutting of a pomegranate. Why cut this fruit? "The pomegranate represents fertility and abundance . . . and it bleeds when you cut it. Some people might want to actually cut something if they want a ritual that closely mimics a *brit milah*. It's a way to acknowledge the role circumcision has played in the history of the Jewish people; it's not just giving the baby a Hebrew name and moving on. And the pomegranate has long been a Jewish symbol."[14]

The puberty milestone marking an adolescent's taking on of the commandments continues to be widely celebrated. In a moment of cynicism, one rabbi I interviewed defined the Bar and Bat Mitzvah celebration as the wedding parents are able to control as a Jewish occasion. Most non-Orthodox parents have no assurance their child will go on to marry at all, let alone wed a Jewish person. At the coming-of-age ceremony, though, parents have a chance to incorporate Jewish rites into a very public ceremony for their child. It continues to be a major event in the lives of Jews, celebrated with much joy and at great expense.

Most Jewish children who celebrate a Bar or Bat Mitzvah do so in a synagogue setting. In larger congregations, the date must be reserved years in advance and children often are asked to double up with a peer because there are more candidates for the ceremony than available Sabbath dates. (The summers and holiday seasons are avoided because guests of the family may not be free to attend.) And for the majority of those who join synagogues, the system continues to work. In a study conducted in the mid-1990s, sociologist Barry Kosmin found that children who recently had celebrated a Bar or Bat Mitzvah in a Conservative congregation identified what occurred in the synagogue sanctuary as the highlight of the experience.[15]

For a growing population of non-Orthodox Jews, though, the demands congregations make of parents and the costs associated with these celebrations are deemed burdensome. To address their needs, a cottage industry of private Bar/Bat Mitzvah entrepreneurs has sprung up, including outreach workers, independent rabbis and cantors, and laypeople versed in synagogue practices. These independent operators prepare children to perform, organize a special service focused entirely on the young child, and even provide a meeting room for the ceremony. Unlike synagogues, which have rules by which families must abide, these independent operators accede to the wishes of families. A study conducted in the Chicago area describes how everything from the rituals included in the service to the prayer books employed can vary greatly. With the families in the driver's seat, services can be highly traditional or divorced from anything resembling a Jewish religious service. Reported one parent: "We found a tutor who told us that she can personalize the service. We don't have to have every prayer. She picks different texts and poems and songs and asks us, 'How do these fit into your family?' The kids were happy with it. It was short and to the point, around an hour and a half." What this represents, the Chicago study notes, is a "shift towards a more personalized, customized Judaism." Such a shift reflects "radical individualism, a trend towards consumerism in Judaism or a generation that 'wants what . . . [it] wants and needs to customize everything.'"[16] Motives aside, the consequences are clear: the ceremonies offered by entrepreneurs offer religion lite without community.

Often connected to the celebration of a Bar or Bat Mitzvah, a new semi-religious ritual has developed in recent decades—the family trip to Israel. Once again, numbers are hard to come by, but a small industry has cropped up in Israel to facilitate family trips to celebrate a milestone event either at the Western Wall (Kotel) or at Masada, the mountaintop redoubt in the Judean desert. Though most popular among Modern Orthodox Jews, these celebratory trips have been embraced by a good number of Conservative families and a smaller number of Reform ones. Not only are extended family members included, but even close friends of the family make the trip to partake in the celebration. Are these trips religious in nature? Insofar as a special religious service is held and a thirteen-year-old is called to the Torah, they appear to be so. More broadly, the trip is designed to link multiple generations of a family to one another and to Israel—in other words, to some transcendent experience of Jewish peoplehood. This is a fairly new ritual and an expensive one, to boot; time will tell whether the changing politics of the American Jewish community—what some have dubbed the "distancing from Israel"—will allow for its perpetuation.

Any survey of Jewish life cycle events involving religious rituals ought to include a discussion of weddings. In recent decades, these joyous occasions have raised complex questions for clergy and families alike. Judging from marriage announcements in newspapers, it is not a foregone conclusion that a wedding of two Jews will be sanctified by an ordained rabbi or cantor, that it will include the traditional wedding blessings, or that it will incorporate anything of Jewish content. Among the majority of non-Orthodox Jews now marrying non-Jews, it is even less likely for the wedding to include Jewish elements: the nature of the ceremony is subject to negotiation and DIY creativity.[17] A friend or family member with a mail-order title may officiate, and the ceremony itself is likely to "draw upon the traditions of both religions," as wedding announcements often put it. Same-sex weddings also require some retuning of the traditional formula.

Moving along in the life cycle, we note that as people in our time tend to live longer than ever before with chronic illnesses or are undergoing treatment for health problems, healing and wellness have risen in importance in public religious life. The clearest expression of this is the foregrounding in synagogues of a petitionary prayer for healing.[18] Perhaps, the popularity of this once fairly obscure prayer can best be understood as an expression of the current spiritual mood of America's Jews. The prayer is both highly personal, for it bids God to remember a particular family member or friend, and also universal in that anyone in the congregation may be similarly engaged. If nothing else, it reflects the growing preoccupation and openness about matters of bodily health. One rabbi of a Reform temple has gone so far as to suggest to me that the future of synagogues will no longer rest on the missions of the past—prayer, study, tikkun olam—but on becoming places for physical healing and good health.

For a small but noticeable number of non-Orthodox Jews, this preoccupation with the body and its health has led to the rediscovery of the Mikveh, the ritual bath. To be sure, the focus is not on ritual purification, but on bodily healing. In the Boston area, a Mikveh has become a center for programming across the denominations. Known as Mayyim Hayim, Living Waters, the Mikveh offers not only a bath for ritual immersion, but also lectures, classes, and other programs to help Jews focus on the salutary powers of the ritual bath. Though it is the largest such center in the United States, Mayyim Hayim is not alone. Here is how a Reform rabbi located on the West Coast describes the new interest he is seeing and promoting in Mikveh: Reform Jews, he notes, can "grab onto the Mikveh, but not in a traditional way. [We] communicate the use of water to transition from sick to healthy, from divorced to ready to start anew, from miscarriage to fertility." In some instances, Reform Jews, he notes, come to the Mikveh to help in recovery from rape or sexual abuse.

Another form of healing service now gaining traction in some Conservative synagogues reappropriates a traditional religious practice that has long fallen into disuse—the *viddui*, a deathbed ritual. As described by one Conservative rabbi who has overseen this practice on a number of occasions, families gather around a terminally ill loved one to exchange expressions of apology, forgiveness, love, and appreciation. The rabbi recites the traditional words of contrition on behalf of the dying patient: when the service is properly done, participants describe what transpired as a cathartic emotional experience.

As much as the renewed interest in the viddui represents a return to tradition, actual mourning practices among the large swath of non-Orthodox Jews are undergoing radical alteration. Most noticeably, the seven days of mourning, known in Hebrew terminology as the shiva, now have been reduced drastically. Death notices in newspapers commonly announce that shiva will be observed for select hours on three days or in some cases on a single Sunday afternoon from two to five o'clock. The choreography of Jewish mourning, with its step-by-step process for reintegrating mourners into the world of the living, is ignored or scaled back by most non-Orthodox Jews.

Symptomatic of the inversion of traditional Jewish religious practices at this fraught time, visitors to the house of the bereaved seem to expect a lavish buffet, with the mourners actually serving the food to their "guests." "At the average *shiva* I'm involved in," reported Lance Sussman, a Reform rabbi in the Philadelphia area, "visitors are greeted by generous platters of corn beef, bagels, lox and cream cheese. In fact, *shiva* is pretty much the last hurrah of deli food."[19] Some enterprising business people have created a new profession as caterers of shiva food,[20] filling a need because visitors are unaware their role is to bring prepared food to the mourners rather than consume a shiva smorgasbord. All of this is a far cry from the traditional seven days of consolation that Jewish communities offered mourners. Vanessa Ochs, a scholar of popular religion, explains the decline in traditional Jewish mourning practices as "an appropriation of certain aspects of American Christian social behaviors following funerals, including an overall mood of 'celebrating the life' of the deceased."[21]

Representing yet another imitation of funeral practices alien to Judaism, cremation of the dead is a growing trend in some sectors of the non-Orthodox community. Estimates of how many Jews opt for cremation range widely by location. Directors of Jewish funeral parlors in Philadelphia approximate the figure at around 10 percent and closer to 8 percent in Chicago. Compared to a national estimate for all Americans of over 50 percent, it seems that Jews remain outliers when it comes to cremation.[22] Still it is noteworthy that such a distinctly nontraditional practice has gained in popularity despite the horrifying associations Jews have when they think of crematoria and despite the long-enshrined Jewish practice of burying the dead. Some prefer cremation because they see it as more environmentally sound, even though huge amounts of fossil fuels are required to consume a human body. Large disparities in costs may be another driving factor: burial is twice as expensive as cremation. Then, too, a social reality may be driving the uptick in cremations: As families scatter over a wide geographic expanse, people assume their children won't visit their graves. Why, then, bother with the expense?

To reverse some of these distortions of long-standing religious practices, most Conservative synagogues and quite a few Reform temples have organized committees of volunteers to provide food to the mourners and see to the proper shiva rituals. A Conservative rabbi in a Midwestern community proudly describes how proper care for the dead and their mourners is a major emphasis of his congregation. He preaches from the pulpit about the special obligations to attend funerals and help with making a *minyan* at graveside, a *mitzvah* especially for those who did not know the deceased well. He asks members to help make a shiva minyan and proudly notes that seventy-five people show up. Members of a bereavement committee cook meals for mourners. In some Conservative congregations, rituals of death are extended to the deceased by a society of volunteers (*Hevra Kadisha*) who assume responsibility for washing and preparing corpses ritually for burial. The literally hands-on approach of these associations brings to light another aspect of DIY Judaism: not relying upon professional funeral homes to perform such a sacred duty.

Without doubt, these efforts to comfort the bereaved represent a return to very basic Jewish understandings of what Jews do for one another. But when they become the primary focus of synagogue life, they distort Judaism.

In conversation with rabbis, it is clear how exasperated they feel over what a Reform rabbi described as his congregants' "death cult." By this he means the best attended service in most Reform and Conservative synagogues is Yizkor on Yom Kippur, when deceased loved ones are remembered in a special set of prayers. Though not nearly as widely observed as in the past, people attend the synagogue to mark the anniversary of a death by saying Kaddish. In many Conservative synagogues, the daily minyan in the majority consists of mourners who come to recite the Kaddish in remembrance of the deceased. Memorial plaques are a preoccupation of congregants who otherwise take little interest in anything else. And for some, membership itself is prized because it ensures that a rabbi will be on hand to officiate at a funeral. None of these activities is to be shunned, but too few other aspects of Judaism are taken so seriously.

How Subgroups Vary

Our discussion of the lived Judaism of non-Orthodox Jews of necessity has been painted with broad brushstrokes to portray overall patterns among amcha, the Jewish folk. To state the obvious, there are numerous exceptions, something that is especially the case in an age of hybridity when Jews pick and choose aspects of the religion they wish to observe and tinker to create their own versions of Judaism. There is no way to account for all these variations. Still, certain demographic groups display distinctive tendencies in their patterns of observance and ritual life, and those are worth noting.

DENOMINATION

Contrary to conventional wisdom, which lumps all non-Orthodox Jews together, denominational allegiances correlate with different patterns of religious behavior. Jews who affiliate with Reform synagogues are not interchangeable with their Conservative counterparts. A common lament of Reform rabbis is that their congregants are unprepared to invest much time in Jewish living. "The God of soccer," one such rabbi laments, "is a jealous God." Missing soccer is punishable; absence from temple service is not. Says another about her congregants: "There is only so much time people are prepared to commit to Jewish things. . . . Don't mess with my schedule. Jewish expression is one compartment; karate is a different one."

The guiding principle seems to be religious minimalism.[23] Reform Jews in the main feel little if any sense of obligation to attend their synagogues with regularity and more generally to invest of themselves in a religious life. This is the conclusion drawn by a social scientist in her assessment of strengths and weaknesses in the Reform population as set forth in the Pew data:

> Many Reform Jews interact with their synagogues only sporadically, when they have a particular need such as a life-cycle event. The Pew data suggest that Reform Jews do not view being Jewish as mainly a matter of religion, but rather of ancestry and culture. It should not be surprising, therefore, that membership and engagement with a synagogue—the home of ritual practice—is not a priority.[24]

Were these Jews to enact their religious lives in settings other than synagogue, this would not be so dramatic. The impression one receives from Reform rabbis is that their congregants enact their religion only in the synagogue, which, as we have seen, the majority attend infrequently. True, a few holiday rituals—breaking the Yom Kippur fast, Passover Seder, and Hanukkah candle lighting—are observed at home. But religious activity seems to occupy a very small fraction of the lives of most synagogue-affiliated Reform Jews, and even less time of the nonaffiliated.

The religious minimalism of Reform Jews, in turn, shapes the worship services of their synagogue. Prayers must be kept short. Friday evening services, the one weekly worship attended by a small fraction of Reform Jews, is attractive in part because it can be completed in an hour. Even the Saturday morning service, which is focused entirely on the Bar/Bat Mitzvah crowd, must be kept to a strict time limit. The same is true of High Holiday services. In some temples this is the case because the sanctuary can accommodate only a portion of the congregants and therefore prayer services are held in shifts. But clergy are acutely aware of the limited attention span and patience of their people. As for observances, Reform Jews tend to favor rituals performed only once a year and even then are highly selective and probably unaware of what they are ignoring.

In response to a question from me about what turns his congregants off, a senior Reform rabbi listed: "(1) brow-beating people about what they are doing wrong; (2) suggesting there is no place for conversation; (3) starting from a position of saying 'no'; (4) remaining oblivious to the short attention spans of congregants." And what does entice them? "Making sandwiches for a soup kitchen. Adult education attracts a certain population. A regular cohort of thirty to forty people attend service on Shabbat mornings and enjoy discussing the *parasha*, the Torah portion of the week. And some people come who love the music and the services." In thumbnail form, this captures what I have heard from over forty Reform rabbis, a good number of whom serve in congregations of many hundreds if not several thousands of members.

Conservative synagogue members and the more traditional sector of Reconstructionist congregations tolerate longer services. Sabbath mornings, when the main weekly service is held in Conservative synagogues, can run three hours. To be sure, congregants straggle in, and few attend from the opening prayer to the concluding one. But most are there for at least half the service. On the High Holidays, the services run considerably longer, with varying attendance at different times of the day. Pressures are mounting in Conservative synagogue to abbreviate the prayer service. "The future of Conservative synagogues is short services," one rabbi flatly declares. Whether this is an accurate prognostication or a self-fulfilling wish is hard to know at present.

As to ritual observances, these too are kept to varying degrees. If we are to judge by the paucity of ritual baths in their synagogues, few Conservative Jews observe laws of family purity, which proscribe sexual contact for a period of time during and after women menstruate. Only a minority of members attend the reading of the Scroll of Esther on Purim, and considerably fewer come to hear the chanting of *Eicha* (*Lamentations*) on the Ninth of Av. And aside from the Day of Atonement, fast days are rarely observed by Conservative Jews. Daily prayer and the wrapping of *tefilin* (phylacteries) are observed by small minorities. (It is doubtful any of these practices register with members of Reform temples.)

Even the less observant members of Conservative synagogues, whose patterns of observance are no different from those of their Reform counterparts, share "the assumption that what happens in the public space of the synagogue should be different from their homes," the rabbi of a large Conservative synagogue contends, "They are willing to give up some of their secular sensibilities in the shul [synagogue]. There still is a different balance of tradition and change than in Reform temples." Note the use of the term "sensibilities" by this rabbi. For the preponderant majority of affiliated Conservative Jews, what they seek is a style of service and a certain ambience. For most, it would be unthinkable for their synagogue to serve nonkosher food or mix meat and dairy during meals—this despite the fact that most probably do so when they eat in restaurants. As distinct from the language of Jewish law, Halacha, employed by the elites of the Conservative movement, ordinary Jews gravitate to a style of being Jewish. The point was conveyed to me powerfully by a Conservative rabbi who expressed his exasperation over the constraints his movement creates when it comes to his officiation at intermarriage ceremonies. "Why," he asked, "should I invoke Halacha on this matter when most of my congregants do not observe Halacha in any other aspect of their lives?"

Still, a significant minority of synagogue members affiliated with Conservative congregations incorporate religious observance into their lives. Significant numbers mark the Sabbath weekly in some way and roughly one-third claim they observe kosher laws at home (as compared to 7 percent of Reform Jews).[25] Even those who mix meat and dairy dishes are likely to avoid forbidden foods, such as shellfish and pork. Among this substantial minority, holidays are celebrated in the home and synagogue attendance on a once-a-month basis is widespread.

In comparing members of Conservative and Reform temples, one additional element needs to be added to the equation—knowledge about Jewish religious culture. Conservative synagogues tend to include a significantly higher proportion of people who have basic synagogue skills and an understanding of how Judaism works. This is most apparent in the dozens of congregants found in many Conservative synagogues who are able to lead the Hebrew services, read Torah, and chant the Haftorah (the portion from latter biblical texts read weekly). Quite a few Conservative synagogue services are run by the laity. Needless to say, not all congregants have those skills, but far larger proportions of Conservative synagogue members than their Reform counterparts have acquired them. This is not a matter of happenstance: though some clearly acquired these skills as part of their Jewish education, quite a few, including converts to Judaism, learned to decode Hebrew and employ the proper cantillation (trope) as adults. Conservative rabbis and cantors make a point of teaching any and all comers, encouraging them as a form of empowerment and involvement. Far less of that is evident in Reform temples where the clergy lead the services and serve as priests or performers of rituals. (According to some Reform rabbis, it is a barely concealed secret that many Bnai Mitzvah also learn their readings from a transliterated text, which they then use to chant their portion in the synagogue.)

The knowledge gap also is evident in home-based religious practices. Conservative Jews and older Reconstructionists, let alone some members of the smaller independent minyanim, know how to lead a Seder, recite the *kiddush* (blessing over wine) and the grace after meals. Here too Reform rabbis report far fewer members who have any of those skills. One Reform rabbi has gone further to argue that by lighting the Sabbath candles in the sanctuary, holding Seders, and having occasional Friday evening Shabbat meals in the synagogue, all ostensibly provided to teach congregants how to do these things on their own, the actual outcome has been greater dependence by congregants upon the temple to do these things for them. And so rituals long understood as being home-based are now exclusively performed in the synagogue.

GEOGRAPHY

How Jews practice their religion is influenced by the larger environment in which they are situated. Jews living in the Bible Belt affiliate with synagogues at higher rates than those who live in highly secular parts of the country. This is most dramatically evident in the sharp contrast in religious participation between Jews living in western states—from the Rocky Mountains to the Pacific, including the small communities in Alaska and Hawaii—and those living in other regions of the United States.[26] When it comes to ritual practices, such as participating at a Passover Seder, attending High Holiday services, fasting on Yom Kippur, lighting Shabbat candles, or keeping kosher, roughly 15 percent fewer western Jews observe, as compared with their coreligionists in the rest of the country. Fewer than a quarter of western Jews affiliate with a synagogue (versus a third of Jews elsewhere). Only 40 percent of western Jews are raising their oldest child in the Jewish religion, as compared with 63 percent in the rest of the United States.

What is driving these trends? The authors of a report about these differences point to two main factors: patterns of family formation and secularity in the local culture. Marriage rates are lower in the West than elsewhere and intermarriage rates for Jews (and others) are considerably higher. Sixty percent of married Jews in the West were found in 2013 to have been married to non-Jews, versus 40 percent in the rest of the country. The higher incidence of intermarriage has an effect on how children are raised and whether their parents participate in Jewish religious life. In addition to encouraging fluid group boundaries, the culture of the West tends toward secularization. Are Jews who prefer to live in this kind of society drawn to the West, or does living in such a setting shape Jewish behavior? Both may be true, but if nothing else they attest to the importance of the larger cultural environment as a factor shaping Jewish religious behavior.

GENDER

Another source of variation stems from gender.[27] The most detailed study of how males and females differ when it comes to Jewish religious practice has documented trends within the Reform movement. The report's title, "Matrilineal Ascent/Patrilineal Descent: The Gender Imbalance in American Jewish Life," neatly telegraphs its main finding: while women are increasing their involvement with Reform temples, males are significantly underrepresented. This pattern holds true also of adolescents in Reform summer camps and youth movement activities. It is even evident in the gender imbalance one can find at biennial conventions of the Union for Reform Judaism.[28] Matters have not reached the same point in Conservative synagogues as yet, where males and females participate at the same rates.

Within the larger population of American Jews, women are 8 percent more likely than men to say religion is very important to them.[29] They also tend to claim certainty about the existence of God or a universal spirit at higher rates than do men. And a gap of 6 percent opens between the genders when it comes to claims of *not* believing in God: 26 percent of men versus 20 percent of women claimed to be atheists.[30] In the previously cited "God survey," many more men than women in the Reform temple surveyed agreed with the claim "there is no God" (33 percent vs. 8 percent) and 44 percent of men agreed that "science can explain everything," as compared to 23 percent of women.[31]

Perhaps these differences begin to explain gender variations in religious behavior. Whereas synagogues traditionally were male bastions, barely setting aside physical space for female worshippers and relegating those women who did attend to a location distant from the "action," non-Orthodox congregations are moving in the opposite direction. Reform and smaller non-denominational congregations show gender imbalances similar to what has long been evident in Christian churches. As Sylvia Barack Fishman, the chronicler of gender patterns in American Jewish life, has put it, "In liberal Jewish America, women have become central and men have become marginal."[32] Fishman goes on to note how these patterns are now trickling down to the younger generation: "In today's America, teenage girls are much more likely to continue their Jewish education after bat mitzvah than boys are after bar mitzvah. Partially as a result, they also have more Jewish friends. The combination of more Jewish education and more Jewish friends is part of what makes American Jewish adult females more attached to Jewishness." Unfortunately, it's getting ever more difficult for these involved Jewish women to find Jewish males who share their religious commitments—and that is both a consequence of and cause for rising rates of intermarriage.

What, then, happens to religious involvement when Jewish women or men intermarry? Relying once again on the work of Fishman, we note strong patterns of differences between the two genders. Jewish-born mothers attend services at the same rate as inmarried Jewish mothers—over half claim to attend at least twice monthly. Slightly under one-third of synagogue-affiliated intermarried men, by contrast, claim to attend that often, and in fact 56 percent claim to attend never or only once or twice a year. (Intermarried men and women who have no synagogue affiliation attend a synagogue at the same rate—hardly ever.)[33]

Large gender differences also are evident in the ways religion plays a role in the lives of families. Fishman reports: "Homes with Jewish mothers tend to have much higher levels of ritual observance than homes that have Jewish fathers and non-Jewish mothers. Whether one speaks of once-a-year rituals like fasting on Yom Kippur, or weekly observances such as Shabbat, having a Jewish mother makes a big difference in American families." Contrary to what we might expect, even the decision to perform a brit milah is far more likely to occur when the intermarried Jew is the mother rather than the father. This goes against the conventional wisdom that Jewish fathers would want their sons to "look like them"—that is, by being circumcised. But writes Fishman, "About one-third of [intermarried] Conservative men and well over half of Reform men married to non-Jewish women report that their male children have not had a *brit milah*. The pattern for intermarried Jewish women is diametrically opposite. Among Conservative women married to non-Jewish men eight out of ten, and among Reform women married to non-Jewish men, seven out of ten report their sons have had a *brit milah*." From her interviews, Fishman learned how rarely Jewish men were prepared to oppose their non-Jewish wives over the issue of brit milah; intermarried Jewish mothers, for the most part, took responsibility to make sure it happened.[34]

INTERMARRIAGE

When we move beyond these gender differences to the broader variations in religious behavior and outlook evident in inmarried versus intermarried families, it is hard to avoid Fishman's conclusion that "in many, if not most, mixed married families religious identity, if any, is ambiguous."[35] These ambiguities are discernible in the blurring of religious practices, if not outright religious syncretism, such as the celebration of both Hanukkah and Christmas, or Passover and Easter in households.

Mixed or confused messages also interfere with the religious education children receive. This is self-evidently so in households where both religions are taught and children attend church and synagogue religious classes. But even in the minority of intermarried homes where the decision has been made to raise children solely in the Jewish tradition, the religious outlook of the non-Jewish parent—often with the best of intentions—is at odds with the Jewish religious school. In a study of families and Jewish education, a team of researchers under my direction interviewed inmarried and inter-married parents. The contrast in outlook of Jewish-born parents and those not born Jewish was often quite dramatic, perhaps best understood as an emphasis among the former upon a Judaism of family and festivals as compared to a Judaism of faith and feelings among the latter. When asked "How do you act as a Jewish parent?" endogamous individuals tended to describe and even list the activities and rituals in which they engaged. For them, the emphasis was on "practice," even when their observance was anything but extensive. One Reform stay-at-home mother phrased her approach succinctly. "I am making Jewish memories." She explained: "I always make latkes for Hanukkah. I even make doughnuts for Hanukkah so they'll think 'mom made doughnuts for Hanukkah.' I make *hamentashen* for Purim. I made challah a few times; matzo ball soup. Generally, we have a big Sukkah party every year, an open house. . . . By helping the children build memories around Jewish holidays and events, I'm a role model."[36]

With the best of intentions, non-Jewish parents raising their children as Jews find it harder to engage in these tactile forms of Jewish activity. They also tend to prefer that religious school instruction focus on faith and ethical behavior. Because of this prioritization of faith, it is hard for them to relate to Judaism's commitments to religious expression intertwined with Jewish peoplehood and also to Judaism's emphasis on religious behavior rather than belief. Little wonder, then, that children who grow up in intermarried homes, even those in the minority of families committed to a Jewish upbringing, do not identify with the Jewish religion in high numbers.[37]

There is much more to be said about Jewish religious practices among the intermarried. Clearly, not all intermarried families are alike. Levels of Jewish connection differ between families with an unambiguous commitment to Judaism and families exposing their children to aspects of two distinct religions; between those residing close to vital centers of Jewish life and those living at a geographic remove; between those where the Jewish partner has benefited from a strong Jewish background and those where the Jewish partner has not (the "socialization" factor). And, as already noted, the gender of the Jewish parent matters a great deal, too. No doubt, quite a few non-Jewish mothers and fathers strive mightily to raise their children as Jews, deliver them to religious school, and attend synagogue services with them. In a small number of cases, the outcomes are impressive and point to a deep religious involvement with Judaism as the children become adults.[38] Overall, though, a mountain of evidence shows that inmarried Jews are considerably more likely to raise their children unambiguously in the Jewish religion and those children as adults identify in the main with Judaism. The same cannot be said for intermarried families, and therefore marital and family patterns are still another circumstance making for variations in religious participation.

GENERATION

It appears that one additional factor is at work—generation. As members of the large millennial generation—those born between 1980 and 2000[39]—have come to assume their places in adult society, a vast outpouring of analysis has picked over every conceivable dimension of their lives. Much of it contends they are like no other generation: their savvy as technology "natives"; their experience growing up in an America where economic growth has slowed to a crawl; their lengthy "odyssey years" spent trying on and casting off jobs, careers, lovers, and interests; their unquestioning embrace of diversity, inclusion, and all manner of sexual orientation; their endless array of choices and their alleged addiction to keeping all their options open—all this and more seemingly sets them apart from their elders.

It is said, too, that they differ in levels of religious participation. A Pew study in 2010 compared millennials to previous generations at the same age and concluded: "Millennials are significantly more unaffiliated than members of Generation X were at a comparable point in their life cycle (20 percent in the late 1990s) and twice as unaffiliated as Baby Boomers were as young adults (13 percent in the late 1970s). Young adults also attended religious services less often than older Americans today. And compared to their elders today, fewer young people say that religion is very important in their lives."[40]

The limited data we have on Jewish millennials indicate they are part of these broader trends. Just as 32 percent of all American millennials claim no religious identification, precisely the same proportion of Jews in this age cohort identify as "Nones." This compares to the 19 percent of Jewish baby boomers who claim no religious identification and 26 percent of gen X Jews.[41] Millennials also join synagogues at lower rates than their elders did at the same age.

A study conducted among millennials in the New York City area also found that religion ranked very low in the priorities of its sample population. Three-quarters claimed to attend synagogue only on the High Holidays. Culture, Jewish humor, and family ranked high for them. But despite their claims of finding religion unimportant, majorities enjoyed celebrating Passover and Hanukkah, and attending Shabbat meals on Friday nights. Females were considerably more interested in religion, and Jewishness generally, than males.[42]

Despite these straws in the wind suggesting either lower levels of engagement or different kinds of participation in Jewish religious life, it remains to be seen how this population identifies with the religion as it grows older. Millennials tend to marry later than did previous age cohorts and to bear children at older ages. Until Jewish millennials form families, it's too early to tell how the responsibility of rearing children will shape their religious participation. Synagogues and a range of Jewish institutions are working hard to draw millennials to programs. Understandably, these efforts are geared toward the presumed interests and needs of millennials in the present. It is not unreasonable to assume, though, that those interests and needs may change as the millennials age. Conventional wisdom has portrayed millennials as drawn to urban living with no interest in the suburbs of their childhoods. But now evidence is emerging of a gradual exodus from urban to suburban neighborhoods, if only because the latter are more affordable and child-friendly.[43] It is not hard to imagine a revival of suburban congregations as millennial families discover their need for local synagogues. By the same token, religious participation may pick up—especially if savvy congregational leaders involve millennials and appeal to their sensibilities.

The previous chapter began with a brief outline of items discovered by the Pew Research Center about the nature of religious life practiced by non-Orthodox Jews in twenty-first-century America. Based on other forms of information, we now can add to this list:

- Even as the category of so-called "Nones" has grown, there still are a considerable number of non-Orthodox Jews who participate in some aspects of religious life. Their involvements are not to be taken for granted.[44]
- Vastly complicating their involvement are grave doubts about traditional conceptions of God. The God of Jewish liturgy poses challenges, even to Jews who are not atheists. Many Jews struggle to square what they know about the injustice and suffering they see around them with the liturgy's insistence on portraying a just deity. Many also have difficulty imagining a God Who listens to, let alone answers, prayers.
- For most non-Orthodox Jews, attendance at worship services is primarily a social and communal activity, rather than one focused sharply on prayer. Jews come to the synagogue to be with other Jews, to feel a sense of belonging, to feel connected to their forebearers who attended some services, and to take pride in their synagogue. These provide a measure of transcendence for them.
- As to the purpose of religion, a good many congregants adhere to a "Golden Rule" Judaism. Behaving as a decent person for most non-Orthodox Jews is the essence of their religion. How they define good deeds often has little to do with any specific Jewish teachings, or if it does, it is based on highly selective readings of Jewish texts. But in their minds, being a good person is the essence of being a good Jew.
- Guiding the decision to observe a particular religious ritual are three factors: (1) personalism—how meaningful the ritual is to each individual; (2) frequency—the less often a ritual is observed, the greater the possibility it will be part of people's lives; (3) life cycle—how entwined

the ritual is with a life cycle event for the family, as distinct from com-munal commemoration, let alone the practices of the Jewish people. In what might serve as the summing up of the Judaism of non-Orthodox Jews, a Reform rabbi succinctly observed: "People want to do things on their own terms."

- These trends describe the predilections of the non-Orthodox popu-lation in the aggregate. But subgroups differ in important ways. Chief among those differences in religious participation are large gaps between Conservative-raised and -affiliated Jews and Reform or nondenomina-tional Jews; gender gaps highlight how women tend to be considerably more engaged in Jewish religious life than men; family configurations are associated with far higher levels of Jewish religious involvement on the part of inmarried Jews versus the intermarried; and generational patterns suggest that, thus far, millennials are less engaged in religious life than were other cohorts at the same age.

- This does not mean non-Orthodox Jews ignore the ritual aspects of Judaism. But they are highly selective in what they choose to observe. More than anything, family is their sacred ground, and aspects of Juda-ism that contribute to strengthening their families will become part of their ritual lives—provided they do not interfere with other meaningful family experiences.

One overarching consideration must be added: for the large majority of non-Orthodox Jews, the Jewish religion plays a role in their lives at peak moments. Jews who maintain a connection to their religion are most likely to turn to Judaism at times of joy or sadness. Family and friends will gather in synagogues to celebrate major life cycle events—the birth of a new child, the puberty milestone of an adolescent, and the creation of a new family unit at a wedding. So too, at times of travail, these Jews will turn to their clergy. According to the rabbis interviewed for this book, the most frequent questions they field are posed by congregants facing a life crisis: how to cope with a major personal failing or the illness of a loved one or with death, and how to help children make sense of human suffering. Not surprisingly, the most widely attended prayers for non-Orthodox Jews is the Yizkor service in remembrance of departed ones—in other words, prayers offered at times of greatest vulnerability and sadness.

These peak moments—both the highs and the lows—tend to revolve around major events in the life of the family. On a lesser scale, year in, year out, family and religion are also intertwined during a handful of annual dates marked on the Jewish calendar, principally when family members attend synagogue together on the High Holidays and celebrate key annual rituals such as the Passover Seder and Hanukkah candle lighting. Family, remarked a wise Reform rabbi to me, is the most important arena of "sacredness in the lives of most Jews today." To be sure, for most non-Orthodox Jews, religious participation is episodic and infrequent; but it occurs at particularly meaningful moments in their lives and those of their family members. In this sense, religion is hardly marginal to what they hold most important.

3

DIVERSITY AMONG THE ORTHODOX

The great divide in American Jewish religious life is between the Orthodox and everyone else. Arguably, it all begins with the way Orthodox Jews relate to the corpus of Jewish observances: they understand Judaism as a package of dos and don'ts. Most observe those commandments with great fidelity, and others are more lax. But unlike their non-Orthodox peers who shy away from "judgmentalism," who claim they don't know precisely how a Jewish religious life ought to be lived (some elites excepted), who deem a pick-and-choose approach as the only sane one in an age of autonomy, the Orthodox understand Judaism as offering a structure of correct behavior, of Ortho-praxis as opposed to correct belief (the literal meaning of Orthodoxy). By regarding Judaism as having an integrity and logic of its own based not solely on subjective feelings but also on externally imposed commandments, they part company with the vast majority of their coreligionists.

To note this is not to suggest that every Orthodox Jew observes all of the proverbial 613 commandments with utmost fidelity. Orthodox Jews are human and subject to all kinds of challenges to their observances. In fact, a trope of Orthodox rhetoric is to confess in public that one has failed to be punctilious in some areas of observance—for example, I fail to pray with sufficient *kavana* (intentionality); I have not set aside enough time for Torah study; I cut corners in the performance of some ritual. But that is a very different approach to religion from what is widely bruited in non-Orthodox circles. It is one thing to admit one has failed to live up to a standard, and something very different to deny that an external standard exists. One does not find among Orthodox Jews an agnosticism about how the "good Jew" ought to behave and practice Judaism. They know what is commanded and what is to be avoided—whether they personally live up to the standards, and perhaps even if they do not necessarily believe God commanded them to behave this way.

Their commitment to observances, in turn, leads to distinctive behavioral patterns. The daily lives of Orthodox Jews are regulated by religious practices, beginning with benedictions uttered when they first arise in the morning and stretching to evening and bedtime prayers. In between, their daily routine requires attention to dietary rules, dress regulations, the recitation of blessings, and Torah study. For many Orthodox Jews, even "private" matters, such as sexual intimacy, charitable contributions, and interpersonal encounters, are governed by Jewish religious teachings. The frequency of their religious participation requires a degree of habituation, which, no doubt, can become rote performance. Alternatively, it can guide the rhythm of one's day. If nothing else, when Orthodox Jews engage in ritual practices with great frequency, we may surmise, the quality of their religious experiences is bound to be considerably different from a Judaism that is a "sometime thing."

But engaging in prescribed religious practices is not the only trait that sets Orthodox Jews apart. In the aggregate, they also are far more knowledgeable about the minutiae of Jewish practices and the basics of their religion. For a good many non-Orthodox Jews, Judaism is shrouded in mystery: it is a foreign way of behaving and being. The great advantage Orthodox Jews have over most of their non-Orthodox counterparts is their relatively high level of Judaic literacy. Rather than rely upon osmosis, imitation, or some vague form of familial transmission, Orthodox Jews have invested heavily to ensure their members acquire the skills and knowledge to live out their religious lives.[1] The Jewish day school movement is overwhelmingly an Orthodox phenomenon, and its educational mission is reinforced by summer camps, youth groups and other informal educational vehicles, and eventually by gap-year study in Israel. To be sure, not every Orthodox Jew is a learned Talmud scholar, but the vast majority of Orthodox males have been exposed to the study of Judaism's major religious texts, such as the Hebrew Bible, Talmud, and codes of law; and though females are given a different type of Jewish education in some sectors of Orthodoxy, they too are exposed to important texts and practices of the tradition. All of this investment in intensive Jewish education provides Orthodox Jews with access to the ways of thinking and behaving promoted by traditional Judaism.

The absence of such an education makes it far more difficult for those not schooled in the vocabulary and concepts of Judaism to relate to the religion. To illustrate the point, let's focus on Hebrew language skills. Without an ability to read Hebrew and understand what one is reading, let alone grasp the biblical allusions sprinkled throughout the traditional liturgy, the prayer book is a foreign document. Reading Hebrew texts in translation is like "kissing your mother through a handkerchief," as the poet Hayim Nachman Bialik put it.[2] By virtue of their intensive Jewish education, Orthodox Jews have at least a rudimentary understanding of the Hebrew liturgy. That is probably true also for the minority of non-Orthodox Jews who have attended a Jewish day school and have studied in Israel. But for the vast majority of American Jews, the liturgy is a closed book. Writing about her own struggles with the Hebrew language, the novelist Dara Horn pulls no punches in explaining why Hebrew proved so elusive for her:

> First, I wasn't Orthodox. No one was sending me to a gap-year yeshiva; no one I knew threw around Hebrew phrases; no one I knew made *aliyah* [immigrated to Israel]. . . . And . . . I never went to a Jewish [day] school. It was clear to me from public school that there were methodical ways of learning languages. In French I progressed from one level to the next, with many tests along the way to ensure I mastered the material. I assumed that a similar method existed for Hebrew in Jewish schools (I now know this is often untrue). But since I never went to a Jewish school, I found myself in different informal Hebrew classes each year with no consistent program.[3]

For Orthodox Jews who have gone through a day school education, their knowledge has empowered them to work with the sources of their religious tradition.[4]

Some observers might argue that Orthodox Jews are also more pious and God-fearing than their non-Orthodox peers. That is *not* the argument here. In truth, we have no way to know how self-consciously Orthodox Jews observe what they do because they feel commanded by God, let alone because they are God-intoxicated. We also have no way to know how much Orthodox observance is governed by what in traditional rabbinic parlance is known as *yir'at shamayim*, fear of Heaven. In a famous essay on the transformation of Orthodoxy in the twentieth century,[5] the scholar Haym Soloveitchik lamented the disappearance of the kind of Orthodox Jew who cried in synagogue on the High Holidays out of awe and fear of a God Who decides the fate of each human being at the outset of the Jewish year. Soloveitchik assumes that the Jews he observed in the synagogue more recently "did not cry from religiosity but from self-interest, from an instinctive fear for their lives. Their tears were courtroom tears, with whatever degree of sincerity such tears have." And, he goes on to note, such Jews harbored a "primal fear of Divine judgment, simple and direct." But these are all his projections: the truth is no human being knows how to measure what is in the hearts of Orthodox Jews or any other kind of Jew; we simply have no way to know what they feel and believe.

It is possible, though, to observe how Orthodox Jews organize their lives. By marrying in their twenties, becoming parents not long afterward, and having more children than their Jewish peers, they set themselves apart. Family formation at a relatively early age, moreover, necessitates engagement with the major institutions of Jewish religious life—synagogues, Jewish schools, and summer camps. In short, Orthodox Jews, by virtue of their commitment to early family formation, of necessity are drawn into communal participation at a time when most of their peers are busy finding their way, a process that may lead to important discoveries or pursuits far removed from any form of Judaism.

Starting a family early, moreover, also requires Orthodox Jews to take on financial responsibilities. The costliest item is a day school education for each child, which has become de rigueur in most sectors of the Orthodox community. Tuition costs range widely, with Haredi schools charging considerably less than Modern Orthodox ones. To reinforce the Orthodox lifestyle, families tend to send their children to summer camps, also not an inexpensive proposition. Orthodox Jews also travel to Israel at far higher rates than do their non-Orthodox counterparts. And then there are other costs: kosher food is pricier than food products not adhering to the Kashrut standards. And the requirement to live within walking distance of synagogues usually drives up housing costs in areas closest to congregations. To be sure, there are some non-Orthodox families who also walk to synagogue, keep kosher, and send their children to Jewish day schools and camps. They are a small minority, whereas Orthodox Jews take these for granted as the price to be paid for being Orthodox.[6]

Varieties of Orthodox Jews

Yet with all these overlapping commonalities, Orthodox Jews are hardly monolithic. To simplify, we identify three broad categories with many subgroups within each. First, there are the so-called Haredi Jews, often described as "the Ultra-Orthodox," a term at once offensive to the Haredim—"ultra" sounds extreme and uncompromising—and to other Orthodox Jews who believe themselves no less faithful to the tradition than the "ultras." The term "Haredi" literally refers to "those who tremble" in fear of God, and in that sense it is a nomenclature that appeals to the self-image such Jews would like to project. We shall see that Haredi Jews fall into multiple subcategories, but what they tend to share is a self-consciously countercultural sensibility reinforced by living mainly among their own.[7] The particular importance of clustering together is that Haredim can insulate themselves *to a significant extent* from influences of the larger society they would prefer to avoid, and simultaneously enforce the religious expectations of their communities, especially through strong social pressures to conform.

The second large grouping of Orthodox Jews, though smaller than the explosively expanding Haredi contingents, identifies positively with modern society, even as its adherents strive to observe the broad range of religious practices. Indeed, Modern Orthodox Jews see no necessary contradiction inherent in the "plural life worlds" they inhabit.[8] How much these Jews will accommodate involves a process of constant negotiation. Modern Orthodox Jews are characterized by their active participation in the wider culture. They tend to send their children to study at colleges and universities, and to pursue occupations in all sectors of the economy. Though they seek housing within easy walking distance of a synagogue, since travel by car or public transportation is forbidden on the Sabbath and holidays, they do not necessarily live in preponderantly Orthodox neighborhoods, and they partake of what modern culture has to offer—including television, movies, and the Internet, all of which Haredi Jews strive to avoid or access very selectively. Such engagement is not seen by these Jews as antithetical to the observance of Judaism.

The third sector of Orthodox Jews consists of Sephardim.[9] Sephardi Jews are outliers in the American Jewish population by virtue of their customs and culture. Most American Jews descend from Ashkenazi ancestors who lived in Europe, mainly in Eastern Europe and Russia, but also in Central Europe. Throughout the Middle Ages and until the founding of Israel in 1948, other substantial and creative Jewish communities flourished in the Mediterranean basin—in North Africa, the Middle East, the Ottoman Empire, and farther east in Iran, Afghanistan, and India. Jews who had been expelled from Spain and Portugal—known in Hebrew as Sepharad—in the late fifteenth century made their way to many of these Mediterranean areas and came to dominate their Jewish communities. Interestingly, even those Jews who come from places such as Iran (Persia), where Sephardi Jews did not influence the culture, now refer to themselves as Sephardim in the American context. (They also reject being called Mizrahim, "those from the East," a designation with class and racial undertones that is commonly used in Israel to distinguish non-Ashkenazi Jews.) The term "Sephardi," in short, has taken on an oppositional quality in America: we are not like the rest of America's Jews and are proud of our distinctive North African and Levantine traditions.

Most Sephardi Jews in the United States would also take umbrage at being called Orthodox. To them, all denominational labels—Reform, Conservative, *and* Orthodox—are Ashkenazi inventions of no relevance to Sephardim, and, even worse, represent misguided responses to modernity. Why, then, do I include the Sephardim with Ashkenazi Orthodox Jews? Primarily because the large majority of Sephardi Jews in the United States live their lives mostly like Orthodox Jews. Their orientations to family and pro-natalism are similar to the Orthodox. They worship in synagogues whose customs are highly traditional and have the markers of what the average Jew would perceive as an Orthodox synagogue: men and women are seated separately, only males lead the services, the liturgy is almost entirely in Hebrew, the prayers follow the traditional structure, and the liturgical music is relatively unchanged from what had been sung in the Old World. (One informed observer noted for my benefit that Sephardim "wanted to be American in all their lives except in their synagogues.") Moreover, to the extent that Sephardi synagogues identify with Ashkenazi institutions, they relate most closely to Modern Orthodox ones, such as Yeshiva University or Haredi ones. And not least, Sephardi Jews are coming under the influence of Ashkenazi Orthodox ways of adapting their synagogues, schools, and other institutions to the American environment. Do some Sephardi Jews join Conservative and Reform synagogues? Yes, but they tend to be the exceptions. Do Sephardi Jews share with other Orthodox Jews a belief that Judaism consists of a clearly defined package of commandments and prohibitions? Most assuredly, even if they do not observe them all. They tend not to have much patience for the reforms introduced by non-Orthodox movements. For the large majority, there is a right way to practice Judaism, even if they personally stray from that way to one degree or another.

The Judaism of Haredim

We begin our survey of the lived religion of "ordinary" Orthodox Jews with those in the Haredi sector.[10] These are the most recognizable Jews by virtue of their distinctive garb, insular ways, and deliberate counterculturalism. Clustering in densely populated enclaves, speaking Yiddish or Yinglish (a mixture of Yiddish, English, and rabbinic Hebrew) among themselves, consciously rejecting much of modish Western culture, and arranging their family lives, daily routines, finances, and politics much differently from their highly acculturated coreligionists, they are a people apart. In recognition of the preferred head coverings of their males, they often are referred to as "black hatters," though not as a term of endearment.[11]

Yet rather than constitute a single uniform body, these Jews demonstrate that there are at least fifty shades of black. The largest contingent consists of Hasidic Jews who divide themselves into at least two dozen sects, each with its own leader. Some are riven internally, as are the two warring factions of the Satmar group,[12] and others simply refuse to cooperate with one another, at times coming to blows. And then there are the historical antagonists of the Hasidim, the spiritual descendants of their Lithuanian opponents; these are the "Yeshivish"[13] whose lives are oriented around upper-level academies of Torah study (yeshivas) for adult men in their twenties and older. To insiders, the subtle but very real distinctions in customs, garb, allegiances, and ways of living that characterize these different subpopulations loom far larger than their commonalities.

Where did the Haredim come from? Until the Holocaust era, the most religiously traditional Jews rarely immigrated to America. For one thing, they were tightly bound to their communities in Eastern Europe; for another, many of their rabbis discouraged relocating to the *Treyfe Medina* (the unkosher land), a country deemed unfit for Jewish religious life. To be sure, some traditionalist Jews, including rabbis, joined the mass migration of Eastern European Jews to this country in the three decades prior to World War I, but they usually failed to transmit their way of life to the next generation. Highly traditional rabbis in particular found America to be a Jewish wasteland where, in their view, learned Torah scholars were marginalized, showboating cantors were all the rage, and Jewish know-nothings dominated the community.[14] Still, despite these abominable circumstances, enough European-style rabbis came to America and managed to establish no fewer than three separate rabbinical organizations during the first two decades of the twentieth century—none of which, however, exercised serious influence over native-born Jews.

The triumph of communism in the Soviet Union and soon thereafter the rise of Nazism—the former intent on destroying Judaism and the latter ruthlessly slaughtering Jews—prompted traditionalist Jews who previously never would have considered coming to American to flee for their lives. Their arrival marked a turning point in the history of Orthodoxy in America. Unlike earlier generations of immigrants from Eastern Europe, they imported sophisticated techniques to cope with modernity.

First came a separatist ideology that stood in opposition to all modern trends in Jewish thought and practice and a self-conception as the only Jews who had stayed true to Jewish tradition.[15] Haunted by the memory of the decimated communities that had nurtured them in Eastern Europe, appalled by the defections of most American Jews to various "deviationist" forms of Judaism—including Modern Orthodoxy—convinced against all odds that the future lay in re-creating what they imagined had existed in the obliterated communities of Eastern European Orthodoxy, they labored far from the centers of Jewish power and influence on rebuilding traditional Judaism on these shores, preferably in isolation. (By virtue of their active engagement with all sectors of Jewish society, Lubavitchers are a major exception, even though they share most of the countercultural values of the Haredim.)[16]

Their distinctive worldview, with its assumption that Judaism will flourish only if Jews sequester themselves in self-segregating enclaves, was, of course, antithetical to the integrationist agenda prevailing in the rest of the American Jewish community. The large majority of American Jews aspired to win complete acceptance and were prepared to pay a high price for it; the Haredim, then as now, insisted on fitting in on their own terms. This unbridgeable divide within the American Jewish populace was captured in Philip Roth's prescient short story of 1959, "Eli the Fanatic." Sent as an emissary by his Americanized Jewish peers to persuade the head of a newly opened yeshiva for Holocaust survivors to dress and behave like an American so as not to embarrass them, Eli regularly must walk past what Roth none-too-subtly identifies as a Gulf gas station.[17] The chasm Roth perceived over fifty-five years ago continues to be maintained deliberately, and is geographically reinforced by the settlement of Haredim in locales far removed from the centers of American Jewish life, such as Lakewood, New Jersey, Orange and Rockland Counties in New York, and several highly insular neighborhoods in Brooklyn.

The tolerant mood of postwar America surely played a role in opening a space for Haredim, along with other minority groups, to live according to their own customs. Like the rest of their coreligionists, the Haredim have benefited from the generosity of Americans who have accorded respect to different forms of religious expression and garb, however alien they may seem. Yet fundamentally, the vibrancy of Haredi life owes the most to their single-minded rabbinic leaders. Finding their Jewish way of life on the defensive upon their arrival in the United States, traditionalist rabbis of the Holocaust era set in place conditions for the renewal of their communities.[18]

The most basic of these was the creation of enclaves for the purposes of segregating their adherents from other Jews and from Gentiles.[19] By fostering a powerful sense of otherness in their followers, leaders of these communities are able to draw sharp boundaries—not so much physical demarcations, but social barriers. Fraternizing with nonobservant Jews, let alone with non-Jews, is frowned upon. Both are stereotyped negatively for their unacceptable, if not immoral, way of life, one that should be shunned by Haredim. Social boundaries, in turn, are reinforced by placing heavy demands on people's time and commitments. Synagogues and schools are what sociologist Ido Tavory describes as "greedy institutions." The "greed" in question is not monetary; instead, the price of acceptance in the community is active engagement with insiders, attendance of synagogues and educational programs, and other forms of participation. All of this reinforces the individual's ties to the community and the power of the community to compel engagement.[20]

Haredi communities also have grown due to their strong pro-natalist orientation. Young people in their late teens or early twenties are paired off by their family members, friends, or professional matchmakers, and once married are expected to produce children quickly and often. In contrast to non-Orthodox Jews who average fewer than two children per household, the yeshiva-oriented Haredim customarily have four to six children; Hasidic families may have eight to twelve.

Though we do not know how far back these high fertility rates go or precisely when they became the norm, their impact on Haredi life today is not in dispute. In Lakewood, New Jersey, perhaps the largest Yeshivish enclave in the country, for example, nearly half the Jewish population in 2010 consisted of children under the age of eighteen.[21] It is doubtful any other locale in the United States has such a high proportion of children. Each year, in fact, the numbers of births keep increasing, which means that within a short time more classes have to be added to local Jewish day schools to accommodate the swelling population.[22] Between 1998 and 2013, the day school population of

Lakewood exploded from fifty-three hundred to nearly twenty-four thousand, and the rate accelerated with time.[23] Even with twelve kindergarten classes in some schools, it is impossible to find room in existing institutions for all the children coming of school age. In September 2012, fourteen new Jewish day schools opened in Lakewood. That did not reduce the pressure to find space to accommodate the even larger cohort of children entering the system the following September.

As for Hasidic families, the epicenter of their activity is located in Williamsburg, Brooklyn, where the dominant Satmar sect is surrounded by many smaller groupings. In that community, nearly half the Jewish population consists of children under the age of eighteen. On a visit to Bais Rochel, a K–12 girls' school in Williamsburg, I was informed that enrollments exceeded three thousand students, making it one of the largest Jewish day schools in the country, matched only by other Satmar schools in Kiryas Joel, New York. As of 2012, Bais Rochel had ten classes of eighth graders, fifteen classes of first graders, and sixteen classes of preschool girls. The upward curve of growth with each entering class could not be more conspicuous.[24]

Hasidic and Yeshivish families residing in nearby Boro Park, Flatbush, and Crown Heights also have high fertility rates: compared to the general American norm of 80 children born per 1,000 women, the birth rate in those two neighborhoods is somewhere between 186 and 192 annual births per 1,000 women. Walking the streets of these communities, one can't miss the sheer numbers of children and the resulting spillover of Haredi populations into contiguous neighborhoods to relieve the pressure for affordable housing. The demographic trajectory, according to one analyst of census data, is for the Hasidic population to more than double in the next twenty years. The Yeshivish lag slightly but also are expected to grow by at least 30 percent with the birth of each new generation.[25] What this means for New York's Jews is already evident: a demographic study conducted in 2011 found that 49 percent of *all* Jewish youngsters under the age of eighteen are being raised in Haredi homes.[26]

Providing a Jewish education for these swelling numbers of children has not been left to chance. Attendance at private Jewish day schools is well-nigh universal from early childhood through high school, and that includes children with learning disabilities. Schoolchildren spend considerably more hours immersed in religious studies than in general-education classes because the former are regarded as critically necessary to prepare them for life in Haredi communities; general-education schoolwork, by contrast, is seen as a waste of time that could be devoted to Torah study or, worse, an exercise that may expose students to heretical ideas or immoral ways of behaving. This, of course, stands in stark contrast to much of the rest of the Jewish community where three to four hours a week of Jewish studies over twenty weeks are the norm in congregational schools, compared to thirty-five hours per week of general education; and even most day schools outside the Orthodox orbit devote considerably less time to Jewish learning than to general studies.

The Haredim have built an extra tier onto their educational infrastructure—at least for males. Young men are expected to pursue post-high-school studies at institutions called *kollelim*, yeshivas of higher learning where adult males continue to study after they have married and begun families. Some seek to attain rabbinic ordination, but most engage in Torah learning for its own sake. This was the dream of rabbinic leaders who arrived during the Holocaust era. Most notable in this regard was Rabbi Aaron Kotler, who arrived on these shores in 1941 from Lithuania and two years later established a high-level yeshiva in Lakewood. His long-term aspiration was to recruit one hundred men in their twenties to devote themselves to full-time study. Today the Lakewood yeshiva enrolls over seven thousand men, making it the largest advanced institution of its kind in North America. Though the Ner Israel yeshiva in Baltimore attracts but a fraction of the student body found in Lakewood, it too serves as a magnet attracting Haredi males. Baltimore today boasts a Jewish population that is 21 percent Orthodox, the highest proportion of any Jewish community in the United States, in large measure due to the anchoring presence of Ner Israel.[27]

Within the Haredi world, devotion to kollel study varies. The Satmar and Lubavitchers, for example, retain men for a year or two of post-high-school Torah study and then encourage them to begin earning a livelihood. In other Hasidic groups, such as the Bobover and Skverer, men linger for more years, in some cases for their entire lives. The Yeshivish, too, maintain an ideal of continued study by adult males until they are well into their twenties. For the most part, though, Haredim studying in American kolle-lim should not be conflated with those in Israel where the government supports yeshiva students and thereby is the enabler of their unemployment. Still, regardless of whether they are Hasidim or Yeshivish, Haredi Jews are intensively schooled in Judaism from early childhood through high school, and often well into their twenties.[28]

None of this would be economically feasible were it not for the remarkable social safety net constructed by Haredi communities to support their own. The expectation of those communities is for every Jew to be engaged actively in Hesed, a term often translated as "acts of loving kindness" but that might simply be defined as giving of oneself. Far from being an invention of the Haredim, Hesed has a long history; but the Haredim have made it an art form by creating hundreds of aid programs, known as Gemachs, a Hebrew acronym for societies extending voluntary aid.

On a stroll through Williamsburg, Brooklyn, a visitor will have little difficulty spotting Gemachs at virtually every turn: down a flight of stairs is a Kallah Gemach storing hundreds of white wedding gowns, shoes, and veils, all donated by wealthier families for free use by brides; on the same street a huge school building hosts two large wedding halls, offering an all-inclusive package, including a single musician and food for 250 guests, at the bargain cost of $10,500; a few blocks over, a store selling kosher meat products at prices subsidized by the Satmar community offers shoppers the ability to contribute funds anonymously so that the poor can be given an added discount. A few blocks on, the Bikkur Holim society, an enterprise run entirely by volunteers, prepares kosher meals daily for shipment to a dozen hospitals and rehabilitation centers in the New York area for distribution to patients; the purpose is to provide free kosher food up to the standards of the most demanding Haredi Jews. Further on, there are "stores" with rack upon rack of used clothing, all free for the taking.

In neighborhoods of dense Haredi concentration around the greater New York and Los Angeles areas, pennysavers list a broad panoply of free services offered by Gemachs. Locked out of your house or car? Haverim will send someone to open your locks at no charge. Are you in need of transportation to medical facilities outside the community? Call Bikkur Holim, which has volunteer drivers lined up to shuttle people to and from those health centers, including family members visiting the sick. Need an emergency ambulance? Call Hatzolah, a volunteer ambulance service started by Satmar Hasidim intent on avoiding the kinds of delays that have cost lives in the past when ambulances did not arrive in time. For disabled children and adults, Ohel and Bais Ezra will help. Bonei Olam arranges free fertility treatments. Or Chodesh offers support groups for people with emotional troubles. To aid bereaved families, Misaskim will literally provide grave diggers, special chairs for mourners sitting shiva, and support programs for orphans. As for goods, one can find Gemachs offering furniture, clothing, and books. Hasidic bridegrooms can even expect to receive the gift of a fur-rimed hat from a Streimel Gemach. And at major medical centers in the greater New York area, Haredim provide free apartments so that family members won't have to travel on the Sabbath and Jewish holidays to be with hospitalized loved ones. The list of possibilities is nearly endless, and because of the value placed upon Hesed, members of the community are constantly dreaming up new Gemachs to address as yet unmet needs.

Current Haredi leaders insist this extensive volunteer effort resulted from the model set by European-born rabbis. As one former insider put it to me, students in yeshivas are taught that "Tzedakah [Jewish giving] is part of your religious direction." Driving this point home, the story is told of the time Rabbi Joel Teitelbaum, the Satmar Rebbe, learned of students in his yeshiva who were shirking their responsibility to make hospital visits to the sick; his response was to threaten closing down the yeshiva.

Without diminishing the remarkable achievement of the Hesed work, a volunteer effort in which all must tithe and give of themselves, we might note the function it plays in making life in poor Haredi communities economically viable by offering so many free services and goods. It also serves as a powerful instrument for building community cohesion, and like all social service programs ties the beneficiaries to the provider. The community has the power to withhold support. In return for Hesed, it expects a high degree of social conformity. In fact, the three key institutions of Haredi life—family, religious schooling, and Hesed—all serve to bind people together within shared and tightly embracing communities.

I should note at this point that nowhere in my discussion have I commented on the piety or profound beliefs guiding Haredi Jews. This is not because they are absent, but because it is so difficult to gain entry to this population and to learn firsthand about the actual beliefs and driving religious concerns of these people. Of course, the official ideologies are accessible, but what really motivates average people is far harder to discern. Moreover, in a community with such powerful forms of social control, it is probably impossible to elicit forthright answers to questions of belief and practice. The argument I am making therefore is not that Haredi Jews are deep believers—there is no way to know—but that they live in communities where religious observance is reinforced and deviations from such practices are punished through social pressures and, in extreme cases, banishment.

This is not to say that there are no defectors or disenchanted Haredim. The Internet has enabled the latter to communicate with one another and has facilitated their learning about the outside world. It is a well-known secret that some Haredim frequent public libraries to gain access to books and online resources about the outside world; this is their illicit way to circumvent the barriers shielding or isolating them from unapproved knowledge. More damaging are the subterranean communities of so-called "reverse Marranos" springing up in Haredi communities. These are individuals who live externally as fully engaged Haredim but privately have lost their faith and when possible find ways to engage in illicit activities. Some stray from their enclaves to the large cities where under the cloak of anonymity they eat in nonkosher restaurants, engage in social dancing, frequent movies, find sexual partners, and in other ways trample on the mores and religious injunctions of their communities. They then return to their home communities and go through the motions of religious participation. They play this double game both because they lack the financial resources and occupational skills to leave their communities and because they wish to shield their family members from ostracism: siblings and children will not be considered as marriage partners for other Haredi Jews if a member of their family has deviated. And so these reverse Marannos hide their skepticism and rejection of Jewish religious practices in order to spare their family members from the harsh fate of social isolation.[29]

Still, a small but growing cadre of Haredi-raised individuals is abandoning that way of life entirely. Precise numbers are impossible to come by, though one Modern Orthodox rabbi claimed his Hasidic relatives explicitly speak of how two or three of their children will "defect," but with families of eight to twelve children, there still will be a large net gain for the family and community. A recent Israeli study claimed that over 10 percent of Haredi-born individuals have left that way of life behind.[30] Circumstances are different, and in some senses more difficult, for Haredim who want to leave their communities in the United States. Lacking the education, family support networks, and cultural savvy to function in the larger society, those who may wish to drop out are thwarted.

A growing literature written by former Haredim about their experiences and a few works of sociology have attempted to trace the lives of those who have largely abandoned Jewish practice. They call themselves OTD—"off-the-derech [path] Jews." A recent survey completed by nearly one thousand such individuals, including Modern Orthodox Jews, offered some suggestive insight into the phenomenon. Among its findings were:

- Most OTD people feel they were "pushed" away from their communities by internal ills such as hypocrisy and the unequal treatment of women, rather than "pulled" by the allure of a different lifestyle. Indeed, the status of women was cited by over one-third of Modern Orthodox women as the reason for their decision to defect.

- Only 21 percent claim to believe in God, but considerably higher percentages observe some religious rituals. Large majorities identify with the Jewish people and with Israel.

- The Internet was not the first means by which they were exposed to the wider culture. Rather, through reading and interactions with outsiders to their communities, these OTD Jews encountered ways of thinking at odds with the worldview of the enclaves in which they were brought up.[31]

To aid these people and connect them to one another, Footsteps was founded.[32] It offers support and counseling to the OTD population and claims to have helped over a thousand such individuals. No one seriously believes this exhausts the pool of such defectors.[33]

Beyond these renegades, some Haredi Jews draw attention to themselves as violators of Jewish law when they find themselves in trouble in American courts of law. The Jewish press seems to spotlight criminals clad in black hats or yarmulkes with far greater zeal than it reports about other kinds of Jewish wrongdoers. And now the Internet further magnifies the reporting. Failed Messiah, an online blog, for example, specialized in documenting in excruciating detail crimes and sins committed by Haredim in every corner of the globe—including cases of sexual abuse, financial irregularities, tax dodging, and various forms of cheating. As when Catholic priests and evangelical preachers who have sinned or worse are exposed, the misdeeds of Haredi rabbis are taken as confirmation that for all their holy-rolling, these people are charlatans.

Does the Haredi population contain more crooks, pedophiles, tax evaders, and embezzlers than the rest of the population? We have no way to know, but probably not. Still, those who project themselves as paragons of religious piety are held to a higher standard: the Haredim, after all, are expected to be free of vice because they are supposed to "tremble in fear of God." Some evidently are not faithfully observing laws, or are selective in what they understand to be incumbent upon the observant Jew. When such deviators are caught misbehaving, other Jews are quick to label them as hypocrites. But there is no gainsaying that the large majority strive to live a religiously observant life, not as a sometime thing but as an all-encompassing one.

Modern Orthodox Jews

Among the severest critics of Haredi Jews are their Modern Orthodox coreligionists. In a slashing commentary, a Modern Orthodox rabbi asks: "Why would a 'secular' Jew be attracted to a 'Torah' lifestyle that purports to demand estrangement from the general society, a cloistered abode, a rejection of general knowledge, an inability to function in the presence of women, a disdain for gainful employment and self-support . . . ? It doesn't seem very attractive, except for one who wants to escape from the world."[34] Were these views idiosyncratic, they would hardly be worth quoting, but they are in fact representative of thinking among large swaths of the Modern Orthodox laity who resent the air of superior religiosity projected by Haredi Jews. (And in turn, the latter make no bones about their contempt for the accommodations of the Modern Orthodox and their rabbis.)

Who, then, are the Modern Orthodox Jews? Relatively small in number, making up just 3 percent of American Jewry as a whole, they strive to forge a synthesis of the modern with traditional Jewish observance. Organizing their family lives far more traditionally than do their liberal counterparts, the Modern Orthodox tend to marry earlier than non-Orthodox Jews and to maintain a fertility rate well above replacement level; only small percentages intermarry. In order to ensure the transmission of their religious commitments, they enroll nearly all of their children in the most immersive forms of Jewish education. Their synagogues in some large centers, unlike most of those in the Conservative or Reform orbit, are teeming with regular worshippers every day of the week. Many sizable ones offer multiple prayer services every morning, afternoon, and evening, accommodating the busy schedules of individual worshippers. Indeed, the growing numbers of Modern Orthodox men who make it a point to pray in a minyan (prayer quorum) thrice daily, even if it means catching an early morning service before work at six in the morning and a late evening service at ten—let alone the minyanim held in offices, sports stadiums, and airports—represent a dramatic new pattern in this sector.[35]

Modern Orthodox synagogues serve a second function, as houses of study. Rabbis report on rising numbers of men and women participating in study classes, and even of teenagers seeking out opportunities to learn on Sabbath afternoons. In a reinforcing loop, as one rabbi notes, "more intensive learning has created greater levels of observance."

Synagogue life, in turn, is undergirded by the life of school and summer camp. Day school attendance from early childhood through high school has become almost universal for Modern Orthodox families. According to Pew data, 90 percent of those between the ages of eighteen and twenty-nine have attended a day school for at least four years—a much higher figure, incidentally, than the one for their parents or grandparents. The figures for summer camps are comparably impressive.

None of this would be feasible without financial resources. Nationally, according to Pew, 37 percent of Modern Orthodox households have incomes of over $150,000, a figure not matched by any other Jewish denomination. In the metropolitan New York area, home to the largest concentration of Orthodox Jews of all stripes, the Modern Orthodox contingent shows the largest proportions earning at least $100,000 or more than $150,000.[36]

This relative affluence makes it possible for some in the community to support key institutions with generous donations, including scholarship assistance for day school families. It also means that a large majority are able to shoulder the costs of Jewish living. Only those with resources—and commitment—can afford to live within walking distance of synagogues, purchase kosher food products, pay membership dues and building-fund assessments to synagogues, and, most expensive of all, cover K–12 tuition costs in day schools and send their children to Orthodox summer camps. Despite this heavy financial burden, there is no evidence that significant numbers have opted for public schools, though it is impossible to know how many decided to limit the size of their families because of affordability pressures.

Finally, none of this comes at the expense of active participation in American society. Just like their counterparts elsewhere in the Jewish community, the Modern Orthodox attend college and earn advanced degrees at far higher rates than most other Americans. Both men and women go on to work, as we have seen, in the more lucrative sectors of the American economy. Some rise to positions of great distinction in their fields of endeavor, including in American public life (e.g., a recent secretary of the treasury, an attorney general, and a former nominee for the vice presidency).

Like their Haredi counterparts, Modern Orthodox Jews are also not monolithic. We shall see in chapter 6 how sharp differences over ideology and religious outlook are threatening to create a rift in the Modern Orthodox sector. In this chapter on the lives of ordinary Orthodox Jews, we focus on matters of practice, behavior, and culture. Simply put, not all Modern Orthodox congregations are the same. Returning from a research trip that took him to five different cities over an extended period, a colleague reported to me how vastly different the congregants were in the Modern Orthodox synagogues he attended. Despite their employing an identical liturgy, these synagogues differed by virtue of how much talking there was during prayers, the subject matter of conversation, the formality or informality of dress, the efforts to include or segregate women, the types of liturgical music sung, and the pronunciation of the Hebrew prayers (Israeli vs. Yeshivish Hebrew).

What accounts for the differences? To begin with, geography is a major factor.[37] There are large differences between congregants in certain neighborhoods in the New York metropolitan area—such as in the outer boroughs, the Five Towns, and other parts of Long Island and Teaneck, New Jersey, on the one hand—and those who live in certain parts of Manhattan or Westchester or more distant suburbs. The former are far more likely than the latter to be punctilious in their observances, though even within each of these locales, members of one congregation may differ considerably in patterns of observance from those in a neighboring Modern Orthodox synagogue. Once one gets beyond the greater New York area, variations become even more common. Visiting a Modern Orthodox day school in Connecticut, for example, I was informed in no uncertain terms by the principal to forget about the kind of Orthodoxy I may have encountered in metropolitan New York: the rules of the game change at the border. And yet in some places where a critical mass of more traditionally educated Modern Orthodox Jews cluster—in North Miami, a few Midwestern cities, such as Chicago, and Los Angeles—a more stringent form of practice exists. And then again in places with small Modern Orthodox communities, a greater latitudinarianism is practiced. Some of this reflects the local culture: how laissez-faire it is about religion and accepting of diversity. But it also reflects the Jewish educational backgrounds of Modern Orthodox congregants, which may have been shaped by study in the major centers of Orthodox life in the United States or Israel.

Much depends also on the presence of enough Orthodox Jews to allow for exclusionary practices. In some parts of the country, congregations are teeming with members and therefore feel no compunction about excluding families that are not sufficiently observant. To the contrary, the dynamic of such congregations is to become more exclusive because that will ensure the retention of the more rigorously observant.[38] In smaller communities, by contrast, where every member who supports the synagogue is irreplaceable, Modern Orthodox Jews assume a "live and let live" attitude. Though it would be unthinkable for Modern Orthodox synagogues in the New York area to keep a parking lot open on the Sabbath and holidays, in other parts of the country where members range in practice, congregations do so. In smaller communities, members of Orthodox synagogues may also affiliate with and support congregations belonging to other Jewish denominations. Their parents may have done the same or their forebearers may have been stalwarts of those neighboring congregations. Some affiliate in order to express solidarity with all the Jews in their communities. None of this would fly in the New York area where lines between synagogues and denominations are etched deeply.[39]

Here is a small sampling of what was reported to me by rabbis of Modern Orthodox synagogues that draw a more eclectic crowd. One rabbi based in a Mid-Atlantic state reports with great satisfaction that thanks to his efforts, 85 percent of his congregants now also attend on the second day of Rosh Hashanah and not only the first day. He also encourages congregants who cannot read Hebrew to hum along with the cantor. (It is unlikely Modern Orthodox synagogues in metropolitan New York attract many Jews who cannot follow the Hebrew prayers or would not attend synagogue on both days of the Jewish New Year.) Another Modern Orthodox rabbi on the West Coast describes how his members struggle with prayers and concepts of God they find troubling. "We want the freedom to believe anything, but also want the freedom to believe in a personal God," he adds. The synagogue is also hospitable to openly gay people.

Investigating the practices of Modern Orthodox Jews in smaller communities, historian Jeffrey Gurock found a good deal of what he calls "heterodoxy within contemporary Orthodoxy." When he reported his findings at a conference of the Rabbinical Council of America, the organization of Modern Orthodox rabbis, he expected to be criticized severely for even suggesting there is such a phenomenon. Instead, he reports, he heard from quite a few rabbis about the laxity of observance among their congregants. "The typical minimally-committed congregant," they related to Gurock, "drove his or her car to the Sabbath services and much like their ancestors . . . parked their vehicles around the corner."[40] This is a world apart from the religious lives of congregants in more traditional Modern Orthodox synagogues, which if anything are being pulled toward a quasi-Haredi orientation and are adopting increased stringencies in their religious practices. Gurock concludes as follows about Orthodoxy in smaller communities: "even in an era of Orthodox triumphalism and the appearance of statistics and anecdotal evidence about an increasingly punctilious Orthodox community in America, there are Jews out on the hustings who as of yet do not—and perhaps never will—harbor staunch traditional religious values."[41]

Yet even in congregations whose members are generally more consistent in their religious practices, there are telling symptoms of an underlying malaise. It is common in quite a few Modern Orthodox synagogues for the prayers or Torah reading to be interrupted repeatedly in order to quiet the loud murmuring of private conversations on both sides of the *Mehitsa*, the barrier separating men and women. No sooner does the rabbi plead for quiet than the talking erupts with full force again. What ensues in many synagogues is a tug-of-war between the clergy who try to quiet the din and many congregants. Rather than berate their congregants, some rabbis work assiduously to shorten services, without skipping any parts of the prayers, and develop a more inspirational ambience.[42] To one Modern Orthodox observer who has prayed in quite a few congregations, the constant talking serves as "the tip of a much more serious problem: a lack of engagement in synagogues in general and in Judaism." To be sure, there is a range of behaviors: In some congregations, a culture has been fostered that discourages conversation and attracts more serious worshippers. But in many others, the high decibel level is unmistakable. It may be indicative of boredom or a lack of engagement with the service. Or it may result from the same phenomenon we have observed among non-Orthodox Jews: the primary purpose of attending prayer services, even in many Orthodox synagogues, is to converse with friends, not to address God.[43]

Variations in religious practice exist not only between congregations but also *within* a good many synagogues. Just beneath the surface in even the more rigorously observant synagogues, it is not hard to find congregants who struggle with contradiction and inconsistency. Balancing between Orthodoxy and modernity can create internal strain or cognitive dissonance. One observer describes Modern Orthodox Jews as perpetually walking a tightrope. Inevitably, as they maneuver hard not to fall off, they sometimes lurch to the right and adopt some characteristics of the Haredim; at other times they swing to the left and compromise on some religious observances. As a result, he add, "everyone in the Modern Orthodox world acts inconsistently."

Without assuming that this is true of "everyone," it is still the case that a good many Modern Orthodox Jews experience strain when working and living in the larger American society, while also trying to observe Orthodox practices. Men must decide whether to wear a head covering (yarmulke) at all times or only in their private lives at home and within their own communities. Women must decide whether to adhere to Orthodox prohibitions against wearing pants (a "male garment") and, if they are married, whether to keep their hair covered. For some Modern Orthodox Jews, cognitive dissonance arises when they attend business meetings and travel. How strictly shall they follow the dietary restrictions of Kashrut? They know that hot food, even when it is dairy or vegetarian, has been prepared in pots that are also used to cook nonkosher meat or seafood dishes; that itself renders the food nonkosher. And yet, they also want or need to interact with business associates and cannot always obtain food prepared to kosher standards. And so they use their knowledge of Jewish law to rationalize: some will eat cheese pizza in nonkosher settings, while others will eschew pizza but not pasta. Why? The latter may have been cooked in a pot that was used for nonkosher food but then was washed; the pizza, though, may have baked in the oven alongside a pepperoni pizza. Others flip the argument and come to the reverse conclusion.

These mental gymnastics occur not only at business meetings. A not insignificant number of Modern Orthodox Jews frequent nonkosher restaurants on vacations or when they are closer to home. Few eat nonkosher meat or seafood dishes, but they will consume what they label "dairy" food—fish and vegetarian hot foods. As related by one observer of the Modern Orthodox scene, the key question is how far a family will travel to avoid being seen in a nonkosher restaurant. Not long ago, when a speaker commented about these patterns in a talk held at a Modern Orthodox synagogue, the host rabbi proudly proclaimed that his people would never do such a thing. His congregants quickly and loudly disabused him of his naïveté.

Almost all nonobservance occurs outside the precincts of synagogues, but one glaring exception highlights the gap between rabbis and their congregants. During the first three-quarters of the twentieth century, social dancing was a commonplace in Modern Orthodox synagogues at Bar/Bat Mitzvah celebrations and weddings. Toward the end of the century, rabbis worked to end the practice, but with limited success.[44] So a tacit compromise was reached: during the early part of celebrations, the focus would be on Jewish-style dancing, with men and women forming separate circles. And then halfway through the festive meal, the rabbis would depart and the celebrants would kick up their heels in coed social dancing. That practice continues often today, but in some settings, the rabbis don't depart but men and women dance together anyway. This blatant disregard of Orthodox teachings highlights the limited authority of rabbinic views among Modern Orthodox Jews and the growing autonomy exercised by congregants.[45]

The purpose of touching upon these matters is not to ridicule, but to underscore that Modern Orthodox Jews are not monolithic in their religious practices (or their deviations from commandments), nor is their chosen course of religious observance uncomplicated by inner contradictions. If anything, new technologies and rising affluence are adding new layers of complexity. A few years ago, the Jewish press was buzzing with articles about Modern Orthodox children who text on the Sabbath despite the prohibition on using electrical gadgets on that day.[46] Some claimed they were addicted to the media and could not resist; others rationalized their behavior, claiming their texts were impermanent and therefore are not akin to writing, another act impermissible on the Sabbath. A new vocabulary arose about those who observe "half Shabbat." These deviations are hardly confined to children. Talk to enough Modern Orthodox Jews and one will hear about parents who turn lights on and off on the Sabbath and watch TV, both violations of Orthodox Sabbath observances. And still these people consider themselves Modern Orthodox, which begs the question of why.

In a widely circulated article,[47] Jay Lefkowitz tackled the question head-on. Describing what he called "social Orthodoxy," Lefkowitz acknowledged the existence of a not insignificant number of Modern Orthodox Jews whose beliefs are not in sync with official doctrines and whose practices stray at times, but who wish to be part of a community of observant Jews and want to raise their children in such a setting. They have concluded their only option is Modern Orthodoxy, and so for social and "peoplehood" purposes, rather than heartfelt religious reasons, they belong to such communities. These social motives, we should note, range from wanting their children to have playmates on the Sabbath and holidays who do not desecrate the traditional observance of those days, to feeling most connected to the kinds of adults who keep traditional observances. What proportion of the Modern Orthodox fall into the category Lefkowitz identified is hard to tell, but, as he notes, 77 percent of the Modern Orthodox surveyed by the Pew study claim absolute certainty about God's existence. Does that mean that nearly one-quarter of Modern Orthodox Jews are nonbelievers? Not necessarily, but it is a small piece of evidence to support his contention that a proportion of Modern Orthodox Jews are not, as he puts it, "doctrinaire" about their religion. Like Lefkowitz, who candidly spoke the truth about his own practices, they too "pick and choose from the menu of Jewish rituals without fear of divine retribution," and root their "identity much more in Jewish culture, history, and nationality than in faith and commandments." Even as we find some Modern Orthodox Jews "sliding to the right" in their religious outlook and practices, others, it appears, are "sliding to the left."[48]

We have provided examples of the latter, but what might the drift to the Haredi camp represent? On a superficial level, the rightward lurch takes symbolic or token form, as when men wear black hats during prayer and women adopt Haredi-style head coverings while otherwise continuing to maintain their very modern style of life. The shift has more far-reaching consequences when families switch synagogues to be among those they deem more punctilious in their observance and enroll their children in day schools whose Jewish studies teachers are drawn from the Haredi community. And then as a kind of finishing school experience, families send their high school graduates off to Israeli gap-year programs at yeshivas and seminaries whose practices and outlook are openly at odds with the Modern Orthodox ethos. It's not easy to know how much of this "slide to the right" is occasioned by a genuine recommitment to heightened observance or an effort to place their children in environments that somehow will lessen the likelihood of their straying from Orthodoxy.

Perhaps most fascinating is the way Modern Orthodox Jews moving seemingly in opposite directions coexist in the same institutions. That kind of coexistence is visibly evident in the ways people dress: men wearing a knitted skullcap can be found seated in synagogues next to ones wearing black satin yarmulkes or fedoras (the black hatters); women wearing wigs or snoods to cover their hair will be found seated next to women who wear fashionable hats and then go bareheaded outside of the synagogue. These seemingly superficial fashions actually are fraught with symbolism in the Orthodox community. What is even more noteworthy is the way some Modern Orthodox synagogues intentionally work to ensure that both types will feel welcome. At the Boca Raton Synagogue, for example, new members are given a special orientation class by the senior rabbi where they are taught the synagogue etiquette of welcoming all Jews, including those who drive to the synagogue on the Sabbath or may have money jangling in their pockets on days when touching money is impermissible. These lessons are distinctly at odds with how many newcomers were raised. They provide further evidence, though, of increasing diversity of observance to be found in Modern Orthodox synagogues.

Sephardi Jews—A Minority within a Minority

If anything, the range of observance among Sephardi Jews is even broader, encompassing what we may call the punctiliously observant, the selectively observant, and the rarely observant.[49] Constituting a minority of no more than 5 percent of American Jews and participating in religious cultures that seem alien to their Ashkenazi coreligionists, collectively they barely register on the radar of most American Jews.[50] Yet they are of increasing importance to American Jewish life. For one thing, they tend to adhere to distinctive religious and cultural traditions and form tightly knit communities centered in synagogues; these groupings have staying power. Second, they are not an insignificant population within Orthodoxy, a fact that has led some Ashkenazi Modern Orthodox synagogues to host separate Sephardi services under their aegis. And at least up to now, Sephardi Jews have succeeded far better than their Ashkenazi counterparts in transmitting to their children a strong Jewish identity and connection to communal life.

There are no authoritative figures on the numbers of Sephardi Jews in the United States, but it is clear that the largest concentration is to be found in the greater New York area. A study of New York Jews conducted in 2011 estimated their numbers at approximately 245,00 people, with the largest concentrations in Brooklyn, Queens, Great Neck, Long Island, Manhattan, as well as Deal, New Jersey.[51] The second significant concentration is found in Los Angeles, though it is not nearly as large as the one in New York.[52] Judging from the presence of Sephardi synagogues, communities exist in locales as far-flung as Chicago, Houston, Miami, San Diego, and Seattle.

Social scientists studying the New York Jewish community, the largest of its kind in the United States, identified key populations of Sephardi families and households containing at least one person of Sephardi background.[53] The largest contingent in the New York area are Israelis of Sephardi extraction. Their families originated in many different lands, and accordingly, those who attend synagogues have joined congregations where the customs of their ancestors' homeland are replicated.

The best-known and second-largest subgroup hails from Syria, though it also includes immigrants from Egypt and Lebanon who have been absorbed through marriage or social interactions into the Syrian communities. Self-styled SYs (pronounced "ess whys") trace their origin to immigrants who arrived early in the twentieth century and then were augmented by refugees fleeing in the wake of Israel's establishment when life for Jews in Muslim lands become perilous.[54] The remaining Jews of Syria were quietly permitted to leave in the 1990s on the condition they not settle in Israel. These too have been absorbed into the SY community of New York.

Jews from Iran constitute a third major contingent of Sephardi Jews in the United States. Persian Jews first began to immigrate in the middle of the twentieth century and then received a major infusion of new blood in the wake of the Khomeini revolution in 1979. Other Sephardi Jews trace their origins in the United States to immigrants who arrived from the Ottoman Empire early in the twentieth century.[55] More recent arrivals originated in Turkey, Iraq, Egypt, Morocco, and Lebanon.[56]

Symptomatic of the information vacuum on Sephardi Jews, one of the largest groups—Bukharans who hail from Central Asia, areas now part of the newly formed republics of Uzbekistan, Tajikistan, and Kyrgyzstan—are virtually unknown.[57] One report puts their figure at fifty thousand souls in Queens alone, though a demographic study of New York Jewry comes in with a lower figure. Their central institutions are in Forest Hills, where they have established their own synagogues, Jewish schools, and community center, but others live in the Rego Park and Flushing neighborhoods of Queens.[58] A leading Bukharan rabbi characterized the religious behavior of his people as "about twenty percent . . . Orthodox, sixty percent are traditional but not necessarily observant, and twenty percent are unaffiliated."[59] Significantly, he employed the term "Orthodox" to refer to the most observant. And indeed Bukhari synagogues conform to Orthodox guidelines. Whereas the percentages vary among other Sephardi groups, the categories and range of behaviors are parallel. For a variety of reasons, including the challenges of access, little will be said here about this group, especially because, as they are the most recent immigrants, so much about their lives in the United States is in flux.

Though they hardly are uniform, Sephardi Jews tend to be strict about certain aspects of the religion. Even those who are not fully Sabbath observant are likely to say the blessings over wine (kiddush) on Friday evenings and mark the arrival of the Sabbath with a festive family meal. High Holiday attendance and the Passover Seder are almost universally observed. Intermarriage and divorce are far less frequent occurrences than among Ashkenazi Jews, perhaps because involvement with the extended family and communal approval are so central to the Sephardi culture: they tend to mingle among their own and also are aware of the social opprobrium attached to intermarriage by their fellow Sephardim. The preference is to marry within the same subethnic group or with someone of a different Sephardi background. With the passage of time, marriages with Ashkenazi Jews are becoming more frequent.

Sephardi Jews differ from their Ashkenazi Orthodox counterparts in the tendency of males to eschew wearing head coverings in work environments. Eating "dairy" or vegetarian food in nonkosher restaurants is widespread. And among some populations, so too is driving to synagogues on the Sabbath. What holds them together despite their different levels of religious practice are strong extended-family ties and a desire to maintain imported religious customs in their synagogues.

Several observers of Sephardi communities described these allegiances as "tribal." And indeed some of these communities try to maintain themselves by marrying within their own subethnic group. Iranian and Bukharan Jews look for partners within their communities, and so do Syrians. The latter, in fact, have gone to the extreme of refusing to accept converts to Judaism on the grounds that such acceptance opens the door to foreign ways of thinking and may encourage intermarriage. A rabbinic edict issued in 1935 by Syrian rabbis in Brooklyn forbids rabbis to convert non-Jews and commits the community to ostracize Jews who have married individuals converted by other rabbis and to reject children of converts. Conversions, according to the edict, are considered "fictitious and valueless." A revision of the edict in 1946 specified "the Congregation's premises will be banned to them [converts and their Jewish-born spouses] for use of any religious or social nature. . . . After death of said person, he or she is not to be buried on the Cemetery of our community." In one notorious case, the Sephardi Chief Rabbi of Israel traveled to Brooklyn to vouch for a convert, but the community rejected his appeal. The daughter of a leading Syrian rabbi has been ostracized for decades because she is married to a convert. The most traditional sectors of Sephardi Jewry self-consciously work to enforce the group's boundaries.[60] That said, the more generations of Sephardi Jews have lived in America, the greater the likelihood of marriage to Ashkenazi coreligionists and, to a lesser extent, non-Jews.

The traditionalism of Sephardi Jews is especially noteworthy in their patterns of family life. They tend to marry relatively young and have children well above replacement level. This is especially true among Syrian Jews, but Iranian and Bukharan populations are not all that different. In their patterns of family formation, Sephardi Jews are akin to Ashkenazi Orthodox Jews. Gender roles also tend to be more traditional among Sephardim. Considerably higher proportions of Sephardi women than Ashkenazi ones engage in traditional roles as homemakers and volunteers, and are less likely to seek employment outside of the home.[61] Sephardi women also earn advanced degrees at lower rates than their Ashkenazi counterparts.[62] Rabbinic observers credit women with keeping their families involved with traditional religion and Sephardi cultural forms.[63]

A variety of other factors account for different levels of religious traditionalism. For one, the number of generations a family has been in the United States will affect how tightly people feel bound to the group. Populations in Seattle and Atlanta that trace their immigration history back nearly a century tend to have a harder time retaining the allegiance of younger people than those who arrived within the past three decades. Marriage to Ashkenazi Jews also leads to a departure from the group. In the perception of rabbis who deal with these populations, Ashkenazi wives often feel uncomfortable in traditional Sephardi synagogues and persuade their husbands to join Conservative or Reform temples. Another factor affecting religious involvement in America is traceable to the exposure of immigrants to modern societies before they left the Levant. Among Iranian Jews, for example, the great divide is between the Teherani and Mashhadi: the former had lived in a more cosmopolitan city and had begun to modernize already in Iran, while the latter held fast to their traditions (in part because they were subject to persecution in Mashhad). In the United States, the Mashhadis are more religiously traditional than the Teheranis.

It is hard to generalize about the religious affiliations of the various Sephardi populations (particularly because surveys don't ask). A study of New York Jews claimed that roughly half the Syrian population is Orthodox, and of these one-third are classified as Haredi. Another 12 percent are Conservative, 18 percent Reform, and 23 percent other. That said, nearly three-quarters of Syrian children are enrolled in Jewish day schools. Among Iranian Jews, day school enrollment varies. Ironically, high numbers of Persian

Jews affiliated with Sinai Temple, a Conservative synagogue in Los Angeles, send their children to the congregation's in-house day school, Sinai Akiba Academy, whereas Persian Jews in Great Neck, New York, have enrolled their children in public schools, even as they attend traditional Iranian synagogues.[64] Perhaps, the key factor here is the quality of the public schools in each area and the high percentage of Jewish children enrolled in Great Neck public schools.

As these communities reckon with the American environment, they are increasingly sending their children to Jewish day schools, which is having an impact on religious life. Graduates of day schools are pushing their families to embrace more consistent patterns of observance. In both the Syrian and Persian communities of New York and Los Angeles, internal pressures are building to adopt a more observant lifestyle, even as some acculturate to American norms and spin away from their communities. Day schools, moreover, are creating a more highly informed population, and that too leads to a push for greater consistency. Among the older generations, Syrian and Persian Jews are not particularly known for their intensive Jewish learning, relying more on folk customs than on knowledge of Jewish law. The Syrian community has been shifting because it has a longer history of sending its children to Jewish day schools. The Persians and smaller Sephardi immigrant groups thus far are less intellectual in their approach to religion and slower to embrace day school education.[65]

When some younger people are sent to Ashkenazi yeshivas for advanced study, they are likely to return to their communities with new attitudes. Those who study at Yeshivish institutions such as Ner Israel in Baltimore no longer identify as Zionist and bemoan the uncritical tolerance for nonobservant Jews in Sephardi synagogues. An example of this shift to greater stringency occurred in a Brooklyn Syrian synagogue where the long-standing custom was to run an early morning service on the Sabbath for members who then would go to work afterward. This service had been sanctioned by a leading Syrian rabbi who permitted such services on the condition that attendees would pray in synagogue regularly on the Sabbath morning and recite the blessing over the wine (kiddush) before going off to their places of business. Under Haredi Ashkenazi influence, these compromises have been phased out. Observers of the scene comment on the adoption from Haredim of new stringencies (*Humrot*) and "superstitions" by sectors of the Syrian community. According to one estimate, 40 percent of Brooklyn's Syrians are now attracted to the Haredi model, while another 40 percent adhere to the Syrian traditions, with the remaining 20 percent steering clear of the divide. As one observer put it, "in Brooklyn, the Litvish [Lithuanian] yeshiva is influencing the Syrian ghetto . . . , instilling obscurantism and fear." The same observer voiced his expectation that the Mashhadi community in Great Neck will experience similar strains as it sends more of its young people to study at upper-level Haredi yeshivas in the United States and Israel.

Overall, though, Sephardi communities accommodate the diverse religious practices of their members. Less observant members are warmly received because the culture encourages hospitality to all who are within the group. Some of the sharp boundaries that exist in sectors of Ashkenazi Orthodoxy are not found among Sephardim. Jews who attend synagogue only on the High Holidays are welcomed and included in religious services, communal events, and family gatherings. By virtue of their family connections and ethnic origins, the nonobservant are treated as insiders.

One factor that facilitates such acceptance is the tendency of those who leave the traditional fold to observe some religious rituals with greater fidelity than do Ashkenazim. A study of Syrians in the New York area, for example, compared the practices of non-Orthodox Syrian and non-Orthodox Ashkenazi Jews: 56 percent of the former claimed to maintain a kosher home versus 22 percent of the latter; 31 percent attended religious services more than once monthly versus 16 percent of the Ashkenazi Jews; and a whopping 80 percent claimed to participate in a Shabbat meal at least sometimes versus 42 percent of non-Orthodox Ashkenazi Jews. These general patterns were confirmed by rabbis who interact with other types of Sephardi Jews. A Los Angeles congregation, for example, rents space in a hotel on Yom Kippur to hold overflow services for its members, most of whom are not regulars, but on the Day of Atonement they stay at the hotel overnight in order to refrain from travel. Considerably more observances are sacrosanct to Sephardi Jews who are not Orthoprax than is the case with their Ashkenazi counterparts.

This chapter began with a claim that the religious lives of Orthodox Jews differ sharply from those of non-Orthodox Jews. After surveying the three major sectors of Orthodoxy, we conclude with another assertion—in this case about an emerging commonality: across the spectrum of American Judaism the ethos of individualism and freedom of choice has spread throughout the Jewish populace. That this is self-evident among non-Orthodox Jews hardly needs elaboration. We have noted already in the previous chapter the liberties non-Orthodox Jews take, picking and choosing from Jewish religious options. More surprising, perhaps, Orthodox Jews also are exercising a significant degree of autonomy in their religious lives.

Rabbis across the spectrum of Orthodoxy speak of congregants who have been shaped by the modern ethos of personalism and autonomy. "What rabbis say does not matter" is a refrain I have heard repeatedly. "Authority is in retreat," declares one rabbi; says another, "People like traditional davening (prayer) and singing; but when it comes to *halakhah* impinging on them, then they resist."

This does not mean the Orthodox necessarily ignore traditional teachings or abandon religious practices. But their relationship to rabbinic authority is changing. To be sure, this is happening far less among Haredim where social controls remain firmly in place. But among the Modern Orthodox and Sephardi populations there is a growing tendency to resist or ignore rabbinic decisors, or at least choose carefully whom to ask for an opinion.[66]

This tendency has been facilitated by the easy availability of information on the Internet. Orthodox rabbis see their congregants venturing online to find answers to their questions—and then governing themselves by conclusions they draw on their own. As noted by Rabbi Yitzhak Adlerstein:

> The Internet has yielded memes that will be bequeathed for generations to come, just as the Enlightenment did. One of them is resistance to top-down authority. The Internet has somewhat leveled the playing field, giving everyone a voice. . . . This democratization of power affects everyone with intoxicating freedom, even those who don't have much to say. Old assumptions about who should speak and who should be silent are crumbling. . . . For better or worse, the Internet and the new technologies

are leaving people more connected, more knowledgeable, and more demanding of personal gratification.[67]

But the Internet alone is not the sole cause of this form of DIY Judaism. An observer of the Modern Orthodox world flatly states that in circles he encounters, few congregants bother to ask questions of their rabbis because they don't want to hear their answers. Instead, growing numbers of congregants arrive at their own *psak* (judgments of what is called for by Jewish law), their own understanding of what is proper. From the perspective of a rabbi who works with colleagues faced with challenging congregational issues, this assessment sounds right: "Rabbinic authority," he avers, "is being ignored."

It is, of course, easy to say in response that rabbis have brought this upon themselves. If they only spoke with authority, the thinking goes, their congregants would pay attention. To be sure, there are a handful of rabbis who command such respect on a national level, even as some congregants regard their own local rabbi as an authority. But in the current environment where individual choice is taken for granted and leaders in general are seen as flawed individuals, even Orthodox Jews do not necessarily seek out the opinion of their rabbis on religious matters. This too is a central feature of the current era of religious recession. Not surprisingly, denominational institutions whose task it is to define proper belief and behavior have also fallen on hard times. Their travails will occupy our attention in the coming pages.

PART II

The Leaky Vessels of

Denominational Judaism

4

IS REFORM JUDAISM ASCENDANT?

Following the model set by their Protestant neighbors who dominated American society for much of the country's history, Jews involved in religious life formed their own denominations during the latter part of the nineteenth and early twentieth centuries. The three major Jewish denominations in order of current size are Reform, Conservative, and Orthodox Judaism.[1] Within Jewish circles, a different nomenclature has been applied to these groupings: usually they are referred to as movements, with the implication that they are trying to move their people in a particular direction. But by the twenty-first century, each of the big three groupings has in its own way embraced a "big-tent" approach with only limited ideological coherence; labeling them as movements may not be especially helpful.

Protestant denominations typically have distinctive theologies, liturgies, and worship practices in addition to organizational infrastructures to carry out their work. So too Jewish denominations have long prided themselves on their clear positions on matters of belief in the divine origin of the Torah, interpretive approaches to Jewish law and Jewish observances, as well as distinct styles of synagogue worship. The latter were particularly important to average Jews who regardless of their knowledge of Judaism could not fail to notice how the public prayer in Reform, Conservative, and Orthodox synagogues differed. As has been the case in Protestant denominations, their Jewish counterparts have been riven by internal battles over matters of practice and ideology, and their leaders have also on occasion lashed out at each other over these issues.

What, then, do the organizations of these Jewish movements do? They strive to set religious policies for their congregations and offer some guidance on governance practices and dues. They issue new liturgical works every few years, ostensibly to synchronize the prayer book with contemporary sensibilities and sensitivities, and not coincidentally to raise revenue through sales to cover their operating budgets. In the recent past, they offered educational services to congregational schools, but of late that function is much reduced. And most important, to one extent or another they run summer camps, Israel trips, and teen programs. (In the past, they also supported campus programs, but now only the Orthodox Union has a campus presence.) The movements often serve as clearinghouses of information about best practices. At conventions and in the pages of in-house publications, ideas are shared, with the expectation that they will percolate down to congregations in far-flung localities. But like national organizations generally in this country, the Jewish religious movements have lost a good deal of their influence and cachet. Localism prevails and national movements are financially strapped.

Why, then, devote attention to these movements? First, because they reflect the views and priorities of the elites. They articulate what leaders would like the masses of average Jews to believe and do. They also offer a prism through which to discern what preoccupies leaders, what they hear from the field, and how they understand the needs of the moment. And the movements, for all their present weaknesses, continue to serve as sorting mechanisms, helping Jews make sense of where they fit into the larger world of Jewish religious life.

Reform's Success as a Liberal Religious Movement

We begin with the oldest and largest of the denominations, Reform Judaism. As one of the most liberal forms of Judaism, Reform seems to pose a bit of a mystery. Here is the larger context: It is by now a well-documented fact that liberal Protestant denominations in the United States have fallen on hard times. In the mainline churches that once dominated American religious life—and from which emerged the country's political and cultural elites—the pews have been emptying since as long ago as the 1960s.[2] As the average age of churchgoers edges ever upward, the challenge of recruiting both members and qualified clergy looms larger still, adding to the general sense of demoralization and desuetude. In the meantime, membership in conservative Christian denominations, particularly the evangelical churches, has been swelling.

Against this backdrop, the relative growth and high morale of Reform Judaism—the Jewish analogue to the liberal Protestant denominations—are nothing short of astonishing. Rather than losing "market share" to its more conservative counterparts, the Reform movement has become the label selected by the plurality of those who identify themselves with the Jewish religion. Nor is its success a matter only of numbers. The movement's internal decisions—on everything from synagogue liturgy to the religious status of gay, lesbian, and transgender Jews to rabbinic officiation at intermarriages—are widely regarded as bellwethers of American Jewish life at large.

Understandably enough, Reform seems to attract the greatest attention when it appears to be acting contrary to type. In recent years, for example, articles in the general and Jewish press have marveled at the release of new Reform prayer books incorporating a much more "traditionalist" attitude toward long-discarded practices and modes of Jewish worship.[3] What could this signify? A healthy openness and self-confidence or, perhaps, a sudden loss of direction?

As it happens, shifts in direction, even radical ones, are nothing new in the history of Reform Judaism. The movement proudly declares its name to be both a noun and a verb, and ever since its emergence in America one hundred fifty years ago, it has self-consciously striven to adjust to the rhythm of the times.

In its first period of growth, Reform appealed primarily to Americanized Jews of Central European origin whose families had arrived here in the early and middle decades of the nineteenth century. By the post–Civil War era, this population had achieved economic success and high social status, and in the process had sloughed off most traditional Jewish practices like observance of the dietary laws (Kashrut) and home-based Sabbath rituals. Their synagogues, too, were undergoing what seemed to be an inexorable tide of reformation, introducing organ music, a formal "High Church" aesthetic, abbreviated services, a liturgy largely in English, and rabbinic sermons delivered with oratorical panache.[4]

On the organizational side of Reform, Rabbi Isaac Mayer Wise of Cincinnati spearheaded an effort to weld individual congregations into a Union of American Hebrew Congregations. This body, in turn, founded the Hebrew Union College (HUC) to train rabbis. By the early twentieth century, Reform Judaism had become the dominant religious expression of the native elite of the Jewish community (as opposed to the newly arrived immigrants from Eastern Europe and their families who, insofar as they affiliated themselves with religious observance, tended to join more traditionalist synagogues).

Historians have debated the reasons for the movement's rapid spread. Much of the debate is academic, but one question has continued to reverberate: was American Reform built upon a structured ideology—on strongly held principles—or did it primarily reflect a series of pragmatic adjustments to the shifting scene? Perhaps the most sustained attempt to articulate a true ideology was the "Pittsburgh Platform" of 1885. According to that document, drafted at a conclave of Reform rabbis, the movement was committed to Judaism as a religion of ethical monotheism; to a highly rationalistic understanding of the deity, presented as a "God Idea"; to the pursuit of social justice for all; and to a definition of Jewishness as solely a matter of confession. On the negative side, much of the ritual structure of Judaism was dismissed as a throwback to an era now rendered anachronistic by the advances of science and human reason. In particular, the movement rejected "such Mosaic and rabbinical laws as regulate diet, priestly purity, and dress." By the same token, it also rejected any national component to Jewish identity or hope for the restoration of Jews to Zion.[5]

We cannot know for certain how ardently these principles were held by ordinary Reform Jews, as distinct from their rabbis. In Reform congregations, however, men were forbidden to wear a head covering or prayer shawl; dietary laws were openly flouted; and the prayer services pointedly eschewed any reference to the national aspirations of the Jewish people.

This period of what is known as "classical" Reform lasted until nearly the outbreak of World War II, when the movement experienced an influx of new leaders with a different set of assumptions. As the children of Eastern European immigrants became a force first within the rabbinate and eventually the membership base, and with the growth of the Nazi menace in Europe, Reform's long-standing opposition to Zionism began to collapse. By 1937, the Reform rabbinate had accepted a neutral (as distinct from hostile) stance on the issue. During the war, this would give way in turn to a positive embrace of the Jewish national movement, compelling anti-Zionist Reform rabbis to break away and found the American Council for Judaism.[6]

Throughout this period, Reform Jews continued to dominate the leadership of the American Jewish community at large—including the top positions within the Zionist camp, occupied by Rabbis Stephen S. Wise and Abba Hillel Silver. But Reform attitudes were increasingly out of synch with the sentiments of the large majority of Jews in the country, a majority now made up of second-generation Americans who held a generally more positive view of ritual observance and found Reform "temples," with their socially exclusive policies and their emphasis on strict decorum, to be alien places.

As the new Jewish majority moved out of the inner cities and into the burgeoning suburbs, Reform began to adapt.[7] Suddenly, temples were sponsoring such formerly unheard-of rites as Bar Mitzvah and, later, Bat Mitzvah ceremonies. The shofar replaced trumpet blasts on the Jewish New Year, and head coverings and prayer shawls made a slow comeback. Some of this "increased ritualism," as it was dubbed by its antagonists, represented a self-conscious effort to compete more effectively with Conservative Judaism, which during the 1950s would overtake Reform as the preferred religious choice of the plurality of American Jews. But many within the movement saw it as a move in precisely the wrong direction, into the benighted past. The historian Jacob Rader Marcus, a revered professor at HUC, spoke for them: "There are today too many Reform Jews who have ceased to be [religious] liberals. Their Reform, crystallized into a new Orthodoxy, is no longer dynamic. . . . We cannot lead our people forward by standing backward."[8] Sounding a similar note, rabbis contributing to a 1960 symposium urged Reform to stick to its pristine agenda. As one respondent declared: "We should not fear to be different."

For the next few decades, the movement zigged and zagged without a defined direction. Clearly, it had repented of large parts of its "classical" ideology. But what it stood for was harder to say. For the centenary of its founding in 1973, the movement had hoped to produce a timely statement of principles; the document finally appeared three years later.

At some point in the 1980s, however, things appear to have changed again, and Reform emerged stronger, more unified, and more confident of itself. This is the Reform we know today. Several related initiatives undertaken by the movement help explain the turn in its fortunes. Their common watchwords are "inclusiveness" and "choice."

For one thing, the movement incorporated sexual egalitarianism as a cardinal principle. Initially this meant that women would be treated as complete equals in all aspects of religious and synagogue life. In 1972, HUC had been the first American Jewish seminary to ordain a woman rabbi, a precedent it followed by becoming the first to graduate a woman as a cantor. Over the ensuing decades, women assumed key positions in the governance of congregations and in the movement's national institutions. In time, Reform also embraced openly homosexual Jews, welcomed so-called gay synagogues into its congregational body, ordained Jews who openly identified as LGBTQ as rabbis and cantors, and sanctioned wedding and/or commitment ceremonies for same-sex couples.[9]

Nor were these the only moves toward inclusiveness. Hoping to retain the allegiance of Jews who had married or who wished to marry non-Jews, significant numbers of Reform rabbis began to bless interfaith unions, thereby overturning a long history of opposition to the practice. Congregations, meanwhile, launched "outreach activities" to draw in intermarried Jews and their families. In 1983, the Reform rabbinate turned aside the accepted definition of a person qualifying as a born Jew—the traditional criterion is a person whose mother was Jewish—so as to include anyone who had one Jewish parent of either sex and who took part in public acts of Jewish identification (for instance, by attending a synagogue).[10]

In terms of demographics, this particular initiative produced dramatic results: by the turn of the twenty-first century, over 25 percent of the member families in Reform temples were intermarried.[11] And no less open-armed was Reform's new approach to diverse types of Jewish expression. In ritual matters, the movement now happily accommodated head coverings and prayer shawls for both men and women during services, while continuing to welcome those who eschewed such garb; synagogues and other institutions began to provide for members wishing to observe aspects of Jewish dietary laws, even as they respected the desires of those partial to prohibited foods. And so forth.

Here the guiding principle has been autonomy and choice. Each individual Jew has the inalienable right to define which aspects of the faith are personally meaningful; so long as these choices were "informed," the movement not only tolerates but endorses them.

On two fronts, leaders have pressed hard for their own point of view; in each case, their instincts have appeared to be wholly in tune with the temper of the times. The first concerns synagogue services, which were deemed hopelessly deadening and in desperate need of revision. As Rabbi Eric Yoffie, the head of the congregational body, put it: "Far too often, our services are tedious, predictable, and dull. Far too often, our members pray without fervor or concentration. Far too often, our music is dirge-like and our Torah readings lifeless, and we are unable to trigger true emotion and ascent."[12] In response, congregations began to experiment with liturgies combining traditional prayers with newly composed prayers and poems; organ and choir music gave way to singing accompanied by flutes, stringed instruments, and drums; rabbis dropped their formal sermons in favor of open discussion. Most noticeably, Reform temples in which congregants were accustomed to sitting passively in pews now freed them to move around the sanctuary—carrying the Torah, dancing during prayers, greeting one another as fellow worshippers.[13]

The final step in this process came with the release of the radically revised prayer book for Sabbath and holidays, followed by a High Holiday *Mahzor*. As was immediately noticed, the new volumes incorporate many more Hebrew prayers than their predecessors and restore much of the structure of the traditional worship service. At the same time, though, in the regnant spirit of inclusiveness and choice, they also provide ample room for each synagogue to tailor the liturgy however it sees fit.

The second front is the political. Until recently, it was possible to find Reform rabbis and lay leaders active in both the Republican and Democratic parties, and the movement's pronouncements on matters of public policy retained at least a studied semblance of political neutrality.[14] This ceased to be the case. In recent years, Reform Judaism, at the prodding of its Washington arm, the Religious Action Center, issued resolution after resolution in support of left-liberal positions across an array of political and social issues. It opposed the war in Iraq; sharply rebuked the Christian right; and vigorously supported the left-wing Democratic stance on gay marriage, health care, and immigration policy. In all of these areas, the Reform movement aligned itself perfectly with positions adopted by mainstream liberal Protestantism. But Protestant denominations had split badly over questions like liturgical innovation, abortion rights, and gay ordination. In contrast, on some of the most divisive issues of our time, Reform leaders not only avoided schism but have evidently built a strong consensus.

Although the new prayer books were completed only after an agonizingly long period of testing and discussion, the movement as a whole seems to have weathered its larger "synagogue revolution" (to use Rabbi Yoffie's phrase) without serious resistance. In the course of that revolution, religious ideology has been replaced by a pragmatic tolerance of pluralism; religious services have become eclectic, drawing upon multiple sources and varying from temple to temple; and congregations have absorbed a continuous and apparently frictionless flow of recruits from the ranks of other denominations, from the gay and lesbian community, and from intermarried households. This is to say nothing of Reform's openly partisan stance on political matters.

In sum, whatever tempests have rocked the ship of liberal Christianity, Reform Judaism would seem not only to have navigated the storms but to be moving forward with the wind in its sails.

The Advantages of Reform

Changing demography has given the movement further cause for optimism about its own bright future. By the end of the twentieth century, the plurality of American Jews who identified themselves as adherents of the Jewish religion claimed to be Reform. And by the time the Pew study was released in 2013, Reform congregations collectively could boast more members than any other Jewish religious movement. A substantial number of Reform temples, moreover, are sitting on significant endowments and collect membership dues from between one and three thousand members. Further adding to the perception of vitality are the successful biennial conventions of the Union for Reform Judaism, which attract some five to six thousand attendees, a figure that dwarfs conventions of the other Jewish religious movements. Described to me by one Reform rabbi as a "typical American pep rally," the biennial attracts a core of committed laypeople who return every other year. Little wonder, then, that morale has soared.[15]

Reform congregations also have a significant advantage over other types of synagogues because they are unconstrained by Jewish law (*Halacha*). This has freed them to improvise and refashion Judaism as they see fit. In a DIY age, this kind of experimentation is perfectly in sync with the spirit of the times. It means that each congregant is encouraged to mix and match whichever aspects of Judaism resonate and to forge a highly idiosyncratic version of Judaism. It also means that the Reform movement, which in the past had clear dos and don'ts about how to dress in synagogue, whether to observe the dietary laws, and how much of traditional Jewish practice was to be defined as outmoded, now takes a laissez-faire approach. Some Reform Jews wear a *kippa* (skull cap) in synagogue, and others do not; some wear a *tallit* (prayer shawl), and others do not.

In the liturgical realm, Reform is also unconstrained by the template of the Jewish prayer service, what in rabbinic language is known as the *matbea shel tefila*. Clergy can pick and choose the prayers to be recited, and add poetry or excerpts from inspirational texts stemming from a wide range of contexts. The publication of new movement prayer books has not stifled the urge of many clergy to fashion services according to their own lights. Indeed, many use the new prayer books selectively.

But the spirit of experimentation has gone well beyond the liturgy. With movement encouragement, some temples have dispensed with prayer books altogether and instead project the prayers, including their translations and transliterations, onto large screens. Worshippers look up at all times, rather than bury their faces in prayer books. An added advantage: there no longer is a need to announce page numbers for worshippers who cannot find the place; it's all before them on a screen. Hands are freed so "you can clap . . . , put your arm around the person next to you, or let a child fall asleep in your lap," adds an enthusiastic rabbi.[16] Visual T'filah, as this method is called, not only offers the liturgy on strategically placed screens, but also employs multiple projectors to offer images of art and other visual stimuli designed to evoke associations. Images of natural settings, for example, are included to stir a sense of connection to the beauty around us, and perhaps a sense of awe when beholding God's creations.[17] And artworks depicting biblical figures referenced in the text—such as renderings of Moses at the crossing of the Sea of Reeds when that event is mentioned in the prayer—are projected.

Liturgical music also has been transformed. Gone are the days of organ music or even solo guitar accompaniment. Some services feature percussion and drum instruments, others electronic keyboards or other electric instruments. Traditional liturgical music has been replaced by compositions employing rock, jazz, and contemporary folk music styles. The Temple in Cleveland, to cite one example, advertises a once-a-month Rock My Soul Shabbat service featuring "a nine-piece band and the congregation in song and prayer for a one-hour service that carries a folksy vibe backed by a wailing clarinet and horns, keyboards, drums and guitars."[18] A West Coast temple offers a monthly Friday evening service employing only acoustic instruments; and High Holidays services are accompanied by musicians playing the cello, viola, bass, tabla, African kora, flute, and percussion instruments. These are but two examples selected from dozens of such innovative musical services. Indeed, it may be hard to find a Reform temple not offering monthly Rock Shabbat services.

To teach congregants the new melodies, the Reform movement has created a career path for "song leaders." The origin of this trend is in the movement's summer camps, each of which employs between five and eleven song leaders. Some of these leaders then go on to rabbinical school, itself an indication of how the rabbinate is increasingly oriented to playing an active role in leading services driven by music. The movement moreover has a cadre of contemporary composers numbering in the dozens who set the liturgy to their own compositions—and are invited by congregations to visit and teach their melodies.[19]

All of this amounts to an enormous investment in refashioning the worship services of Reform temples. The technology itself, including high-tech projectors and screens as well as sophisticated sound systems, is costly. What is clear from speaking with clergy is how much time the staff in Reform temples invests weekly to coordinate the services, keeping them fresh and lively. Friday night and High Holiday services have become major productions.

A second great advantage enjoyed by Reform congregations derives from their success in having cornered the market of intermarried families seeking synagogue membership. Overall, a third of Reform temple members, according to the Pew study, are intermarried. And among those members between the ages of thirty and fifty, more than half are in mixed marriages. Inmarried members are so outnumbered in the younger age cohorts that a prominent movement leader reports on being asked by an endogamous couple whether they ought to belong to a Reform temple, since nearly all their peers were intermarried. That said, the Reform movement has been able to keep its membership figures from shrinking thanks to the large numbers of non-Jews who are synagogue members.[20]

Not least, the movement is enticing to some Jews for its historical commitment to social justice. Translated into more current vocabulary, this means that Reform is seen as the Tikkun Olam movement of American Judaism. And indeed Reform temples steer members to volunteer in programs for social and environmental causes, lobby for legislation favored by the movement, and enlist youth to aid the poor and needy in their localities. To some Reform rabbis, this commitment is a winning position. In conversations, several used almost the exact same words to note how Reform is "best positioned to lead American Judaism in the twenty-first century" through its "amalgam of tikkun olam and a strong emphasis on personal meaning."

Countertrends

But is the movement thriving as heartily as its upbeat leaders and spokesmen insist? Is it, by its own standards, succeeding in not only retaining its members but also inspiring them to intensive religious engagement?

The answer is a highly equivocal one, and it begins with some stark demographic facts. Only a minority (36 percent) of those raised Reform actually belonged to synagogues when surveyed in 2013. (An even smaller number—28 percent—report any involvement at all in Jewish organizational life; and barely half give to Jewish causes.) More than half, moreover, say they have not attended a synagogue within the past year.

Nor is there any evidence that Reform synagogue membership has grown over the past few decades due to the successful transmission of Jewish commitments from one generation to the next. If temples are holding their own, it is mainly by attracting people from outside, chiefly from the Conservative movement (roughly 28 percent), which has been commensurately shrinking, and from the ranks of Gentiles married to Jews. Whatever this says about Reform's appeal to outsiders, it suggests a serious weakness when it comes to inculcating a strong sense of Jewish religious identification and commitment in those raised within Reform itself.

What is the cause of this weakness? A study of schooling under Reform auspices conducted in 2007 points to one culprit: the lack of a proper education. For the overwhelming majority of children in the movement, formal Jewish schooling ends at Bar or Bat Mitzvah age. More than half drop out of supplementary classes after the seventh grade; of those who continue their studies, two-thirds are gone by grade nine or ten.[21] Despite the declared aspirations of the movement to engage Jews in "lifelong Jewish learning," its teens and adults have so far declined to heed the message.

The same goes for regular attendance at religious services. According to the Pew study, just over one-third of Reform Jews who affiliate with a synagogue claim to attend services once a month or more, a figure that drops to 17 percent for all *self-identified*, but not necessarily affiliated Reform Jews. As with survey findings about church attendance, these figures are inflated considerably if we judge from figures reported by rabbis. Sabbath-morning services in most Reform temples attract only the family and friends of the Bar or Bat Mitzvah for a ceremony in which, in the words of the former head of the Union for Reform Judaism, "worship of God gives way to worship of the child."[22] The central weekly religious gathering remains a one-hour service on Friday evening. And as we have noted, much effort has been invested to rethink the music, choreography, and atmospherics of those services. Rabbis do report a consequent uptick in attendance, though the increase is incremental and rarely do the regulars constitute more than 10 to 15 percent of the congregational membership. Due to the great investment in refashioning the Friday night prayer service, a rabbi proudly reports attendance has now risen to one hundred at Friday evening services—out of a congregational membership of six hundred fifty families; other rabbis refer to two hundred regular worshippers in congregations of twenty-five hundred or even four thousand members.

And then there is the question of continuing adult education. Rabbis celebrate the unexpected revolution that has brought a cadre of dedicated learners to synagogue on Shabbat mornings to engage in study. "No one could have imagined this revolution," enthused one rabbi. And no doubt, the Shabbat morning study groups are uplifting to rabbis as opportunities to engage in high-level study with a committed core. But as the same rabbis will admit, the regulars at these study sessions number somewhere between twenty-five and forty learners, out of a membership in the thousands. They draw heavily from the population of professional Jews—and often attract local Christian clergy and other interested outsiders. True, other adult learning opportunities also attract small numbers, mainly empty-nesters and young mothers hoping for some guidance about raising Jewish children. All very well and good, but the large majority of members do not avail themselves of opportunities to study and deepen their Judaism.

Off the record, many Reform rabbis are forthright about the difficult situation they have inherited. One speaks about the "terrible Judaism" her congregants have been taught over the years. Others bemoan the low levels of literacy that complicate efforts to improve the quality of prayer services: when few people can read, let alone understand the Hebrew, what is accomplished by reappropriating the original Hebrew text in new prayer books? "Reform Jewish education," reports another rabbi, "did not prepare people for the new style of worship. People don't have the toolkit to experience this type of service. Spirituality in people's lives may not be Jewish; it may be yoga." Other rabbis speak of their frustration with the inability of parents to help their children prepare for a Bar/Bat Mitzvah, because the parents themselves have little knowledge to share. A low level of Judaic literacy is the Achilles' heel of the movement.

When the overwhelming majority shun religious study, how are individual Reform Jews expected to make the "informed choices" on which the movement prides itself?[23] When the majority of synagogue members absent themselves from religious services and partake of very few religious rituals at home, where is the evidence for what some refer to as a "return to tradition" among the laity, as distinct from the elites? And when the overwhelming majority of synagogue members cannot be counted on to participate in religious services other than on the High Holidays, what precisely is thriving in Reform temples?

The initiatives to include once-marginalized populations show equally ambiguous and no doubt unanticipated results. Reform institutions are open as never before to women, welcoming them into positions of authority and leadership. Yet even as women have moved from the periphery to the center, Reform men have been moving rapidly in the opposite direction. As numerous congregational rabbis have testified, the declining presence of men is palpable in the sanctuary, in committee meetings, in national study programs, even in the biennial conventions of congregational leaders. Matters have reached such a pass that some rabbis have taken on the challenge of attracting male worshippers as a cause.[24]

Boys, too, seem to have drifted away. Youth groups and summer camps are filled with female teens who, according to one West Coast rabbi, "wonder where their male counterparts are." In one recent study, boys made up only 12 percent of participants in a leadership camp for ninth graders. On college campuses, similarly, Reform programs struggle to attract males. In the professional schools of the movement, men now constitute a minority of students training to become rabbis, cantors, and educators.[25]

"If you look carefully at the most hands-on people who are running Jewish institutional life today, you are seeing fewer and fewer men," notes a prominent movement leader—an observation manifestly not true of other denominations but very true of Reform. And an analogous situation seems to obtain on the home front. The sociologist Sylvia Barack Fishman, in a re-

port cited earlier, has found that within Reform families, fathers participate much less than mothers in the Jewish upbringing of the children.
This is particularly the case among intermarried Jewish men—to the point
where Fishman concludes that "Reform Jewish men who marry non-Jewish
women [are] the 'weak link' in American Jewish life today."[26]

In a movement so proudly identified with egalitarian ideals, the fact that
men are fleeing institutional life is mystifying—unless we posit a vast gap
between Reform's professed values and the religious desires of its male adherents. In any event, the ironic fact remains that a movement that led the
way toward sexual equality in Judaism is now the least balanced internally
between the genders. On this score, too, Reform today resembles liberal Protestantism, where men form a dwindling minority in the pews, in congregational leadership, and in the seminaries. Even within Reform, however, few
count this fact as a sign of success.

Similarly fraught with complications is Reform outreach to the intermarried. The numbers themselves are undeniably impressive. Among intermarried families in the United States, at least 70 percent of those joining a
synagogue opt for Reform.[27] But this large population has posed a massive
educational challenge. How are synagogues to teach non-Jews about Judaism while simultaneously working to increase the knowledge of their Jewish
members? Many Reform rabbis have waved away this dilemma by noting
that in their congregations, Jews and non-Jews possess the exact same (i.e.,
minimal) level of Jewish literacy. Others acknowledge the seriousness of the
problem, but are at a loss to remedy it.

Also unaddressed are the potential challenges of integrating Christians
into the religious life of congregations, however well-meaning they are. A
Reform rabbi has recounted to me his baffled reaction when seated across
from a woman who had a blackened cross etched on her forehead, having
returned from Ash Wednesday services just in time to participate in a meeting of the temple's education committee. Apparently, no one else thought
it odd for a communion-taking Catholic to sit on a governance committee
setting policy for a synagogue. As Reform temples now make few distinctions between Jews and Christians (or adherents of other religions) in the
synagogue, are we to believe that religious practices are unaffected? Growing

religious syncretism, let alone confusion about what is condoned by Judaism and what belongs to other religions, doesn't disappear just because it is ignored.[28]

One of the places where the proverbial rubber hits the road is in congregational schools. Reform temples now draw at least half their enrollment from families in which one parent was not born Jewish and only a minority of these parents have converted to Judaism.[29] One can only sympathize with teachers trying to cope with the mixed signals sent to children about the diverse religious practices on display in the homes of intermarried families. So far, there seems neither much willingness to recognize the sheer magnitude of the responsibility the movement has taken on nor any sign of appropriate resources being channeled to address it through schools, camps, youth movements, or college programs.

In fact, there is little critical talk at all about the consequences of having integrated so large a population of non-Jews and their families into Reform synagogues. Non-Jewish parents who devotedly bring their children to services and classes are now publicly honored as "heroes."[30] But the movement has been silent on the need to maintain an unambiguously Jewish orientation within the family so as to minimize confusion among the children and foster their strong identification with Judaism. In 2005, Rabbi Yoffie floated the idea of tactfully conveying to Gentile spouses that they were welcome to convert to Judaism and would be eagerly embraced.[31] The response from the movement's rabbinic and lay leadership was swift and direct. His proposal was deemed to be deeply offensive to the sensibilities of both non-Jews and their Jewish family members, and was soon a dead letter.

According to the head of a major Reform organization, intermarriage is now so taken for granted in the movement that most Reform Jews no longer see anything problematic about it. To the contrary, as a Reform rabbi has noted to me, "The Jews in the pews see blending in as great." Intermarriage is now portrayed as "a shining example of the victory of American Jewry" in winning acceptance. This has created a bind for the minority of Reform rabbis and rabbinical candidates who do not wish to officiate at so-called "inter-weddings"—and who know that they may be denied a pulpit for sticking to their principles. Movement policy still formally discourages rabbinic officiation at such unions, even while respecting the right of individual rabbis to follow the dictates of their conscience.[32]

Inclusiveness, in short, has brought a number of short-term gains to Reform while exacting a very high price in unintended consequences. So has the movement's stress on the principle of individual choice.

For one thing, by emphasizing autonomy, Reform Judaism has inadvertently weakened the commitment of many of its adherents to the collective needs of the Jewish people. Though the leadership remains intensely attached to Israel and to the welfare of Jews around the world, and has invested in a Reform presence in many parts of the globe, a connection to the Jewish people does not rank high in the priorities of many self-professed Reform Jews. Undoubtedly, this connection is even more attenuated among intermarried families and their children. But the emphasis on personalism has clearly enfeebled the allegiances of many born Jews as well. Rabbi David Ellenson, the past president of HUC, declared that the future of American Judaism is "contingent, to a large extent, upon the success Reform rabbis will have in instilling communitarian religious values and commitments."[33] It is hard to fathom how rabbis will succeed at this task given the movement's insistence on the priority of individual choice.

To make matters worse, while rabbis must respect the autonomous right of their congregants to choose which aspects of Judaism they value, congregants need not and do not necessarily respect the autonomous choices of their rabbis, let alone their rabbis' authority to create a hierarchy of choices rooted in traditional Jewish texts and practices. In this connection, it is by no means clear that many of today's Reform Jews have adopted the positive approach of a sizable number of younger rabbis toward those traditional practices.

The Reform movement has wagered its future on the gamble that a coherent and vibrant Judaism can be built on the idea of a big tent, on the informed choice of each Reform Jew, and on a highly elastic definition of both "Reform" and "Jew." Both in what it cannot accept and in what it cannot *not accept*, the movement is very much at one with the individualistic and "pluralist" ethos of contemporary American culture. But for how long will significant numbers of people continue to be drawn to, or stick with, a religious movement that cannot or will not define criteria for committed living, and that (except when it comes to politics) has self-consciously shunned imperatives and obligations?[34] The Pew data suggest the answer has already emerged: Though over 44 percent of synagogue members over the age of fifty-four identify as Reform, that share drops to under one-third among the synagogue-affiliated between the ages of forty and fifty-four, and 21 percent of those between twenty-five and thirty-nine. In this regard, the dramatic decline of liberal Protestant denominations may truly serve as a warning of what lies ahead for Reform Judaism.

5

CONSERVATIVE JUDAISM

A REAPPRAISAL

"In the United States, 'Conservative Judaism' is a synonym for failure." So concluded the Israeli journalist Yair Ettinger after interviewing a spectrum of American Jewish religious leaders.[1] For many who share this perception, the central issue is the movement's numerical decline over the past quarter century. In the decades after World War II, and as recently as 1990, the plurality of American Jews self-identified as Conservative. By 2013, the Pew Research Center reported the Conservative proportion had fallen to 18 percent, as compared to 35 percent who identified with the Reform label and 10 percent with Orthodoxy.[2] That quantitative loss means there is a smaller population of synagogue members, fewer students enrolled in Solomon Schechter day schools and congregational supplementary programs—though not in Ramah summer camps—and more limited financial resources for the Conservative movement.

Beyond the decline in numbers, the movement also shows evidence of having lost its way. Some insiders desperately want to distance themselves from the Conservative label because, they believe, it alienates the large majority of American Jews who identify as liberal;[3] meanwhile, others advocate abandoning a commitment to Halacha, Jewish law, because religious laws tie the movement's hands when it comes to accommodating new ways of thinking.[4] "Tradition and Change" was once proudly broadcast as the encapsulation of the movement's core values, but developments in recent decades have demonstrated just how difficult it is to reconcile the two parts of this slogan—to the detriment of the former.[5] And then there is the interminable process by which the movement addresses new challenges: almost inevitably when questions of religious policy arise, movement leaders engage in wrenching debates, until they eventually accede to what they regard as modern imperatives. To outside observers, the cycle of temporizing, followed by eventual capitulation, seems to reflect a retreat from bedrock commitments.[6]

Few questions in recent times have highlighted the movement's anguished self-doubts as the debate over the religious status of homosexuals.[7] Hot-button issues of this sort have historically proved agonizing for the movement—as they have not been for Orthodoxy, which has tended to side almost automatically with traditional religious laws, or for liberal denominations, which have reflexively accommodated themselves to societal change. By contrast, the underlying assumption of Conservative Judaism has been that any dissonance between shifting social mores and long-established religious laws should and can be reconciled or harmonized.

In the question under discussion, that assumption proved untenable. The issue was this: how can one maintain fidelity to the Torah's explicit prohibition of male homosexual intercourse, as well as later rabbinic rulings extending that negative judgment to lesbianism, while simultaneously remaining open to new social perspectives and scientific research on the nature of sexuality? After deliberating over the matter for a period of years, the movement's Committee on Jewish Law and Standards voted to approve not one but three different and frankly contradictory rulings. All three welcome homosexuals into Conservative synagogues. Two, however, uphold the traditional disapproval of homosexual behavior and ban openly gay men and women from holding positions of religious leadership, while the third, even as it restricts male homosexual activities to specific acts not prohibited by the Bible, nevertheless sanctions the ordination of gays and lesbians.[8] When the ballots were tallied, it emerged that, on the issue of gay ordination, equal numbers had voted in favor and against, enough in each case to leave both as equally valid positions for Conservative Jews.[9]

Movement officials lauded the committee's work, characterizing its acceptance of diametrically opposite rulings as proof positive of Conservatism's commitment to religious pluralism. But to judge from a follow-up opinion poll, rabbis and presidents of Conservative synagogues felt otherwise. Two-thirds of the former claimed to have been "somewhat embarrassed" by the rulings, and over half of the lay leaders pronounced themselves "confused."[10]

When it came to actually implementing policy, institutional leaders lacked the luxury of embracing both positions simultaneously but were forced to choose between them. Within weeks, the two US seminaries of the Conservative movement announced that they would admit gay and lesbian Jews as rabbinical students without further delay. Sensing they had the upper hand, proponents of gay equality now began to press the view that, as one rabbi put it, welcoming people of all sexual orientations should be, for Conservative Judaism, "a value and not an option"—that is, declining to subscribe to complete gay equality in religious life, as two of the three approved legal rulings do, should no longer be tolerated.[11]

The controversy over the status of homosexuals illustrates the extent to which Conservative Judaism is continually whipsawed between contradictory impulses: conserving Jewish law and accommodating new mores; aspiring to build as big a tent as possible for diverse points of view and, alternatively, defining itself more sharply and thereby risking the loss of some members but gaining a more distinct profile within the larger marketplace of American Judaism.

Balancing Polarities

From its inception, Conservative Judaism has struggled to maintain a balance of one kind or another. There are even two dueling historical narratives about its origins. According to one account, the movement emerged in the closing decades of the nineteenth century as a response to the seemingly inexorable advance of the more radical antinomian impulses of Reform Judaism. Some locate the historical turning point in a notorious "*treif* banquet" that marked the ordination in 1883 of the first graduates of the Reform movement's rabbinical seminary—a dinner that, according to one report, featured "littleneck clams, frogs' legs and crabs, topped off with roast beef, ice cream, and cheeses."[12] Scandalized by this brazen flouting of Jewish dietary laws, a group of traditionalist rabbis and lay leaders rallied to found the Jewish Theological Seminary (JTS) in 1886. Graduates of JTS soon assumed pulpits around the country and brought their congregants around to the more tradition-minded Conservative position.[13]

In this telling, the Conservative movement was founded by an elite with a clear religious agenda whose essentially conservatizing purpose was captured in its name. But a second narrative traces the movement's origins less to a religious impulse than to a broadly social one: namely, the upwardly mobile aspirations of the second generation of Eastern European Jews whose families had arrived during the great mass migration that lasted from the 1870s to America's imposition of entry quotas in the 1920s. As the children of these immigrants climbed the socioeconomic ladder, they grew disenchanted not with Reform but, on the contrary, with Eastern European–style Orthodoxy and its Yiddish-speaking rabbis. They sought a refined synagogue service, sermons in the vernacular, mixed seating of men and women, and a shift from an adult-centered religion to a child-centered one. Reform temples would not do; they were often socially exclusive enclaves, and their services were too church-like to appeal to the children of Eastern European immigrants. Instead, this generation overwhelmingly opted for the Conservative synagogue.

Thus the second narrative, first presented by the sociologist Marshall Sklare over sixty years ago.[14] In this telling, Conservative Judaism arose as a modernizing movement in defiance of Orthodoxy, and its religious conservatism was more nostalgic than ideological in nature.

Both accounts contain much truth. Between the teens and the early 1950s, the Conservative movement grew like Topsy because it attracted large numbers of Jews seeking a modern American synagogue that would not require of them a high degree of religious observance. At the same time, much of its leadership, religious and lay alike, observed Judaism in a traditional fashion, keeping the Sabbath and holidays and adhering to ritual obligations even as the majority of their fellow congregants behaved very differently. Thus, from the beginning, the movement was based on the marriage of an anti-Reform elite ideology with anti-Orthodox folk aspirations.[15]

The movement bridged this chasm by offering something for everyone. Its synagogues followed the traditional liturgy and Torah reading in Hebrew, but included some English-language prayers. Sabbath and holiday services were central to synagogue life, but the key gathering time was the "late" Friday-evening service, held hours after the Sabbath had begun in order to accommodate working people. The rabbi prided himself on his oratorical prowess, delivering English-language sermons mainly about the issues of the day, even as he still insisted on his status as an arbiter of religious law. Almost all Conservative congregations utilized the Hertz edition of the Torah whose commentary rejected modern biblical criticism, but rabbis and teachers drew upon the latest scholarship in their adult education classes. The kitchens of Conservative synagogues were strictly kosher, but only in a fraction of members' homes were Jewish dietary laws observed. The movement's elite walked to synagogue on the Sabbath, while the folk drove.

Though there tend to be gaps between religious leaders and the laity in most denominations—Jewish and otherwise—the Conservative movement has long lived with a chasm. This is how a Conservative rabbi in the last quarter of the twentieth century mordantly described the gap between clergy and their congregants in his movement: "We rabbis are their problem and they are ours. We remind them that the institution stands for something, and they remind us of how little influence we have. If we talk of God or Jewish law, they act as if we breached a tacit understanding."[16] Undoubtedly, a good many congregants remained impervious to the religious teachings of their rabbis. But indifference, alone, does not tell the whole story.

On a fundamental level, congregants and their clergy held sharply different views about the demands of Judaism. Following the pioneering work of Charles Liebman, we may best understand the gap within the Conservative movement as a classic example of folk versus elite religion. Whereas the latter "is the symbols and rituals (the cult) and beliefs which the leaders acknowledge as legitimate," and also the hierarchical authority structure of the movement itself, "folk religion is expressed primarily through rituals and symbols . . . that may be rooted in superstitions" or distorted understandings of elite religion. "Folk religion tends to accept the organizational structure of elite religion, but to be indifferent to the elite belief structure."[17]

Liebman's analysis was brought to life for me several decades ago when a colleague told a story about his childhood to illustrate how this gap played out in an ordinary Conservative family. Customarily, the family ate Sunday dinners at a local nonkosher burger joint. But one Sunday, crisis erupted when the waiter mistakenly brought cheeseburgers to the table, rather than the plain burgers that had been ordered. And so seated around their table, the family sought to apply their understanding of rabbinic laws: Is it sufficient, they wondered, to scrape the cheese off the burger? Or must they return the cheeseburgers and exchange them for plain burgers? From the elite point of view both options were nonsensical because no burger served in a nonkosher restaurant would be acceptable: it possibly included meat of an animal not deemed kosher, one definitely not slaughtered according to Jewish ritual, and the burger was prepared on a grill used to cook prohibited meats. But from the perspective of the Conservative folk religion, these were eminently reasonable options for a family that did not mix meat and milk, but had no compunctions about eating meat not slaughtered in accordance with Jewish laws. Like many other Conservative families, this one adhered to its own folk understanding of what is permissible and impermissible, rather than jettisoning all religious regulations.

For a long time, the movement was successful in managing its balancing act between elite and folk religion. Contributing significantly to that success was the fact that Conservative synagogues functioned as, in Sklare's terminology, an "ethnic church."[18] They placed a strong emphasis on rallying support and collecting money for Zionism in the decades leading up to the establishment of the state of Israel in 1948. Later on, while continuing to mobilize in support of Israel, they flocked to the cause of Soviet Jewry in the 1970s and 1980s. They did all this by creating a comfortable environment for second-generation Jews to enter American society together, as members of a club. More than anything else, perhaps, most Conservative Jews were bound to their synagogue and to one another by the bonds of ethnic solidarity.

There were strains, of course. But these, while palpable, were also bearable because the movement was constantly expanding and experimenting. During the peak growth years of the 1950s, as Jews moved to the beckoning suburbs, it was not unusual for the movement to add over a hundred new congregational affiliates annually. "New Jewish Community in Formation: A Conservative Center Catering to Present-Day Needs" proclaimed the title of one contemporaneous article.[19] It was not alone in remarking upon the dramatic expansion of the movement, which by the late 1950s claimed a plurality of American Jews affiliated with a religious denomination.

Nor was this just a matter of numbers. The movement's rabbinic leaders achieved renown as spokesmen for American Judaism and as interpreters of Jewish civilization, and some of its lay leaders were figures of national stature. The movement itself was widely admired for its experiments in youth education, initially in its Ramah summer camps and later in day school education. Indeed, in surveying the achievements of the movement over the course of its entire 120-year history, one cannot but be struck by the sheer extent of its contribution to the cultural and social capital of the American Jewish community, if not of Jews worldwide.

Conservative Judaism has produced a body of scholarship and religious literature informed by an admirable attempt to negotiate polarities. "We are the only group," declared Louis Finkelstein, chancellor of JTS from 1940 to 1972, "who have a modern mind and a Jewish heart, prophetic passion and Western science."[20] At JTS, Finkelstein famously gathered key exponents of differing, even clashing, schools of thought. He himself, and Talmudists like Louis Ginzberg, represented a traditionalist approach to Jewish law and observance even as Mordecai Kaplan, perhaps the most radical Jewish religious thinker of his time, sought to persuade rabbinical students of the need to "reconstruct" Judaism thoroughly to suit the American moment. Later on, Finkelstein balanced Saul Lieberman, an outstanding interpreter of Talmud, against the neo-Hasidic and socially activist inclinations of Abraham Joshua Heschel.

Over the decades, whether despite or because of the tension among divergent constructions of religious reality, the result has been a remarkable library of learning in the fields of rabbinics, theology, history, and literature.[21]

Conservative institutions have also nurtured a core cadre of congregants and leaders profoundly engaged with traditional Jewish religious practices, the Hebrew language, and the Jewish people.

The Current Malaise

It is in light of these manifold achievements that the weaknesses of today's Conservative Judaism are so striking and potentially damaging not only to insiders but to all who care about the vitality of the American Jewish community. Most apparent to informed observers is the movement's demographic fall, masked until now by the large bulge of mid-twentieth-century recruits who are passing from the scene. In the single decade of the 1990s, membership in Conservative synagogues contracted from 915,000 to 660,000,[22] dropping the number of affiliated Conservative Jews below that of their Reform counterparts for the first time in a half century. By the time of the Pew study in 2013, the estimated number of synagogue members had declined to around a half million.[23]

Even more ominously for the future of the movement, its members tend to be older than Jews in the Reform and Orthodox movements, and the majority are empty-nesters. Not surprisingly, children enrolled in Conservative educational programs number not much more than 50 to 60 percent of those in Reform programs.[24] Once the home of second- and third-generation American Jews, Conservative synagogues are much less successful at attracting the fourth and fifth generations, relying instead on smaller cadres of recent immigrants from South Africa, Israel, Latin America, and Iran.[25]

Where have all the Conservative Jews gone? By far the majority of "switchers" have found their way into the Reform camp; 28 percent of the members of Reform temples claim to have been raised Conservative, according to the Pew data. Conventional wisdom attributes most of this defection to the inhospitality of Conservative synagogues to intermarried Jews. As rates of intermarriage have skyrocketed among people raised Conservative, the argument goes, the latter have gravitated to Reform temples whose rabbis are able to officiate at interfaith weddings, and they readily incorporate children of intermarriage into their congregations and schools. Once intermarried Jews join Reform temples, moreover, they tend to bring along their parents, who often wish to participate in services with their children and grandchildren.

Additional factors also are at work. One is geographic mobility: during the past quarter century, vast numbers have migrated from Mid-Atlantic states or the Midwest, places with a strong Conservative presence, to the South and West, where Reform congregations are readily available but Conservative synagogues are not. Nor have these "Jews on the move" bothered to found new Conservative synagogues themselves. Although that fact has something to do with the movement's structural incapacity to seed new congregations as aggressively as does Reform, it also speaks to the kind of Jewish culture in these locales (as noted in chapter 2).

Some mobile Conservative Jews are also attracted to the style of a particular Reform temple, its rabbi or other religious functionaries, or the services it offers. But the major factor seems to be that too many individuals raised in Conservative synagogues have received a minimal Jewish education, which has left them unable to participate in religious services that, after all, are almost entirely conducted in Hebrew and presuppose a certain level of Jewish literacy. Because members of Conservative synagogues are also more likely than a few decades ago to play an active role in reading Torah and leading religious services, those Jews lacking the Hebrew skills and synagogue literacy gravitate to Reform temples whose services include far less Hebrew and whose members are expected to observe far fewer Jewish rituals and holidays.

On the other end of the religious spectrum, interestingly, a smaller but noteworthy minority of Conservative Jews has been gravitating to Orthodox synagogues. According to the Pew data, 13 percent of affiliated Modern Orthodox Jews were raised Conservative. These particular switchers tend to be among the best-educated products of day schools, summer camps, and youth programs, usually the offspring of the most active and religiously engaged members of Conservative synagogues—young people, in short, who have been groomed to assume leadership roles in their parents' movement. Anecdotal evidence suggests that many of them are drawn to Orthodoxy less for its ideology than for its strong communal life. They are seeking a religious support system for themselves and their children, one that will reinforce observance and participation—something that relatively few Conservative synagogues can provide.

Some departing members are also drawn to Orthodox "outreach" congregations, especially the hundreds of Chabad centers run by the Lubavitch Hasidic group. It is hardly a secret that Orthodox outreach workers have long looked upon Conservative Jews as "low hanging fruit" because they are familiar with the structure of traditional prayer services and have a working knowledge of Jewish holidays and rituals. Another cohort, young and often single, has abandoned the movement to create nondenominational prayer groups whose style, however, is distinctively Conservative, combining the traditional liturgy, mixed seating, and equal leadership roles for men and women with, in many cases, a heavy dose of left-wing "social justice" activism.

The upshot is a substantial hemorrhage by multiple cuts. The movement has bled members of all ages to its religious left and right, to new nondenominational groupings, and to a phenomenon once widely described but no longer mentioned in polite company: assimilation. Because the outflow is multidirectional, the movement has been at a loss to decide which populations to focus on or to calculate what it would take to woo them back. Besides, an approach that might work to retain the intermarried could alienate those seeking a ritually observant community; what might attract social activists could drive away members committed primarily to the needs of the Jewish people; efforts to enliven religious services and thereby draw in younger Jews might be off-putting to older members.

Matters are exacerbated by the structural weaknesses of the movement. Though it is configured like a Protestant denomination—an umbrella organization for congregations, two seminaries, separate organizations for rabbis, cantors, and educators, and still others for women's and men's auxiliaries—Conservative Judaism never developed a system of internal governance that would enable it to function cohesively. No single person or institution is regarded as authoritative. JTS has long claimed centrality as "the fountainhead" of the movement, but every chancellor in its history has been at loggerheads with his counterparts in other Conservative institutions.[26] Conversely, some of the movement's most important initiatives—the camping network, day schools, experiments in religious innovation and synagogue renewal—were forced upon chancellors by frustrated local leaders.

Having never learned to work together effectively in the years of growth, the major institutions now flail about at cross-purposes in a time of crisis. In the recent past, at least two hundred Conservative synagogues have disengaged institutionally from the movement, and the former West Coast affiliate of JTS now claims no allegiance to Conservative Judaism at all. Nor has the movement created a forum for conducting a conversation with the rank and file on the question of what a serious effort at renewal might look like.

There have been such efforts in the past, and there is even a rhythm to them. Whenever the movement has taken a dramatic step away from traditional religious behavior—sanctioning driving to synagogue on the Sabbath, ordaining women as rabbis—it has balanced it with a campaign to encourage more intense and widespread religious observance. But the latter effort, predictably, has fizzled for lack of follow-through from the top or of interest on the part of the movement's various constituencies. Often, there has not been even a semblance of coordination. In the months leading up to the decision on the status of homosexuals, for example, leaders of Conservative institutions, nonplussed that the issue had been allowed to come to a head before congregants were prepared for so major a change, scrambled ineffectually to delay the vote.

Perhaps the most serious sign of disarray at the center is the movement's failure to capture the imagination of the philanthropists who sit in the pews of its synagogues. As a consequence, its overarching institutions limp along with insufficient financial support. On the domestic scene, no serious funding has gone into seeding potential affiliates in places of new Jewish settlement; Conservative groups on college campuses receive virtually no backing; and even some of the day schools that were once the pride of the movement have folded or assumed a nondenominational identity for want of financial support. Internationally, the movement has established virtually no presence in former communist lands, and only a few congregations in Western and Central Europe. It has also permitted its operations in Israel to starve for funding, even though the sums needed to keep them afloat were smaller than the annual budget of a single midsized synagogue in North America.

The Question of Ideology

In religion as in other areas of life, disunity and disorganization can be symptoms of a deeper confusion. A wag once memorably classified Orthodox, Conservative, and Reform Judaism as, respectively, "crazy, hazy, and lazy." The "hazy," at least, is not inaccurate.

Of all the movements, Conservative Judaism has been the least able to condense its religious ideology into a single message. Instead, it has relied mostly on assertions of what it is not—for example, it disagrees with the movement on its right for one reason and with the movement on its left for another—rather than on affirmations of what it is. An easily identifiable set of associations, a clear "branding," has been lacking. But, for reasons I have spelled out, there is also a vicious circle here. Lurking in any effort to sharpen the movement's definition has been the perpetual danger that it will expose irreparable fault lines.

For much of its first century, the movement strove to paper over its ideological divisions by stressing the commonalities of synagogue practice, allegiance to JTS as the spiritual center, and the shared identification of all Conservative Jews with the Jewish people. Rather than making strong statements, it preferred to invoke a vague but innocuous slogan: "Tradition and Change." Not far beneath the surface, however, rabbis holding opposing views on the nature of belief and doctrine seethed with resentment. Their disagreements burst forth at rabbinic conventions, which were often rife with controversy over religious policies and the proper interpretation of Jewish law. Significantly, it was not until the late twentieth century that the movement even tried to produce a statement of principles. Attempting to harmonize irreconcilable beliefs, the resulting document, *Emet ve'Emunah* ("Truth and Faith," 1998), was virtually incomprehensible.

As historical irony would have it, *Emet ve'Emunah* appeared at a moment when the movement had already shed its own extreme left and right wings. In the mid-1960s, the Reconstructionists, who regarded Jewish observances as no more than folkways, convinced their aged leader Mordecai Kaplan that his program for Jewish life could be implemented only through the creation of a separate movement from the one in which he had spent his career. Two decades later, traditionalists who found no religious justification for ordaining women as rabbis departed when the movement embraced egalitarianism. Yet the secession of these extremes did not so much resolve as lay bare and perhaps even sharpen the continuing fact of internal disagreement.

When religious traditionalists dominated the movement's key institutions, the tactic adopted by proponents of innovation was to argue for pluralism. Rather than accept a single understanding of Jewish law, they pleaded, let multiple voices be heard. Let there be majority and minority rulings, with both treated as equally valid, and let each rabbi decide what is best for his or her congregation. During the past quarter century, the pluralists triumphed, winning the battle over women's religious status and most recently over homosexuality.

Now, suddenly, pluralism does not look so attractive. How can it be, the innovators ask, that the Conservative movement, which trains women to become rabbis and cantors, still permits its congregations to refuse to hire women for those positions? How can a movement undertaking to ordain gay and lesbian Jews tolerate legal opinions that would bar homosexuals from positions of religious leadership?

The Conservative movement thus finds itself locked in a conundrum. Unable to agree on a Jewish way of behaving, it has long touted a "big-tent" approach to religious practices and expectations. This, understandably, has left large numbers of its adherents ideologically confused, even as it has created ample room for those not so confused to press for greater clarity—and then for the authority to impose it. These days, such clarity is to be found mainly among the devotees of "progress," which is to say conformity with contemporary social mores.

Strength on the Ground

Has the Conservative movement played its historical role, and should it call it quits? In 2004, the head of Reform's rabbinical association giddily predicted the demise of Conservative Judaism within two decades.[27] More recently, Norman Lamm, the former president of Yeshiva University, publicly prognosticated "with a heavy heart, we will soon say Kaddish on the Reform and Conservative movements."[28] And, as we have noted, it has become the conventional wisdom in some quarters of the larger Jewish community to write off Conservative Judaism as a failed experiment.

Shorn of any context, demographic trends within the movement seem to point to failure. But before rendering judgment, a more thoughtful approach might first ask: a failure as compared to what? Viewed in a vacuum, the Conservative condition appears bleak. But the movement operates within a larger American Jewish context. True, the declines in Conservative identification are noteworthy relative to surging Haredi Orthodox populations and the stable Modern Orthodox numbers. But those are standards no other non-Orthodox group has matched. The more pertinent question, then, is this: How do Conservative Jews stack up against the other non-Orthodox populations?

On every measure of religious participation, Conservative Jews today score higher than all other Jews except the Orthodox. They are the most likely to attend religious services with some regularity, to observe Jewish holidays in their homes, and to put a strong emphasis on Jewish education. The positive effects of a Conservative Jewish upbringing are most dramatically evident among the younger population of Jews, those thirty to forty-four years old. In comparing Conservative-raised with Reform-raised individuals in this age group, we find that the former are far more likely to fast on Yom Kippur; twice as likely to belong to a synagogue and to feel that being Jewish is very important to them; three times as likely to send their children to day schools; four times as likely to light Shabbat candles usually; and five times as likely to maintain what they regard as a kosher home.[29]

This engagement has redounded in numerous ways to the benefit of the Jewish collective. More than any other non-Orthodox group, Conservative Jews give to Jewish causes, support Jewish organizations, travel to Israel, and socialize primarily with Jewish friends. Much of Jewish organizational life, moreover, is beholden to Conservative Jews working as professionals and volunteer leaders and investing themselves in the needs of the Jewish people.

Moreover, though it is true that the movement has declined numerically, not all of its "defectors" have abandoned Judaism. Certainly, those who have joined Orthodox synagogues and attend Chabad have not given up on Judaism. Independent minyanim and synagogues disproportionately attract Jews raised in the Conservative movement—especially in leadership roles—and these settings are among the most dynamic on the contemporary Jewish religious scene. Many of those who affiliate with Reform, Reconstructionist, and nondenominational congregations are bringing their knowledge and experience of Judaism to bear in those settings. Rabbis of congregations to the left of Conservative Judaism are forthright about how much they rely upon the more traditionally educated (by which they mean mainly former Conservative Jews) to support their efforts at synagogue renewal, especially through the infusion of Hebrew into the worship services. Defections from Conservative synagogues most assuredly have hurt the movement, but many of those who left have become assets in other Jewish religious settings. The movement failed to retain their allegiance, but it did not fail in producing a good many involved Jews.

Nor is it true that the majority of local synagogues are floundering. The vacuum created by ineffectual national leadership has opened space for congregations to experiment and find their own solutions. Unquestionably, congregations generally have experienced a decline in membership, and in some areas of the country that has led to mergers or congregations closing their doors. In the face of these hard realities, energetic synagogue leaders, clergy and board members alike, have sprung into action. If anything, the weaknesses on the national level have spurred synagogue leaders to launch new initiatives to stave off decline within their own congregations. Viewed from the perspective of those congregations, a somewhat different portrait emerges.

Tales Out of Shul

Sometimes it takes an outsider to see what is actually happening on the ground. Around the time of the High Holidays in 2015, the environmentalist Alon Tal, a Conservative-raised Jew who had lived in Israel for forty years, traveled around the United States to spend some time in congregations of his erstwhile movement. "In recent years," Tal reported, "I have read many a eulogy for what used to be the largest Jewish denomination. So imagine my surprise to discover myriad robust, creative and spiritual Conservative communities—not only hanging on, but flourishing."[30] To say the "myriad" Conservative congregations fit this description is, no doubt, an exaggeration. But Tal is on to something when he observes a tonal shift in a good many local congregations.

Driving these changes are rabbis who are reshaping the language of synagogue discourse and creating a different kind of ambience. They are doing so, moreover, after taking a long, hard look at their congregants and asking themselves whether the movement's tried-and-true messages resonate any longer. Conservative rabbis in growing numbers are concluding that the language of obligation to observe the commandments is a nonstarter with their congregants. Something else is needed to touch people's souls. A female rabbi based in a Mid-Atlantic state put it this way: "Judaism no longer comes from membership, obligations, or the Holocaust. It's now about meaning." Says a male rabbi based on the same coast: the new Conservative Judaism is "all about spirituality, personal growth, connection to people, with far less talk about community, though daily minyan [public worship] is important to members" because it provides for those who need to say Kaddish. Says another Conservative rabbi on the West Coast about his members: "They don't want a formal, stodgy, movement Judaism. They seek intimacy, genuine connection."

How this new emphasis gets translated into synagogue life varies greatly. An East Coast rabbi reports that most of his members have little interest in attending services weekly. He therefore teaches them how to engage in home rituals, such as reciting the *Shma* with their children at night, or reciting the kiddush, the blessing over wine, on Friday nights and the Havdala to mark the end of the Sabbath. In a Mid-Atlantic congregation, a rabbi senses that "a minority of his congregants are in a post–Bowling Alone phase. . . . People want a synthesis of community, intellectual pursuit and ritual, not separated but combined. There is a hunger for a mix of these." This rabbi encourages his congregants to perform more rituals outside the synagogue's walls: he shows them how to build a Sukkah and suggests they enjoy the holiday in the company of neighbors—Jews and non-Jews alike;

he acquaints them with rituals previously unknown to them, such as the sending of *mishloach manot*, Purim baskets filled with delicacies, and selling their *hametz* (leavened foods) before Passover. He also teaches them how to conduct the Seder as a thoughtful event in the lives of their families, and steadfastly refuses to run a community Seder because he wants his people to embrace home-based rituals. In pursuing this course, his self-professed slogan is "Returning Judaism to the Jews." Implicitly, he also is returning Judaism to the home.

By contrast, two co-rabbis in a western congregation self-consciously build upon the perceived wish of their members for religion to help them develop character. Not only do they teach Jewish texts stressing the importance of generosity, kindness, and even silence, they also emphasize how the performance of commandments is part of a collective responsibility Jews have toward one another. In the view of these rabbis, "People are interested in boundaries and Halacha, but as a tool for observance. They are not interested in the ins and outs of it. They need to see Halacha as a means to a religious end." These rabbis voice disappointment with their movement for issuing Halachic rulings without addressing what is actually on people's minds: "Why be Jewish still? How does observance reach up to God? The *Teshuvot* [responsa] of the Conservative movement do not answer people's real questions." And so in their synagogue, these rabbis draw connections for congregants between the performance of individual mitzvot (commandments) and the attainment of a spiritual and religious life.

In a Bay Area congregation, the rabbi takes still a different approach based on his perception that "many people feel very alone and isolated. They don't know their questions are religious. . . . People bring a sense of loneliness and come to not be alone." The issues are especially acute for younger people, he contends: "The God they are not interested in is a personal God who intervenes in history and commands in discrete language. That kind of God keeps them away. . . . Young people feel they have a soul even if they don't believe in God." As for the role of synagogues: "It roots them in something ancient. Shuls evoke a shared tradition. . . . A shul that works is a place where people's souls feel tended to. . . . People want to be held," he states. "They look for a rabbi who is very human in the moment."

And in congregations across the country, synagogues are experimenting with blending mindfulness with aspects of the prayer service. Some offer special contemplative services. Others provide classes on meditation. And in very specific ways, rabbis use their time on the pulpit to teach a Torah that might touch the hearts of congregants by demonstrating how Judaism can enrich their lives, their relationships with family members, and their connection with others. Clearly, they are playing to the personalist ethos of the times. Simultaneously, though, they are resisting the push to privatism. Even as they teach and preach increasingly about the ways Jewish texts and observances give meaning to the lives of individuals, they also stress how participation in community, rather than following one's individual bliss, is the way to a fulfilling life. Rabbi Michael Wasserman put the argument as follows:

> Instead of moving the discussion away from obligation toward personal benefit, we should re-emphasize obligation in a new, more serious way. We should say out loud what people already know at an unspoken level: that there is no meaning without obligation. To experience meaning is, by definition, to feel that something larger than us has a claim on us, that we are not in this world for our benefit alone. To the extent that synagogues offer meaning, it is by responding to the deepest human need of all: the need to be needed. Instead of eliminating obligation from our discourse, we ought to call for a more substantive, more meaningful sense of obligation.[31]

Even as Conservative rabbis are increasingly disinclined to speak about Judaism as a set of obligations to God, they are more inclined to preach openly about the responsibilities congregants have toward one another. Some congregations create a system of shared responsibility to attend the daily minyan and thereby make it possible for mourners to recite the Kaddish. Some rabbis speak from the pulpit about the mitzvah of accompanying the dead to their final resting places, and dozens of members show up at cemeteries for the funerals of near strangers. Some congregations create committees to offer support to young couples and others to provide kosher meals to families struck by illness or death. It has even become more common for Conservative congregations to organize Hevra Kaddisha societies whose task it is to prepare the dead for burial according to traditional Jewish customs.

Increasing levels of participation are most evident in the synagogue sanctuary. Conservative synagogues have educated congregants numbering in the dozens, and even in the hundreds, to take turns reading Torah. To make this possible, clergy, especially cantors, invest a good deal of effort training men and women in cantillation skills and Hebrew language reading so they can chant the Torah, *Haftarah*, and *Megilot*, sections from the biblical text of the week or holiday. The deliberate effort to "empower" congregants to play an active role in services extends to the musical sphere. Not only do some congregants lend their voices to leading the services, but some are orchestrating the music to accompany the services.

Heightened attention to music, indeed, is yet another commonality of many Conservative synagogues. Like their counterparts in other movements, Conservative rabbis and cantors have come to understand the importance of music as a way to shape the mood of the service and especially to spur congregational participation. Toward that end, a revolution has taken place over the past two decades that has seen increasing numbers of Conservative synagogues introduce musical instrumentation in the Sabbath and holiday services. A survey conducted in 2013 under the auspices of the United Synagogue of Conservative Judaism found that half of the congregations surveyed used instruments during services. A minority of these did so only before the Sabbath and holidays actually began, but 70 percent of congregations using instruments reported doing so on the sacred days. Some included instruments in the main service, while others held multiple concurrent services so people could pick the style that appeals to them. Large majorities of reporting congregations also indicated a significant increase in attendees when musical instruments were introduced, higher levels of congregational participation in those services, and the presence of members who usually do not attend services—though they also noted some drop-off on all these measures after the novelty had passed.[32] In some parts of the country, notably California, the inclusion of musical instruments has become so important that one rabbi has flatly claimed a Conservative synagogue eschewing the practice cannot survive.

What makes these trends especially noteworthy is the absence to date of an accepted opinion by the Conservative movement's Committee on Law and Standards addressing the range of religious questions posed by the use of instruments at prayer services on the Sabbath and holidays.[33] Among those are matters of custom as well as Halacha, including refraining from activities that may lead to the desecration of the Sabbath, the category known as *Shevut*.[34] Is it permissible to set up and then disassemble on the Sabbath the apparatus, electronic and otherwise, used by bands? May Jews perform or only non-Jews? If Jews do perform, is the playing of stringed instruments permitted if it may lead a performer to repair the instrument should a string break midway during the service—an impermissible action on the Sabbath? Are some instruments, such as drums, therefore preferable because they are less likely to need repair? The list goes on. But to repeat: there is no approved responsum addressing these issues.

And so we come to yet another commonality in a good number of Conservative synagogues: a pragmatic if not improvisational approach to Halacha. To be sure, departures from traditional practices despite the absence of official movement sanction are justified by rabbis as being, as one put it, a *"leshem shamayim* [for the sake of Heaven] question—what can we do to help reach beyond ourselves and feel connected to God, the tradition, self in a way that is meaningful for our congregants—especially since they don't speak the language of the *siddur* [prayer book]."[35] Rabbis and their congregations are taking a far more accommodating approach when they see attendance flagging; and they are willing to make far-reaching changes to draw in those who find the services alien or incomprehensible.

The same pattern is evident in the face of high intermarriage rates. Rather than signal disapproval, congregations are moving toward what they see as greater hospitality. With no clear direction from central offices, rabbis and congregations are improvising policies on the role Gentiles may play in the religious service, honors they will receive, public recognition of forthcoming intermarriages, and even the attendance of rabbis at such ceremonies. To date, the movement has drawn the line at officiation, and therefore a small minority of Conservative rabbis who dissent from that policy are dropping their membership in the Rabbinical Assembly.[36] But on many other matters, local rabbis and congregations are setting their own policies, whether the national movement is ready or not.[37]

There is nothing especially new about this: well before the Law Committee sanctioned driving to the synagogue on the Sabbath in the 1950s, synagogues had made their parking lots available to members on sacred days. So too synagogues included women in the religious services before the Law Committee issued responsa to justify such departures from traditional practices. This dynamic was acknowledged already by a mid-twentieth-century rabbi active in the Law Committee when he explained the many halakhic changes introduced by the movement: "All these and similar enactments were in effect 'takkanot' [a type of Talmudic legislation], though in some cases the rabbis were not consulted when innovations were begun. Mixed pews [and] the use of the organ . . . were long left in limbo by the scholars, while congregations proceeded to act on their own."[38] Changes in religious policy have been driven from the bottom up for a long time in the Conservative movement.

Nor is it especially novel that today rabbis are taking the lead in reshaping their congregations to fit what they perceive to be the needs and sensibilities of the hour. Conservative rabbis have been doing that virtually from the start of their movement. The difference now is one of emphasis: whereas mid-twentieth-century rabbis believed that oratory and formal services would offer the grandeur their congregants desired, and post-1960s rabbis created less formal, more participatory services to match the spirit of the times, rabbis currently are playing to the themes of the day: inclusiveness, spirituality, musical creativity, shorter services, nonjudgmentalism, personalized attention, caring communities, relational Judaism, and Judaism beyond the walls of the synagogue.

The jury is still out about how well this new type of Conservative synagogue will fare in the long run. Will the uptick in attendees hold firm once the novelty of musical instrumentation at prayer services has worn off? Will efforts to welcome intermarried families succeed if religious services continue to adhere closely to the traditional Hebrew liturgy? Will synagogues successfully educate the next generation to participate in an all-Hebrew service so the Conservative style of prayer will persist? And if Conservative synagogues curtail prayer services to accommodate those who cannot follow the Hebrew, will they be able to distinguish themselves from other liberal congregations? Will the de-emphasis of Halacha coupled with stronger attention to diversity, inclusiveness, and personalism in the longer term satisfy those who seek coherence? These are inescapable questions with fraught implications for the future of the Conservative movement and its adherents.

For the present, something unexpected is happening in a sizable number of Conservative synagogues. The departure of a not-insignificant number of former congregational members has not broken the movement, but instead given many congregations the license to rebuild. Those members who remain tend to be more active. They are forging more cohesive, participatory, and spirited communities.[39] And their leaders tend to understand that twenty-first-century Conservative synagogue life needs considerable reshaping if it is to address the needs and aspirations of current congregants. They are working to create joyful and emotionally satisfying communities consonant with the style of the Conservative movement. It appears that the balance has shifted in these congregations: the elite meet the folk where they are. However one judges these efforts, there is little doubt that local synagogues are the laboratories where a new Conservative Judaism is emerging.

6

THE BATTLE FOR THE SOUL OF
MODERN ORTHODOXY

On the current American Jewish religious scene, one group stands out for its seeming success in transmitting a strong commitment to Jewish religious practice from generation to generation. Small percentages of Orthodox-raised Jews, to be sure, continue to go "off the derech [path of observance]," but the percentages are relatively small; the large majority remain committed to religious observance. This in itself represents a major reversal in fortunes, a departure from two centuries of decline. Orthodoxy has largely stanched the hemorrhage of defectors who have been abandoning traditional Judaism in droves since the early nineteenth century, and now attracts a substantial group of recruits raised in the other movements of Judaism or in secular families. In absolute numbers, the size of the Orthodox population is increasing due to the above replacement level of births. And as a proportion of the larger American Jewish population the Orthodox share is also growing because of the movement's success in socializing younger generations to live as religiously observant and engaged Jews, while the other Jewish religious movements have experienced a sharp decline in the numbers of children in their synagogues and have lost a substantial proportion of their adherents to assimilation.

By far, the major growth sector of Orthodoxy is to be found in the Haredi communities. The Modern Orthodox, by contrast, are stable but not growing—both because their children are more likely than the Haredim to defect and also because their fertility rate is not sufficiently above replacement level to make up for those losses. This demographic reality itself has affected morale. But the deeper source of trouble in the Modern Orthodox camp is ideological conflict within its elites and a loss of confidence in those leaders among some of the rank and file.

These internal tensions within Modern Orthodoxy are the focus of the present chapter. A battle now rages for the soul of this sector, a tug-of-war over both practices and ideas that is pitting rabbis against each other, even as some laypeople work to push their synagogues onto new paths, and others largely tune out their rabbis. At bottom, this internal struggle is over nothing less than the foundational assumption of the movement: that it is indeed possible to combine fidelity to traditional Judaism with modern values and understandings.

Pressure from the Right

To grasp the dynamics of the current struggle, it is critical to understand that it is playing out against challenges from both the "traditional" and the "modern" sides of the equation. The traditionalist challenge derives from the increase and growing self-confidence of the Haredim.

Historical antecedents to the current stand-off between the modern and Haredi sectors of Orthodoxy are not far to seek. During the mass migration of Russian, Austro-Hungarian, and Romanian Jews at the turn of the twentieth century, some rabbis strove to re-create the all-embracing religious culture of Eastern Europe in the New World setting. Jeffrey Gurock, the foremost historian of American Orthodoxy, labels these rabbis "resisters"—the main object of their resistance being the intrusion of American ways into their lives. Against them stood more moderate immigrant and native-born rabbis whom Gurock labels "accommodators." Each group established its own rabbinic organization (or, in the case of the resisters, three separate organizations).[1]

As the immigrant population adapted to America, the accommodating or Modern Orthodox position triumphed. Symptomatically, Modern Orthodox rabbis played an outsized role as chaplains during World War II;[2] in the postwar era, the dominant face of American Orthodoxy was that of Yeshiva University(YU)–trained rabbis (and their counterparts at the Hebrew Theological College in Skokie, IL) who were joined together in the Rabbinical Council of America (RCA). The Modern Orthodox ideal was conveyed by the motto of YU, *Torah u'madda*, usually translated as Torah and secular knowledge or, more broadly, Jewish learning combined with Western culture. For second- and third-generation American Jews attracted to this synthetic ideal, the figure they looked to was Rabbi Joseph B. Soloveitchik, who embodied the ideal through his mastery of rabbinic texts and his broad knowledge of and continuing engagement with Western philosophy.

But even as Modern Orthodoxy reached the peak of its influence, an influx of Holocaust-era refugees from both Nazism and communism gave a powerful boost to the resisters' cause. The newcomers came with an ideology of separatism that had developed in Europe and found institutional expression in the Agudath Israel movement established in the early part of the century. As the Haredi Rabbi Yaakov Weinberg of Baltimore's Ner Israel yeshiva put it: "there is an 'otherness' to us, a gulf of strangeness that cannot be bridged, separating us from our compatriots."[3]

During the second half of the twentieth century, the key lines of division hardened. The Haredi resisters were intent on rejecting much of "enlightened" Western culture—whose bankruptcy, in their view, had been exposed in the depravity of the Holocaust—and no less bent on insulating themselves from what they saw as the corrupting morals of secular modernity.[4] The accommodators, for their part, while recognizing that not everything condoned by modern fashion was in sync with traditional Judaism, were open to absorbing "the best that has been thought and said," regardless of its source. They flocked to universities and entered the professions, working side by side with non-Jews. They also maintained connections with Jews who were not traditionally observant but with whom they were prepared to work toward common ends. The most noteworthy common end was Zionism, which they embraced despite its largely secular leadership—a step shunned by the resisters, many of whom remain staunchly non-Zionist to the present day.[5]

In the face of withering criticism hurled at them by their critics among the resisters, Modern Orthodox Jews insisted on the legitimacy of their way of life—stressing, in addition to the embrace of Zionism, the value of what Jews can learn from Gentiles; full participation in the larger society (bounded only by strict adherence to Jewish ritual observance); and the provision to girls and women of the same kind of Jewish education received by boys and men (though not necessarily in mixed-gender settings). As we have seen, this insistence paid off handsomely.

Now, however, several developments have combined to give rise to a well-founded anxiety. One source of concern, alluded to above, is demography. Just a few decades ago, the modern sector constituted the large majority of Orthodox Jews; in our time, it has become vastly outnumbered by the Orthodox resisters and is on track to decline even further. As compared with the 3 percent of American Jews who (according to Pew) identify themselves as Modern Orthodox, 6 percent identify themselves as Haredi. In absolute numbers this translates into an estimated 310,000 adult Haredim compared with 168,000 adult Modern Orthodox Jews. The disparity only widens when we look at younger age cohorts. Those raised Modern Orthodox constitute 18 percent of American Jews over sixty-five, but only 2.9 percent of those between eighteen and twenty-nine. Something closer to the reverse holds among those raised Haredi, who constitute only 1.6 percent of Jews aged sixty-five and older but rise to 8 percent of the eighteen- to twenty-nine-year-olds.

And then there are the children. A 2011 population study of Jews in the New York City area estimated the number of Haredi children at 166,000, roughly four times the number of Modern Orthodox children.[6] Marvin Schick, who used different categories in a national census of day schools he conducted during the 1998–99 and 2013–14 school years, found barely any change in Modern Orthodox numbers and a slight decline in Centrist Orthodox enrollments. (The latter grouping represents the more traditionalist wing of Modern Orthodoxy.) By contrast, the numbers of children in Yeshivish schools were up by 60 percent and in Hasidic ones by 110 percent.[7]

To be sure, this is not the only circumstance depleting the numbers of Modern Orthodox Jews in the United States. Another one, ironically, stems from the movement's great success in imbuing its young with Zionist values. Precise numbers are lacking, but by some estimates as many as 20 percent of Modern Orthodox youngsters who spend a year or more in Israel during their gap year between high school and college end up making their homes there for at least some period.[8] Needless to say, settling in Israel is socially and religiously approved behavior within the Modern Orthodox world; but that does not diminish its demographic impact on the community as a whole.

Still another worrying sign is the not insignificant rate of defection to more liberal movements. Thus, among those between the ages of thirty and forty-nine who have been raised Modern Orthodox, 12 percent have moved religiously leftward. (The commentator Alan Brill may have been the first to coin the term "post-Orthodox" for this population.)[9] True, as noted above, Modern Orthodoxy is much more successful than liberal denominations at retaining its members, and it continues to attract substantial numbers from them; but the losses hurt.

If the relatively static size of their community and the sheer demographic heft of the Haredim afford grounds for worry about the long-term viability of the Modern Orthodox way of life, beyond this concern lies another, related one: what some Modern Orthodox rabbis describe as a crisis of confidence among their laity. A salient symptom of that crisis, visible even among some otherwise highly acculturated Modern Orthodox families, is the decision to gravitate rightward toward Haredi or semi-Haredi schools and synagogues. Such families are driven, contends one of their rabbis, by "religious insecurity and feelings of guilt about that insecurity." This rabbi therefore sees his role as twofold: insisting on the validity of Modern Orthodoxy even as he encourages his congregants to intensify their commitment and practice.

As it happens, the Pew data suggest that the movement rightward may be balanced by a movement of Haredi Jews traveling in the opposite direction. Moreover, those joining "right-wing shuls" do not generally move into Haredi communities. It would thus be more accurate to see the so-called "slide to the right" as a matter less of massive defections to the Haredi camp than of a shift *within* Modern Orthodoxy, led in this instance by those inclined to adopt aspects of Haredi life while remaining nominally Modern Orthodox.

In some cases, the "slide" takes merely symbolic or token form, as when men wear black hats during prayer and women adopt Haredi-style head coverings while otherwise continuing to maintain their very modern style of life. More significant, and much more distressing to stalwarts of Modern Orthodox values, has been the assimilation—some would say infiltration—of a "neo-Haredi" worldview into some of the movement's key institutions.

Since the passing of Rabbi Joseph B. Soloveitchik from the scene some thirty years ago, the Yeshiva University world has lacked an authoritative figure who personifies for the broader public the synthesis proclaimed in YU's motto of *Torah u'madda*. Meanwhile, a "neo-Haredi" group of *roshei yeshiva*—the term, often translated as deans of talmudic academies, more accurately connotes advanced teachers of rabbinic texts—has planted its flag at YU's Rabbi Isaac Elchanan Rabbinical Seminary (RIETS), which educates, ordains, and shapes the religious and halakhic worldview of Modern Orthodox rabbis.[10] In addition, Modern Orthodox day schools often employ Haredi teachers who likewise communicate their ideology to impressionable students and may encourage them after graduation to attend an Israeli yeshiva or girls' seminary where neo-Haredi perspectives predominate. (Symptomatic of their disdain for the schools in which they teach, they choose to enroll their own children in Haredi schools.) The gap-year experience has led a proportion of post-high-school males and females to "flip out," or abandon Modern Orthodoxy for a Haredi lifestyle.[11] Of late, some longtime Modern Orthodox synagogues have also taken to hiring Haredi or neo-Haredi rabbis to fill their pulpits. And the community as a whole has become dependent on Haredim who fill certain ritually critical roles, including as scribes who write Torah scrolls and other religious documents, kosher slaughterers, and supervisors of kosher food production.[12]

Most subversive of all has been the internalization of the idea that Haredi Judaism represents the touchstone and arbiter of Orthodox authenticity, period.[13] This has placed Modern Orthodoxy on the defensive, handcuffing it to a way of thinking at odds with its founding assumptions. Willy-nilly, by absorbing the resistant mind-set, important sectors of the movement have thereby undermined Modern Orthodoxy's accommodative ideology and, worse, have made it more difficult to help their members navigate as observant Jews who embrace modern culture.

Pressure from the Left

If the challenge represented by the Haredim exerts pressure on Modern Orthodoxy from one direction, another and equally great challenge makes itself felt from the opposite direction. To Rabbi Yitz Greenberg, speaking at a forum on the Pew study, Modern Orthodox Jews live "on the same [cultural] continuum" as their non-Orthodox counterparts, being no less "exposed to the attractions of modernity and the acids of skepticism/historical criticism/social mores," and no less likely to succumb to those twin forces, both the "attractions" and the "acids," than are Conservative, Reform, or for that matter nonaffiliated and secular Jews. Rabbi Greenberg even attributes the "demographic decline" of the movement primarily to this factor.[14]

Actually, as we have seen, the problem is not (or not yet) one of serious decline but rather one of demographic stasis. But there can be no doubt that Modern Orthodox Jews have become at least as alert to the most controversial issues roiling their movement from the left as from the right. To adapt Jeffrey Gurock's nomenclature of resisters versus accommodators, which he applied to the struggle within the larger Orthodox world between the Haredim and the Modern Orthodox, we may say that Modern Orthodoxy itself is now beset by a no less bitter or momentous struggle: between its own internal resisters attracted to Haredi Judaism and accommodators more willing to adapt Jewish law to twenty-first-century ethical sensibilities.[15]

Undoubtedly, the most hotly debated set of issues concerns the status of Orthodox women. Gender equality is now taken for granted in most Modern Orthodox homes, and holding males and females to different standards is increasingly unthinkable. Still, the religious status of women in Modern Orthodoxy is far from resolved. Drawing the greatest heat are the following concerns: What are rabbis prepared to do to release "chained" women (*agunot*), whose husbands have refused to grant them a proper writ of divorce?[16] How much Torah and Talmud ought girls and women be encouraged to study? May women serve as clergy, either with the title of "rabbi" or some other official designation?[17] May they conduct their own prayer services, lead parts of mixed services, or wear tefilin during public worship? May women serve as synagogue presidents?[18] And why should it not occur to some girls that they too might don tefilin (phylacteries), traditionally the accoutrements of male worship?[19]

Another focal point of debate centers on the proper treatment of homosexuality and homosexuals in the Orthodox community. As is true in society at large, younger Modern Orthodox Jews tend to be considerably more open-minded about matters of sexual orientation than their elders. For some, this issue creates severe internal conflicts. The head of a Modern Orthodox day school describes what he has observed:

> In my experience, many, if not most, 20 to 40-year-olds in the modern Orthodox world struggle with the issue of homosexuality and the divinity of the Torah. They believe in a kind and just God and they want to believe in the divinity of the Torah. But at the same time they feel fairly certain that being gay is not a matter of choice. In the apparent conflict of these ideas, the first two premises seem to be losing ground. Students today do not find solace in the argument that the issue mirrors other questions of theodicy—children born with severe disabilities, tsunamis or other natural disasters, or the proliferation of cancer, for example. This generation by-and-large views this particular challenge to faith as irreconcilable.[20]

It is noteworthy that in the eyes of this observer, there is no resolution—and that is bound to have consequences for belief and the acceptance of religious authority.

Though they loom largest, questions about the status of women and homosexuals hardly exhaust the list of troubling issues.[21] Others concern how the community should relate to non-Orthodox Jews; the authority exercised by the Israeli Chief Rabbinate in matters pertaining to American Orthodox Jews; the authority of congregational rabbis vis-à-vis that of *roshei yeshiva* (rabbinic authorities based within yeshivas); the latitude, if any, for interpreting the theological category of "Torah from Heaven"—that is, the belief that the Torah was dictated verbatim by God to Moses; and more. In short, the same culture wars that have engulfed non-Orthodox Jews, Catholics, and Protestants now rage in the Modern Orthodox world.

This is not the place to discuss the complex legal and theological arguments on these issues advanced by different rabbinic authorities. Suffice it to say there are deep differences over who is credentialed to issue legal rulings and how flexible is Jewish law. On one side, Modern Orthodox resisters argue they are constrained by halakhic precedent even when it comes to mitigating the suffering of agunot. On the other side, accommodators tend to interpret Jewish law as in some degree subject to historical circumstances. Blu Greenberg, the preeminent leader of Orthodox feminism, has encapsulated the latter view tersely, declaring that "where there's a rabbinic will, there's a halakhic way." Many advocates of new thinking see the principal driver of change as the larger Orthodox community, with rabbis lagging behind.

While such disagreements on matters of Jewish law occupy the foreground, a series of cultural forces in the background are seen by all as shaping current debates. Rabbinic authority is waning. Rabbis across the spectrum of Modern Orthodoxy, resisters and accommodators alike, point to a community that has absorbed American understandings of the sovereign self. "What rabbis say does not matter" is a refrain I have heard repeatedly. In one Haredi school, the head of Jewish studies states without any prompting, "In today's age, the model of rabbinic authority does not exist. We don't live in ghettoes anymore, so you have to reach students where they are. Saying 'because it is so' no longer works."

In private conversation, the same lament recurs regardless of ideological position, although some go on to lay the blame for the loss of rabbinic authority on their opponents. On the accommodative side, the prevailing sentiment is that hidebound rabbis have brought this situation upon themselves because, when it comes to the demands of modernity, they are "oblivious and clueless." From the resisters, one hears that the accommodative wing has undermined the authority of recognized legal decisors by running to peripheral figures who are only too willing to approve innovations. Many sense their loss of authority so keenly that they shy away from asserting their views on the major cultural issues of the day even when they personally feel strongly about them.

Accelerating these trends is the new reality of the Internet. Thanks to it, states one rabbi, "everybody has a right to have a position; everyone has a *de'ah* [opinion] about everything." Educated Jews can look up answers to their own questions and choose from the answers available online. Many feel empowered in this role simply by dint of their day school education and by the time they have spent studying in Israel, even as they are also encouraged by modern culture's stress on individual autonomy to act according to the dictates of their conscience.

In this connection, day schools themselves are faulted by some for inadequately preparing their students to cope with the intellectual and moral challenges they encounter once they enter college. Rabbis on both sides agree that the failure lies in the deliberate neglect of questions of belief, theology, and the "why" of observance. From my own visits to Orthodox day schools, I question this critique. To me the problem seems more fundamental: there is no way fully to prepare Orthodox young people for the transition from their insular and homogeneous communities to the environment of the university, where the reigning values are so at odds with traditional Judaism. Be that as it may, however, efforts to remediate the situation are being made by rabbis in both the resistant and accommodative wings who are undertaking to teach their congregants about what is relevant and meaningful in Judaism rather than focusing solely on the study of texts. "I used to give heavy-duty classes on *rishonim* and *aharonim*," one rabbi on the side of the accommodators informed me, referring to rabbinic commentators writing during different eras. "Now I teach about *derech eretz* [proper behavior], women and ritual observance, and *tz'dakah* [Jewish giving]."

One thing is certain: an estimated 70 percent of Modern Orthodox college students are enrolled in secular institutions of higher learning, and the impact of their experience there cannot be ignored.[22] True, many of the parents and grandparents of current students also attended secular colleges, but it can be postulated that academic values and assumptions have changed since then, or that they are instilled far more explicitly than they were in the past, or both. On every campus today, incoming students are required to attend an intensive orientation program during which they are exposed to strongly formulated judgments about diversity, tolerance, and correct thinking. In this hothouse atmosphere, how is it possible for Orthodox students to argue in defense of the differentiated treatment of women in the domains of religious observance and leadership? Can one conceivably emerge from a college experience today without having encountered attitudes toward sexual behavior at odds with traditional Orthodox beliefs?

Making it still harder to shelter today's Modern Orthodox Jews is that they have strayed beyond the commuter colleges favored by an earlier generation. Once on campus, moreover, they are also less likely to shy away from courses on sexual roles, psychology, comparative religion—or modern biblical criticism—that will challenge views they absorbed during their day school years and from their elders.

As with the challenge from the Haredim, so with the challenge from "modernity," one can trace the effects on the institutional level as well as the personal. Acknowledging the seriousness of both challenges, some among Modern Orthodoxy's accommodative leaders and activists, male and female alike, have been pushing to reinvigorate and reinforce the movement's founding ethos from within. To generalize, one might say that these efforts are aimed simultaneously at fending off the inroads of "Haredization" and at incorporating, to some unspecified degree, the "open" ethos of modern liberal culture.

In 1996, an organization, Edah, was founded with just that dual purpose in mind. Its leader, Rabbi Saul Berman, issued a pamphlet spelling out "a variety of Orthodox attitudes to selected ideological issues"—with the emphasis on "variety." The issues ranged from the treatment of women in Jewish law to the meaning of *Torah u'madda,* from pluralism and tolerance within Orthodoxy to outreach aimed at non-Orthodox Jews. A year later, Edah was joined by the Jewish Orthodox Feminist Alliance (JOFA), whose declared mission is to advance "social change around gender issues in the Orthodox Jewish community."[23]

Although Edah folded after a decade, JOFA continues with its work. And in the meantime, a number of other institutions and initiatives have arisen, each dedicated to fostering change in the Modern Orthodox world. They include Yeshivat Chovevei Torah (YCT), an accommodative rabbinical seminary competing with YU's RIETS, and Yeshivat Maharat, which styles itself as the "first institution to ordain Orthodox women as clergy"; both of these institutions are associated with a camp that has come to be called Open Orthodoxy.[24] Allied with them is the International Rabbinical Fellowship, whose announced aim is to stand up for "the right, responsibility, and autonomy of individual rabbis to decide matters of *halakhah* for their communities."[25]

In the same orbit, if not necessarily of the same mind, are women-only prayer groups as well as "partnership minyanim" where men and women share the responsibility of leading different parts of the prayer services in a manner deemed acceptable to select rabbinic authorities.[26] To disseminate new thinking, Modern Orthodox bloggers have been busy putting forth more "progressive" perspectives. One of them, the website TheTorah.com, grapples with the findings and conclusions of modern biblical scholarship, long regarded as inherently incompatible with the teachings of traditional Judaism.[27]

It is not unusual for some Modern Orthodox Jews and their rabbis to pick and choose among these activities. Members of women's prayer groups, for example, may confine themselves to that initiative alone. Some students at YCT may support partnership minyanim (groups supporting the maximal participation of women as prayer leaders, according to the standards of some respected Modern Orthodox decisors),[28] while other students do not. Some students at YCT and Yeshivat Maharat decline to identify themselves personally with Open Orthodoxy. Interestingly, it has been estimated that as many as forty rabbinical students at RIETS itself would participate in a partnership minyan even though several of the leading Talmudists at that institution have unequivocally proscribed such prayer services.

In sum, it is problematic to assume that individuals, even if they share a willingness to stretch the boundaries of Orthodoxy, form part of a common accommodative camp. Nor is it possible to quantify the number of Modern Orthodox Jews sympathetic to any of these efforts, though most observers assume it is relatively small and limited to a few centers of liberal thinking in New York, Washington, Boston, and Los Angeles. Still, just as it means something that Modern Orthodox congregations in, for example, St. Louis and Kansas City have sought out women to serve in a quasi-rabbinic role, it seems safe to assume that the hundred or so rabbis ordained so far at YCT and now occupying positions on campuses, in day schools, in chaplaincies, and in pulpits all around the country have had an impact of their own. In time, the cadre of women being ordained at Yeshivat Maharat will also serve as an important influence. The same can be said for the ideas making their way into every corner of the Modern Orthodox community through the reach of the Internet.

Yet if the scope of dissatisfaction in the "modern" camp is hard to measure, the role of gender in defining the battle lines is evident. Whereas biblical criticism, for example, agitates a few, questions related to the status of women have prompted the sharpest controversies and deepest divisions. Traditionalists in the Rabbinical Council of America have drawn a line in the sand opposing partnership minyanim, religious services in which women play some role as prayer leaders.[29] The same organization adamantly "reaffirmed the traditional Orthodox position against the ordination of women, regardless of title, and the hiring of women in rabbinic positions in Orthodox institutions," a rejection of Yeshivat Maharat and the hiring of its female graduates.[30] And as a further irritant, women who wish to attend daily prayer services, often to say Kaddish for a deceased loved one, sometimes find themselves marginalized by Orthodox congregations—at times literally forced to stand in a hallway or silenced when reciting the prayer.[31]

But nothing has aggravated tensions more than ongoing battles over the status of agunot, women chained to husbands who refuse them a divorce. In a recent flare-up, a new rabbinic court was set up by Orthodox rabbis of some repute to aid such women; and in short order, it was shot down by leading decisors at Yeshiva University. "From start to finish this is a great mistake," wrote Rabbi Herschel Schachter; only "great scholars of the generation" should be dealing with such weighty matters, this about a problem that has festered for decades without resolution. In communities where some women are assuming leadership roles within their synagogues and even more have active careers, leaving the fate of "chained" women solely in the hands of male rabbis is a difficult, if not impossible, pill to swallow for a good many female, as well as male, congregants. Understanding the realities, the head of the new court put it this way: "This is a war," observed Rabbi Simcha Krauss. "We're fighting for these women. And if we win, the whole community wins. And if we lose . . . more is lost than we can ever know."[32]

Toward a New Synthesis?

The most basic consequence of these ongoing skirmishes over religious law and policy is an increased awareness that the ground is shifting. As one observer has put it, "everyone knows the lines are moving." The same individual notes how "in shuls, people talk about how far to the Right modern Orthodoxy has gone."[33] Meanwhile, for those opposed to Open Orthodoxy, the ground is similarly perceived to be shifting, albeit in a distinctly different if not heretical direction.

The discomfort has led some rabbis to speak of a widening chasm within the movement and the inevitability—if not the desirability—of a schism.[34] On the resisters' side, those insisting that lines must be drawn have mostly limited themselves to fighting against new practices rather than ostracizing people,[35] although, in a few synagogues, men who participate in partnership minyanim have been banned from leading services in their home congregations, and there are concerted efforts to bar YCT graduates from being hired by major Modern Orthodox synagogues. Some resisters have also taken to dismissing their opponents as closet Conservative Jews; to one prominent rabbi, the Open Orthodox should be known as "the observant non-Orthodox."[36]

For their part, advocates of Open Orthodoxy have shown little hesitancy about castigating their traditionalist opponents as reactionaries. Resentment toward Yeshiva University boils over in statements that the institution has fallen under the sway of rabbis with no understanding of today's world and has become intellectually bankrupt. By contrast, Open Orthodox rabbis pride themselves on their hospitality to those who are not Orthodox. "We create an open space and do not say 'no,'" one leader declares. Another draws the distinctions differently: "YU is modernist; [its people] think they are right.

They draw lines in the sand. YCT people are postmodern. We see no conflict between intellectual openness and using critical tools, even as we remain committed to *halakhah*."

It is this willingness to live without drawing lines in the sand that is currently seen as the defining feature of Open Orthodoxy, according to its most prominent—and controversial—exponent. Rabbi Avi Weiss has put the question thus: "Is our focus on boundaries, fences, high and thick—obsessing and spending inordinate amounts of time ostracizing and condemning and declaring who is not in—or is our focus on creating welcoming spaces to enhance the character of what Orthodoxy could look like in the 21st century?" His answer forms a credo of sorts for Open Orthodoxy:

> The dividing line within Orthodoxy today revolves around inclusivity. Is Orthodoxy inclusive of women—encouraging women to become more involved in Jewish ritual and Jewish spiritual leadership? Notwithstanding the Torah prohibition on homosexuality, are those in such relationships included as full members in our synagogues, and are their children welcomed into day schools? Do we respect, embrace, and give a forum to those who struggle with deep religious, theological, and ethical questions? Do we insist upon forbiddingly stringent measures for conversion, or do we, within halakhic parameters, reach out to converts with love and understanding? Should Orthodox rabbinic authority be centralized, or should it include the wide range of local rabbis who are not only learned but also more aware of how the law should apply to their particular communal situations and conditions? Are we prepared to engage in dialogue and learn from Jews of other denominations, and, for that matter, people of all faiths?[37]

Caught between the rival camps are those in the middle who feel sympathy for both sides and want a peaceful resolution that will keep everyone in the same camp. At a celebration of rabbis recently ordained by Yeshiva University's RIETS, a keynote speaker emphasized a single theme: we at YU are open; we have always stood for openness. Was this a peace offering to the progressive side of the spectrum, another salvo in the battle over legitimacy, or perhaps both? Others watch in embarrassment as "the hotheads" denounce each other. And in Modern Orthodox congregations around the country the question is whether the pronouncements of rabbinic organizations will hold much sway. In most quarters, there is a sense that the current situation is unsustainable.

Of course, it is possible to view the factionalism within Modern Orthodoxy as a sign of vitality. Thus, one might say that differences have arisen because those on each side, equally committed to the Jewish future, are alarmed by the unhelpful ideas or policies being promoted by their counterparts on the other side. One might even remark that, in the fastidiously "nonjudgmental" climate prevalent today in the rest of the American Jewish community, it is refreshing to encounter Jews prepared to stake a claim to what they see as true, necessary, and obligatory.

Worth noting, in any event, is that the programs and institutions spawned by rival factions are stimulating a welcome spirit of creativity. As Yehuda Sarna, the rabbi of New York University's Bronfman Center, has observed, "There are multiple Torah and college options, multiple rabbinical schools, multiple forms of Orthodox Zionism, multiple ways of engaging with modernity, multiple entry and exit points to the community."[38] One merely has to cite the range of Orthodox websites issuing commentaries on the weekly Torah portion, and compare those offerings with the paucity of non-Orthodox counterparts, to appreciate the dynamism. The same can be said about bloggers in all sectors of the Modern Orthodox community who address everything from matters of theology to preparing brides for their wedding night.

Moreover, despite conflicts over practices, Modern Orthodox Jews of all stripes observe the same religious common core—daily prayer, kosher food restrictions, laws of family purity, Sabbath and festival celebrations. In fact, one of the contentions of the accommodators is that they are in no danger of going the way of Conservative Judaism precisely because they live and work in religiously observant communities, whereas Conservative rabbis historically made legal decisions for communities that did not observe Jewish law. Open Orthodoxy can experiment with new ideas and interpretations, they contend, because the commitment to Jewish law will keep them and their followers in check.[39]

In "The Rise of Social Orthodoxy," Jay Lefkowitz put this perspective succinctly: "I imagine [that] for many others like me, the key to Jewish living is not our religious beliefs but our commitment to a set of practices and values that foster community and continuity."[40] Assumed in this formulation is that practices and values will remain unaffected by changing beliefs. But is that right? In fact, as we have seen, a whole set of core Modern Orthodox assumptions is under assault both from forces outside Modern Orthodoxy and from the partisans of those forces within, and there is considerable evidence that some practices, and even some values, are changing as a result.

Thus far, the Modern Orthodox world has managed to flourish and persist by creating a community of practice and by focusing most of its intellectual energy on intensified Talmud study. This is not to be minimized. The movement's vibrant communal life, high levels of observance, and serious engagement with traditional texts are monumental achievements. But, caught as Modern Orthodoxy is between the absolutism and insularity of Haredi Judaism and the realities of an open and radically untraditional American society, are those achievements sufficient to retain a population well integrated into American life and profoundly influenced by its mores, assumptions, and values?[41]

The urgent question for Modern Orthodoxy is which values can be accommodated without undermining religious commitment and distorting traditional Judaism beyond recognition—and, conversely, what losses will be sustained if Modern Orthodoxy should undertake more actively to resist the modern world in which its adherents spend most of their waking hours?[42] The same urgent question, mutatis mutandis, has confronted other Jewish religious movements in the past, and has continued to haunt their rabbis and adherents long after they made their choice of a path forward. That is one reason why today's unfolding culture wars within Modern Orthodoxy carry far-reaching implications not only for that movement but also for the future of American Judaism as a whole.

7

WHO NEEDS JEWISH
DENOMINATIONS?

It's hard to avoid the conclusion that the organized denominations of American Judaism have fallen on hard times. It's not just that each struggles with questions of definition and purpose; the division of Jews into neat denominational boxes causes resentment. "Conservative? Orthodox? Reform? Labels are for clothes . . . not for Jews" proclaims an ad placed by an organization of Orthodox outreach workers.[1] But beyond the forced choices Jews are asked to make are the realities of their lives, where hybridity is common and picking and choosing among the offerings of different synagogues is not only possible, but seen by many as desirable. The very notion of adherence to one denomination is treated by many as an unacceptable imposition, a constraint upon their individuality and eagerness to experiment. Denominational switching has become widespread, with the result that the movements appear to be leaking vessels.

The Decline of the Denominations

Drastically limited finances are both symptoms and causes of the malaise. It has not helped the denominations that their institutional structures are severely compromised by inadequate funding. During the Great Recession organizational budgets were slashed and long-standing programs were eliminated by the national congregational arms of the Conservative and Reform movements. Neither has recovered.[2] Hardest hit have been the education departments of each movement and support for campus activities—precisely those programs that nurture the next generation of Jews. Both organizations are trying to reinvent themselves as service organizations primarily concerned with their own constituents, the synagogues. The Orthodox Union, the largest and best funded of several Orthodox congregational bodies, has been spared these cutbacks because its budget comes mainly from the OU Kashrut supervision department, a lucrative enterprise.[3]

The fiscal problems reflect a deeper malaise in the Conservative and Reform movements. Both have suffered from declining numbers of congregational members, and therefore, not surprisingly, synagogues have had to curtail their dues paying to the United Synagogue of Conservative Judaism and the Union for Reform Judaism.[4] It is hard to know exactly how many Jews still affiliate with each movement's congregations because those numbers are closely held by synagogues. Whether the national offices have accurate numbers is unknowable, though that does not impede their making what seem to be inflated claims about the size of their following. As the two movements sign up intermarried families, we also have no idea how many synagogue members are Jewish. Though some large congregations in each movement are enjoying healthy membership enrollment, a good many others have suffered a steep decline and are making do with more limited resources. And for all the bravado of national leaders and a few self-satisfied congregational rabbis already cited, the pithy observation of a prominent Reform rabbi about the view from the trenches is probably equally true for both movements: "Nobody is in a triumphalist mood. The wind is not in our sails." Even in the leadership circles of Modern Orthodoxy, sobriety has replaced the triumphalism of the recent past: the defection of some who were raised in the movement, laxity of observance in some quarters, and the increasingly nasty skirmishes among different sectors of Modern Orthodoxy have tempered the self-confidence of leaders.

In my interviews with over 160 rabbis of all denominations, it was also striking how few expressed particular pride in their movement's national leadership (with the noteworthy exception of Chabad emissaries). In fact, hardly anyone acknowledged getting much help from the national offices. Congregational rabbis felt they were largely on their own, and to the extent they relied upon others for advice, they turned to peers, not to the denominational bureaus. The congregational arms came in for particular scorn for offering little help.

From the vantage point of most rabbis I interviewed—across the spectrum—the pronouncements of national officials are irrelevant, if not a source of ongoing chagrin. One is reminded in this connection of Rabbi Irving "Yitz" Greenberg's mordant pronouncement a few decades ago: "I don't care what denomination you belong to, as long as you're embarrassed by it."[5] Much resentment has accumulated over the years about the high-handed ways of movement leaders. Several Reform rabbis, for example, vented their ire to me about leaders of their national organization who seem to feel that *they* are the movement, whereas rabbis are convinced *the synagogues* ought to be at the center. A Reform rabbi decried the role of central leaders who claim to speak on behalf of his movement without any process of vetting those views ahead of time. The same may be said of Conservative Judaism, though of late the major arms of the movement have coordinated to issue joint position papers.[6] As for Orthodoxy, with its multiple subgroups and competing organizations, there is no centralized leadership but rather a multiplicity of voices, usually sharply at odds with one another. Voicing a sentiment of many colleagues across the denominational spectrum, a Conservative rabbi articulated the irrelevance of denominational pronouncements to his primary commitments: "I make my own garden grow. I go back to my Kehilla and teach people how to daven [pray], and I lead them."

If that were not sufficient, denominationalism itself has come under serious, and not entirely friendly, scrutiny in light of developments during the latter part of the twentieth century. In the 1980s and 1990s, denominational leaders engaged in a number of very public spats, primarily though not exclusively over "Who is a Jew?" debates in Israel. As the rhetoric became increasingly inflammatory, leaders in other sectors of the American Jewish community began to worry about the damage heated exchanges were inflicting upon the cohesiveness of American Jewry.

The dismay over denominational rivalries was captured in a series of publications toward the end of the century. First came an essay in the mid-1980s by Rabbi Greenberg, provocatively titled "Will There Be One Jewish People in the Year 2000?"[7] Warning of an impending schism, Greenberg identified two developments propelling a crisis of religious polarization: "the demographics of separation—an explosion in the numbers of Jews of halachically contested or unmarriageable status; and the denominational politics of separation—interdenominational alienation, de-legitimation, and the shift of the balance of power within each movement toward those who seek to resolve problems by internally acceptable solutions to the utter disregard of the other denominations."[8] Equally troubling to Greenberg was the hardening of positions within the various denominations that was resulting in unilateral decision making, with no regard for how such actions would affect other groups of Jews.

Symptomatic of the concern at the time about religious polarization was a pronouncement in the 1988 *American Jewish Year Book* deeming intra-Jewish religious conflict "the issue that most worried American Jewish leaders."[9] By the end of the nineties Samuel G. Freedman had documented just how destructively the conflict of "Jew versus Jew" had played out in several local communities.[10] Freedman's work echoed concerns raised already in the early 1990s by my own book, an analysis of the underlying causes for heightened religious tensions, and starkly warned that "the divided world of Judaism imperils the unity of the Jewish people in America."[11] Little wonder, then, that some concluded the denominations were more of a headache than they were worth.

Forging a Transdenominational Culture

One response to these misgivings was a concerted effort to privilege transdenominational programs over those offered by the individual movements. Fearing that American Jews were retreating into self-isolating and mutually hostile camps, federations of Jewish philanthropy, major Jewish organizations, and key funders launched a series of initiatives to bring Jews of different outlooks together. These so-called pluralistic efforts were especially pronounced in new types of educational programming. Here are some of the most noteworthy examples:

- For college and post-college young adults, Birthright Israel has provided ten-day free trips to Israel for those who have not previously been there on trip with their age peers. Birthright Israel is open to anyone who identifies as a Jew. It has thus far sent over a half million young people from the United States, alone, to Israel. Its orientation is transdenominational.[12]

- New centers for Jewish learning open to all comers have emerged in recent decades that pride themselves on their nondenominational orientation. Among them is Mechon Hadar in Manhattan and the Hartman Institute, based in Israel, both offering programs in synagogues and Jewish Community Centers around the country. Neither is affiliated with one particular movement. Hartman in fact runs study programs for rabbis and laypeople that intentionally bring together individuals of different Jewish religious outlooks expressly to encourage them to learn with and from one another.

- The most successful adult education efforts are nondenominational in orientation. These have included the Florence Melton Adult Mini-School and the Meah Program, first developed by the Hebrew College for the Boston Jewish community and later sponsored by the Jewish Theological Seminary. The largest Jewish adult education program nationally and internationally is the Jewish Learning Institute, which attracts Jews of all kinds to study its curricula under the religious auspices of Chabad.

- Efforts to bridge day schools have also made considerable headway. Community day schools offering a pluralistic, nondenominational approach numerically have outgrown both the Conservative movement's Schechter network and the Reform movement's Pardes schools. And though clear lines of denominational boundaries persist, a new umbrella organization called Prizmah has merged four separate support agencies on the theory that despite ideological differences, day schools across the spectrum share many common challenges.[13] Similar efforts were also launched to support Jewish summer camps, preschool education, and congregational schools, regardless of denominational differences.[14]

- Several other kinds of institutes also work with clergy spanning the denominational spectrum. The Institute for Jewish Spirituality runs retreats for rabbis and cantors designed to help them rethink their professional work and recharge through meditation, spiritual exercises, the study of Hasidic and Mussar texts, and exposure to Eastern religious thinking. Rabbis without Borders, as its name implies, is also cross-denominational in its scope, and likewise encourages rabbis to develop initiatives that go beyond conventional institutions and the confines of denominationalism. T'ruah, the Rabbinic Call for Human Rights, brings together rabbis and rabbinical students for training in advocacy work on behalf of domestic and international human rights issues.[15] Like the Hartman program in Israel, these three efforts based in the United States intentionally encourage clergy of different outlooks to learn from one another and work cooperatively.

- Two initiatives under the auspices of the Wexner Foundation have engaged with future lay and professional leaders, bringing promising young people together from around the country to annual retreats. The Wexner Heritage Program, which offers an intensive two years of study for women and men interested in playing a role as volunteer leaders, has created cohorts in midsize and large communities around the country. A second effort brings together graduate students who are preparing to serve as religious and professional leaders of Jewish institutions. The Tikvah Fund is another foundation that has taken on an operating role, offering seminars of varying lengths for high school, college, and rabbinical school students and midcareer advanced professionals.[16]

- Several rabbinical schools have been founded with the express purpose of drawing students from different sectors of the community into trans-denominational settings. Perhaps, the most successful was founded in 2003 and is based at the Boston Hebrew College. And with campuses in New York and Los Angeles, the Academy for Jewish Religion offers part-time study, again without a denominational orientation.

- Synagogue 2000 and now Synagogue 3000, as well as the now defunct Synagogue Transformation and Renewal (STAR) initiative, have worked with a mix of synagogue professionals and lay leaders to help them re-envision their congregations and clarify the missions of their institutions. The largest federation of Jewish philanthropy runs its own Synergy

Program in New York City, to support all types of Jewish congregations in the organization's catchment area.

- Limmud conferences have proliferated around the United States based on a community-wide model pioneered in the United Kingdom. These annual local or regional gatherings bring together Jews of all outlooks for a weekend of study, conversation, cultural celebration, and fellowship. Just as the original Limmud strives to bridge the variety of Jews in Great Britain, the offshoots in this country celebrate Jewishness in all its forms and for all kinds of Jews.

The list of such programs undoubtedly could be expanded considerably. What they all share in common is a *transdenominational orientation*. Each intentionally brings together Jews of different religious outlooks, usually reflecting the spectrum of Jewish religious life in this country, ranging from Renewal, Reconstructionism, Reform, Conservative, and Modern Orthodox Judaism. All types are represented; only the Haredi and Hasidic worlds of Orthodoxy are not at the table (but some of them are seated at the head of the table as teachers). The implicit message of such gatherings is twofold: Jews face many common challenges and have much to learn from one another; that which divides us is less important than the common concerns and texts we share.[17] Not surprisingly given these goals, rabbis representing the range of denominational views are far more likely in recent years to study together privately, and they often schedule public programs to model for their congregants how Jews of different outlooks can study the same text while holding firm to distinctive ways of reading those texts.[18]

These settings also help foster new relationships. Participants understand one another better, even if they do not necessarily agree. Not surprisingly, when studying or working side by side, participants form friendships, thereby lessening ideological and religious tensions. In brief, these programs have nurtured a degree of empathy among Jews of disparate backgrounds.[19]

Funders and major organizations encourage these trends and often foster cross-denominational cooperation. Quite a few of the large membership organizations, federations, and family foundations were deeply shaken by the rancor of the highly public religious disputes that punctuated Jewish communal life during the last fifteen years of the twentieth century. They feared that religious divisiveness would subvert efforts to address issues of common concern, such as the battle against anti-Semitism, efforts to support Israel, and fund-raising to support pan-Jewish causes. They also regarded such divisiveness as undermining their own work, which tended to focus on bringing together Jews of all outlooks. In their effort to encourage cross-denominational cooperation, these groups have often banished religious disagreements to the margins, employing a variety of techniques to downplay or ignore denominational differences. Some have bypassed rabbinic leaders entirely, working instead with laypeople, who are seen as less likely to engage in spats. The common assumption is that the primary sources of friction are turf issues and rabbinic pride, not matters of religious principles or faith. Or perhaps it is felt that religious differences are so intractable that they should be set aside in favor of less divisive matters. In either event, the result has been a concerted communal predisposition to sweep those differences under the communal rug.

Funding institutions have also created a reward system to encourage civil behavior and a renewed appreciation for the overarching needs of the Jewish people (*klal yisrael*). Some federations either explicitly or implicitly condition their support for schools on the participation of principals and teachers in cross-denominational activities and affinity groups: heads of all the local day schools are expected to attend meetings of the principals' council, and teachers at all types of supplementary religious schools are expected to attend in-service study days. When there is interest in founding a new day school, federation officials are likely to exert pressure to ensure it will be cross-denominational or "pluralistic" if it is to secure communal funding. Jewish philanthropists are taking a similar tack, and a few large foundations have even pledged to withhold grants from institutions whose leaders engage in "sensationalism and slander" directed at other Jewish groups.[20] In short, quite substantial groups on the Jewish scene have deliberately employed the power of the purse to press for cross-denominational cooperation—or at least a muting of denominational combativeness.

The New Anti-denominationalism

The various Jewish religious movements are also under attack from a more hostile foe—anti-denominationalists who seek to dismantle the organizational structure of American Judaism. "Denominations are yesterday's news," declares a key backer of the New York Limmud conference, a program designed to bring together Jews of many "backgrounds."[21] Increasing numbers of Jews today eschew a denominational label when they are surveyed about their preference: according to the 2013 Pew study 30 percent claim to be nondenominational—up from 18 percent twenty-three years earlier.[22] And so some have come to believe that denominational identity is on the decline, and perhaps the very language of denominationalism is outdated. The religious movements are seen as creations of elites who have manufactured false distinctions among Jews. They are also regarded as poor reflections of a far more complex reality; as Jews increasingly pick and choose in order to form their Jewish identities, they do not fit neatly into denominational packages. In contrast to the transdenominationalists, the postdenominational groups do not seek a pluralism based upon Jews with clear denominational identities coming together to engage in study or religious activity; instead, they wish to see an end to the false and unnecessary denominational distinctions altogether—because they are useless at best and harmful at worst.

A variety of factors are stimulating this interest in postdenominationalism. Certainly, the overt conflict among the movements from the mid-1980s to the mid-1990s repelled quite a few Jews: if this nasty infighting is the consequence of having separate Jewish religious movements, some contended, a plague on them all. Critics of the denominations are convinced, moreover, that these groups deserve to be consigned to the dustbin of history because they serve no compelling purpose: if so many Jews are disengaged from Judaism, the argument goes, it must be because the movements are outmoded. Indeed, two Jewish academics have argued that "a Jewish world without denominations" might have a better chance to retain the allegiance of Jews.[23] In their view, "drift and alienation from organized Jewish life continue, in part, because denominational packaging no longer appeals to a growing number of hungry spiritual consumers." In other words, the denominations are *a cause* of the declining engagement with Judaism. Along similar lines, a Jewish Renewal rabbi named Gershon Winkler, who promotes a concept he calls "flexidoxy," believes that many American Jews are "turned off by the rigidity of established 'standards' found in every Jewish denomination." He blames the religious movements for the lack of interest of many Jews, who need to learn that "the broader spectrum of Judaism that shines far beyond and above the particular party-line versions they have been fed by every denomination."[24]

Besides, the real distinction between the movements, in the view of some, comes down to a choice between heteronomy and autonomy, between Orthodox Jews who accept externally imposed limits on their action and everyone else.[25] Since the Orthodox share of the population is roughly 10 percent, it is clear that the overwhelming majority of American Jews behave as autonomous beings and share a common desire to construct their own version of Judaism rather than accepting a received version. Postdenominationalism provides an option to draw upon the best in all the non-Orthodox movements—the social action of Reform, the Conservative movement's mediation of tradition and modernity, the neo-Hasidism animating Jewish Renewal, and so on. A mélange is preferable to homogeneity. In such circumstances, labels are constricting, rather than liberating.[26]

Some have discerned a strong generational element in this new postdenominationalism. Writing in 2003 of younger Jewish adults, Rabbi Leon A. Morris has claimed his generation "is characterized by the idea of hybrids, not just with regard to being Jewish and American but by additionally defining ourselves in a myriad of complex ways." Younger Jews "resist categorization. We don't want to be labeled. We seek a model of Jewish life that is self-designed." As a result, he claims, "we create Judaisms as diverse and individualistic as the Jews who practice them." And in a concluding affirmation that might leave some heads spinning at denominational headquarters, he declares: "perhaps in the new century, each one of us is Reform, Conservative, Orthodox, and Reconstructionist."[27]

It is not clear as yet how pervasive or deep postdenominational longings are. Few proponents of this position have articulated how it might work in practice.[28] It suits Orthodoxy, some say, to maintain that Jews are all on a continuum of observance: some are more observant, some less, but everyone is trying to do better (i.e., by becoming more observant). Samuel G. Freedman reports the motto of an organization called Olam, which purports to welcome all Jews to the "Ashkefardi-Ultrarefconservadox Generation," but, upon closer inspection, betrays that "beneath the rhetoric of mutual respect, Olam [was] proselytizing for wayward Jews to adopt Orthodoxy, the one true faith."[29] In some instances, then, the language of postdenominationalism may be more lip service than anything else.

It also remains to be seen whether younger Jews who are deliberately eschewing denominational labels will eventually change their attitudes when they discover how dependent they are upon denominational institutions to educate and socialize their children in schools, youth movements, summer camps, and the like. Still, there is far more talk today about jettisoning the denominations and far more publicly voiced criticism of their failings. As a result, the movements are on the defensive.[30]

The Broader Context

It would be a mistake to attribute the diminution of the denominations solely to the inner dynamics of American Judaism. Altered circumstances beyond those movements have also tended to marginalize them. Three of these are especially salient: First, denominationalism itself is in deep trouble at its source—American Protestantism. The number of nondenominational churches in the United States has skyrocketed in recent decades. According to a study by the Hartford Seminary, if all these independent churches would combine, collectively they would become the third largest Christian body in this country, after Catholics and Southern Baptists.[31] In addition, it is arguable that the key divide today is not between Protestant denominations but within them. The culture wars are creating links across the denominational lines to connect like-minded conservatives across the spectrum and also like-minded liberals, regardless of their denomination, over public policy questions such as reproductive rights, gay marriage, stem cell research, and so forth. Denominations have been riven by these types of issues. It also has not helped denominations that high rates of religious switching are depleting the ranks of some of the oldest and once dominant Protestant mainline denominations.

These developments, in turn, are not occurring in a vacuum. National organizations of all kinds, religious and secular alike, have to deal with the fallout from declining membership and support. That process began in the closing decades of the twentieth century when expressive individualism triumphed on the American scene and resulted in ever more Americans detaching themselves from distant national institutions.[32] Analyzing these developments, Yuval Levin adds: "Over the past several decades people have been increasingly able to tailor their experiences and connections with others as they choose."[33]

That is true also for local houses of worship, which have been dropping their membership in or distancing themselves from national denominational structures. The most successful denominations are decentralized. They don't assume themselves to be holders of authority, but serve as conveners. Moreover, new networks are arising in the church sector that are nondenominational. Even within some denominations, religious leaders are defining their own path. Among the Methodists, for example, two hundred top pastors are convening without denominational leadership but are banding together to address their common challenges. The eclipse of Jewish denominations is consistent, then, with much wider trends weakening centralized national structures.

A second external factor accounting for the sidelining of the Jewish religious movements in recent years, undoubtedly, is sheer distraction. American Jews are preoccupied with threats to Jewish security that emanate from without. As levels of anti-Zionist activity have risen and often crossed the line into blatant anti-Semitism, external threats have captured the attention of American Jews. People can focus only so much attention on their problems, and that attention has been riveted on the threats from without rather than on inter- and intradenominational disputes.

Third, the internal crisis confronting American Jewry—declining involvement in Jewish life—is blamed on synagogues and religious institutions, and so the religious movements are portrayed as the problem, rather than part of the solution. As growing proportions of American Jews disengage from organized Jewish activity, are less inclined to join any Jewish organizations and support Jewish causes, move to areas at a great geographical distance from central Jewish institutions, and intermarry at staggeringly high rates, the very institutions that might help reverse these trends are portrayed as irrelevant, out of touch, or responsible for what ails American Jewry. It has become fashionable to portray all legacy institutions as hopelessly archaic, and none more so than religious ones. Given these perceptions, the denominations have been largely sidelined.

Denominations for What?

The denominations have not helped themselves by pretending to play an authoritative role in shaping the religious lives of American Jews through ideological pronouncements. Ideology may be of interest to the elites, but the "folk" have their own agendas. As one observer of the Modern Orthodox world put it to me, "religion is not as important to your average congregant as it is to the rabbis." If this is true of Orthodox Jews, it is even more the case for the non-Orthodox. And yet, the movements persist in defining themselves in ideological terms. Orthodox rabbis affirm with great certainty that their Judaism is distinctive because it alone is based on the firm belief in a literal understanding that the entire Torah, including rabbinic teachings, was revealed at Sinai to Moses. Since the other movements deviate from this understanding, they are deficient and have no standing in the eyes of Orthodox leaders. What is unknowable is how many rank-and-file members of Orthodox synagogues, including Haredi ones, actually believe in a literal definition of Torah Mi'Sinai, that the entire Pentateuch was transmitted to Moses by God.[34] In the case of Conservative Judaism, the ideology of the movement portrays it as committed to Halacha, Jewish law, even though no one seriously argues that most members of Conservative synagogues act upon such a commitment in their daily lives. And as for Reform, the motto of the movement is "informed choice," yet it is universally understood that with few exceptions Reform congregants are neither well-informed nor even aware they are making choices.

Even the elites of those movements are not necessarily on board when it comes to ideology. I am reliably informed by participants in numerous biennial conventions of the Union for Reform Judaism that for the past three decades the only dependable way to ensure a standing ovation has been through the by now routinized lip service paid to "a woman's right to choose." Nothing about living a Jewish life evokes a similarly high level of enthusiasm among the assembled rabbis and lay leaders. In the Conservative movement, the Committee on Jewish Law and Standards is the authoritative voice of proper religious observance. But when it came to granting full synagogue honors to women or introducing musical instrumentation during the services or officiating at same-sex weddings, quite a few of the rabbis did not wait for a definitive ruling by the law committee. They did what they felt they had to do, with no sanction. Even in the Modern Orthodox sector, the vehement opposition of the Rabbinical Council of America to partnership minyanim and women's services has barely registered with those who disagree, including some rabbis who are members of that organization. Decrees from on high are having relatively little resonance, but the denominations persist in issuing them.[35]

If ideology and religious pronouncements are of such small interest to ordinary Jews, for amcha, why do they join synagogues affiliated with specific denominations? The movements, in fact, serve as sorting mechanisms, bringing together like-minded or, more accurately, like-behaving Jews. Based on our earlier discussion about the religious practices of ordinary Jews (chapters 2 and 3), we can identify some commonalities shared by Jews in each movement based upon the following five criteria:[36]

1. **Frequency of Religious Activity:** In the aggregate, Jews in each movement engage in religious activities roughly as often as their fellow congregants. The denominational gradient is fairly obvious. Orthodox Jews participate in Jewish life more than do Conservative Jews; and the latter do more Jewish religious things than Reform Jews. This is certainly the case when it comes to attendance at synagogue services. Orthodox Jews attend considerably more often; Reform Jews tend to go infrequently over the entire year; Conservative Jews show up less often than Orthodox Jews but more frequently than Reform Jews. The same holds true for the observance of Judaism's rituals. Reform Judaism does not proclaim that observances like candle lighting or reciting kiddush on Friday nights or fasting on Yom Kippur are unnecessary; nor does Conservative Judaism teach the irrelevance of rituals like keeping

kosher in the home and outside or dismiss the fast days as unnecessary. But the adherents of those movements generally ignore these practices of their own volition. They want to observe, but only up to a point. They, then, choose a synagogue whose members tend to be as observant or unobservant as they are. To do otherwise would be to set oneself up for discordant and uncomfortable interactions with fellow congregants.

2. **The Locus of Religious Activity:** Adherents of the different movements differ in *where* they observe their Judaism. The large majority of Reform Jews confine their religious activities to the synagogue. A small number may light Hanukkah candles and have a perfunctory Seder at home; some will even say a quick blessing over the wine on Friday nights, but probably not recite the full kiddush. How do we know? Reform rabbis report on how little the children in their religious schools have seen of Jewish observance in their homes.[37] Reform Jews think of their synagogues the way Christians regard their churches: religion takes place only in their sacred precincts. Conservative Jews are far more likely to do Jewish things in the home. They are more likely to have a Seder that pays some attention to the Haggadah, to light candles on Friday night, to hold a break-fast meal at home after Yom Kippur ends, to light Hanukkah candles, and, in growing numbers, to build a Sukkah. Perhaps most telling, a quarter of Conservative-raised Jews claim to keep a kosher home, a figure that rises to 41 percent among those between the ages of thirty and forty-nine. (Comparable figures for Reform-raised Jews are 9 percent and 7 percent. In other words, rates of keeping kosher at home are declining among younger Jews raised Reform and rising among younger Jews raised Conservative.) As to Orthodox Jews, they not only infuse their homes with religious practice but also take their religion on the road by making allowances for eating kosher food when traveling; joining Torah study circles not necessarily based in synagogues; involving themselves in their children's Jewish day school. In the aggregate, and with exceptions, adherents of these movements differ in *where* they let Judaism into their lives.

3. **The Preferred Style of Synagogue Worship:** Until recently, Jews sorted themselves by the type of worship service they expected to find in a synagogue. Orthodox synagogues would recite the entire traditional liturgy in Hebrew. Reform services included a good deal of English, were accompanied by an organ or guitar, and drew selectively from the traditional liturgy; they also were shortened considerably, so that attendees knew precisely when they could expect to leave. For their part, Conservative synagogues combined a bit of both: services were conducted almost entirely in Hebrew, followed the traditional liturgy with a few, relatively minor exceptions, involved a good deal of congregational singing but rarely accompanied by any musical instruments. The prayer services in Conservative synagogues differed from Orthodox ones mainly in the adoption of a triennial reading cycle for the weekly Torah por-

tion, rather than completing the entire Torah reading each year; some repetitions were dropped; and of course the men and women sat together. In the twentieth century, synagogue attendees could reasonably anticipate what to expect in a synagogue once they knew its denominational affiliation, even if they were attending an out-of-town synagogue for the first time. With the introduction of elaborate musical instrumentation, Rock Shabbat services, Friday Night Live musical compositions, and other such innovations, the style of non-Orthodox synagogues has changed, and lines between Reform, Conservative, and nondenominational services are blurring. It remains to be seen whether Conservative synagogues have been wise to relinquish one of their most prominent selling points: their distinctive religious services. To be sure, some may argue that despite the different musical arrangements, the services remain largely unchanged because the main weekly service in most Conservative synagogues is held on Saturday morning, while in Reform temples the main service is held on Friday night. The two liturgies are vastly different, and the "feel" of a worship service on Friday nights is not at all like one on Saturday morning. Although the jury is still out, it is clear that the style of service in the past was something that attracted attendees because it was reliably consistent across each denomination.

4. **The Character of Social Networks:** The sorting mechanism offered by synagogues of different stripes is associated not only with ritual practices, but also with the social network congregations provide. Simply put, members of these different types of synagogues have sought out other Jews whose Jewish lives are congruent with their own. In the case of Reform Jews, as a congregational rabbi in that movement put it, people seek to join a "self-selected periphery." They deliberately decide "I don't want to be with people who take this too seriously. Who practice more than I do. Who will make me feel badly about my limited observances." Conservative Jews also seek out a synagogue where their level of involvement is not criticized. Regular attendees of Conservative synagogues will never interrogate an infrequent attender and ask why he or she has not come more often or has failed to help make up a minyan. The tacit rule in both Reform and Conservative synagogues is to be nonjudgmental. Welcoming and hospitality come with no strings attached. By contrast, Orthodox congregants exert a significant degree of peer pressure to ensure having a minyan, and there are clear expectations of attendance and observance. Some Orthodox Jews may chafe under these pressures, but more may also welcome them as a way the social group keeps them in line.

5. **Connections to the Jewish People:** Synagogues communicate messages about the responsibility Jews have to one another and the Jewish people globally. The choice of a congregation for many Jews also involves, however subtly, a decision about how engaged a congregant wishes to be with other Jews. Reform Jews as a group are increasingly dissociating themselves from the Jewish people. A good

deal of this is being driven by the large numbers of intermarried families whose own relationship to the Jewish people is tenuous, if not fraught with tension. It is also driven by resentments, too often fueled by rabbis, over the treatment of non-Orthodox Jews in Israel. Conservative synagogues until recently were the most oriented to the needs of the Jewish people, klal yisrael. They served as marshaling grounds for raising money for Israel at times of crisis. Today, some Conservative synagogues are riven by disputes about Israeli policies. Whether these controversies will come to overshadow their commitment to the Jewish people as a whole is not at all clear. For their part, Orthodox synagogues have focused primarily on the needs of fellow Orthodox Jews. They also have become bastions of support for what are considered to be a more hardline set of policies pursued by the Israeli government. Of all the factors accounting for the decision of Jews to join a congregation, the way congregants relate to the wider Jewish population is currently a wildcard. It is impossible to predict whether this relationship will unify or splinter congregations.

The combination of the previous five items can work together to provide or sustain a Jewish identity for members of different kinds of synagogues. Whether such an identity is shallow or profound varies greatly. It is evident, for example, that in the latter part of the twentieth century, the reflexive answer of the plurality of American Jews was to self-identify as Conservative. Many were not members of a Conservative synagogue, but the Conservative label was the default option. Today it appears that the Reform label has become the fallback for those who feel they are Jewish but not too Jewish. Perhaps in time, "none of the above" will become the vanilla option. But even such loose identifications are not entirely without meaning. A sizable proportion of congregants and former congregants take a measure of pride in their synagogues, relate to their style of worship, feel comfortable in the company of fellow synagogue members, and practice Judaism in ways comparable to other members of their synagogue or temple.

To note these patterns is not to attribute all religious behavior to social preferences alone: in subtle and overt ways, fellow congregants share common values and assumption. One need only attend to the buzzwords (and pieties) popular in the synagogues of each movement to note how a common language of discourse binds adherents of each Jewish denomination—and how such language differs from one denomination to another.[38] Haredi speak differs from Modern Orthodox language, no less than Conservative and Reform public discourse differ from each other. This is most obviously the case in how Judaism's commandments and verities are discussed in public settings, such as from the pulpit; but even private conversations of fellow congregants around a Shabbat or holiday table reflect these different types of discourse. Denominational identity creates parameters for how to speak about what it means to be a Jew, and, in turn, the synagogues of different denominations adapt to the language their adherents are prepared to hear.[39]

A Role for Denominations

If our analysis of why people join a particular denominational synagogue is correct, the gap between what interests average Jews and the preoccupations of denominational leaders could not be more vivid. The personal considerations we have listed are a far cry from the issues that seemingly agitate national spokespersons. During the closing decades of the past century, Conservative Judaism and to a lesser degree Reform suffered through divisive battles over the religious status of women and gay Jews, issues that still agitate Modern Orthodoxy. One can make a strong case for why these questions required resolution. Many Jews found traditional stances immoral and cruel. Many were put off by exclusionary policies. Something had to be done to open opportunities for these Jewish populations to participate equally in religious life. However, at some point responsible leaders need to ask themselves whether the enormous investment of energy and time on these issues has been wise. While such public controversies dominated, other pressing issues were left to fester—and today the movements live with the consequences.

Take the battles over the admission of women to rabbinical schools of the non-Orthodox seminaries: with the resolution of that issue, the population of *eligible* students doubled for the simple reason that half of all Jews—women—who had been refused consideration in the past now could apply for admission. But rather than see a dramatic rise in the numbers of applicants, these schools have experienced plummeting enrollments over the course of the past few decades. In September 2015, all the non-Orthodox rabbinical seminaries in the United States *combined* enrolled fewer than one hundred *entering* students, a figure dwarfed by admissions at the same schools before women were admitted.[40] Matters are even worse in synagogues: battles have raged about the inclusion of women, the LGBTQ community, and inter-married families. Now that these questions have been largely resolved across the board in non-Orthodox synagogues, all the evidence suggests that the number of regular attendees is down and fewer members observe even the most popular of Jewish rituals—attending a Seder and lighting Hanukkah candles, let alone the more demanding practices.

The new openness is *not* the cause of declining numbers. But despite the great emphasis on inclusiveness and despite the considerable creativity un-leashed by the expanded roles of women and other previously marginalized groups, it is a fact that Jewish religious life attracts a smaller proportion of the Jewish populace. The very public battles over inclusion have been *neces-sary*, but their resolution has hardly been *sufficient* to address subterranean developments eroding Jewish religious life.

What might the movements learn from the experience of the past few decades? First, they might disabuse themselves of the notion that their ideo-logical pronouncements make much of an impact on average Jews or even synagogue leaders. Particularly in the current age of hyper-individualism and declining authority, members of synagogues are not going to toe a line prescribed by a distant denominational office. Only the encounter with clergy and fellow Jews in their own social networks is likely to effect changes in be-havior. Second, the dabbling of the denominations in public policy matters of little direct connection to Jewish life is at best of little importance to the average Jew, and at worst a cause of resentment to those who dissent from positions espoused by their movements in their name. Instead, a clearer focus on their religious mission might energize these denominations so that they actually serve as movements rather than trade organizations.

And what is that mission? Above all it is to serve as the conscience of their constituents, reminding those who attend to the day-to-day affairs of con-gregations to keep their eyes on larger goals. To do so, the denominations may have to dispense with snappy "branding," and to reimagine themselves as something more than political sloganeers. They will need instead to speak the truth about perennial challenges.

None of those challenges is more important than the responsibility to educate and socialize young people as future adherents of their denomination. How ironic, then, that both the Reform and Conservative synagogue arms have drastically cut back on educational services and seem so blasé about the low proportion of teens who enroll in their movements' youth arms—and this is not to speak about the vacuum they have left on college campuses. They will also have to pay more attention to linking the generations in order to enable Jews of all ages to participate in the task of socializing young Jews as adherents of Judaism and active members of the Jewish people. And they will have to offer educational programming so that "lifelong Jewish learning" is an actual option in their synagogues. These may not be sexy initiatives, but if the denominational arms ignore them, who will make the case for their importance?

The denominational arms also have a role to play as the conscience of their movement by reminding local congregations about the long-term needs of the American Jewish collective. Synagogue leaders understandably worry about the fiscal health of their own institutions. They may pay far less attention to the *needs* of Jews in their community, including those who are not members. Slashing programs that draw only small groups, or failing to budget for programs that bring in nonmembers like millennials, may seem fiscally prudent but are shortsighted in their obliviousness to the missed opportunities to engage Jews who currently are not members but may well be drawn into active participation if given the chance. The denominational offices have a role to play in educating synagogue boards about long-term considerations that go beyond the bottom line.

There's also a role to be played by the denominations as conveners of high-level discussions and research about ways to strengthen Jewish life today. Rabbi Dan Ehrenkrantz, former president of the Reconstructionist Rabbinical College, put it well in defining the proper role of the movements: "Jewish institutions . . . should be evaluated based on their missions and visions and their successes and failures in bringing their visions to life."[41] Denominations have access to powerful technologies to facilitate conversations. They should be harnessing the new social media to involve their members in discussions about the deeper questions of belief, practice, and participation facing today's Jews.

Finally, the movements need to focus on raising funds and then directing them to initiatives that further their missions. The movements have been starved for funds because they have not persuaded donors of the importance of what they do and the efficacy of new initiatives. If the Reform movement has decided its summer camps are the key to an educational renewal of their young people, its national institutions should be raising the money to make it possible for all interested families to send their children to those camps. (Both the Reform and Conservative movements take great pride in their camping systems, but inexplicably seem satisfied to attract only an estimated 8 to 10 percent of their potential pool of children.) If the Conservative movement identifies Jewish day schools as the best vehicle for nurturing literate and observant young Jews, it ought to marshal the resources to help those schools rather than allowing them to flounder on their own or, in the case of over two dozen, to sink. The movements also ought to identify new initiatives to help underserved populations—teens who participate in youth movement programs at embarrassingly low rates, college students who receive little attention and even less support from their movements, the disengaged millennials who have at best an episodic connection to Jewish life. Perhaps by demonstrating their capacity for getting these kinds of things done, the movements will make it self-evident why they still are needed.

PART III

Where Religious Renewal Flourishes

8

NOT YOUR GRANDPARENTS'
SYNAGOGUE

In recent decades, conventional wisdom in leadership circles of the American Jewish community has singled out synagogues as an unlikely place to look if one wants to find a flourishing Jewish religious life. In the often self-serving telling of those who are promoting alternative religious settings, Jewish congregations are moribund, interested primarily in their own self-preservation, rather than the promotion of a living, passionate Jewish life. Symptomatic of how the synagogue is discussed, a panelist speaking to Jewish activists of the millennial generation asked his audience, "How many of you think the davening [prayer] at your congregation is really awesome?" When only a handful of people raised their hands, the speaker pounced: "Why would I come to your congregation to participate in worship that even you find uninspiring?"[1] At least three assumptions are embedded in this vignette: synagogue services need to be "awesome," and if they are not then they are "uninspiring"; the only possible reason to attend a synagogue is to have an extraordinary experience; and imposing such high expectations upon synagogue services, week in, week out, is reasonable. It's hard to think of another institution in Jewish life held to such unrealistic standards.

It's not that all the criticism directed at synagogues in recent decades is wrong.[2] Public worship in many synagogues *had* become stale and routinized. Attendance was declining. And as the wider culture has changed its expectations of what a house of worship should properly offer, many synagogues were insufficiently nimble to "get with the program." But the criticism was and continues to be overwrought because it assumes that what turns Jews off stems necessarily from the shortcomings of synagogues, rather than from wider patterns of disconnection evident across American society. The phenomenon captured by Robert Putnam in his landmark study *Bowling Alone* has been widely noted, and its consequences are evident in the decline of all kinds of American institutions where "social capital" is at a premium. Across the board, American institutions have trouble retaining members and attracting people on a more than sporadic basis. Why would synagogues be different?

Equally important, whatever the merit of criticism leveled at synagogues in the recent past, it is now outdated because of the considerable efforts invested to reshape religious services in all kinds of congregations. Compared to just a few decades ago, most synagogues are very different places today. As will become evident in the coming pages, much thought, creativity, and financial investment have gone into transforming the core functions of synagogue life.

The House of Prayer—Beit Tefila

Even upon superficial examination, it is evident that a good many synagogue sanctuaries *look* different today. Some synagogues have gone so far as to renovate their buildings to accommodate smaller, more intimate prayer settings. An observer of congregational trends reported that it had become impossible to keep count of the number of congregations "that are lowering their *bimah* or removing their fixed seats so that people can sit in a semicircle and see one another, rather than sitting in long, straight rows."[3] One Reform temple replaced its sanctuary, which had once seated two thousand members, with two large rooms that would work well on ordinary Sabbaths.[4] Some Conservative synagogues have reconfigured their sanctuary space so that the *shaliach tzibbur*, the prayer leader, now stands in the midst of the congregation, rather than on a stage in front of the congregation. In a related move, rabbis and cantors in many synagogues make a point of sitting within the assembled congregation, rather than on the bimah where they otherwise would hover above and far away from the worshippers. Even a number of congregations that have not undertaken new construction have moved their smaller services into rooms that allow for informal seating arrangements: moveable chairs make it possible to adjust the seating configuration depending on the numbers of people attending. All of these physical changes to the prayer settings have been made in order to create a more intimate, interactive, and warm ambience.

The smaller worship spaces, in turn, have made it possible to provide a variety of religious services within one congregation—in the words of one such Reform temple, affording "multiple worship opportunities." This reflects a desire to cater to the different tastes and needs of individual members.[5] Conservative synagogues, for example, offer concurrent services on Friday nights and Saturday mornings geared to those seeking either a more traditional service or a more experimental one, to those who wish, or don't wish, to have a service accompanied by musical instrument. On Sabbath mornings, larger Conservative synagogues may have as many as five or six concurrent services, including Tot Shabbat, youth and teen services, and several minyanim for adults.[6]

In the Orthodox orbit, multiple prayer services have proliferated less because they offer variety than to address changing and increased demands. As rising numbers of Orthodox Jews have spent time studying at yeshivas and seminaries in Israel, they became accustomed to praying three times a day, every day; as a result, Orthodox synagogues, which a generation ago might have had trouble rounding up ten men for a weekday minyan, may have a hundred or more attendees for morning and afternoon/evening prayers.[7] Some young women, having adopted the same regimen, now attend weekday services, a phenomenon virtually unknown in previous generations, and one sometimes requiring rearrangement of the prayer room to provide a screened-off space for the female participants.

Explaining why his congregation sponsors *seven* separate Shabbat morning services attracting thirteen hundred worshippers on a regular Sabbath, and *five* separate services on weekday mornings, the rabbi of Young Israel of Woodmere explained: "People come from different homes, different traditions. People studied in different schools. Some people like a smaller minyan. Some people like a bigger minyan. Some people like a quicker minyan."[8] A popular alternative for those interested in a faster pace than offered in the main sanctuary is the so-called *hashkamah* or early morning minyan that begins at seven thirty or eight in the morning, an hour or more before the regular service. Dispensing with sermons and other time fillers and zipping along at a brisk pace, the hashkamah minyan resembles the yeshiva prayer service many men encountered during their gap year in Israel.

There are some downsides to the multiplication of services under one roof. For one thing, fragmentation can diminish allegiance to the synagogue itself, which in turn can affect the cohesiveness of the entire congregation, not to speak of raising money. "The fund-raisers can't give the same pitch. It's easier for people to say, 'I gave at the other minyan.' There's not that critical mass," argues one observer. Also, rivalries can erupt between competing services. Still, many synagogues have concluded that the risk is worth taking because members enjoy the intimacy of smaller services and the enhanced opportunities for active lay participation. To counter the dangers, some congregations have instituted a kiddush buffet (after services) to bring everyone together and maintain a sense of common purpose.[9] In an era when Americans demand multiple options, alternative minyanim provide points of entry for Jews seeking different styles of religious services.

As for the worship services themselves, both Reform and Conservative clergy invest a good deal of effort in scripting precisely how things will be done each week. Reform rabbis, particularly, invoke the language of "high production values" when they describe the care they take to ensure that the music, choreography, and sermon are all integrated into a well-produced and fresh service, with all the components bound together by a common theme. Knowing that they have people for only one hour once a week at the Friday evening service, they leave little to chance.

Unquestionably, the greatest effort goes into enlivening the services with music. Liturgical music, as we have already noted in chapter 4, has assumed a central place not only in the Reform movement's "prayer revolution,"[10] but in all kinds of synagogues. The importance of music was articulated by a Modern Orthodox rabbi, who wrote:

Nothing . . . comes close to the power of communal song. The energy that fills the room when all of the voices have joined as one is incomparable.

Achieving this does require a rigid insistence that all of those who want to lead services comply with the communal singing standard, and the synagogue must provide opportunities for training. But the benefit in terms of renewal of interest and active participation in prayer is enormous.[11]

Few who are engaged in synagogue revitalization would disagree, and it is therefore no accident that congregations of all kinds have developed new approaches to music in order to overcome sterility and rote renditions of prayer services.

For some congregations on the more traditional end of the spectrum, the music of Shlomo Carlebach has offered a new way: "Call it Modern Orthodoxy meets the holy rollers—a joyous, some say ecstatic, Judaism," wrote one journalist of Carlebach's "heart-stirring melodies."[12] In Conservative synagogues Hasidic *niggunim*, wordless songs, are introduced to infuse even more music into the service and perhaps make the setting more comfortable for those who find it difficult to recite the Hebrew liturgy. For their part, Orthodox synagogues draw eclectically upon music popularized in Israeli yeshivas, Hasidic circles, and elsewhere, which are then adapted to accompany the liturgy. In all kinds of synagogues, music is deliberately used to stimulate spirited singing by the congregation.

Reform temples and some Conservative synagogues, as already noted, employ musical instruments to stir all participants—clergy and congregants alike—to engage in spirited prayer. Many Reform temples try to offer a different musical sound each week of the month. On one Friday evening, the prayers may be accompanied by rock music, on another week by jazz, on a third by a guitar and folk music, and on a fourth by more traditional cantorial music. Some Reform temples even like to revert to the "High Church" style of the past, occasionally trotting out the long-discarded Union Prayer Book that was in vogue during the first half of the twentieth century, accompanied by organ music. In all of these different types of services, laypeople are given the opportunity to perform and even showcase their own compositions. To hear Reform rabbis tell it, the quality of the music, the choreographing of where clergy stand and how they sing together, the ambience they hope to create all are born of hours of staff meetings devoted to deliberate planning.

As part of their effort to invigorate the services, many congregations encourage members to get into the rhythm of things by clapping, swaying, and expressing their fervor in other physical ways. In line with that approach, dancing is encouraged if the spirit moves congregants. In Orthodox synagogues, men will dance around the *shulchan* (table) where the Torah is read to celebrate a joyous occasion, and the same is likely to occur in Conservative synagogues, except that women join in too. Especially on Friday evenings, welcoming the Sabbath may be accompanied by snake dancing lines. Nothing better highlights how far synagogues have traveled from their earlier emphasis on strict decorum. The staid prayer customs of the past have been replaced by an effort to stimulate participation, emotional connection, and *ruah* (spirited worship).

This shift has been most dramatic in Reform temples, where in the past congregants were figuratively locked into fixed pews. Now Reform rabbis proudly speak of encouraging their congregants to move around and become part of the action. One rabbi, for example, describes how on Rosh Hashanah, thirty shofar blowers are stationed throughout the building in order to make it possible for congregants to gather around the nearest one. Similarly, multiple Torah reading stations are placed throughout the synagogue and congregants are invited to encircle the readers. The goal is to draw congregants into close proximity and thereby bridge the distance between officiants and congregants.

Toward that same end, Conservative and Orthodox synagogues encourage members to help lead parts of the service. In both types of synagogues, congregants not only read Torah but also serve as prayer leaders. A fair number of Conservative synagogues have dispensed with a cantor, relying upon congregants to play that role—or as is more often the case, expecting the rabbis to lead services. Orthodox synagogues have come the farthest distance in this regard. Gone are the days when they conducted their Sabbath and festival services with pomp, relied upon star cantors, and featured a sermon with suitable oratorical pyrotechnics.[13] Today, laymen rather than professional cantors lead the prayers, generally in the style of the yeshiva world. And, given the sophistication of many of the members, pulpit rabbis can no longer get away with conventionally edifying sermons, and so they either deliver talks that are highly textually based or offer critiques of what are perceived as pervasive problems in the community, such as the evils of gossip and the dangers of family strife.

This, in turn, brings us to the creative ways rabbis and cantors have developed to move their congregants during the prayer services. On Yom Kippur, a Reform rabbi prepared her congregations for the Yizkor memorial service not by offering a sermon, but by encouraging them to engage in a meditation exercise. She asked them to visualize being in a garden with a loved one who is no longer alive: "What do you want to talk about and tell the person? What do they want to tell you that they hadn't ever said?" "People sobbed," the rabbi reports. Another rabbi invites congregants to hand in cards anonymously before Yom Kippur in which they confess their sins. On Kol Nidre evening, she then reads aloud the anonymously written pleas for forgiveness offered by congregants who have embezzled money, engaged in infidelity, or acted abusively. Still another Reform rabbi invited congregants to toss cards containing sins for which they seek forgiveness into a figurative pyre in the synagogue during the part of the Yom Kippur service devoted to the sacrifices offered by the High Priest in Jerusalem's temple to atone for the sins of his community. A Conservative synagogue offers a less fraught example: it invites a few congregants to speak publicly about the personal meaning a section of the High Holiday liturgy holds for them. In all these instances, the goal is to encourage congregants to get in touch with emotions that may lie deeply buried and to connect to those feelings during the prayers. The risk, of course, is that such exercises may come across to some as voyeuristic, highly intrusive, or just plain melodramatic; the benefit is they may help bring the prayer services to life for congregants.

Even a somewhat safer exercise can be seen as going too far. One Rosh Hashanah, a Reform rabbi invited congregants to speak before each shofar blast about what they intend to do over the coming year about three issues the rabbi felt ought to be uppermost when entering into the New Year—gun violence, gay rights, and human trafficking. The latter topic proved so unsettling to young people in the sanctuary that the rabbi publicly apologized for having created "an unsafe space for children" by raising the topic of contemporary slavery. Still, she adds unrepentantly, "tradition is there to support us but we do what we need to do to bring it alive." Needless to say, this kind of emphasis is designed not to foster a sense of connection to other Jews but to rally people to support a cause or spur introspection and evoke deeply personal responses.

Nowhere is this turn to the personal during worship services more evident than in the nearly universal foregrounding of a petitionary prayer, asking God to fulfill one's needs. Such prayers have always been part of the traditional liturgy, but over the past two decades or so congregations of every stripe have come to emphasize one particular prayer—the *mi sheberach* blessing for the sick. Matters were not always so. In Reconstructionist and Reform synagogues the prayer had long been anathema—in the former because the movement's theology denied the prayer's underlying assumption of a personal God directly involved in the lives of people, and in the latter because classical Reform services had no place for individual prayers. But with the setting of the mi sheberach to the music of Debbie Friedman, it has become ubiquitous in Reform temples and even among Reconstructionists. Today, even in most Orthodox congregations, worshippers line up to ensure that a synagogue functionary will include the names of friends and relatives who are ill when the petitionary prayer is recited, or, as in virtually every Conservative synagogue, members stand at their seats and state the name of the sick person at the appropriate spot in the communal prayer.

It would make for a fascinating study to understand why this once fairly obscure prayer has assumed such importance and ubiquity: Is it because more people are living with illness? Has research on the efficacy of prayer inspired people to participate?[14] Is the mi sheberach popular precisely because it is both highly personal and universal?[15] What is beyond dispute is that the prayer for healing gives expression to the quest for personal "meaning" in congregational worship, and illustrates the commitment of synagogues to touch congregants' lives.[16]

House of Study—Beit Midrash

In addition to their role as places of worship, synagogues also have served as houses of study. Traditionally, synagogues offered males the opportunity to study a classical text because such learning was regarded as a religious activity. Indeed, the study sessions would conclude with the *kaddish derabanan*, a prayer devised by the rabbis to sanctify the act of study. To this day, Orthodox synagogues and some Conservative ones conclude study sessions with the recitation of this Kaddish.

For the most part, though, synagogues currently sponsor classes for less religiously explicit reasons.[17] They regard themselves as educational institutions about all kinds of topics, and frankly also realize that offering classes and lectures is a way to bring people into the building. Indeed, a study of adult Jewish education found that the synagogue is the most commonly utilized site for such classes, followed by Jewish community centers.[18]

In all kinds of synagogues, it has become part of accepted synagogue culture for people of all ages to engage in learning. This may take the form of skill building, such as classes in reading Hebrew, Torah cantillation, kosher cooking, or crafting Jewish ritual objects. Reform and Conservative synagogues offer intensive adult Bar/Bat Mitzvah programs for those who never received a strong education when they were young. They also educate far more non-Jews than in the past, particularly parents who are raising their children as Jews and want guidance about the teachings of Judaism. And congregations of all kinds offer a multiplicity of opportunities to study texts, with classes on the weekly Torah portion, Talmud, Jewish history, and Jewish customs and practices among the most popular.

None of this is especially new. But what does set the current programs apart is their greater emphasis on teaching skills for practicing Judaism outside the synagogue. A number of Reform Temples and Conservative synagogues have gone so far as to reconfigure their congregational schooling so that it includes a significant amount of practical information for implementation at home. Parents and children together learn how to prepare the Sabbath table for a Friday night dinner, how to recite the Havdala at the end of the Sabbath, how to cook traditional foods for the Sabbath and holidays, and so on.[19]

Perhaps, the most novel of such "how to" classes are ones devoted to exploring how to pray. Rabbis who have participated in programs focused on their own meditation and prayer practices are experimenting with ways of sharing with interested congregants what they have learned. Some have en-rolled their congregations in a program named Prayer as Practice that brings experienced educators to their synagogue. The underlying assumption of this and other programs is that prayer requires practice and focus; it is an ac-quired skill, not an innate one for most people.[20]

Yet another characteristic of current educational trends in synagogues is the commitment to breaking down the walls separating the classroom wing of the building and the sanctuary. This is not literally the goal, but figura-tively synagogues are working to integrate education so that it is not seen solely as an activity for children. To the contrary, congregational school-ing strives to involve parents in educational efforts and the sanctuary is no longer regarded as an adults-only domain. Reform and Conservative syna-gogues alike run programs leading up to the Bar/Bat Mitzvah that are de-signed to engage parents and their children in Jewish study.[21] They are work-ing to undo what one Reform rabbi has described as the dry cleaning model of Judaism—"drop the kids off; the synagogue makes them Jewish; and the parents then pick them up."

To overcome this mentality, growing numbers of congregations run fam-ily education programs.[22] The logic behind this approach is to involve the family as a partner in the process of Jewish education. This means, notes the principal at a Reform temple, that "if your goal through family education is to have an impact on the ways families are Jewish together, then you have to be with the family together."[23] This family-oriented approach represents a break from the past in how synagogue educators viewed their role and mobi-lized parents as allies.

Synagogues work not only to bring parents into the school, but also to engage children in the religious life of the congregation outside of the school. Symptomatically, rabbis in all the denominations have been appeal-ing to congregants to welcome children into the sanctuary rather than ban-ish them to youth services. "These young kids who come to shul are learning to be shul-goers," wrote Rabbi Eliezer Havivi, a Conservative rabbi, to his congregants, "and they and their parents are the future of our congregation, and of the Jewish people. If they go only to Junior Congregation, they'll think that that's all there is."[24] Adds his colleague, Rabbi Menachem Creditor: "A sanctuary is not a sanctuary from children. It is a sanctuary we've built for our children, and their children after them."[25] Such a perspective is vastly different from the formal approach to synagogue decorum that once dominated. It stems from an understanding of how habituation and a sense of comfort within the synagogue sanctuary are critical in the formation of future synagogue participants.

A number of congregations go considerably further by involving youth in leading the services. This, of course, is on display in almost all synagogues when a Bar or Bat Mitzvah celebrant plays a central role in the proceedings. Not a few synagogues also invite specific grades to lead the services several times a year, in part to teach the youngsters about the liturgy and in even larger measure to attract their parents to the synagogue on those occasions to observe their children "perform." Some congregations go further and involve students in the congregational school on a regular basis in leading the services. Often, such an approach is born as much of necessity as of an educational philosophy: smaller congregations need teens to help make the minyan and lead the services. This is why a small Conservative synagogue in the Midwest launched its Shabbat School. By meeting on the Sabbath, the school could bring students and their parents together in the synagogue on the Sabbath, and in the process enable students to enact during the services what they were learning in the school. Through a deliberate effort on the part of the rabbi and lay leadership, a cadre of young people was prepared to lead the prayer services—no small achievement.[26]

Synagogues that take social action seriously regard their efforts in this realm as educational too. Congregations of all stripes sponsor a range of activities designed to model behavior and engage their members in programs to aid other Jews and/or the broader communities in which they live. In more traditionally oriented congregations, these programs range from providing clothing and food for impoverished Jews to organizing visits to members of the community who are ill to raising money for Jewish institutions in this country and abroad. As one moves across the spectrum from Orthodox to Reform, the programming of congregations becomes less parochial. On the left of the spectrum, synagogues might involve their members in soup kitchens and shelters for battered women, create a market for selling organic food, engage in a blood drive, and organize members to volunteer at agencies for the needy and sick. Rabbis and other synagogue leaders freely concede they are intentionally widening the scope of their work in order to bring in Jews who are not interested in the traditional activities of synagogues—prayer and education. "For better or worse, American Jews of my age," said one thirty-something rabbi, "have for the most part not grown up davening [praying]. Only a certain number of people will be attracted to synagogue for three hours of praying on a Saturday morning." Yet even in congregations where prayer is not a foreign experience, leaders are intentionally sponsoring a range of so-called tikkun olam initiatives out of a clear understanding that synagogues teach members how to act responsibly and thereby they build social capital.[27]

Education of a different sort occurs when synagogues engage with hotly contested social issues. Social policy questions stirring debate within the larger society have impinged on synagogue life, most obviously through changing social attitudes regarding feminism and sexual orientation. These and other issues have spurred rabbis and educators in synagogues to explore how Jewish texts approach such matters. There are serious questions to be asked about how politicized and ideological discussions in synagogues ought to be: such engagement may please some, but can alienate others and certainly may detract from the core mission of synagogues. But some contemporary hot topics impinge directly on how the synagogue conducts its ritual life, and these are much harder to sidestep. Surveying the world of American synagogues at the end of the twentieth century, the anthropologist Riv-Ellen Prell assessed the impact of these controversies:

> Since the 1970s, the synagogue has been anything but an uncontested bedrock of American Jewish life. . . . Synagogues . . . have been responsive to cultural and social change and the challenges posed. Rabbis have fought aggressively on all sides of issues to allow their synagogues to reflect passionately held principles about gender equality, the rights of homosexual Jews, access of the intermarried, and the maintenance of Halakhah. Thus, there has been nothing bland about American synagogues. To the contrary, they have become important testing grounds, even battlegrounds, for shaping American Judaism.[28]

Assuming the accuracy of this assessment, perhaps it's time to reconsider whether synagogues are as boring, lifeless, and moribund as their critics have suggested.

Israel in the Religious Life of Synagogues

If the synagogue continues to be a testing ground for the shaping of Judaism, one of the most contested issues confronting Jewish religious institutions in recent years has been Israel. As recently as fifteen years ago, this observation would have been shocking. Full-throated support for Israel was a given in Jewish religious institutions at least since the Six-Day War in 1967, and in many cases well before the establishment of the state. In recent years, though, Israel has become a divisive topic in some congregations, leading Jews to resign their membership and in other cases creating deep rifts among congregants—and between some congregants and their rabbis.

Before turning to instances of conflict, we note that Israel has served as a point of consensus among American Jews during the second half of the twentieth century—and in many congregations to the present day. True, some peripheral groups in the Reform movement and the Haredi worlds distanced themselves from Israel. But the mainstream movements and their synagogues staunchly and openly advocated on its behalf. At times of war in Israel, American synagogues served as marshaling grounds for massive fund-raising campaigns on behalf of the Jewish state. As recently as the mid-1990s, an Israeli historian observed: "It is justified to speak about a Zionized American Jewry represented in large measure by its religious movements."[29] The truth of that observation was evident in the pronouncements of the three major religious movements, the advocacy work they supported, the Jewish educational programming they sponsored, and the activities of their synagogues.[30]

Indeed, Israel has literally been put on display in synagogues of all kinds. Many congregations place the Israeli and American flags in the front of their sanctuary or social hall. For a period of time, it was popular to face parts of the buildings, particularly sanctuaries, in Jerusalem stone.[31] Synagogue displays often include photographs of members taken during group trips to Israel. Not to be overlooked are Israeli-imported *kippot* (skull caps) and *talitot* (prayer shawls) donned by worshippers. And then there are the gift shops, which, in the words of one historian, "introduced countless American Jews to Israeli culture and life."[32] Not a few synagogues publicize their connection to Israel by posting large signs on their grounds announcing, "We Stand with Israel."

No less important, in virtually every non-Orthodox synagogue prayers are pronounced in Israeli Hebrew—or at least in Sephardi Hebrew. Few American Jews have mastered the precise Israeli inflection, but Ashkenazi pronunciation has virtually disappeared, despite the fact that the preponderant majority of American Jews descend from Ashkenazi families.[33] Sephardi Hebrew is so ubiquitous that few can even remember when congregations altered their practices. Of course, it had taken decades for the changeover to occur, but in the 1960s and 1970s, *Shabbos* became *Shabbat*, *Gut Yontif* became *hag sameah*, and the Sephardi pronunciation became ubiquitous in non-Orthodox synagogues. For their part, Orthodox synagogues continue to adhere to the Ashkenazi pronunciation even today, mainly because so many of their members attended US and Israeli yeshivas where the pronunciation of prayers and other religious texts has continued to be Ashkenazi—even though it is not uncommon to hear Sephardi Hebrew in such synagogues as well.

Music has served as still another means to connect worshippers in synagogues to Israel. It has become common for Sabbath and festival prayers to be sung to the melodies of Israeli songs. Writing of his upbringing in an Orthodox synagogue during the 1950s, Lawrence Grossman recalled that "the *hazzan*, on festivals, would chant the prayer '*ve-havienau le-tzion berinah*' ('bring us to Zion in joy') and the subsequent request for the restoration of the sacrificial system to the tune of *Hatikvah*, and the congregation would spontaneously rise."[34] Other examples of this same tendency in synagogues of all stripes are the singing of a passage from the *Kedushah*, the focal point of the cantor's recital of the service, to the tune of the (formerly) popular Israeli song "Erev shel Shoshanim," and setting the words of the liturgy appealing to God to return to Jerusalem ("*veliyerushalyim ircha berahamim tashuv*") to the iconic Naomi Shemer song of 1967, "Jerusalem of Gold." Up to the present day, cantors and prayer leaders routinely adapt the words of the prayers to Israeli pop tunes, melodies composed for Israeli song festivals, niggunim (wordless melodies) composed in Israeli yeshivas and Yemenite, or other Middle Eastern Jewish tunes that arrive via Israel.

Prayers specifically for Israel are often offered at dramatic and very public moments of the religious service, underscoring even more that country's significance. The prime example is the *Tefila Li'shlom Ha-Medinah* (Prayer for the Welfare of the State), recited in many synagogues just after the Torah reading and before the return of the Torah scroll(s) to the ark on the Sabbath and festival days. In many congregations, it is customary to stand during its recitation.[35] Most controversially, it begins and ends with messianic overtones, referring to the establishment of the state as the "first flowering of our redemption," and concluding with an explicit plea for the arrival of the Messiah "to redeem those who long for Your salvation." The prayer was adopted in its totality by Modern Orthodox congregations, but Haredi congregations of the Agudath Israel outlook, not to speak of Hasidic ones, refrain from reciting it due to its messianic overtones.[36] Conservative, Reform, and Reconstructionist prayer books offer abridged versions, and the prayer's messianic and militaristic references have occasioned fresh debate among non-Orthodox Jews in recent years, too.[37]

Israel figures in the liturgies of the various movements in other ways as well. In every service, the traditional prayer book asserts the sanctity of the land of Israel and the historical aspiration for a Jewish return to Zion, and Modern Orthodox congregations unself-consciously apply the themes to contemporary Israel.[38] Reform, Reconstructionist, and Conservative prayer books have reworked such references in keeping with the theological outlook each movement takes toward the current reality of Israel. Summing up his survey of these revisions, David Ellenson, a leading scholar of American Judaism, concludes:

> The exclusively nationalistic or secular elements of the Zionist dream and contemporary incarnation of those political elements in the state are underplayed, if not entirely rejected. . . . Universalism informs and animates this vision of the Jewish state, a vision that is highly consonant with the American and Diasporan context that inspired it.[39]

Since American Jewish religious movements express through liturgy both their religious conceptions of Israel and their self-understanding as American Jews, those attending synagogues of all stripes are exposed to repeated reminders of Israel's religious significance.

In addition, many synagogues hold special services in honor of Israel. These include celebrations of *Yom Ha'Atzma'ut* (Israel Independence Day) and *Yom Yerushalayim* (Jerusalem Day, marking the city's unification in 1967). *Hatikvah*, the national anthem of Israel, and popular Israeli tunes are sung on such occasions, and some celebrations also feature Israeli-style foods. Many synagogues recite special prayers for Israel and host guest speakers on Israeli subjects. On the more somber side, some American congregations mark the eve of Israel Independence Day with a special service to mourn those who lost their lives in Israeli wars. Tisha B'Av, the fast day commemorating the destruction of the two temples and loss of Jewish sovereignty in ancient times, is marked in traditional synagogues with prayers for the restoration of that sovereignty, and non-Orthodox congregations as well sometimes incorporate Israel into the day's services.[40]

Most conspicuously, Israel figures in synagogues through the countless sermons offered by rabbis and articles in congregational bulletins. Sometimes these are occasioned by newsworthy events occurring in the Middle East, the anniversary of Israel's founding, or the presence of an eminent Israeli guest. It is of significance that appeals for Israel are often delivered on the High Holidays when the greatest number of Jews attend synagogue services.[41]

While all of these trends persist in most congregations, public discussions of Israel have become more fraught in some synagogues (and other Jewish institutions) over the past two decades. As has been documented by a series of surveys, segments of the American Jewish population are fractured over Israeli policies. A minority of Jews show evidence of "distancing" themselves from Israel, though observers are divided as to whether the increasing proportion of Jews who claim to feel distant from Israel as one moves from older to younger age groups represents a sea change in attitudes toward Israel or a tendency of younger Jews to harbor more critical attitudes toward Israel's treatment of Palestinians, which modulates as they grow older.[42] Regardless of the longer term implications, congregants are divided and what once was a surefire feel-good sermon topic for rabbis is now a third rail to be avoided. An online survey completed by some 550 rabbis in 2013 found that one in five feared some kind of sanction or retribution from their congregants for voicing their "honest opinions about Israel or particular government policies." A similar percentage also indicated they have been "strongly criticized . . . for views [they] have voiced on Israel." In turn, this has affected the programming these rabbis are prepared to organize.[43]

A second issue of no less potency concerns the status of non-Orthodox groups in Israel. That the Israeli religious establishment acknowledges only Orthodox rabbis has long served as an irritant. It has come to symbolize the lack of legitimacy accorded to non-Orthodox Jews, as is evident in the transformation of the Western Wall into a Haredi-controlled Orthodox synagogue and the continuing denigration of non-Orthodox versions of Judaism—in word and practice. The lack of Israeli government funding for non-Orthodox synagogues is a further cause for dismay. And then the ugly incidents at the Western Wall itself where women have been attacked both verbally and physically for holding their own services further inflame a wide swath of American Jews.[44] News stories about these developments inevitably filter back into synagogues, often reported by rabbis from the pulpit.

The upshot is a good deal of restiveness if not resentment in the pews of non-Orthodox synagogues.[45] In a minority of synagogues, the leadership has opted to forbid sermons about Israel entirely, lest such public discussions erupt into ugly arguments among congregants. In others, rabbis continue to speak about Israel but the thrust of their remarks is about how American Jews have to find ways to get along with one another and fashion responsible and respectful ways to engage with the topic.[46] Israel has not disappeared from synagogue life, but as a matter of public discussion it is handled in a gingerly fashion.[47]

What this means for the long-term attachment of American Jews to Israel is hard to predict. But the obverse side of this issue is no less important: What does it mean for Jewish religious life in this country if Israel is regarded as a third rail to be avoided? Perhaps the focus of attention will shift to other causes, such as tikkun olam or Jewish learning. Alternatively, less politicized aspects of Israel, including spiritual and religious innovations by Israelis or

Israeli cultural creativity, may become the focus. Perhaps the vacuum created when Israel is no longer such a strong focus would open space for other forms of religious renewal in synagogues and other places for congregating.

More likely, Israel will remain a central theme of sermons and its influence on the culture of synagogues will not diminish. Those congregations that banish overt discourse and symbolic references to Israel will suffer great harm because they will try to sanitize Judaism of core elements—kinship and land. What relevance would reading the Torah and latter biblical books have if Israelite origins become irrelevant? And perhaps equally important, what damage would it do to congregations were they to efface Israel, which has served as a glue unifying Jews for at least the past seventy years? For all their misgivings about particular Israeli policies, synagogue-going Jews continue to identify with the Jewish state and care about its welfare. It's hard to think of anything that arouses more passion and continuing concern.

House of Gathering—Beit Knesset

Even as they have served as places where sharply clashing views have aired, congregations simultaneously have striven to present themselves as warm and welcoming environments. Synagogues across the board are paying far more attention than in the past to the needs of individual members and hence all the talk about "inclusiveness," a term that has different meanings depending on the setting. Non-Orthodox synagogues strive to welcome Jews thought to have been marginalized—women, singles, gays and lesbians, intermarried Jews, Jews of non-Caucasian appearance. Orthodox synagogues include members who come from different backgrounds and with different experiences, and therefore have varying sets of expectations about the style and pace of religious services.

The most dramatic expression of the new inclusiveness is evident in the altered roles women have assumed since the feminist revolution of the 1970s. Where once women and girls had been relegated to a passive role, assuming no leadership responsibilities either in the sanctuary or governance spheres, they now are treated as equals of men in virtually all non-Orthodox congregations. Bar Mitzvah boys and Bat Mitzvah girls are expected to take on exactly the same responsibilities during their rites of passage, and those egalitarian assumptions persist into adulthood. Women play equal roles in board leadership, and congregations of all stripes (even Orthodox) have elected women as presidents.[48] While there is still talk of a glass ceiling for female rabbis, change appears to be in the offing in this realm too: females outnumber males as students in most rabbinical schools that accept women, a phenomenon that is even more pronounced in cantorial schools. Particularly on the West Coast, some of the largest Reform temples now are led by female rabbis and cantors, a trend that will undoubtedly make its way eastward.

The exception proves the rule: Orthodox synagogues still maintain a physical partition between the seating areas for women and men, and the focal points of worship activity—the prayer leader and the Torah reading—are situated in the men's section. It is nonetheless noteworthy how Orthodox congregations have worked to involve women in ways that are permissible within the framework of Orthodox understandings of Jewish law. When the Torah is removed and returned to the ark during services, some Modern Orthodox synagogues pass it through the women's gallery on the Sabbath and holidays, and create a place for women to dance with the Torah on Simhat Torah; some have hired women to serve as religious leaders, though lacking the formal title of rabbi; some have welcomed women's *tefila* groups into their building.

A similar revolution has brought LGBTQ Jews out of the closet and into active leadership roles in congregations. That gays and lesbians have been members of synagogues for a long time is beyond dispute, but they were expected to remain closeted. As the gay rights movement developed, around two dozen synagogues were established specifically for LGBTQ people. Now that most non-Orthodox synagogues explicitly welcome Jews regardless of sexual orientation, the future of those gay synagogues may be clouded. Though resistance is still strong in Orthodox congregations, those in the "open" camp are gradually becoming more hospitable to same-sex couples and their families.[49]

Congregations are also working to address the specific needs of other subpopulations, including those not part of a traditional Jewish family unit—singles, divorced people, widows and widowers, and intermarried Jews. Some congregations organize special support groups for the latter, where couples discuss their responses to challenges inherent in being intermarried.

As for single people, congregations have long struggled to create a welcoming environment for people who have not married or are no longer married. The tendency of synagogues is to focus mainly on families with children, as is evident from the hoopla surrounding Bar/Bat Mitzvah celebrations and child-oriented holiday celebrations, such as Purim carnivals. The consequence is that only 22 percent of single Jewish adults, according to the Pew study, claim to belong to a synagogue. Given these low numbers, congregations are concluding that they cannot afford to marginalize singles. Some run singles programs for older adults, and others provide support groups for the recently divorced. Still, the pediatric mission of many synagogues gets in the way of fully integrating single adults.[50]

Attracting younger Jews who may not have married or do not have children has become a goal of some congregations. Generally, the synagogues most willing to invest in such efforts are in urban centers where large numbers of millennials have settled. One of the most successful synagogue programs for this age group, the Riverway Project, is run by Temple Israel in Boston, a Reform synagogue. Its success stems from the willingness of its leadership to go outside the walls of the synagogue to meet millennials where they live. "We're continually trying to be a synagogue without walls," says the rabbi who currently runs the program. "I'll go anywhere and I'll meet with anyone who's curious. It entails a whole lot of creativity and a decent amount of risk. A bar is not my favorite place to pray, but we went there last year and we're going there two times this year."[51] In Dallas, Sheerith Israel, a Conservative synagogue, created a program called Makom, which has grown to serve some fifteen hundred young Jewish professionals.[52] Like the Riverway Project, it aims to "take the synagogue outside the synagogue, free it outside the walls of the building, and bring it to the streets," said the founding rabbi. Among its most successful programs is a Friday night service welcoming the Sabbath, followed by a dinner served in a loft.

Sinai congregation in Los Angeles, a Conservative synagogue, offers a different model, one focused on once-a-month Friday evening services. Led until recently by Rabbi David Wolpe and Craig Taubman, a musician, the Friday Night Live aims to "create an experiential take on the Friday night service . . . offering a concert experience with unique, melodic interpreta-

tions of traditional prayers, special guests, a short sermon and a social component—a singles event for young professionals at the end of every service."
In its heyday, some fifteen hundred millennials attended the services.[53] Still a
different model has been tried by the Sutton Place Synagogue in Manhattan.
In partnership with several suburban Conservative synagogues, this congregation offers programs for millennials whose home congregations want to
ensure they have a place in the city to participate in synagogue life.[54] Though
these types of programs have proved a success, they are also controversial in
synagogues because of the costs they incur to host nonmembers. They do so
out of a commitment to the larger community. Fortunately, some attendees
eventually join the sponsoring synagogues, and some become leaders.

Of late, some synagogues have focused special attention on their population of older adults in recognition of their unique needs. A Conservative congregation in Maryland, for example, installed moveable chairs to permit the
widening of aisles in order to accommodate walkers and wheelchairs. It also
streams the rabbi's classes online for those members who lack the mobility to
come in person to the synagogue but wish to continue their Jewish education.
Some Conservative congregations run cultural programs specifically for their
older members. Even more ambitiously, Central Synagogue, a Reform temple
in Manhattan, has run discussion groups on what Rabbi Rachel Cowan refers
to as the "spiritual agenda" of older adults, "many of whom are battling with
questions of identity as they retire, live with loss, and adjust their priorities."[55]

Informing all of these efforts is a desire to forge what is often described as
a "caring community" built on relationships.[56] Congregations in all the denominations have expanded their activities for mutual support. Synagogues
now have teams of members in the health care field who serve as consultants
for fellow congregants in need; they have organized members to visit the
sick and prepare meals for the bereaved; and Hevra Kadisha groups (burial
societies) have proliferated beyond the Orthodox community.

Another dimension of the widespread effort to build caring communities
is the new emphasis on hospitality and attentiveness. Synagogues organize
welcoming squads for newcomers. Going still further, a Conservative congregation in Detroit sets aside time for a "*simha* moment," when "everyone
has the opportunity to tell the congregation something good that happened

to them during the prior week." And congregants "bless each other at the end of services. It's not quite a group hug, but it's important that you are not ignored when you come to the synagogue."[57] And at a Reform temple in Maryland, a number of services over the course of the year are set aside as "Sacred Story Shabbats," when, instead of the usual talk about a topic in the Torah portion, members narrate their personal spiritual journeys to an audience of fellow congregants. Each member focuses on a theme, such as "A Sanctuary in My Life" or "When I Have Experienced the Presence of the Divine in My Life." At the close of services, the congregation breaks into groups of ten to talk about themselves.[58] The common thread here is the attention given to individual experience in a very public setting.

To keep members in the building and encourage social "connectivity,"[59] synagogues of all kinds serve food in great abundance. Late Friday evening services routinely include a "collation" of coffee (always decaf) and pastries. On Shabbat mornings, study groups in Reform temples begin over bagels and lox. And in most synagogues, there is a kiddush collation after Sabbath morning services. The same goes for the holidays. Increasingly, congregations are introducing a "break fast" for the community of worshippers at the end of Yom Kippur. Every synagogue offers a kiddush in its Sukkah on the holiday of Sukkot. After the reading of the Scroll of Esther on Purim evening, *hamantaschen* and drinks are available; and refreshments and alcoholic beverages are to be had on Simhat Torah.[60] The communal Seder is a commonplace at many synagogues on Passover night. And then there are the light spreads available before and after committee and board meetings and educational and other programs, and the more elaborate meals prepared by women's auxiliaries for the entire congregation at all kinds of festive occasions. All of this is the source of much mirth, but in truth it is hard to find a congregation that does *not* use food as a lubricant for community building.

The Synagogue in the Context of American Religious Trends

None of this would come as big news to informed observers of Christian (and perhaps other non-Jewish) congregations in America. To begin with food, note how a student of Protestant churches describes "food-centered social events":

Church dinners and coffee hours . . . are crucial to the religious life of many Americans. For these people participating in a community is often the most important motivation for attending church, and shared meals are often more important to creating community than are shared worship experiences. The meals are a place where religious identity is shaped, community is built, and memories are created. They may not be religious, but they're not just another meal.[61]

Beyond the specific issue of food, what is noteworthy is the extent to which building community is a central preoccupation of churches, and is now driving synagogue transformation as well. Churches, too, have grown far more interested in the choreography of services, the uses of space, and, of course, music. This is how Robert Wuthnow, one of the leading students of contemporary American religious life, has described changes in Christian worship:

Some of the nation's fastest-growing churches attribute their success to what leaders enthusiastically refer to as contemporary worship. This is a distinctive innovation that has emerged largely since the mid-1970s. Pioneered by young pastors and lay volunteers at fledgling nondenominational churches, it has grown to the point that many traditional churches have started borrowing from it as well. Contemporary worship lives up to its name. It incorporates musical instruments (such as electric guitars and keyboards) and lyrics unheard of in churches a generation ago and makes use of new communication technologies such as home-produced videos and the Internet. It is meant to attract people with little interest in historic approaches to worship. Some of its advocates further distinguish it by arguing that it offers immediacy, relevancy, and intelligibility, rather than permanence, and that it is an expression of a new generation trying to find its voice in the church.[62]

It is not difficult to find strong parallels between most new trends in synagogue life and prevailing patterns in churches, from the concern with women's equality and gender-neutral language to the harnessing of new technologies for worship and study, from the quest for inclusiveness to less formal styles adopted by clergy,[63] from the growing acceptance of LGBTQ individuals to the creation of niche congregations serving specific age groups, people of the same sexual orientation, or like-minded political views, to the goal of creating "caring communities."

A recent study reports on Christian congregations that make "community building . . . an explicit focus, a subject of conversation not left to chance but carried out through organized programs":

> Beyond making some effort to care for those members who are experiencing a personal crisis, and beyond the informal groups of friends that are found in all congregations, these congregations engage in a conscious attempt to provide members with experiences of community and an opportunity to discuss what that means. There is an explicit language of community-building employed here, an elaborated discourse about what it means to be a community. This is in contrast to the family congregations, where "family" as a term is used frequently, but what it means to be a family is seldom explicitly articulated.[64]

Members of such community-building churches self-consciously refer to themselves as a "community of like-minded people" or "a caring community."[65] Is this not precisely what efforts at creating a relational Judaism promote? It is difficult to avoid concluding along with Heinrich Heine, who wrote nearly two centuries ago about his former coreligionists, "*Wie es sich christelt, juedelt es sich*"—as do the Christians, so do the Jews. Only, perhaps, in their heavy emphasis on textual study do synagogues depart very far from emerging church practices.[66]

The Limits of Synagogue Revitalization Efforts

There is much to admire in the new American bid to revitalize religious congregations, and specifically the hard work of reimagining synagogue life. Many concerned Jewish communal leaders, as we noted at the outset, regard the revival of synagogues as vital for the health and growth of the entire

Jewish enterprise. Fortunately, many synagogues are neither resting on their laurels nor resisting change. What we have surveyed should give pause to those who are convinced that synagogues are unchanging and unimaginative. Quite the contrary, to employ a term popular in the Reform movement, synagogues across the board have been undergoing a massive "revolution" in prayer and practices. That some may wish for faster change or more radical transformations does not negate the far-reaching rethinking of the religious mission congregations aim to fulfill.

Yet even as congregations experiment with the liturgy, music, and choreography of worship services, even as they expand their educational reach, and even as they work on building meaningful relationships among members, a note of caution is in order. To illustrate the nature of the dilemma, let us note one of the success stories—the now ubiquitous monthly Rock Shabbat on a Friday evening in Reform temples that attracts more worshippers than any other service, aside from those on the High Holidays. When I inquired of rabbis why they don't repeat this kind of service twice a month or weekly if it is so popular, the uniform answer was that their people will attend only once a month, at most. The obvious question to consider, then, is why these Jews are unwilling to participate more frequently. The usual answer is because synagogues are boring. But if they come once a month, does the problem lie with synagogues or has it more to do with congregants' limited attention span for matters religious, given all the other options in life? It seems infrequent synagogue attenders intentionally cap how often they will set foot in the sanctuary for services, no matter how enticingly the worship service is delivered.

What this means is that with all the considerable effort that has gone into rethinking how to engage synagogue members and enliven the religious services, in the aggregate, it seems, the needle has not moved very far. A comparison of synagogue attendance rates reported by the 1990 National Jewish Population Study and the 2013 Pew study provides a picture on the macro level of American Jewish life. It reveals four important takeaways: (1) the proportions of Conservative and Reform members who are regulars— once a week or more—have pretty much held steady; (2) the once or twice a month crowd has increased slightly in Conservative synagogues, but declined a bit in Reform temples; (3) members who attend Conservative synagogues only a few times a year and nonattenders have declined a small percentage, but the few times a year crowd in Reform temples has soared from 45 percent to 60 percent; and (4) those who attend least frequently are dropping their memberships, especially in Reform temples.[67] These trends, we should emphasize, occurred precisely during the period when efforts to transform synagogues were most intensive.

None of this negates the fact that some synagogues have done better at attracting their members to services. Undoubtedly, too, many congregations can become more appealing through greater creativity, assuming they have the resources of personnel and finances to engage in change. But perhaps synagogues have struggled to attract more regular worshippers because prayer itself is difficult, particularly for highly educated American Jews. In their study of moderately affiliated Jews who maintain some formal affiliations but are not engaged actively in Jewish life, Arnold Eisen and Steven M. Cohen identify the gap between private and public prayer as a primary challenge:

> The most striking finding of our study in connection with God and the synagogue is that, for the most part, the Jews we interviewed do not make any straightforward connection between the two. They believe in God far more than we expected, or than survey data about American Jews led us to believe. They are also surprisingly content with, and even fondly attached to their synagogues. They told us time and again that they do not come to synagogue expecting to find God there, or stay away because they do not. The words in the prayer book do not particularly interest them. The God described and invoked in those prayers is very different from the one in which they believe—too commanding, for one thing, and . . . far too "Jewish." They are distinctly uncomfortable with the act of prayer. And yet, they pray.[68]

Here, then, is the deeper dilemma facing synagogues and their members: a great many Jews have difficulty engaging in *public prayer* and finding it personally meaningful.[69] Like their Christian counterparts, Jews have moved away from what the sociologist Robert Wuthnow has called "a traditional spirituality of inhabiting sacred places" to a "new spirituality of seeking," exchanging the sublimity of churches and synagogues for "the new spiritual freedom" to be found through privatized, inner experiences.[70] If that is a correct diagnosis, there is a limit to what changes in synagogues can accomplish on their own. It is doubtful that extensive efforts to transform synagogues into warmer, more spirited, caring places will win back the large majority of Jews who do not relate to public prayer or see much significance in connecting with a caring community.[71]

Moreover, dual-earner families have to make hard decisions about how to use their limited non-work-related hours most efficiently.[72] Synagogues feel compelled to make allowances for what one rabbi has called the "McDonald's generation, fast food for the soul," an impatience with religious services that stretch on.[73] Many congregations have sharply curtailed services to fit into neat packages of an hour on Friday night or two hours on Shabbat morning, but whether such a step makes for a more satisfying synagogue experience, let alone allows for the leisurely reading of the Torah and serious prayer, is another matter.

Not least of the challenges is the prevailing culture of middle- and upper-middle-class Americans. Here is how one of the more innovative younger rabbis has described the challenges faced by synagogues:

> How does a culture of narcissism, over-entitlement and personalization manifest itself in terms of Jewish communal engagement? How can an iPod generation find rigorous exploration of Talmud and Jewish literature compelling and life-sustaining? How can those taught to walk away/ delete/unfriend on a whim be taught [and] . . . be stimulated to discover a spiritual practice that actually requires practice? Is there a way to cultivate a sense of obligation, enchantment, spiritual hunger in a generation that is essentially able to log off or sign out in all other aspects of life?[74]

The author of these words has not given up on finding ways to touch the lives of her own congregants. Still, her realistic assessment of the current climate should give pause to those who dismiss synagogues as failures.

In the years to come, American synagogues will undoubtedly continue to address the difficulties Jews experience when they participate in public worship, and in the course of doing so will engage in further experimentation. What should be clear from this overview is just how much effort already has been invested by congregational leaders to renew and enliven religious practices in their synagogues.

9

ORTHODOX OUTREACH

NOURISHING THE JEWISH WORLD

- On Tuesday evenings at Detroit Partners in Torah, between two hundred and two hundred fifty men and women gather to study Jewish texts in paired groups.[1] Each partnership or *Hevruta*, to use the rabbinic term, consists of one Orthodox and one non-Orthodox person. Together the partners select an aspect of Judaism they wish to study, rather than engage with a text chosen for them by the program. Over time, Hevruta partners become friends, invite each other to family celebrations, and through study enrich each other's understanding of Judaism.[2]

- Between 2009 and 2015, the Jewish Women's Renaissance Project (JWRP), has brought over seven thousand women for eight-day trips to Israel on a program that has become known informally as Birthright for Mommies. JWRP works with over a hundred fifty organizations around the world, including US federations of Jewish philanthropy to recruit women. "During the trips," states Lori Palatnik, a former Aish HaTorah worker and the founder of this initiative, "we strongly emphasize that the women must take this inspiration home and assume spiritual responsibility for their families, communities and even the Jewish people." When surveyed after the trip, 61 percent of participants (almost all are not Orthodox) claimed increased observance of Shabbat and over 20 percent enrolled their children in a Jewish day school.[3]

- In a Boca Raton Chabad center, over two dozen men and women gather to study texts on how the Jewish tradition understands the need for leaders to strike a balance between humility and self-assertion. That week, the exact same texts and subject matter were studied in over 265 locations in North America. Under the guidance of the Jewish Learning Institute, the largest Jewish adult education program in the country, roughly fifty-five thousand adults, almost all of whom are members of Conservative and Reform synagogues or are not affiliated with any congregation, engage in the study of religious topics with Chabad teachers, both male and female.[4]
- Some sixteen thousand teens in the United States participate annually in programs of NCSY, the youth movement arm of the Orthodox Union. Over one-third of these attend with some regularity by going on weekend retreats and enrolling in immersive learning programs and trips, including to Israel. Roughly half of the participants in NCSY attend public or nonsectarian private schools; presumably almost all are from non-Orthodox homes. NCSY represents a major initiative by Modern Orthodoxy to play a role in outreach.[5]
- A swank new synagogue in Soho, a hipster section of Manhattan, has been founded by an Orthodox married couple, formerly connected to Chabad. Featuring loft parties, cocktail gatherings, comedy club routines, and a savvy online presence combined with Shabbat meals, talk of spirituality, and challah baking, the synagogue has attracted hundreds of post-college millennials to its artistically stylish quarters. As independent Orthodox outreach workers, the couple take a decidedly laissez-faire approach to Judaism: "We are not saying, why [on the Sabbath] do you have a phone in your pocket, why after services are you going to Balthazar [a hip eatery], or why are you dating a non-Jewish person?" says the rabbi. "It's not my place. We are here to inspire them and open up their eyes and enable them to reconnect and to grow."[6]

What these and many other initiatives reflect are the variety of efforts by Orthodox Jews to help strengthen Jewish religious life among their less engaged coreligionists. An army of outreach workers—professionals and volunteers—drawn from different sectors of the Orthodox community is spreading throughout the country, establishing beachheads in areas of relatively sparse Jewish settlement and running intensive programs in cities and suburbs with dense Jewish concentrations—all with the aim of helping non-Orthodox Jews connect to some aspect of their religious tradition. Though regarded by some as competition for existing synagogues and denominational institutions, these Orthodox outreach workers tend to see themselves as partners in rebuilding a rapidly assimilating Jewish community.

The Contours of Orthodox Outreach

Orthodox outreach, or *kiruv* (literally, "bringing close," meaning closer to God and the commandments), first began in the United States after the Second World War.[7] Inside the Modern Orthodox sector, educational programs were launched by the National Council of Synagogue Youth (NCSY) and the Young Israel movement to teach returning war veterans and Jewish children enrolled in public schools about traditional Jewish observance.[8] By the 1950s, the Torah U'Mesorah movement was energetically planting Orthodox day schools in communities around the country, most of whose students did not come from fully observant homes.

Then, sometime in the mid-1950s, the leader of the Lubavitch Hasidim, Rabbi Menachem Mendel Schneerson, recruited the first small cadre of emissaries to fan out to communities across the United States and abroad with the mission of remaking those communities.[9] Kiruv efforts picked up steam in the 1960s with the opening of yeshivas in Israel aimed at potential *baalei teshuva* (returnees to Jewish practice) and the founding of beginner services in American Orthodox synagogues. By 1988, enough personnel were engaged in kiruv work to warrant the creation of the Association of Jewish Outreach Programs, or AJOP.

Since the 1990s, the kiruv project has really taken off, led by Chabad—the Lubavitch Hasidic movement.[10] One of the distinguishing features of Chabad's efforts is its programming for Jews of all ages and types of Jewish interests. For younger Jews, Chabad runs early-childhood programs, Hebrew schools, day schools, and day camps. At a time when Jewish teen programs are languishing, Chabad has created CTeen, which is attracting ever larger numbers to its seminars, holiday events, and Shabbatons.[11] Chabad also operates on 162 college and university campuses across the country. Its campus center at SUNY Binghamton, to cite one such program, regularly attracts three to four hundred students to Shabbat dinners.[12] And when students graduate from college, Chabad has created emissaries whose primary task is to reach young singles and newly married couples in their twenties and thirties. In Dallas, for example, an emissary has converted a former bookstore into a meeting place for Jewish singles; he finds potential participants by frequenting bars preferred by this demographic.

For adults, Chabad centers also offer a panoply of activities: daily and Sabbath services, High Holiday prayer venues, educational lectures, and social programs. Some Chabad emissaries run hiking and skiing programs where they can connect with Jews in recreational settings. According to one report, female emissaries of Chabad are experimenting with "Jewish yoga" as another means of reaching Jews through their avocational interests. To this mix Chabad adds initiatives directed at subpopulations of Jews, including immigrants from the former Soviet Union and their offspring, Israelis, French speakers, and families with special-needs children.[13]

Of particular note is the Jewish Learning Institute (JLI), by far the largest internationally coordinated adult-education program on Jewish topics, offering the same set of courses at hundreds of Chabad locations around the world, all on the same schedule. This means that Jews who are traveling can follow the same course from session to session, even if they find themselves in a different city each week. In the calendar year 2015, nearly sixty thousand American Jews were enrolled in JLI courses, including programs geared toward women and to teens.

The Chabad network is striving to create a seamless transition, so that young people who attended its camps or schools will gravitate to a Chabad campus center when they arrive at college and later, as adults, will join Chabad synagogue centers. No other Jewish movement offers this kind of cradle-to-grave set of services. The participants in these programs, needless to say, range in their Jewish commitments, but with the exception of a small minority, all are drawn from the ranks of the non-Orthodox.[14]

That does not mean, though, that Chabad is solely a vehicle for outreach. Many thousands of Jews regard a Chabad center as their synagogue, and when they travel they seek out a congregation belonging to the same "franchise." Moreover, insiders contend, the fact that there is a gap between the religious practices and ideology of synagogue members and the movement's elite parallels exactly what is happening in the Conservative and Reform movements. Chabad efforts began with a mission to inspire Jews to take on additional observances, but in time its contours have grown more similar to other Jewish religious movements—except that Chabad's mission is to serve all Jews, whether or not they are "members" of their centers.

Unfortunately, neither demographic studies nor the national office of Chabad provides an estimate of how many Jews in the United States participate in Chabad programs, let alone consider Chabad to be their synagogue. There is an exception: when a question was posed about participation in a Chabad program in a survey of Jews in Dade County, Florida, it elicited a stunning set of findings: 26 percent of Jewish households in that county claimed they had engaged with Chabad programming during the year prior to the survey (2014), a figure that rose to 42 percent of Jewish households with children at home. The youngest families were the most likely to have attended Chabad.[15]

A closer look at Chabad centers in a variety of states reveals some eye-opening levels of participation.[16] Two centers in Dade County, in Bal Harbor and Aventura, alone claim to host thirty-five hundred people on Yom Kippur and some seven thousand participants a year in their various programs. A Chabad in the San Fernando Valley in greater Los Angeles claims attendance by fifteen hundred people on Yom Kippur and an average of three hundred every Sabbath. Some thirty-five hundred people participate in its programs annually. All of these places run summer day camps and have Hebrew schools. To be sure, most centers attract smaller numbers, but collectively the various Chabad programs touch the lives of as many Jews as do Reform or Conservative synagogues. It therefore should not be surprising that large structures are being constructed by Chabad centers to house the plethora of their activities.

As stunning as the Chabad network is in its scope, the explosion of kiruv work now emanating from non-Hasidic yeshivas also is remarkable. In contrast to Chabad, which for a century has embraced a mission to reach Jews of all stripes (a strategy devised in part by Chabad leaders who were living under communist oppression), the Yeshivish world historically has been far more insular. But over the past two decades that has been changing. The yeshivas have been sending their students across the country to establish study centers for all comers. First on the scene was Aish HaTorah,[17] which runs seminars on leading a Jewish life, with locations in some fifteen US cities and a presence on nearly as many university campuses. In short order, Aish was joined by community or outreach kollelim—centers of study for advanced yeshiva students.[18] Their growth has been explosive: some sixty-five community kollelim now dot the American landscape, with talk of opening an additional thirty. The men and women involved in community kollelim are expected to divide their days between their own continuing study and then teaching local residents in classrooms, small groups, or personalized one-on-one sessions. Thus far, there has been no shortage of personnel available to recruit, with the Lakewood Yeshiva, Ner Israel in Baltimore, and numerous Israeli yeshivas providing a large pool of talent, and post-high-school seminaries training women who join their husbands as teachers for the kollelim.[19]

Several important distinctions within the outreach world are noteworthy. True to their Yeshivish orientation, Aish HaTorah and the kollelim stress study, rather than prayer. Aish contends that its classes offer more relevant and practical topics than the more academically inclined kollelim, though the latter offer a good deal of personal guidance in one-on-one conversations with participants. And though study classes are hardly absent from Chabad centers, as should be evident from the vast JLI infrastructure, the primary orientation of Chabad *shluchim* and *shluchos* (male and female Chabad emissaries) is encouraging people to take action—that is, to take on one more mitzvah, commandment. The Yeshivish approach, by contrast, is predicated on the assumption that learning will lead to greater ritual performance. "You can't love something you don't know," a kollel rabbi informs me. And then he invoked the regnant assumption of these study centers: "Once you start learning, things will fall into place."

Whatever may click for participants does not happen solely by serendipity. Orthodox outreach is prescriptive in its approach to learning. Teachers try to avoid being heavy-handed, but they do not shrink from speaking explicitly about God's will. Clear declarative sentences define what is expected of Jews: "If you desist from eating pork products you are heeding what God wants of Jews." "Keeping the Sabbath accords with God's will." This matter-of-fact certitude distinguishes Orthodox outreach from the far more nuanced and hedged way Judaism is taught in most other sectors of the Jewish community. A kollel rabbi recounts the following conversation he had with an adult member of a Reform temple who came to study with him: "You're different from my Reform rabbi," said the student; "you want me to grow as a Jew." To his credit, the kollel rabbi suggested that his Reform counterpart probably also wants the man to grow as a Jew. The difference may lie in the certainty with which God's will is invoked by Orthodox outreach workers and their commitment to state without equivocation, "this is what Judaism says you should be doing."

To hear outreach professionals tell it, their approach does not fall on deaf ears. In private conversation, many, in fact, express amazement at how far some of their students have come. A kollel rabbi speaks of a twenty-something man who loved eating pork but eventually decided never to touch the stuff again after study and conversation with the rabbi. A convert to Judaism through the Reform movement transformed her house to meet kosher standards under the tutelage of a Chabad rabbi who never expected such a development. And younger people who were raised with a minimal Jewish education take on a Haredi lifestyle under the influence of Aish HaTorah or other campus outreach programs. (A leading innovator among kiruv professionals was not even Jewish when on a lark he accompanied a Jewish friend to an outreach yeshiva in Jerusalem and was hooked; eventually he converted to Judaism.) Outreach workers are well aware of their limited influence over the decisions their students will make, but they work with great intentionality. As a kollel rabbi put it: "We can't control the results. We can only inspire Jews" to observe Judaism's commandments.

The various outreach groups also differ in whom they define as their target audiences. It has become a truism among kiruv professionals that younger people—teens, students on campuses, and the post-college set in their twenties and thirties—are likely to be the most receptive to the outreach message. Younger people are not yet set in their ways, and many may be seekers. Much of outreach effort in the past, therefore, tried to reach people under the age of thirty-five. Certainly, the huge Chabad infrastructure and increased presence of kollel personnel on campuses are indicative of this orientation, as are the teen programs and outreach to the post-college set.

Some of these assumptions, though, have come under question in recent years. A Chabad rabbi whose portfolio is to work with young people in their twenties and thirties explained to me how challenging he finds it to connect with individuals who have never experienced defeat or loss. Until they do so, he contends, they are unlikely to be seeking for answers; they have lived charmed lives and have not felt the need to explore the large existential questions. Parents of younger children may make for a more receptive audience as they are seeking guidance about how to raise their children as good human beings and as Jews. The targets of the Jewish Women's Renaissance Project clearly are young mothers, and of late fathers too. In brief, outreach workers are rethinking the importance of age and stage of life when considering their opportunities to make the greatest impact.

In recent years, some outreach groups have expanded their purview to work with an unlikely group: Orthodox Jews. Off the record, individuals engaged in outreach work speak candidly about day school graduates and current members of Orthodox synagogues who are not "inspired Jews." Some drop out of Orthodoxy already during their college years; more mature adults may have become mechanical in their observances. For this reason, the Orthodox Union's Jewish Learning Initiative on Campus, for example, has placed married couples on over twenty campuses with the express purpose of strengthening Orthodox life and not incidentally to reach Orthodox-raised college students who may be wavering in their commitments. And even beyond the campus, Chabad centers, Aish HaTorah branches, and kollelim also attract Orthodox-raised individuals.[20]

Perhaps the most surprising reversal in the field is the outsize role now assumed by the so-called Yeshivish sector, the groups most likely to live in insular enclaves, rather than the Modern Orthodox one.[21] One might have expected the Modern Orthodox who interact with all kinds of Jews and are more conversant with the wider culture to spearhead outreach. But it is the graduates of Haredi yeshivas who staff Aish HaTorah, community kollelim, and a variety of other initiatives. A good deal of this is attributable to economics. Modern Orthodox Jews must earn substantial salaries if they are to afford the much higher costs of living in a Modern Orthodox community, as compared to a Haredi one: housing and schooling, for example, cost considerably less in Haredi communities.[22] Modern Orthodox Jews simply cannot afford to become professional outreach workers. There also is the question of mission: Haredi Jews may be more driven to draw nonobservant Jews to Judaism because their yeshivas imbue them with a sense of mission to reach assimilating Jews before they are lost to Judaism.[23] And not least, in an odd way, the Haredi world is better positioned to engage in outreach because it has no fear of associating with non-Orthodox Jews. The Modern Orthodox, by contrast, with their deep division over Open Orthodoxy, are more vulnerable to de-legitimation if they make common cause with non-Orthodox Jews.[24]

There are exceptions, such as NCSY with its active programs in public and nonsectarian private schools, the Manhattan Jewish Experience (a Modern Orthodox outreach effort aimed at young professionals), beginners' services in a few Modern Orthodox synagogues, and the not inconsiderable numbers of Modern Orthodox Jews who volunteer to teach in outreach programs, such as Partners in Torah. According to one count, some two hundred rabbis serving in struggling Modern Orthodox synagogues around the country are reaching out to the broader community, if only because their congregations cannot survive without an influx of non-Orthodox Jews. Needless to say, some reach out because they are committed to the cause. Still, the outreach enterprise is primarily in the hands of Haredim.

How many people staff this multitude of programs? Precise numbers are hard to come by, but Chabad claims to field 1,740 couples in the United States alone (a figure that has increased fivefold over the past quarter century). Since both spouses engage in outreach work full time, that means nearly thirty-five hundred shluchim and shluchos are engaged in kiruv. Moreover, many Chabad schools, centers, and programs are staffed by younger people who are training to become emissaries. They are augmented by a back-office staff, which puts out publications, maintains the chabad.org website, prepares educational materials, and coordinates programs. Chabad alone, therefore, probably accounts for over four thousand people engaged full time in kiruv. Then there are the two thousand non-Chabad outreach workers who constitute the membership of the Association of Jewish Outreach Programs.[25] Not to be overlooked are perhaps as many as two hundred Modern Orthodox outreach workers and many dozens of independent operators, some devoting all their time to the effort and most doing it part time.[26]

All in all, the estimated six to seven thousand men and women working across the country in kiruv—that is, with non-Orthodox Jews—constitute more than double the number of active Conservative, Reform, and all other permutations of liberal rabbis *combined*.

What Are the Goals of Orthodox Outreach?

By subsuming all these activities under the catchall of kiruv, I am intentionally transgressing one of the pieties of the Orthodox outreach movement. For some purists, the term rightfully should be associated only with those who aim to bring nonobservant Jews to Orthodoxy. This all-or-nothing conception was perfectly captured when one Haredi rabbi told kiruv workers that they "have accomplished nothing" if the subject of outreach does not "go all the way."[27] Under that conception of kiruv, Chabad is merely a "service organization," offering kosher food and holiday celebrations to travelers who find themselves in remote locations of the globe, helping Jews with other needs, and running glitzy holiday programs, but expecting little of the Jews they serve.[28] Indeed, most Chabad emissaries would concede their proximate goals are modest. As one emissary explained it to me, Chabad efforts have "a non-result orientation. Our job is to love our fellow Jews, regardless of outcomes. Chabad does not regard its work as a waste of time if people don't become *frum* [observant]. Any mitzvah is a positive step."

But for all the disdain directed at Chabad's latitudinarianism, outreach workers across the spectrum concede that they, too, realize their limita-

tions. In my conversations with more than three dozen outreach professionals connected with the range of organizations, the same pragmatic themes
emerged:

- "We plant seeds but don't know what impact we have."
- "Everyone is on a journey."
- "Kiruv works on the *ta'amu u'reu* model. Give people a chance 'to taste
  and observe' traditional Judaism, and then they may come back for
  more."
- "I can only teach Torah, but people have free will; we can't coerce
  behavior."
- "My goal is to increase knowledge of all Jews so they can make in-
  formed decisions."
- "I judge success by how many people come to engage in Torah study."
- "We don't make anyone frum. We build a community of interested
  people and break down apathy."

These kinds of comments are not only stated off the record. The website of
Aish HaTorah asserts: "Judaism is not all or nothing; it is a journey where
every step counts, to be pursued according to one's own pace and interest."[29]
Kollel leaders explain their belief that the act of studying Torah will draw
some people to observances, but they are vague about the process and outcome they pursue. Even in their promotional literature, outreach centers eschew terms such as kiruv, and instead stress how they seek to aid "people on
a path of spiritual growth." Once they get beyond the insular world of the
yeshiva, outreach workers quickly learn their limitations and privately lower
their expectations. Not for nothing do some speak of the "Chabadization of
Orthodox outreach."[30]

Just how difficult it is to bring less observant Jews to Orthodoxy is illustrated by rough numbers. Though no systematic record keeping exists, well-
placed people in the outreach world estimate that there are roughly two
thousand new recruits to Orthodoxy in the United States annually, with as
many as 30 percent consisting of college students.[31] As recently as the 1990s,

these numbers were thought to be twice as high. Many outreach workers acknowledge that the likeliest targets of opportunity historically have been drawn from Conservative Jewish homes where they had been exposed to some measure of traditional Judaism. With the demographic contraction of that movement, the low-hanging fruit of the past is not nearly as available today, and therefore the pickings have grown slimmer.[32] Conversely, as ever more Jewish children come from intermarried households, the task of bringing Jews to observance has grown more complex—not least because according to the Orthodox definition, children of a non-Jewish mother are not considered Jewish and therefore a large proportion of those encountered by outreach workers must first undergo a conversion to Judaism before they can be drawn into an observant form of the religion.[33]

But even beyond these technical questions of Jewish law, outreach workers speak of the many Jews they encounter every day who are estranged from their religion. One leader in the field describes how when he began several decades ago, "there were Jews with some connection to tradition, a relationship to Israel and memories of grandparents who were observant." Today, many Jews on campus no longer fit that bill. "Millennials," he declares flatly, "are the enigma of all Jewish life." Enigma or not, the work of outreach has not gotten easier.

The numbers suggest there are more than three full-time outreach workers for every single "success." That is a rate unlikely to impress potential funders as a winning investment. But from the perspective of outreach workers, there are mitigating circumstances. First, winning over two thousand annual recruits translates into a quantitative net gain because these individuals will marry other Jews and raise far more Jewish children than they would have otherwise done. Theology plays a role, too. If one believes that drawing even a single Jew to God and the commandments is a mitzvah, a religious imperative, quantity is far less of an issue. Some have their eye on an even higher religious aspiration because they regard each Jew brought closer to observance as a contribution to Jewish "national *teshuva*"—the return to God's ways that is a necessary prelude to the coming of the Messiah.[34]

Not all funders of outreach programs share these goals.[35] As is the case with so much of American philanthropy of late, metrics (quantifiable data) are all the rage. Donors are increasingly linking their largesse to quotas: One funder insists that each campus outreach worker annually must draw in at least seven college-aged newcomers to Orthodox observance. Not surprisingly, these pressures have resulted in creative bookkeeping—and demoralization when unrealistic goals cannot be met. They have also prompted pushback on the part of those who understand the realities of American Jewish life. Outreach, they argue, is a retail operation. It requires intensive one-on-one work, and the decision of a nonobservant Jew to become Orthodox often results from the combined efforts of many outreach workers in a variety of settings.[36] For every recruit to Orthodoxy, moreover, there are dozens who choose not to go the distance. An outreach worker has likened the process of engaging Jews to moving people through a funnel that is wide at one end and quite narrow at the other. Outreach programs cast a broad net to bring people to programs that require little of participants, other than a willingness to socialize with other Jews. Kiruv workers then try to identify those who seem interested in a bit more—perhaps some study opportunity, theological conversation, or religious participation. As these seekers move along from one program to the next, only a very small minority come out of the funnel as Orthodox Jews.

And what about the rest? In off-the-record interviews with outreach workers associated with Chabad, Aish HaTorah, Modern Orthodox organizations, and community kollelim, I received the same response, sometimes offered with a shrug, sometimes with strong conviction: *If the Jews whom I have taught and mentored become more active in their Reform or Conservative synagogues,* they say, *or in their federations or Israel-oriented organizations, or in their willingness to marry another Jew and raise a Jewish family of any kind, I consider that to be a success.*

A good many non-Orthodox leaders probably would respond to this flat assertion with incredulity, for it has become an article of faith that Orthodox outreach is cultlike and intentionally designed to raid the non-Orthodox sectors of the Jewish community. With a few exceptions, this is simply false. In fact, what is actually happening is far more interesting: kiruv has become a powerful vehicle for reengaging Jews with the *non*-Orthodox sectors of the community. Leading members of Conservative and Reform synagogues attend Chabad educational programs or community kollel study sessions and then return to their home congregations, probably as better-informed Jews. Individuals who have had little contact with organized Jewish life are turned on to Judaism by kiruv workers and in many cases find their way into non-Orthodox synagogues or secular organizations.[37]

Their numbers are not negligible. Though no one has collected definitive figures, a quick back-of-the-envelope estimate yields eye-opening results: Assuming that there are between six and seven thousand kiruv workers today and each interacts annually with an average of no more than one hundred non-Orthodox Jews (a conservative figure given the size of most Chabad centers and the popularity of kiruv events sponsored by other organizations), the collective impact of Orthodox outreach may touch between six and seven hundred thousand Jews *each year*,[38] rivaling the impact of the Conservative and Reform movements, and in the majority of cases *complementing* and *enhancing* the work of those movements.

The Growth of the Field

How might we explain the vast expansion of Orthodox outreach efforts over the past two decades? Economic necessity surely plays a role: As ever more students attend Haredi advanced yeshivas or women's seminaries while simultaneously eschewing a university education, a vast pool of people with expertise in Torah but no other marketable skills must find opportunities to earn an income. Take, for example, the Lakewood Yeshiva, which currently enrolls close to seven thousand men in study that leads to rabbinic ordination and post-ordination study. Some of these students will find their way to colleges and universities afterward and train to become professionals; many others will go into business; but a significant proportion will have to find employment in one form or another of Jewish education. Kiruv work is a natural fit, as it is fundamentally about teaching Torah (the one type of knowledge these yeshiva products have in great abundance). As Adam Ferziger, a historian at Bar Ilan University, has noted, "the Orthodox outreach 'industry' has opened new vistas for Haredi employment."[39] Predictably, the heads of yeshivas have begun to pay attention to the success of Chabad emissaries in supporting their own families through kiruv work and now encourage their students to enter the field.

It is doubtful they would have done so, however, without significant shifts in the landscape of Jewish life. For much of the past two centuries, traditional Judaism has hemorrhaged vast populations to other Jewish movements or secularism, leading the Orthodox world to adopt a defensive, self-insulating posture. But in recent decades, this strategy has been rethought in some quarters because Orthodox Jews no longer see themselves as a beleaguered minority. Once a net loser of adherents, Orthodox Jewry in most places around the globe has now stabilized and, if anything, is growing. Much of this population increase, as we have seen, is the result of high fertility rates. Though there unquestionably are dropouts from Orthodoxy, these numbers pale compared with the number of defectors from other religious movements. Orthodoxy is also attracting followers who were raised in families adhering to those movements.

Demographic resurgence has been coupled with a newfound sense of self-confidence, born of a conviction that the Orthodox alone will continue to thrive while the other religious movements of American Judaism are in steep decline; and born, too, of a realization that they have little to fear from interactions with their nonobservant coreligionists. The prophet of the turn to assertive kiruv was Menachem Mendel Schneerson, the last Lubavitcher Rebbe, who threw down the gauntlet as early as 1951. Employing martial imagery, he justified an aggressive campaign as follows: "Orthodox Jewry up to this point has concentrated on defensive strategies. We were always worried lest we lose positions and strongholds. But we must take the initiative and wage an offensive."[40] This strategic doctrine has gradually gained a following in other quarters. It is now understood that there is much to be gained spiritually, financially, and demographically from intensive efforts at reaching out to those who may be brought closer to God and the commandments of the Torah. Orthodox outreach thus represents a shift from fearful defensiveness to a heady sense of mission, whose goal is nothing less than the rescue of Jews for God and Judaism before they are lost forever.

Problematical Dimensions of Outreach

Not surprisingly, what some kiruv insiders see as an intoxicating cause is the object of much criticism, if not scorn, in other sectors of the American Jewish community. Conservative and Reform rabbis routinely tangle with kiruv workers, in some cases fighting tooth and nail to keep them out of their communities. A Chabad rabbi reports that when he tried to participate as a worshipper in a campus prayer service, he was barred by the Hillel rabbi; others claim they have been subjected to orchestrated shunning campaigns. Some of the tension has resulted from strong ideological differences, as when Chabad emissaries erect Chanukah candelabras in public spaces that raise the ire of liberal rabbis concerned about church/state infringement.[41] But much of the recrimination revolves around more prosaic concerns. Kiruv workers are accused of poaching members from existing synagogues, even as they claim to be serving only the unaffiliated. And then there are congregational rabbis who resent the razzle-dazzle of episodic mega-events staged by kiruv workers. "Sure they throw a dandy Purim carnival or matzo-baking party, but they can invest heavily in such one-offs because they don't have to maintain a synagogue year round and address the daily needs of congregants," a Conservative rabbi, speaking for many others, bitterly contends.

Whether or not Orthodox outreach programs *intentionally* lure people away from conventional synagogues is hard to document. It stands to reason, though, that among the hundreds if not thousands of people Chabad and other outreach groups claim they see at their High Holidays services, a considerable number attended Conservative or Reform synagogues in the past. These people may have stopped paying congregational dues because they attended synagogue only on rare occasions, such as the High Holidays. For considerably lower sums or a voluntary contribution, they can get seats on Rosh Hashanah and Yom Kippur in the Orthodox outreach centers. Moreover, over the past two decades, these centers have increasingly drawn younger families who previously had not been members of a synagogue. A good many of those unaffiliated Jews probably would have joined Conservative and Reform synagogues in much the same way as did their parents. With well over a thousand Chabad and other Orthodox outreach centers springing up over the past two decades, it is apparent that some of their growth has come at the expense of denominational synagogues. Little wonder, then, that leaders of non-Orthodox congregations are resentful.

Financial considerations further inflame tensions. Kiruv workers are accused of undercutting the costs of synagogue membership by offering free or inexpensive High Holiday seats, charging modest fees for Hebrew school, and, most galling of all, managing entirely without synagogue dues—thereby undermining the business model of most synagogues, which is predicated upon mandatory membership fees. To add insult to injury, rabbis of liberal congregations charge kiruv workers with hypocrisy for talking about *raising* levels of observance even as in actuality they expect *less* of their people. Bar and Bat Mitzvah preparation is an especially sensitive issue. Synagogues require children to have spent a minimum number of years (usually at least three) studying in a congregational school as a prerequisite for celebrating their milestone in the synagogue sanctuary; kiruv workers often waive such requirements and "Bar Mitzvah" kids who have had little or no Jewish education. The disparity between the stated objectives of outreach and this lowering of standards is a special provocation for many rabbis and synagogues, especially given their heavy reliance on Bar and Bat Mitzvah preparation as the hook to draw families to join.

Perhaps the most severe critics of kiruv emanate from within the Orthodox world. Chabad in particular is faulted for its minimalistic expectations and for peddling a form of "Judaism lite." "Why not aim higher and bring nonobservant Jews to full Orthodox observance?" they ask. "Is this the best use of Orthodox Jewry's limited resources?" Still others fault the bumbling nature of the enterprise. "The *kiruv* world is still dominated by amateurs advising amateurs," writes Rabbi Avraham Edelstein, himself an Orthodox rabbi. The field offers "little sustained professional training and mentoring in specialized areas."[42]

And then there is the criticism about the intellectual shallowness of some programs. One frequent target is the Bible Codes seminars run by Aish HaTorah to demonstrate that buried in the biblical texts are references to all sorts of historical events, including the assassination of Yitzhak Rabin and the assault on the Twin Towers on 9/11. To arrive at these hidden clues, one simply ignores the actual sentence structure of the Torah and, voilà, references to events that have occurred millennia after the text was written may be uncovered by stringing together contiguous letters vertically, horizontally, or diagonally![43] Chabad, too, has been faulted for farfetched teachings, as when dinosaur fossils are explained away as items intentionally planted by God to test our faith in the accuracy of the Genesis narrative. Why engage in such sophistry, many in the Orthodox and non-Orthodox communities wonder?

From an ethical perspective, others worry that the pressure to win recruits is leading some to engage in disingenuous advertising. "Kiruv workers can sometimes rope 'em in by painting an unrealistic canvas, describing only the beauty of the frum community," laments another Orthodox rabbi. Some kiruv workers, like other men and women with a mission, are not immune from the seductions of deceptive practices.

The Dilemmas of Outreach Workers

Even within the outreach community some are queasy about the enterprise because it places Orthodox Jews in compromising situations.[44] Here is but a partial list of the kinds of predicaments in which they often find themselves:

- Activities such as traveling in a car, smoking, going to work, and using electrical devices are all considered to be desecrations of the Sabbath if performed on that day of the week. A Jew who desecrates the Sabbath is classified by Halacha as being an *akum*, literally a worshipper of stars and astrology, or an idolator. Those classified as akum may not be granted synagogue honors, such as being called to the Torah for an *aliya* or lead services or be counted as part of the minyan (the prayer quorum). The predicament is that, by definition, virtually all who attend services in kiruv synagogues desecrate the Sabbath according to Orthodox lights. How are they to be treated? If they are barred from full participation, they may never return—and then they certainly would not have the chance to learn about the error of their ways. If they are included as full participants, the prayer service will not have proceeded properly and that means the kiruv workers will not have fulfilled their religious obligations by praying in such a setting.[45]

- May an outreach worker invite someone to attend Sabbath services or a Shabbat meal knowing that the invitee will desecrate the Sabbath by driving in a car when returning home? The kiruv worker is torn between providing opportunities to the nonobservant to experience Jewish life guided by Orthodox standards and avoiding a situation that will result in Sabbath desecration, but thereby foreclosing the opportunity for the nonobservant Jew to participate.

- One of the features of outreach centers is a lavish food spread typically prepared for attendees. But the question arises, may one offer a nonobservant Jew a meal if that Jew in all likelihood will not say grace after meals? By actively feeding a fellow Jew, the kiruv worker is creating a situation whereby Jewish law will be desecrated.[46] The alternative is to inform the nonobservant Jew of the requirement to say grace after meals, but if the individual declines to do so, the kiruv worker will have made matters far worse from the perspective of Jewish law because the failure to utter the correct blessings will result from an intentional decision, rather than inadvertence—that is, ignorance.[47]

- May a male kiruv worker teach women who are not dressed properly according to standards of modesty Haredi Jews believe are required by Jewish law—such as, if their clothing is too revealing, their hair is not covered, they are wearing trousers? The outreach worker is caught between the goal of teaching Torah to the nonobservant and his understanding of the proper standards of modest dress.

- The pervasiveness of intermarriage creates a host of dilemmas: May a child born of a non-Jewish mother be enrolled in a kiruv school or summer camp? At what point should a kiruv worker make clear that he or she does not consider such a child to be Jewish according to Halacha and therefore would not allow such a child to celebrate a Bar or Bat Mitzvah? If the kiruv worker speaks openly about the standards of Halacha, families may be driven away before there is even a chance to draw them into Jewish life; on the other hand, if this information is withheld, parents may feel mistreated when told that despite their child's years of studying Judaism, the kiruv worker does not accept the Jewishness of that child.

These and a host of other questions have been posed to rabbinic decisors. Indeed, so many responsa have been written about the Halachic ramifications of outreach work that two separate Hebrew volumes have been compiled for the benefit of outreach workers.[48] Yet even with all this guidance, the enterprise remains fraught. A leading rabbinic figure of the Haredi world warned kiruv workers in a message quoting his own father:

> "Always remember that you are not *HaKadosh Baruch Hu's apotropis* [the Holy One's guardian]." He is responsible for the results, not you, and you have no right to bend Shulchan Aruch [the code of Jewish law] in the pursuit of "better results." . . . None should go into *Kiruv* imagining that he will always be able to preserve "West Point standards" in the field. . . . "We are not talking about doing anything in contravention of Shulchan Aruch" . . . just the fact that any *Kiruv* professional in the field will find himself engaged in many types of activities that he never imagined himself doing in the yeshiva or Kollel.[49]

The author of these words clearly is concerned about the pitfalls those working in the field may encounter, and the seductions of working to rescue Jews from assimilation. Accordingly he advises outreach workers to check in weekly with their mentor to make sure they do not go astray, a practice followed by some outreach professionals. Still the internal tug-of-war persists in the work of kiruv. As one Chabad emissary put it to me, "I struggle every day whether I am going too far and where to draw the line. But if we don't observe Halacha, what are we doing?"[50] He is hardly alone in his daily wrestling with these dilemmas.

The Rewards of Outreach Work

Despite the criticism and potential pitfalls, thousands of outreach professionals continue to go about their work. Presumably, they are heartened by an indisputable reality: Jews are voting with their feet, coming to outreach centers to study, engage with other Jews, and deepen their understanding of Judaism. Judging from the testimonials they offer when asked, they value the altruism, deep religious conviction, and love for fellow Jews outreach workers convey.

Are these perceptions accurate? In many cases, most assuredly: the mission of Orthodox outreach has attracted some remarkably dedicated and generous human beings to what they regard as holy work. In one important sense, though, the accuracy of these perceptions is less significant than the many opportunities for encounter created by the kiruv movement and the ensuing bridging of a vast social gulf between Orthodox Jews and other sectors of the community. Through these efforts, Orthodox Jews now have a human face, and, as one Chabad emissary has put it, "the fear factor of being in a frum [devout] environment" has lessened. Outreach has diminished the hostility of a good many non-Orthodox Jews toward the Orthodox.

And what about the reverse: Do those who work in outreach rethink their stereotypical views of Jews who differ from them? And are they in any way influenced by the Jews whom they encounter? At this point, one can answer these questions only with more questions. For example, one may wonder about the impact of new social media upon the thinking of those who employ them. Chabad.org receives more unique visitors than any other Jewish website in the world, with Aish HaTorah not far behind.[51] Are these simply examples of new forms of technology employed in the service of tradition? Or have the technology and the new social media brought about any deeper reordering of the relationship of kiruv organizations to the Jews they aim to reach?[52]

Or to cite another suggestive development, what does it mean that a large gap is opening between kiruv workers and their Orthodox critics? It is an open secret that a growing divide now separates Chabad emissaries in the field from fellow Lubavitchers who reside and work in isolated enclaves in Brooklyn. Kiruv workers situated in the gamut of outreach programs say their critics don't understand the hard realities of Jewish life in America. A pulpit rabbi operating in the Modern Orthodox community but sympathetic to kiruv has castigated the Orthodox world precisely for its insularity: "To effectively inspire people to become observant, the effort must be done in isolation from the established Orthodox community," Rabbi Ilan Feldman laments. "*Frum* communities as *cultures* are simply not conducive to outreach," he believes, because those communities have a defensive perspective and don't welcome Jewish seekers who are not yet planted in the Orthodox life.[53] Put differently, outreach workers of necessity develop a far more empathic understanding of the non-Orthodox population than do other sectors of the Orthodox world.

It's too early to tell how much those engaged in Orthodox outreach will absorb the cultural assumptions of the Jews they serve, but inevitably they are more likely to see a recognizably common Jewish humanity when they work with Jews who are not like them. Particularly in an age such as ours of extreme polarization and deep concern about incivility in American Jewish life, the possibility of rapprochement between some sectors of the Orthodox community and other types of Jews is good news indeed.

And so too is the fact that with the growth of the kiruv movement, the American Jewish community can rely upon a new resource to complement existing religious movements, synagogues, and educational institutions in their collective mission to inspire Jews of all ages to draw closer to their religious tradition. The lives of hundreds of thousands of non-Orthodox Jews have been touched by Orthodox outreach activities. The vast majority have not taken on an Orthodox lifestyle, but large numbers have given Judaism a second look, learned about their religion, and taken on some observances they had previously regarded as too alien to contemplate. The army of outreach workers is reshaping Jewish religious life in this country.

10

LOOKING FOR JUDAISM IN
UNCONVENTIONAL PLACES

Every year since 1990, the Burning Man festival, described as a "celebration of freedom, self-expression and art," is held on the desert sands of Black Rock, Nevada.[1] Attracting as many as seventy thousand participants—almost all not Jewish—for a week of revelry, Burning Man does not appear at first glance to be a setting conducive to any form of Jewish religious activity. And yet, as the sun sets on Friday afternoon, some seven hundred Jews gather for a Kabbalat Shabbat service (welcoming the Sabbath), followed by a Sabbath dinner for four hundred. Describing the religious service at a recent gathering, one activist makes clear that organizers "adhere to the spirit of the law rather than its letter, honoring the religious rites of Jewish ancestors *and* innovating to transcend them. . . . Like singing one of the traditional prayers to the tune of Leonard Cohen's 'Hallelujah.' Or like swapping a traditional prayer for an original, secular song. . . . It looks like simplifying the traditional words of prayer as much as possible, or choosing to sing *niggunim*, wordless prayers with learnable melodies, so that every guest can add their voice in the absence of prayer books or longtime familiarity." In a setting self-consciously dedicated to radical self-expression, some Jewish participants come together to demonstrate that radical also can mean "a return to what's elemental."[2]

Across the country on the East Coast, every November for over thirty years, an Orthodox prayer service has been held at a different unconventional site: close to the marshaling area for the New York Marathon. On

the Sunday morning of the race, three separate services are held to accommodate the runners' varied start schedules. Proudly announcing a record-
setting minyan, one report noted that no participants came close to winning
the marathon or setting a new record, but the 140 people who attended represented a new high and the service ran extra-long because the date of the
race coincided with the Jewish New Moon (Rosh Hodesh), when additional
prayers are recited. To accommodate the runners, the minyan organizers
take responsibility for transporting talitot (prayer shawls) and tephilin (phylacteries) to a Manhattan synagogue near the finish line.[3]

These two examples hardly exhaust the list of unconventional forms of
Jewish religious congregating. Rabbis organize Shabbat and holiday services
on ski slopes, on wilderness hiking trails, or in desert sites.[4] The Coachella
Valley Arts and Music festival in Southern California hosts a Shabbat tent
attracting several hundred attendees swarming through the festival grounds
to hear various genres of music performed on multiple stages.[5] One year,
when the festival fell on Passover, the tent housed Matzachella for Jews looking to participate in a brief, ten-minute Seder. Not infrequently, at professional sporting events such as baseball games and tennis matches, minyanim
sprout up for those who wish to engage in daily prayer at the assigned times.
Morning prayer services on flights to Israel have long been a staple, and one
can find observant men gathering in airport terminals while awaiting their
flights. All of these are examples of Jewish religious gatherings in out-of-the-
way spaces. For outsiders, they are interesting curiosities, though they tend
to be ad hoc in nature.

The American Jewish scene in recent years also has given rise to less tran-
sitory, yet equally experimental forms of Jewish religious congregating. Indeed, one of the more striking features of American Judaism in the twenty-
first century is the proliferation of start-ups and other efforts to spur "disruptive innovation" in much the same way as is evident on the wider American religious scene.

The goal of these new initiatives is to create *un*conventional settings for
religious expression. An informed observer of the current scene has unabashedly celebrated the "renaissance in Jewish religious life . . . happening
in new spiritual communities . . . unbound by conventional expectations

about the roles and parameters of a synagogue."[6] Several dozen Jewish religious start-ups meet in places intentionally chosen because they do *not* look like a synagogue: they meet in night clubs, bars, performing art spaces, lofts, bookstores, warehouses, and other rented properties. In no small measure, their allure lies in the distinctly non-synagogue ambience they create. "Give them a space they can love, and they will come," asserts a founder of one such group, while offering a variation of "if you build it [differently], they will come."[7]

But it is not only a matter of meeting in offbeat settings. In one way or another, Jewish religious start-ups are deliberately rejecting conventional synagogues as hopelessly out of step with today's Jewish population. To simplify, we note three different lines of criticism leveled by these groups. One critique focuses on the structural inadequacies of conventional synagogues. Governance is top-down, rather than flat, as suits the tastes of the current age. By concentrating authority in the hands of clergy and a lay elite, synagogues, some contend, are out of step with the democratic and participatory expectations of today's Jews. Not surprisingly, start-ups strive to spread responsibility for running religious services and programs among a large number of people and claim to reject a hierarchical governance structure. Moreover, critics of how synagogues are structured contend the model of membership dues is neither affordable nor reasonable: Why pay for services one rarely uses? The funding model must change to a fee-for-services arrangement, it is argued, rather than maintaining uniform membership dues unconnected to the frequency of use.

A second critique contends that synagogues are simply bad at what they *do*. Worship, to begin with, is dull, routinized, and incomprehensible to all but the initiated. Who wants to sit passively through a service, while the clergy run the show? For spirited worship to happen, congregants must be taught how to pronounce the words and sing the melodies—and then encouraged to pray with intentionality (*kavana*, in Hebrew). As to the overall synagogue experience, it currently fails to touch the lives of congregants, contend the critics. For services to be meaningful they should appeal to the heart and mind: they ought to relate Jewish texts to what is relevant to the lives of worshippers and offer them genuine community, a highly participatory service, and opportunities to act upon their social and political ideals. Here too, the critics contend, synagogues fail.

Hovering behind much of the dissatisfaction with conventional synagogues is what might be labeled a generational critique: synagogues, it is said, hold no appeal for younger Jews. To cite one such critic, "For many of my [age] peers, Judaism exists as something behind a piece of glass in a museum. It's pretty to look at, but not something my peers feel they can touch or play with or engage with."[8] Millennials, born toward the end of the twentieth century, it is widely asserted, find the services boring, and just as fatally synagogues are focused on a demographic that includes few millennials—family units with children or empty-nesters. As long as millennials have not formed families of their own, they will have no interest in joining or even attending a synagogue, contend the critics who write off synagogues as generationally "challenged."

Niche Synagogues—Then and Now

The impulse to create alternatives to the denominational synagogues, of course, hardly began with the current generation. During the latter decades of the past century, several new types of synagogues were established by Jews who were dissatisfied with the existing options. Today, perhaps as many as three hundred such congregations remain. We might refer to these as niche congregations, employing a term popular in Christian circles. The sociologist Nancy T. Ammerman defines niche churches as congregations that "do not serve a specific locale. They reach beyond an immediate neighborhood to create an identity relatively independent of context. . . . The implications of a mobile, cosmopolitan culture where congregational choice is the norm, make such specialized religious sorting more and more likely."[9] Many, though not all, of the models described in this chapter may be described as niche synagogues that draw attendees from outside a single neighborhood or suburb because they offer a distinctive religious ambience.

Orthodox outreach centers, as we have already seen, fit this description. At the other end of the ideological spectrum are fellowships and congregations that describe themselves as liturgically and socially progressive. That is, they compose their own prayers, resist the "corporate" culture of conventional synagogue life,[10] pride themselves on their openness to previously marginalized groups such as gays and lesbians, the intermarried, and singles, and embrace the causes of the political left. Unlike Orthodox outreach congregations, founded by rabbis looking to recruit congregants, the progressive groups are a grassroots phenomenon: Jews banded together, initially without professional assistance, often intentionally eschewing rabbinic leadership.[11] By 2016, some 116 of them affiliated with the National Havurah Committee,[12] approximately 97 were linked to the Federation of Reconstructionist Congregations and Havurot,[13] and another 40 were linked to Aleph: Alliance for Jewish Renewal.

Structurally, these three bodies are not easy to disentangle, as a number of congregations belong to more than one. At least a half dozen Havurot belong to the Jewish Renewal network, and others are Reconstructionist. For quite a while their leaders were intertwined: many Renewal and Havurah people were either ordained at the Reconstructionist Rabbinical College or taught there, and their members still attend retreats together at places such as Camp Isabella Freedman in Connecticut.

The Reconstructionist movement is the best known of these groups. It has, in fact, the infrastructure of a Jewish denomination—an umbrella organization for synagogues, a rabbinical seminary (in 2012 these two merged), and an association of rabbis.[14] Reconstructionism also has the most defined ideological positions, originating in the views of its founder, Rabbi Mordecai Kaplan (1881–1983), although the clarity and direction of the movement became murkier in the decades following his death, just as all the movements have become less ideological. In the more established congregations the Sabbath morning service is the focal event of the week, whereas in the smaller *havurot* twice monthly Friday evening services are central. Reconstructionism proudly embraces an especially large percentage of intermarried families.

A sampling of mission statements put out by Reconstructionist congregations highlights their overall direction. Congregation Dor Hadash in San Diego describes Reconstructionist beliefs in Kaplanian terms: "In our spiritual search many of us see our texts and traditions as a record of human endeavor, sacred but not supernatural in origin. Many Reconstructionists view God as the power within us that encourages self-fulfillment and ethical behavior, the spiritual energy that works through nature and human beings, and the inspiration for all that gives meaning to life."[15] The Ann Arbor Reconstructionist synagogue prides itself on "shared leadership among a broad range of members and the active participation of all members in community life. Events will be held in wheelchair accessible locations. Non-traditional households are welcomed. . . . We each agree to provide funds within our means so that economic hardship will not hinder participation."[16] A third congregation, the Reconstructionist Synagogue of the North Shore (Long Island, New York), describes on its website its eclectic style of worship: "A Billy Collins poem and an ancient Hebrew melody. A middle-eastern chant and a favorite congregational tune. Our worship services place an emphasis on group participation, as our members engage in lively discussions and spirited singing, using a modern prayer book that helps worshipers of all backgrounds connect to the service in a meaningful, interactive way."[17]

The hallmarks of Reconstructionist congregations are to experiment with the liturgy and jettison aspects that do not speak to current sensibilities. They are outspokenly left-wing in their political and social orientation. Rejecting hierarchy, they have reinterpreted the role of the rabbi, making him or her a facilitator of democratic decision making rather than the decision maker on ritual matters. The emphasis on inclusion of groups that are allegedly excluded from other synagogues, such as the handicapped and indigent, is a point of pride. But it has created some discomfort in Reconstructionist synagogues that have undertaken capital campaigns to build permanent structures, since raising the necessary money entails breaking with their "anti-hierarchical approach to fund-raising" and potentially embarrassing people who cannot pay their share.[18] These countervailing needs have prompted some congregations to study what they refer to as "the Torah of money." In all of these ways, Reconstructionist congregations have signaled their displeasure with conventional denominational synagogues.

As to the religious services themselves, they vary greatly by congregation. Only a minority attract the kinds of congregants Mordecai Kaplan invented

Reconstructionism to address: the Judaically well educated who can follow the liturgy and a fair number of whom can read Torah and lead the prayers. In these places, rabbis play a facilitative role, rather than serving as the religious authority. The larger number of congregations today, albeit those with smaller membership numbers, tend to attract Jews with little Jewish learning. Worship services consist of congregants seated in a circle, led by a rabbi who plays the guitar and is heavily involved in leading readings and discussing them. There is much talk of spirituality and of progressive politics, I am told by Reconstructionist rabbis. The buzzwords to be heard in such synagogues are "values-based decision-making" and "inclusivity," and there is a clear slant toward "universalistic Jews who are anti-particularists"—or so lament a few more experienced Reconstructionist rabbis. "The rich mix in the Reconstructionist movement of particularist and universalist emphases is now fading," one such rabbi complains. "The universalist tendency is being driven by the top leadership of the movement." Says another about the road not taken, the leadership of the movement has chosen to pursue "a low bar Judaism," rather than become the movement of deep learning and knowledge. Given the movement's historical commitment to intellectual and cultural pursuits and its emphasis on Jewish peoplehood in the past, the current path represents a sharp break from Kaplanian Reconstructionism.

But then again the ideology of Mordechai Kaplan is hardly a factor any longer in Reconstructionist synagogues. As one Reconstructionist rabbi put it to me: "I stopped talking about ideology a long time ago. I rather talk about life. . . . Lived practice, rather than ideology, is so important." To be sure, Reconstructionists still pay lip service to Kaplan's method—his conception of Judaism as an evolving civilization and his receptivity to radical change. The content of his teachings, though, is an afterthought at best. What rabbis in the movement seem to take most pride in is the emotional connection they forge with congregants and the experiential dimension they bring to congregational life—precisely the same goals cited by rabbis of every denominational and unconventional movement today.

Jewish Renewal and the network of Havurot share the Reconstructionist niche, but differ primarily in the liturgical realm. Reconstructionist congregations follow their movement's prayer book; the others experiment both with the content of the prayers and with deportment during prayer. As one Reconstructionist rabbi put it to me, "Renewal is the ecstatic wing of Reconstructionism." From the Renewal perspective, the large quotient of Hebrew and traditional liturgy in Reconstructionist synagogues render their services stiff and staid. Renewal congregations favor body movement, meditation, wordless song, and the like. The point is driven home by a newspaper reporter who visited Makom Ohr Shalom in Woodland Hills, California, where the Yom Kippur services were led by the now deceased spiritual founder of Renewal, "Reb Zalman" Schachter-Shalomi: "Picture 20 massage tables, with people lying down and being gently touched, with music playing in the background. On Yom Kippur."[19] To be sure, Renewal has become somewhat less touchy-feely under its more recent leadership, but it nevertheless remains highly experimental.

With the passing of Reb Zalman, a new generation of younger rabbis has assumed prominence. Perhaps the most successful such congregational rabbi has been David Ingber, whose congregation on the Upper West Side of Manhattan is formally nondenominational, but "has ties to the Renewal movement."[20] Romemu, as it is called, is influenced by New Age and Eastern religions but also retains a fair amount of traditionalism, perhaps a vestige of Ingber's Orthodox upbringing. The Shabbat morning service was described to me as having "a very traditional feel" through the conclusion of the Torah service; at that point, additional (Musaf) service is eliminated. On Friday nights those who wish to join in dance during the service may do so, but unlike other Renewal services that leave time for meditation after tunes have been sung, Romemu's service tends to move along briskly. The rabbi's sermons may feature Hasidic and Buddhist texts, as well as contemporary meditations. As is the case with so many of the start-up congregations, Romemu is inconceivable without the active presence of its rabbi. For all the talk about dispensing with hierarchy, Romemu is the expression of Ingber's sensibility and talents.

Finding a good definition of Jewish Renewal is not a simple matter, given the improvisational style and ever-shifting nature of this movement, the absence of a guiding leader or leadership council,[21] and a deliberate refusal to create an infrastructure to speak for the movement.[22] Here is a stab at a working definition offered by an insider:[23] "Jewish Renewal is essentially an attempt to revive, recontextualize, and reform Jewish spiritualist movements that have most recently manifested in Hasidism but have roots in premodern Jewish pietism. It is a reformation of Jewish spiritual practice in the spirit of humanism and global consciousness." To this we might add several other ingredients: Renewal prides itself on its syncretism, drawing upon the wisdom of all religions; it welcomes non-Jews and presents itself as a universalistic rather than particularistic form of Judaism; and it knows of no single way to pray.

Both Renewal congregations and Havurot tend to be small fellowships that meet a few times a month, lack large congregational structures, and focus on prayer, education, or social causes.[24] Jewish Renewal groups involve themselves with kabbala, neo-Hasidism, and meditation. Convinced that only "a paradigm shift" will "develop a spirituality through which Judaism can transform itself,"[25] they incorporate aspects of Eastern religions into their prayers, proudly borrowing "openly and liberally from other faith traditions and speak[ing] of ourselves as JuBus, Jufis, and Hinjews."[26] The Renewal movement has issued a prayer book, *Ohr hadash: New Paths for Shabbat Morning.*[27] Independent Havurot are liturgically eclectic, using works and performing practices that originate in various religious movements.[28]

Another niche is occupied by the gay and lesbian synagogues. The first of these, Beth Chayim Chadashim of Los Angeles, was founded in 1972.[29] By the beginning of the current century, some nineteen such congregations had been formed—eleven of them were independent, seven belonged to the URJ, the Reform movement's congregational arm, and one belonged to the Reconstructionist Federation.[30] Prayer services in gay and lesbian synagogues tend to follow Conservative or Reform practices, and congregations employ the prayer books of these denominations. As the rabbi of Bet Mishpachah in Washington, DC, put it: "When people come to our synagogues they're coming for the same reasons that any other Jews come to synagogue. With few exceptions, we say the same prayers. It's not really different in content."[31]

Even so, these synagogues have developed their own liturgical and theological responses to issues of particular concern to their members, ranging from prayers acknowledging discrimination against LGBTQ individuals to meditations on the ravages of the AIDS epidemic, from attention to gender neutrality to the inclusion of non-Jewish partners in the services.[32] Since their members are now having more children, these synagogues are increasingly grappling with the tension between demands for congregational supplementary schools and the resentment of older members who say that they established these synagogues as "adult places in an era when gay couples didn't often have kids."[33]

The future of gay synagogues, however, is hard to predict. On the one hand, some of the larger ones on the East and West Coasts are attracting substantial percentages of their members from the heterosexual population; as many as one-third of San Francisco's Sha'ar Zahav are thought to be heterosexual, as are half of Atlanta's Congregation Beth Haverim. Simultaneously, with the shift in policies on gay issues in Reconstructionist, Reform, and Conservative synagogues, homosexuals and lesbians feel more welcome to join conventional synagogues. "There are [LGBTQ] people," said Idit Klein of Keshet, a national Jewish LGBTQ advocacy organization, "who wanted to go to a 'regular' shul. Or wanted a rabbi. Or wanted services every week. Or wanted a particular service or a shul with its own building. Or a host of other reasons that people will choose one shul over another." Gay synagogues also face the same challenge all non-Orthodox ones encounter: generally, people join only when they are raising children, and fertility among non-Orthodox Jews is down considerably.[34] Ironically, then, the future viability of gay synagogues may depend on their success in attracting gay and lesbian Jews who have children, and also their straight counterparts.[35]

Still another niche is occupied by so-called Humanistic communities and congregations, which are dedicated to secular Judaism. Beginning with the founding of the first of these in a suburb of Detroit by Rabbi Sherwin Wine in 1963, the movement has grown to some twenty-six communities in the United States, under the umbrella of the Society for Humanistic Judaism.[36] Humanistic congregations draw upon the traditional liturgy as well as other Jewish texts when they engage in communal gatherings, but, as committed secularists, they do not pray, although they do celebrate life cycle passages so as to "allow the family and community to reinforce their unity and to articulate the values that make life worthwhile."[37] One Humanistic congregation in Washington, DC, eventually withdrew from the society because it was partial to a more traditional liturgy, and accepted as members Jews who believed in God. This congregation pushed the envelope by saying the *Sh'ma*, a central prayer of traditional Judaism that affirms belief in one, indivisible God. The recitation was prefaced with the words: "In concert with what Jews have said for thousands of years, let's rise and say the *Sh'ma*. We are doing this as a tradition, not as a prayer."[38]

Founded during the last third of the twentieth century, all of these types of niche synagogues reflect a sensibility of an earlier time. All struggle to draw millennials, but mainly attract aging baby boomers. Though some speak bravely about being the wave of the future, all these types (as distinct from individual congregations) seem to have stagnant membership numbers. One Reconstructionist rabbi forthrightly explained her belief that her movement would remain small by noting that all non-Orthodox synagogues are struggling to attract new and younger members; given the static demography of Reconstructionist synagogues over the past quarter century, there is little reason to believe that movement will attract larger numbers in the coming decades. With the complete acceptance of the LGBTQ community in Reform and Reconstructionist synagogues and a fair number of Conservative ones, the continuing need for gay synagogues also is not clear. And the Humanistic synagogues are a fringe. Judging by Renewal's ordination of some two hundred members, that movement may have legs, though only a fraction of its rabbis serve in synagogues of any kind, and many of those who do so, officiate in congregations holding dual affiliation with Reform or Reconstructionism, for example. We lack survey data on the numbers, but all told these groups collectively may attract fewer than fifty thousand adult adherents, half of whom belong to Reconstructionist synagogues.[39] Still, they have their own committed members and serve as models for those seeking to establish alternatives to conventional denominational synagogues.

New Spiritual Communities for a New Era

Since the closing years of the twentieth century, new settings for Jewish religious gathering have appeared. Driving the creation of these start-ups has been a widespread anxiety in the Jewish community about low levels of participation by younger Jews in organized Jewish activities. "Engagement of young people is almost a preoccupation in the Jewish community," contends Pearl Beck, a demographic researcher; another social scientist stated matters more baldly: "It's a very real fear. And the smaller the community, the more significant it is. . . . It's really difficult for them to do anything that's going to attract young Jews."[40] With a third of younger Jews claiming to identify with no religion and an evident graying of congregational membership, these trends have occasioned much soul searching in established synagogues, new research about what makes millennials tick, and a cottage industry of advisors claiming to know how to lure this population to participate in Jewish life.

Two examples of this advice industry's output may suffice to capture the conventional wisdom. One comes from the ROI Community, which specializes in investing in promising young leaders:

> Young people today have varied and complex identities, of which "Jewish" tends to play just one role—and oftentimes, not even the main one. While these millennial leaders may therefore not find their calling in traditional Jewish institutions in which Judaism is expected to be top priority, they do see themselves fitting into a Jewish network that encourages them to explore the multiple layers of their identities on their own terms, and create Jewish communities that jibe with their other deeply held values—*Tikkun Olam*, education, environmentalism, social justice and more. This realization alone—that Jewish life is important to the millennials who are most active in building the future of this world, albeit in new and evolving ways—is inspiring.[41]

Though it is not clear whose education or what kind of learning is one of the "deeply held values," the rest of this description focuses on causes thought dear to the hearts of this generation. Also of note is the apparent irrelevance of specifically parochial Jewish activities, let alone of belief, religious practice, or Jewish learning.

A second column directed to millennials takes up the question of religion head-on: "You have the power to shape your Judaism your way. You can create communities that are meaningful to you, with rituals that take advantage of the best our tradition has to offer, combined with values that you would be proud to pass on to your children and share with your friends."[42] Here the working assumption is that carefully selected rituals may hold some attraction. But the overarching conception is of a Judaism that millennials will craft on their own based on their unique values and needs. Together these two strands—the emphasis on universalistic causes and the selective appropriation of Jewish rituals—inform the thinking behind a good deal of the spiritual life being created for millennials.

Three very different types of religious start-ups have been formed to address millennials. Receiving the most attention are rabbi-founded and -led "spiritual communities," which sometimes are referred to collectively as Emergent Congregations.[43] The second, also organized and led mainly by rabbis and other Jewish professionals, meets at varied intervals and cannot be described as communities, so much as gathering venues for those who wish to attend Jewish events episodically. And the third consists of Independent Minyanim, mainly founded and led by gen Xers, that is, those born between 1966 and 1979 who are neither baby boomers nor millennials. What sets these Indie Minyanim apart is their commitment to what they describe as "quality" prayer, above all else, and their eschewal of rabbinic leadership. Though these three types of gathering places share some commonalities, they differ fundamentally in goals and sensibilities.

We begin with the rabbi-led spiritual communities. Some such as Ikar in Los Angeles, Lab Shul and Romemu in Manhattan, Mishkan in Chicago, and Sixth and I in Washington, DC, are primarily designed to offer worship services with a twist that appeal especially to younger Jews. A few other start-ups regard themselves as communities first, and only secondarily as places of worship. Among these are the Kavana Cooperative in Seattle and the Kitchen in San Francisco. The latter two, as their names imply, emphasize social gatherings, potluck meals, and an innovative sensibility. That said, they also focus on Judaism. As one report has put it: "They use buzzwords like 'high-content

Judaism' and 'DIY Judaism.' They have 'spiritual directors' instead of rabbis and 'live entertainment managers' in place of cantors. Their services tend to be lively and musically oriented, and they are explicitly committed to welcoming all comers, regardless of level of religious practice or sexual orientation—or even whether the participants are Jewish."[44] In their self-presentation, all of these groups stress their "inclusive[ness] without being 'lite.' "[45] As Rabbi Sharon Brous has put it about her community, "At Ikar we strive for an environment that really welcomes and embraces everyone—including folks who are ambivalent, atheist or just cynical about community, ritual, even God. . . . And at the same time, we don't lower the bar for them. If we did, they'd walk in and run out."[46] Mishkan's statement of core values laments that "too many religious experiences feel like we leave our real selves at the door when we walk in. At Mishkan we create containers for real self-expression through music, text, meditation, breath, and through creating a space that is comfortable enough for us to laugh, cry, dance, sing out, be silent, pray . . . whatever is real for each person. This is a safe space to be one's self."[47] Lab Shul is perhaps the most radical in its approach to prayer: At its High Holiday services, "all traces of patriarchal, hierarchical and hetero-normative language, including the classing [sic] art/thou, He, and even the word God, have been removed. Instead of using the baggage-laden G-O-D, we've replaced it with terms like 'source of life,' and 'deepest source.' We're hoping more expansive, inclusion imagery will translate to a more welcoming, inclusive service."[48]

"Inclusiveness," of course, is one of the aspirations of contemporary Jewish life, and usually is a code word for the full equality of the LGBTQ Jews and the welcoming of individuals living in all kinds of family configurations, especially with non-Jews. In the new spiritual communities, the goal also is to provide a comfortable experience for Jews who have little formal training in Jewish religious living. Lizzi Heydemann, rabbi of Mishkan, has stated her special sensitivity to "the common story of American Jews who feel alienated from Jewish life because they have little knowledge of Jewish ritual and Hebrew."[49] This sensitivity also extends to non-Jews. In the Kitchen in San Francisco, some 40 percent of attendees are not Jewish, according to the estimate of its leader, Rabbi Noa Kushner. Acceding to what journalist Peter Beinart describes as the "little tolerance for tribal distinctions their parents and grandparents took for granted," the Kitchen addresses itself to anyone who wishes to be "doing Jewish," rather than simply "being Jewish." No doubt part of the attraction of these new spiritual communities lies in downplaying Jewish peoplehood commitments and receptivity to the active presence of non-Jews, a policy that works well in a Jewish society where intermarriage and interdating have become the norm, and where younger Jews increasingly wish to spend time doing Jewish things with their non-Jewish friends.[50]

A further defining feature of the new spiritual communities is their undisguised commitment to what they call "progressive" politics. Mishkan proudly declares on its website its commitment to "working with local community organizing groups, service agencies, and taking inspiration from the many people in our community involved in the work of social change, Mishkan is constantly working toward greater social justice, locally, nationally and globally."[51] The Kitchen calls its children's program Freedom School because "we believe learning Torah will move students to justice." And Ikar announces its "expectation . . . that every member . . . participate in the work of tikkun—healing" by fighting poverty, gun violence, and environmental degradation.[52] Not surprisingly, given their politics, the leaders of these communities tend to be more outspoken critics of Israeli policies than are rabbis in more conventional synagogues.[53]

Indeed, one way these communities set themselves apart from conventional synagogues is in their sharp tilt to left-wing politics. Whereas Reform and Reconstructionist synagogues have long paid lip-service to tikkun olam, their programs have tended to favor more moderate positions espoused by the Democratic Party. The new spiritual communities, by contrast, are inclined to the policies and preoccupations of the left wing of that party.[54] Those Jews who do not support these particular ideological agendas or prefer their synagogues to focus on prayer and learning, rather than politics, may not find the new spiritual communities to their taste.[55]

Pop-Ups

In contrast to the community-building efforts of the "spiritual communities," a range of what might be called "pop-up" gatherings offer a more episodic set of experiences. The logic behind these start-ups is the imperative to go where the Jews are, rather than sit back and wait for them to find their way into a synagogue. Organizers intentionally create settings where young singles and newly married Jews tend to cluster, hoping these millennials will find it enticing to attend Jewish events in their own neighborhoods. The further assumption is that through a mix of programs, few of which offer anything resembling a prayer service, younger Jews who have no interest in prayer will be drawn by the ambience, cultural cachet, and social opportunities. That these groups meet only sporadically offers still another incentive. No one is expected to attend on a weekly basis; if pop-ups can attract millennials once a month or a few times a year that is seen as a success.

In the case of Ohel Ayala, the intention is simply to provide free High Holiday services in several locations around New York City, but no further follow-up during the rest of the year.[56] Unlike other pop-ups, Ohel Ayala offers a highly traditional Conservative prayer service. By contrast, the pop-up Because Jewish deliberately targets secular Jews who "want to create something that feels authentically personal and at the same time genuinely spiritual," says its organizer, Rabbi Dan Ain. "There's a real niche of people who experience spirituality in communal concert settings, who go to festivals, to Burning Man, and to Phish shows. The idea is to create a context where people can tap into Judaism through what they love doing." Because Jewish offers a Friday night "jam series" consisting of candle lighting, blessings over wine and challah, and then interviews and performances by pop artists. Saturday Mornings offer some kind of Sabbath programming for "people who feel most comfortable in non-traditional spaces." And Korban Shabbat invites participants to offer something of themselves at their gatherings—reciting poetry, singing Hasidic niggunim, performing shamanic drumming, leading meditation, and playing guitar. The goal is to help people who normally would have no contact with Jewish life on the Sabbath to express what is in their hearts in some form of prayer, with the rabbinic leader serving as the curator.[57]

A different approach to creating a "customized Judaism" seems to be at work on the West Coast when East Side Jews meet in Los Angeles. At least once a month, programs are offered "around a Jewish holiday, ritual or just plain social activity, giving the gathering an irreverent, artsy and enterprising spin." Just how irreverent may be gauged by two examples: at a Havdala event, called "Sacred/Profane," attendees "dunked homemade French fries in turmeric and curry, drank beer and listened to the Jewish adult-film actress Nina Hartley lecture on 'Sacred Sensuality.' Another time, they celebrated Rosh Hodesh on the rooftop of the Wi Spa, calling it 'Once in a Jew Moon,' during which men and women made their way through an Asian-style mikveh and, afterward, gathered under the open sky for Torah study."[58]

Not all programs offering pop-up options are so unconventional. The Well in Detroit, for example, which originally began under the auspices of a local Reform temple, has created partnerships with a range of communal institutions. Its programs float between a variety of institutions and center around Jewish holidays and rituals. Like so many other pop-ups, the offbeat venue is part of the attraction, but the Well is primarily designed to offer "effective (and replicable) liberal Jewish outreach," as distinct from what is offered by Orthodox groups. On Sukkot, programs are held every evening during the holiday's eight days; the venue is a Sukkah, albeit one decorated unconventionally as an art installation. On the second day of Rosh Ha-shanah, almost five hundred millennials cast off their sins at a communal Tashlikh ceremony. Shabbat picnics are held, as are women's Rosh Hodesh groups. The Well works hard to engage young adults in planning these pro-grams for their peers, and does not shy away from asking participants to make a financial contribution or donate food. Refreshingly, the organizers recognize that "free is false, and is a disservice to our community."[59]

Another model is offered by Moishe Houses, a network of some fifty-eight centers scattered throughout the United States that offer a variety of Jewish social and religious programs geared toward millennials in their twen-ties.[60] Begun in 2006, Moishe Houses offer rent subsidies to young Jewish adults who are prepared to use their house as a neighborhood center for Jewish programs, everything from Shabbat dinners to Purim parties, social action activities, and Jewish study circles. As part of their contract, house mates agree to post pictures and written descriptions of their events on the Moishe House blog site, as well as to start one of their own. The stated goal of the effort is to use the house as a base to have "more Jewish adults actively live vibrant Jewish lives in their homes and communities."[61]

Moishe Houses vary greatly from place to place, but Friday evening Shabbat dinners are a universal feature, as is the celebration of Jewish holidays. As at the pop-ups, attendance is episodic for most participants. But as is the case in the spiritual communities, the Moishe Houses are staffed by a set number of designated volunteers who are responsible for hosting events of a Jewish nature. Some houses even have a formal association with a rabbi. As for attendees, writes one observer, most "are 'not Jewish in the rest of their lives' in the traditional sense. They may not be celebrating holidays on their own, they may not be attending Shabbat services at a synagogue, and they may not have a family back home with whom to enjoy 'Jewish life.' Moishe House is the surrogate that provides these experiences for them."[62]

Indie Minyanim

Rounding out the picture are fifty Independent Minyanim established by and for young Jews[63]—that is, those born since the end of the baby boom, both singles and younger couples.[64] Some are partnership minyanim within the Modern Orthodox orbit. Most are largely stocked with Conservative-raised and -educated Jews, and define themselves as Egalitarian Traditional. They tend to meet only on the Sabbath, and some only hold services either on Friday evening *or* Shabbat morning. They do not strive to provide the accoutrements of a synagogue, such as weekday services, rabbinic leadership, and a congregational school for children.

All are conservative in the sense that they are looking to create "quality" prayer employing the traditional Hebrew liturgy, even as they strive to be "inclusive." The latter tends to entail the respectful acceptance of different family configurations and the presence of intermarried couples, but in this setting it also means a receptivity to including Jews who may lack a strong Jewish educational background. In the Indie Minyanim, as they often are called, this is easier said than done. Mechon Hadar, the fountainhead institution of the Indie Minyan movement, devotes a substantial section on its website to the challenge of "being inclusive in davening without sacrificing quality." Simply put, if the goal is to offer "quality" worship services, how does a minyan ensure that people who lead the services or read Torah are up to the task? "Minyan standards and quality control" are major preoccupations in these settings. Some groups offer classes to individuals interested in learning how to lead the prayers. Several require Torah readers to be tested "two days before Shabbat to make sure they are ready." The Indie Minyanim also post recordings of model prayer services and Torah readings on their websites for members to emulate. Ensuring the preparedness of prayer leaders while simultaneously encouraging novices to learn the skills necessary to lead tefila is a tightrope walked with great care by the Indie Minyanim.[65]

It bears emphasizing that all of this effort expended by Independent Minyanim is performed by volunteers. Though a few have hired some part-time help to deal with bookkeeping matters, the actual work of running the minyanim is done by laypeople. In this sense, the Indie Minyanim are vastly different from the "spiritual communities" and pop-ups. That this volunteering is performed by young adults in their twenties and thirties who are primarily concerned with launching their careers and family formation further suggests how much altruism and commitment are to be found in these Indie Minyanim. Not for nothing have they been described as "very pragmatic and self-sufficient. . . . They emphasize lay leadership, and are less interested in rabbinic authority and in creating superstructure buildings than they are in building their community."[66]

What sense might we make of the combined efforts of the "spiritual communities," the pop-up efforts, and the Independent Minyanim? Some have suggested that they are but a twenty-first-century variation of the independent Havurot of the 1970s and 1980s.[67] The latter too were highly critical of synagogue life, especially the uninspiring quality of prayer services and the cold formality of social interactions. But the current religious start-ups differ from those Havurot considerably. To begin with, the Havurot tended to be elitist and appealed to highly educated young Jews. The Independent Minyanim are most similar to the Havurot in that regard, but with their strong emphasis on serious prayer and their high level of traditionalism, the Independent Minyanim offer a very different version of congregating. As to the spiritual communities, with their programs attracting many hundreds of participants, they hardly are like the intimate fellowships created by the

Havurot: they are increasingly becoming synagogues with their own buildings, strict dues structures, and congregational schools for children of members. And the pop-ups, in strong contrast to the Havurot of yesteryear, have not as yet managed to create anything resembling tight social communities.

Today's religious start-ups are better understood on their own terms, rather than as replications of earlier forms. This is most dramatically evident in the indispensability of rabbis in all but the Independent Minyanim. Despite all the opposition to hierarchy and the efforts to involve participants actively in the running of services and programs, both the spiritual communities and the pop-ups exist only because of the efforts of rabbis who organize them, raise the money to fund them, and run the services. They are very much top-down operations. It is no small irony that with all the talk of replacing the clergy-led synagogue, spiritual communities are entirely dependent upon charismatic rabbis and a staff of music leaders, some of whom are treated as national rock stars. These groupings hardly are structured in a manner designed to offer "flat" governance.

A second characteristic of the unconventional groupings is their dependence upon an urban environment. Few of these groups have emerged in the suburbs where most Jewish families continue to live.[68] Millennials, of course, tend to cluster in urban spaces, and so it is understandable that the various programs to attract them are held in cities. The question for the near-term future is whether millennials will continue to live in urban settings where space to raise a family is at a premium and housing costs are considerably higher than in the suburbs. If aging millennials decamp to the so-called "leafy suburbs," will these new models follow? Indeed, are they even feasible in places that lack the critical mass of Jews available in cities?

Still another question about the unconventional religious settings for millennials is how well their product will wear as their populations grow older and develop new needs, such as religious schooling for their children. Some of the older Independent Minyanim and even the spiritual communities are already facing these challenges as their members age and as they attract multiple generations. Do they purchase their own buildings and offer the range of programs found in conventional synagogues, or do they insist on appealing to people in their twenties and thirties who have not yet formed families, letting older members find other places to worship and educate their children? It is already an open question whether younger millennials, those born during the tail end of their age cohort, are drawn to the spiritual communities where the majority of attendees are married with children.[69]

The additional wild card in these calculations is how denominational synagogues respond to the challenges posed by the unconventional settings. If history is a guide, synagogues will adapt the ideas and methods of their critics. The Havurah concept was co-opted by synagogues: when the independent Havurot emerged in the early 1970s, hundreds of synagogues simply divided their members into smaller Havurot; and many of these continued to meet over the course of decades. There already is evidence that the spirited style of prayer, the outreach to millennials, and the stress on meditation and other spiritual practices pioneered by the start-ups are being brought into conventional synagogue life. The catalysts for change generally are younger rabbis who have been influenced by the innovations of start-ups and trained in places such as the Institute for Jewish Spirituality and Rabbis without Borders to replicate the style of those places within conventional synagogues.[70]

It remains to be seen whether the millennials and gen X populations attracted to unconventional religious settings will eventually make their way into more conventional synagogues. For the present, it is enough that the nascent start-up sector is growing in size and spreading to increasing numbers of communities. Not least, the leaders of these groups are developing new approaches to draw Jews into religious settings and are introducing a fresh sensibility that speaks to swaths of Jewish millennials.[71] As such, they represent a third prong in the effort to draw Jews into religious life—the first being conventional synagogues that are reshaping their approaches to worship and study; the second consisting of Orthodox outreach groups, which touch the lives of many hundreds of thousands of non-Orthodox Jews; and the third being the numerically smaller but intensely experimental start-ups, which are innovating new ways to conduct prayer, approach study, and build community.

CONCLUSION

A NEW REMIX

Each summer in recent years, between a hundred fifty and two hundred adult Jews of all ages gather at a retreat center in the lower Berkshire mountain range to sing Jewish songs and teach one another new melodies. Participants are drawn from the full spectrum of religious backgrounds, from former Haredi Jews to adherents of Conservative, Reform, and Renewal Judaism. The focal point of the weekend is the celebration of Shabbat, a time to engage in prayer and learning Jewish songs, which, as the organizers point out, are "inclusive of a wide range of Jewish ancestry and religious practices." Not all the songs are religious: some are drawn from the secular Yiddish ambience, the Jewish labor movement, and Judeo-Arabic folk culture. Most, however, are religious in nature, including, as the organizers state, music sung to liturgical texts, *piyyutim* (religious poetry) and Hebrew chants; some are wordless melodies (niggunim), generally of Hasidic origin, appropriate for religious settings.[1]

Let My People Sing, as this annual gathering is called, admittedly draws only a small fraction of the American Jewish population, although it is spreading gradually to communities around the country.[2] Its importance lies not in the number of people who participate but in the sensibility it reflects. It is pluralistic both in the broad spectrum of Jews it attracts to learn from one another and also in the wide-ranging provenance of melodies taught and sung. Both types of inclusiveness are intentionally built into the retreats whose object is the remixing of Jewish music—and Jews.[3]

The terminology of "remixing" originates in the musical sphere and refers to combining different media or elements of music to create new versions of older music. New technologies have simplified the process of remixing music. But the term, imprecise as it is, has come to represent an approach to other spheres of culture, not only music. "With remix," explains a self-styled video remixer, "we can reedit tired narratives into more subversive ones or pay homage to the awesome narratives that do exist."[4] Though taken from a context far removed from Judaism, this description captures the sensibility now animating a range of current initiatives, including Let My People Sing, to reshape Jewish religious life in the United States (and for that matter in Israel and some other countries). The tinkering at times is subversive, and other times it pays homage to traditional Judaism.

Evidence of remixing is apparent, as noted in the first chapters of this study, in the highly personalized selectivity exercised by many Jews involved in some form of religious activity. Jews across the spectrum tend to decide for themselves which mitzvot (commandments) they will observe and which they will ignore. From an outsider's perspective these choices may appear arbitrary and inconsistent, though presumably they make perfect sense to an individual. (By what logic, to mention an example already noted, would a Jewish man faithfully wrap tefilin, but scoff at kosher food laws?) Noteworthy too is the receptivity of Jews to traditional practices that in the past were foreign or even repugnant to them, such as deciding suddenly to observe one of the kosher dietary laws, even while continuing to reject others—for example, no longer eating pork but continuing to enjoy seafood. And conversely, among some observant Jews in both the Conservative and Orthodox camps, major efforts have been under way to make it possible within the structure of Jewish law for women to play a much larger role in religious life than had been sanctioned in the past.

The spirit of remixing is even more evident in major initiatives to spur renewal in Jewish religious practice. Synagogues, as we have seen, are literally incorporating newly composed music into the worship service, often combining the traditional *nussach* (liturgical music) with Hasidic, Israeli, and contemporary American compositions. Congregations also are experimenting with dance and various forms of Eastern meditation practices, even as they adhere to the traditional liturgy. In some congregations, as we have seen, the Yizkor service designed to remember the deceased has become a time not only to recall the departed, but also to converse with them imaginatively; and the High Holiday services in some synagogues include opportunities for the *public* confession of sins (albeit the confessants are shrouded in anonymity). The intentional incorporation of Hasidic and Mussar teachings into liberal synagogue settings offers still another incongruous remixing of vastly different religious outlooks. These and other examples attest to how once marginalized religious views and practices are now given fresh meaning through a process of reframing, juxtaposition, and integration.

Perhaps nowhere is the remix of tradition with radical innovation more evident than in Orthodox outreach settings. The rapid adoption of new Internet tools, such as social media, by Chabad and Aish HaTorah, owners of probably the two most widely visited Jewish websites in the world, speaks to the eagerness of these outreach groups to harness new technologies. Many hundreds of videos have been posted by these sites offering Torah study, homilies, and religious guidance. Their efforts are all the more remarkable given the hostility to the Internet within the Haredi world of which they are a part. Even more radically, Orthodox outreach groups have worked around long-established Halachic precedents about who may be counted in a minyan, how much modesty of dress is required, or whether one may teach Torah to non-Jews or enable the desecration of the Sabbath by another Jew (for instance by inviting someone who will arrive by car to a Sabbath meal). In the name of kiruv, some Orthodox outreach synagogues adopt practices unthinkable in congregations of any of the liberal movements. A Chabad rabbi, for example, explained to me how he keeps his people in the synagogue during the long High Holiday services: as the prayer leader recites the traditional liturgy, the rabbi conducts a discussion about facets of the holiday, *by talking over the prayer leader*.

Almost by definition, many of the unconventional settings for Jewish religious gathering offer a variety of remixes. A well-known new spiritual community, for example, regularly serves light refreshments *in the sanctu-*

ary during the service in order to revive the energy of congregants. In some Renewal settings, yoga and other forms of physical expression are common features, as are dance and movement. Among start-ups, the balance of tradition and innovation is usually tipped toward the latter, so that a recitation of kiddush and HaMotzei, the blessing over wine and bread, is the only traditional feature at Friday evening gatherings. That balance, of course, varies greatly from one type of unconventional setting to another, but the object of many of these gatherings is to merge elements of Judaism with hipster culture. Why else hold a Shabbat gathering in a bar, event space, or warehouse? It is precisely the mixing of the conventional and unconventional that is thought to be attractive to younger Jews who otherwise might shun a Friday evening Sabbath gathering.

Collectively, the many hundreds of local synagogues, outreach centers, and start-ups engaged in the efforts to remix Judaism for the current age constitute a large nationwide movement. Of course, not every place of Jewish religious gathering vibrates with religious intensity, nor are all Jewish clergy engaged in a well-conceived plan to draw Jews into some form of religious life. Undoubtedly, quite a few congregations fail to inspire. Still, my interviews with many dozens of rabbis and volunteer leaders about their activities impressed upon me just how much energy and idealism they invest in the task of building religious connections. Many rabbis speak with emotion about their sense of urgency and commitment, if not mission, to draw Jews closer to religious engagement. What makes this all the more remarkable is the clear-eyed way they see the challenges: whether they are pulpit rabbis, educators, outreach workers, or organizers of religious start-ups, they speak with realism about the powerful forces they are up against—and yet nonetheless, they persevere.

They operate in a broader American cultural environment that has internalized a set of "isms" highly antithetical to traditional religion. Large portions of the American Jewish populace, like so many of their neighbors, have come to value *voluntarism* (an insistence on radical choice), *DIY-ism* (the license for invention), *personalism* (the quest for personal meaning), *universalism* (the abnegation of parochial collective identity), and *moralism* (the emphasis on the moral and ethical value of rites and customs).[5] What this has meant is that ever more Jews choose whether they wish to identify as Jewish and then define for themselves what such a decision means. As for Judaism itself, the primary purpose of religion in the eyes of a large swath of the Jewish population is to live as a "good human being," with decency defined in highly ideological, if not politically correct, ways set forth by the wider culture and only marginally related to traditional Jewish teachings.

Perhaps no such culturally approved norm is more sacrosanct than the myth of the "sovereign self" as the primary determinant of how each Jew will choose to enact a Judaism of personal meaning.[6] As autonomous individuals, the thinking goes, all Jews exercise the right to cobble together a religious life as they see fit, even if such a Judaism has little connection to a recognizable form of Jewish behavior and sees no virtue in working for the interests of the Jewish people. With such personal license also comes freedom from other people's judgment: no one has the right to define what kind of religious observance is proper for anyone else.

Missing from this calculus about the inevitable triumph of autonomy is an awareness of how much humans are shaped by cultural and social expectations. Not for nothing do some speak of a "herd of independent minds"— that is, those who claim to act independently but actually are guided in their choices by their social group, or what Harold Rosenberg described as "mass culture."[7] The sovereign self is a cultural construct. And what appear to be autonomous decisions usually are the outcomes of peer influences.[8]

Moreover, the constant harping on autonomy ignores the many ways modern people constrain themselves in nonreligious settings for the sake of the social and communal good. Rabbi Jacob J. Schacter put it well when he punctured the myth of individual autonomy as the overriding ethos of our times: "a closer look at contemporary notions of autonomy yields the inescapable conclusion that they are, in fact, bankrupt and empty of meaning. All people make decisions to limit their autonomy—and do so all the time—to get through life. All people abide by laws, whatever they may be; the dream of unbridled liberty and autonomy is a foolish one."[9] Religious communities, like other mediating institutions standing between the individual and the government, have a role to play in challenging their adherents to live up to ideals and values beyond their own short-term needs. They can—and do—shape behavior through education, inspiration, and calls for joint action.

For the moment, though, the unquestioning acceptance of autonomy as an ideal has given many Jews license to act as they see fit. If the grounds for defining Judaism are personalist, one picks and chooses from the religion that which is personally fulfilling. If the DIY mind-set empowers Jews to reinvent Judaism, then tinkering makes perfect sense. And if universalism negates the collective needs of the Jewish people, asking anyone to desist from certain behaviors because they are not good for the health of the Jewish people either makes no sense or is seen as an unwelcome intrusion into deeply personal decisions.

One of the effects of this emphasis on choice and empowerment is a diminution in the authority of religious leaders. As the larger culture ostensibly encourages individuals to make their own decisions, and as online services have made vast quantities of information available, there is less of a perceived need for authoritative clergy. Instead, the wider culture encourages each person to exercise authority to decide on religious matters individually. And in making religious choices, and other kinds too, instrumentality becomes a major determinant. Does this work for me? Does it help me navigate? These questions loom large in the current age of seemingly limitless choices. The upshot is a challenging environment for religion as individuals arrive at their answers in highly subjective ways because everyone is faced with different sets of questions and challenges.[10]

In the course of this continual negotiation, religion has been at a great disadvantage. Sociologist James Davison Hunter has noted how religion almost always capitulates to the larger culture.[11] It is likely, he writes, "that the cognitive bargaining between the structures and processes of modernity and a religious belief system taking place in the arena of people's world views would result in cognitive contamination of the religious world view. This would be due to the massive plausibility structures available for the modern rational and secular world view,[12] and the comparatively small and fragile plausibility structures available for any form of religious world view."[13] In practice, utilitarian, therapeutic, and secular liberal assumptions guide the behavior of contemporary American Jews, far more than do Jewish teachings.

These shifts in outlook are not mere abstractions: they have real-world consequences. When religion is redefined to serve the personal needs of individuals and offer therapeutic help, it cannot set forth obligations. The most glaring example of how this has worked may be found in the discourse surrounding intermarriage, which has shifted from what Jewish religious teachings expect of Jews and what is good for the Jewish people to what is good for a particular couple.[14] With the transformation of societal attitudes about individual choice and privacy, it became far more difficult to make a case for public opposition to such marriages—even though the majority of religious leaders understand that intermarriage creates a major obstacle to the transmission of Jewish identity from one generation to the next. The case for endogamy collides with American individualism because it calls upon individuals to limit their choices in deference to the needs of the Jewish people. Soaring rates of intermarriage, in turn, have driven vast numbers of Jews away from Jewish engagement.[15]

In other areas of religious life too, it has become considerably more difficult to make the case for why Jews should relinquish leisure-time activities in favor of synagogue attendance, limit the kinds of foods they eat in order to keep kosher, or even observe major Jewish holidays on the designated calendar date, rather than when it is most convenient. In our current hyper-individualistic age, people don't want to be told what they should do, not a small challenge for religious leaders responsible for presenting a religious tradition replete with commandments and prohibitions.

Not surprisingly, then, rabbis are increasingly loath to offer prescriptive messages about the observance of Judaism. "Thou shalt" and "thou shalt not" have given way to a very different kind of religious language. Judgmentalism is deemed repugnant, and though the language of mitzvah is still invoked, it has been stripped of its meaning—commandment—and now refers to the performance of a good deed.

In place of the traditional religious categories, a new vocabulary has entered religious institutions, designed to fit the current cultural climate. The evidence is all around us: in books promoting "empowered Judaism" and "relational Judaism," blogs singing the praises of DIY Judaism, slogans celebrating a "Jewish renewal" or a "Jewish renaissance" in America, and more. In what has been called the big tent of the new Judaism, the theme of inclusion reigns, with synagogues declaring their intention to create caring communities, family-friendly environments, and, especially, homes for "diversity." An advertisement for an educational retreat in Atlanta holds out the promise of having it all: "An Open, Remixable, Meaningful, Connected Jewish Life."[16]

Surely the most striking features of this vocabulary are its stance and its tone: idealistic, expansive, and upbeat. Presenting Jewish life positively and without fear, it dismisses talk of Jewish vulnerability or of threats to Jewish vitality in the United States. For the newly expansive approach, it is an article of faith that Judaism benefits from diversity and openness, which in turn help foster creativity and even a "renewal" of Jewish life. Seeking to be inviting and enticing to Jews and Gentiles alike, the new language of American Judaism shuns prescriptions and limits its demands to the doing of "good" as defined by universal ethical principles. It is no coincidence that the ideas and attitudes embodied in the new American Judaism are largely indistinguishable from the cluster of ideas and attitudes that inform liberal American culture at large.

There is little reason to doubt the sincerity of those who reframe Judaism in the language of the wider culture, although it is not a stretch to imagine that some are employing tropes tactically as a means to speak to the Jewish folk in a language with contemporary resonance. Like Christian clergy, many rabbis are reshaping their religious teachings to make common cause with the individualistic ethos of the times. The uncanny resemblances between Christian and Jewish religious remixing and the common emphases upon self-expression, meaning making, empowerment, meditation, spirituality, caring, inclusion, and diversity all suggest that religious leaders are struggling to accommodate to the wider culture while they build a big-tent religion to satisfy all comers.

Like their Christian counterparts, rabbis also are promoting religion as a means to personal fulfillment. Religion, the argument goes, satisfies a quest for meaning and human connection in an increasingly disconnected society. It lifts the individual out of the quotidian and injects an element of intentionality in the lives of religious adherents. As a case in point, we note the "selling" of the Sabbath as an Internet-free time zone to society at large: it's not a day of rest commanded by God and regulated by complex commandments; it's a day to engage in all manner of activity, except for the "plugged in" sort.[17] Engagement with a religious community, it is often said, offers an experience of peace, calm, and introspection to counterbalance the frenetic pace of life in our times. These widespread—and laudable—arguments for religious engagement now have made their way into the Jewish sector too where religion is presented as an antidote to the stresses and emptiness of contemporary life.

The synagogue, in turn, is now reconceived as a place where Jews can attend to their well-being. For some it will serve as a place to find serenity: the synagogue is portrayed as an island of calm ideally suited for individual congregants to commune with their innermost selves. The growing popularity of meditation services is symptomatic of the accommodation to this orientation. Taking the logic of well-being to its extreme, as noted earlier in the book, a Reform rabbi now conceives of the synagogue as a place to focus on physical wellness. Appealing to the subjective wants of individual Jews is one path taken by congregations, but it is not the only one. Rabbis of all denominations increasingly offer words of Torah about how to behave kindly toward others—family members, friends, fellow congregant, and, for that matter, humanity at large. Common to these themes, of course, is a view of the synagogue as a therapeutic environment—for the body and soul.

And then there is the turn to universalism, couched as globalism, another buzzword of the current age. There is nothing new about this direction: it was noted already in the 1950s by sociologists Marshall Sklare and Joseph Greenblum when they described "the effective redefinition [of Jewish holidays] in modern terms."[18] What is noteworthy today is how pervasive this process has become, so that every Jewish holiday is likely to be reinterpreted in universalistic terms: Tu Bishvat, the New Year for trees, which barely registered on anyone's radar at midcentury, is now a holiday focused on global sustainability; Purim commemorates all forms of discrimination and abuse; and Passover is about liberation, broadly conceived and without any necessary Jewish content.[19] As for the High Holidays, they provide an opportunity in many synagogues to recommit to the great causes of our time, such as fighting gun violence, human trafficking, and substance abuse. In the quest to help Jews relate to their own religious traditions, the meaning of holidays is continually reframed in the language of contemporary causes.

A case for making Judaism more relatable is not hard to imagine, and may go something like this: If synagogues and other religious settings hope to attract people, they must employ an idiom and set of concepts with contemporary resonance. Failing to do so would relegate Jewish institutions and Judaism to the margins. Only the most insular of Jews will find Judaism meaningful if it does not speak to twenty-first-century sensibilities. Moreover, as they reframe Jewish teachings, religious educators and leaders must be savvy in how they deliver their messages. None of this is especially new: all forms of modern Judaism have taken this approach to one extent or another. And premodern Judaism was hardly insensitive to changing cultural assumptions in the societies where Jews found a place for themselves. If there appears to be something radically new in our times, it is the nature of contemporary culture with its individualistic, hedonistic, and secular orientation, not the tactical accommodation to it.

Yet even if one accepts this rationale, several difficult questions remain unresolved: How much accommodation is possible without distorting Judaism's teachings? Can a minority religion flourish if it presents itself as a pale imitation of the dominant civic culture, rather than as a counter-cultural movement? What remains distinctive about Jewish teachings? And when the larger culture moves on, will Jewish leaders be sufficiently nimble to adapt to the next wave of cultural preferences?

If the bid to reframe Judaism to appeal to changing sensibilities has a venerable history, the same cannot be said of several other approaches set forth by current enthusiasts of Jewish religious renewal. Here is a sampling of some questionable, if not overwrought, assumptions that have gained purchase in recent years:

First, for religious institutions to thrive, they must operate more like businesses, preferably "disruptive" ones. To the extent that synagogues have budgets and pay salaries, their leaders necessarily must be mindful of the bottom line. Even medium-sized congregations may spend over a million dollars annually, and the larger ones have budgets many multiples greater. There is little doubt, furthermore, that many contemporary rabbis conceive of their role in part as marketers of their places of religious gathering. "Kiruv is all about relationships, so are sales," affirms an Orthodox outreach worker. The rabbi of a prominent Modern Orthodox synagogue explicitly notes his responsibility to "market" his synagogue. Quite evidently rabbis of non-Orthodox synagogues, which tend to have larger membership rolls, are hardly oblivious of the need to compete by promoting their congregations and delivering services attractively packaged.[20]

But some are under pressure from within and without to conceive of their synagogues as business operations.[21] The Jewish press is replete with articles making this case. A proponent of this approach contended that synagogues can be salvaged only if they "learn from Netflix and other companies and industries that explored new possibilities and pursued innovation." Invoking the voguish language popularized by Clayton M. Christensen, a professor of business administration, the author depicts synagogues (and other legacy institutions) as artifacts of an earlier era desperately in need of "disruptive innovation." Indeed, Jewish survival is attributed to the fact that "the Jewish people have innovated, adapted and changed."[22] Giving a moment's thought to this line of argument, is it not possible that the synagogue also has survived precisely because of what has *not* changed? This, in fact, is the contention of still another article with a corporate orientation, but in this case one that urges synagogues to focus their energies on what they do uniquely, rather than offer "high production" values incapable of competing with professional shows or yoga when high-class studios probably can do a better job. "Rather than abandon the traditional mantle for other, lighter ones that feel more colorful and cool and contemporary," the article sensibly concludes, "synagogues should reiterate that their predominant commitment is, as it has always been, to the collective practice of religious ritual."[23]

Second, in contrast to the hard-nosed apostles of business strategies, other purveyors of advice suggest moving in the exact opposite direction, urging a greater stress on spirituality. Synagogues are failing, they contend, because they provide insufficient room for spirituality. As most observers will concede, the term it-self is imprecise: to wit, spirituality in a Jewish context may refer to helping Jews reflect on their connection with God, exposing them to the spiritual literature of the Jewish tradition, sponsoring healing and/or meditation ser-vices, bringing Jews to sites of natural beauty to inspire moments of awe, or incorporating the spiritual practices of other religions into Judaism, among other options. Any of these measures may be designed to stimulate worship-pers and add an element of meaningfulness to their prayer routine.[24]

Still, the connection between spirituality and religiosity is a matter of much dispute. It is commonplace to hear people define themselves as "spir-itual but not religious,"[25] and nearly as common to hear others challenge the claim that these two are necessarily antithetical. Given the rich literature of many religions about the spiritual quest and the attestation of many over the millennia that their religious connection has been heightened by spiritual experiences, it would be foolhardy to dismiss spiritual yearnings. It would be just as misguided, though, to conflate spirituality and religiosity. The for-mer need have no connection to the latter, even if religious engagement may include a rich spiritual life. Exercises in spirituality may add intensity and meaning to religious activity and especially prayer. But spirituality without a grounding in religious practices and community is ephemeral.[26]

Sociologist Nancy T. Ammerman, the author of a major study of Ameri-ca's "spiritual tribes," offers a blunt appraisal of how the trend toward spiri-tuality has benefited religious life only minimally:

> People who do not have a religious community or some circle of focused spiritual conversation do not do very well at maintaining a spiritual out-look on life. Engagement in spiritual practices, pursuing some sort of active connection to a power beyond oneself, is not something people do *instead of* participating in a religious community. *Engagement in orga-nized religion and engagement in spiritual practice go together.* . . . One of the most striking results of our research . . . is the degree to which *par-ticipation in organized religion matters.* The notion that spirituality exists as some sort of individual path or arrives fully formed out of the cultural ether is utterly absurd.[27]

The takeaway for synagogues and other places of Jewish religious gathering is that by introducing spiritual practices, they may heighten religious experience for some congregants. But those practices are no substitute for all the other activities that sustain a religious congregation.

Third, it has now become commonplace to speak publicly of synagogues, along with other so-called "legacy" institutions, as passé. Contracting membership numbers and plummeting attendance figures offer proof positive to some that longtime institutions are incapable of attracting younger Jews, especially millennials. As the latter are the focus of greatest anxiety, a whole range of unconventional programming has arisen to address their particular needs. And those initiatives tend to stress the offbeat, to downplay the traditional activities offered by places of Jewish religious gathering, and to be driven by a conviction that only experimentation will salvage Judaism.

Symptomatic of this uncritical approach, if not boosterish perspective, is the following description of so-called "new spiritual communities," the unconventional settings discussed in the previous chapter: "What the[y] . . . have in common is that they utilize a particular idiom unique to contemporary American culture that attracts other Jews with similar interests. The richness of the Jewish heritage is literally being re-invented in our time by the way in which Jewish wisdom is being applied to the challenges that confront our world today. If properly nurtured and encouraged, these 'communities of meaning' can form the nucleus of an American Jewish renaissance."[28] The first two sentences, as we have seen, are descriptive of many dozens, if not hundreds, of conventional synagogues across the spectrum. Why, then, assume that a handful of "new paradigm spiritual communities" alone will lead the way toward a renaissance of religious life?

A second characteristic of this way of thinking about Jewish religious renewal is its love affair with the offbeat, its romanticizing of novelty. Uncritically swallowing the "disruption" mantra of our times, this way of thinking assumes that only change, not tradition, will attract, let alone offer "meaning." The popular Jewish press inflates the importance of start-ups, rarely stopping to ask tough questions about them, even as it continues to demand accountability from synagogues. While synagogues come in for severe criticism when they lose members and are forced to merge or close their doors, little attention is directed to a basic characteristics of start-ups: most fail and close up shop. The novelty they offer during their usually brief existence overshadows their failings.

It's not only that the bar is set so low for these places, but they also are spared criticism because of the belief that innovation for its own sake may be enough. We don't know what the Judaism of tomorrow will look like, goes the reasoning; therefore, let's figuratively throw things against the wall to see what will stick. And what does stick will become the Judaism of tomorrow. Aside from offering a cavalier conception of how religion evolves, this unprincipled approach also displays little respect for Jewish religious perspectives and practices that have had quite a long run.

Fourth, it is taken as a given that today's Jewish population is unusually hard-pressed for time due to unprecedented responsibilities. Jewish religious institutions must cater to distracted and impatient people, if they are to attract them. The only way to deal with the flighty impatience of our times is to accommodate it. "The future of the Conservative synagogue," a congregational rabbi flatly informed me, "is short services." A Reform congregation redefined short by announcing a new eighteen-minute Friday night service. Lest there be any confusion about the intent, the new service was unself-consciously billed as an experience in "Shabbat Lite."[29] That other synagogues have offered brief, one-hour services for many decades with little evidence of an uptick in regular attendance does not seem to have made an impact on this kind of thinking. Perhaps, as they look out upon their congregants and see many furiously working their smartphones during worship services, some rabbis conclude they have no choice but to cut down on the time congregants are expected to spend in the synagogue sanctuary. It is doubtful abbreviated services will persuade those who are addicted to their smartphones to attend to the prayers.

Even if they resent being expected to sit through services, congregants for their part have very high expectations of their clergy—or so we are told. Here is an advice columnist setting rabbis straight about what is expected of the clergy: "Young adults are interested in having a personal relationship with a rabbi. The caveat often is that the rabbi must speak their language, must not make them feel judged based on their life choices (e.g. who they love, what they eat, which holidays they observe), and must eliminate bureaucracy (making an appointment to see the rabbi through her/his administrative assistant isn't the same as dropping a text or Facebook message with a question)."[30] This is just the opposite of what service programs claim they are doing, and yet those programs are treated as successful ventures for attracting younger Jews. Only religious institutions are asked to aim so low. It's hard to imagine this approach will serve as a solid foundation for building a "meaningful" religious life.

In place of these highly dubious prescriptions, a different set of guiding emphases may have a longer-lasting impact on religious participants—especially because they have had a far longer track record. One is an acknowledgment that the *frequency of participation in religious life matters*. When religious engagement is a sometime thing, relegated to a few peak moments annually, it is unlikely to carry much meaning. This is hardly an alien concept: it is a truism that a minimal investment of time and energy tends to yield only small returns. Why, then, expect otherwise when it comes to religion? And yet, in some quarters this obvious point is ignored. One of the low points during my interviews came when a promoter of start-ups explained with great enthusiasm how a fabulous new initiative meets one Friday evening a month and includes but a glancing reference to the Sabbath coupled with extensive comedy and musical entertainment. When asked why the program expected so little of participants and offered minimal religious content, the reply was, "I would be thrilled if Jews engage in something Jewish once a month." Perhaps this was a statement born of realism, but why aim so low? Judaism not so long ago was conventionally described as "a way of life." Now it is an episodic thing. If religious practice is limited to a few occasional acts, it won't get much traction and it also will be very difficult to transmit to the next generation. What message, after all, do parents convey to their children if they themselves set aside little time for religious participation?

Nearly a century ago, Franz Kafka already made the point in his famous "Letter to My Father":

As a young man, I could not understand how, with the insignificant scrap of Judaism you yourself possessed, you could reproach me for not making an effort (for the sake of piety at least, as you put it) to cling to a similar, insignificant scrap. It was indeed, so far as I could see, a mere nothing, a joke, not even a joke. On four days in the year you went to the synagogue, where you were, to say the least, closer to the indifferent than to those who took it seriously, [you] patiently went through the prayers as a formality, [you] sometimes amazed me by being able to show me in the prayer book the passage that was being said at the moment, and for the rest, so long as I was present in the synagogue (and this was the main thing) I was allowed to hang about wherever I liked.[31]

Kafka refers solely to synagogue attendance, but *Judaism is a religion to be observed in all settings.* By now, large sectors of non-Orthodox Jews have adopted a Christian approach to religion: rituals are confined to the house of worship and religion is expressed elsewhere through moralism or living life according to the Golden Rule. The result is a minimalistic and enervated Judaism. Opting not to pull his punches, a leading Reform rabbi described his people as having little sense of Judaism as a "thick culture," one with its own language, conceptual vocabulary, rituals, etiquette, and worldview. That absence may characterize the lives of a good many Jews, but it could not be further from what is needed for a vibrant, living Judaism to thrive.

If Judaism suffuses life, it will gain cultural "thickness" and staying power. It will inform ethical decisions, choices of what to eat, how to spend one's time, and how to think about marriage, sexuality, and family formation— to cite just a few areas of religious concern. The relegation of Jewish religious practice to the synagogue is not only unfaithful to the teachings of Judaism, but deeply destructive. The home is classically the place of observance, family celebration, and mourning. It is in the home that the Sabbath and holidays are to be marked, and where the shiva, the week of mourning, is observed. If innovators are eager to revive Jewish religious participation, a good place to begin is by teaching Jews how to live their Judaism at home, in the workplace, and in all settings of their lives.

None of this is to suggest that the synagogue is irrelevant. The unrelenting assault on synagogue life over the past three decades (see the beginning section of chapter 7) has done deep damage to an irreplaceable institution.

It is one thing to say that Jewish religious life properly is to be expressed by Jews wherever they find themselves. It is another to dismiss synagogues as hopeless because they fail to live up to unrealistic expectations.[32] There is a reason synagogues have been central to Jewish life for over two millennia. Of course, the liturgy has evolved, as have the music and choreography of worship services. But to imagine that the Judaism of the future will dispense with synagogues is delusional.

Jewish prayer occurs ideally in a quorum (minyan), and other religious activities require a scaffolding provided by people and institutions. *It takes a synagogue community to create a social support system for Jewish religious life.*[33] Ritual, whether it is combining the four species on the holiday of Sukkot or fasting on Yom Kippur, is given meaning and support by a community of Jews who engage in the same acts. Community offers a plausibility structure for religious behavior, especially behavior deemed alien by the larger culture. Religious community, as we have already noted, offers a counterweight to the modern preoccupation with autonomy.

Nor is community limited only to fellow congregants. Identification with other Jews across the generations (synchronically) and in their current habitations around the globe (diachronically) reinforces Jewish religious life. A connection to generations past serves to anchor Jews in an ongoing historical trajectory they know will also continue after them; linking oneself to this chain of tradition provides a form of transcendence. And identification with Jewish people in other communities both adds to the cultural richness and diversity of Jewish civilization and is a mission to aid kinfolk. *Those who contend that the ethnic dimension of Jewishness is not only passé but also unnecessary ignore the power of Jewish peoplehood to provide religious meaning.* The writer Yossi Klein Halevi said it well: "Because Judaism is a particularist faith intended for a particular people, unlike the universal faiths of Christianity and Islam, strengthening peoplehood is a religious category, a precondition for the fulfillment of Judaism itself."[34] With the establishment of the Jewish state, which among other things is home to the largest Jewish community in the world, a connection to Israel, its people and culture, is an essential dimension of Jewish religious life.

Judaism also is sustained by literacy. It's not only that the liturgy is in a for-eign language, Hebrew, but the Jewish religion emerged in an environment entirely different from contemporary America. To make sense of such an alien religious culture requires knowledge. The classical texts of the Jewish religious tradition are written in biblical and Rabbinic Hebrew, which are not the same as modern Israeli Hebrew. They also are written in an idiom requiring an insider's knowledge of their meaning. For this reason, recent trends in religious education, which focus on positive experiences and/or social action activities rather than on acquiring the language and conceptual skills necessary to live as a Jew, are doing no one any favors.[35] There are, of course, more and less stimulating ways of teaching, and it is important to engage students in active learning. But if Jews are to live a religious life, they will need to be educated, and not only up to age thirteen when most Jew-ish children begin to drop out, but as teens and adults when they have the maturity to work with religious texts in a sophisticated fashion.

Finally, an overarching consideration: *in our age, it is more important than ever for Jewish religious expression to be guided by intentionality.* Following Michael Berger, a professor of religion who has argued for the necessity of building intentional communities in our current age of weakening "natural communities," I borrow his definition of intentionality as "an implied vi-sion of an ideal—that for an act to be truly religious, to 'earn' that adjec-tive, it must be performed thoughtfully, mindfully, with deliberateness and intent."[36] This expectation is not unique to Jews: other Americans also are turning to a more intentional practice of religion. It's not only that contem-poraries want to engage with religion with heightened self-consciousness and deliberativeness; they scorn rote observance.

For Jews, there is an additional need for intentionality, and that is be-cause of their religion's countercultural outlook. As a minority, Jews have maintained their distinctive religious culture with the help of props sup-porting their way of life—propinquity (Jews living close to one another), an allegiance to Jewish peoplehood based on kinship, and the absorption of identity through an osmotic process. These three props have eroded consid-erably in the modern era, and especially in recent decades. For Jewish life to thrive in the current environment, a far more intentional approach to religion is necessary than that in the past.

Berger spells out what this intentionality must include: "having the ability to explain one's practice in Jewishly meaningful terms, ground[ing] one's decision-making in Judaism's rich tradition, and lend[ing] 'Jewish significance' to one's daily or regular activities."[37] Such a religious practice requires knowledge, including an understanding of the Jewish religious vocabulary and concepts. It also would stress content over process: it is not enough for a worship service to have "high production values" or a Shabbat event to pay brief attention to the blessing over wine and bread, while ignoring the deeper meaning of the day of rest. Helping Jews infuse religious practice into all aspects of their lives would take precedence over one-off gatherings.

Perhaps most refreshing, intentionality as understood by Berger offers a major shift in emphasis: it directs Jews to discover Jewish significance in the quotidian. In this sense, intentionality will counter the relegation of Judaism to the margins of people's lives. Equally important, it holds the promise of reversing the presentism and universalization that currently so dominate discussions about religious life. Instead of reinterpreting Judaism's holidays and rituals to conform to the passing fads and preoccupations of the wider culture, now the goal will be to help highly acculturated American Jews internalize the vocabulary and conceptual framework of the Jewish tradition. In the process, they may gain an appreciation for ways of behaving and thinking that animated Jewish life in the past and may enrich Jewish life today.

In our current age when hyper-individualism reigns and so many Jews imagine it necessary to recast their distinctive religion in "universal" terms, the rebuilding of Judaism will require a renewed appreciation for Jewish memory, community, and particularistic content. American Jews might well find sustenance and inspiration in these old/new commitments as they create the next iteration of a new/old Judaism.

Notes

Notes to Introduction

1. Pew Research Center, "U.S. Public Becoming Less Religious" (November 3, 2015), http://www.pewforum.org/2015/11/03/u-s-public-becoming-less-reli gious/. In 2011, sociologist Mark Chaves flatly declared "no indicator of tra ditional religious belief or practice is going up" within the broader American public. "If there is a trend, it is toward less religion." Chaves, *American Religion: Contemporary Trends* (Princeton, NJ: Princeton University Press, 2011), 110.

2. Not surprisingly, demand for clergy has declined severely, prompting a sharp contraction in the numbers of people studying at seminaries producing minis ters for mainline congregations. See Ian Lovett, "Seminaries Reflect Struggles of Mainline Churches," *Wall Street Journal*, August 10, 2017, https://www.wsj .com/articles/seminaries-reflect-struggles-of-mainline-churches-1502357400.

3. Sarah Eekhoff Zylstra, "Pew: Evangelicals Stay Strong as Christianity Crumbles in America," *Christianity Today*, May 5, 2015, http://www.christianitytoday.com /gleanings/2015/may/pew-evangelicals-stay-strong-us-religious-landscape-study .html. The magazine, it should be said, is directed to an evangelical readership.

4. Jeffrey M. Jones, "Sept. 11 Effects, Though Largely Faded, Persist," Gallup, Sep tember 9, 2003, http://www.gallup.com/poll/9208/sept-effects-though-largely -faded-persist.aspx. Notwithstanding the title of this article, it contends that church attendance and assessments about the importance of religion in people's lives spiked in the months after 9/11, but then settled back to their earlier levels within two years.

5. Chris Pleasance and Kelly Mclaughlin, "Hundreds of Thousands Crowd the Heart of Philadelphia to Bid Farewell to the Pope," *Daily Mail*, September 27, 2015, http://www.dailymail.co.uk/news/article-3251252/Cheering-faithful-wait -hours-heart-Philadelphia-hopes-catching-glimpse-Pope-Francis-celebrates -historical-outdoor-Mass-expected-1million-spectators.html#ixzz3yqeD9lR9.

6. Patrick Henry, "'And I Don't Care What It Is': The Tradition-History of a Civil Religion Proof-Text," *Journal of the American Academy of Religion* 49, no. 1 (March 1981): 35–49.

7. I have co-authored one such study with Steven M. Cohen, titled "The Pew Survey Reanalyzed—More Gloomy News but a Glimmer of Hope," *Mosaic*, November 2015, http://mosaicmagazine.com/essay/2014/11/the-pew-survey-reanalyzed/.

8. For upbeat assessments of what can be if only the right steps are taken, see Sidney Schwarz, ed., *Jewish Megatrends: Charting the Trends of the American Jewish Future* (Woodstock, VT: Jewish Lights, 2013), especially the editor's introductory and concluding essays.

9. For two examples of works that argue for radical revision, see Arthur Green, *Radical Judaism: Rethinking God and Tradition* (New Haven, CT: Yale University Press, 2010) and Shaul Magid, *American Post-Judaism: Identity and Renewal in a Postethnic Society*, Religion in North America (Bloomington: Indiana University Press, 2013). The latter argues that "Jews . . . are inventing new forms of religion, 'new' Judaisms through syncretism . . . and by creating new rituals to mark communal, national, and global events that have nothing to do with Jews, Jewish history or Jewish myth" (34).

10. Sociologist of religion Peter Berger has dilated on the roles of capitalism and American democratic norms in shaping attitudes toward religion: "All of life becomes an interminable process of redefining who the individual is in the context of the seemingly endless possibilities presented by modernity. This endless array of choices is reinforced by the structures of the capitalist systems, with their enormous market for services, products, and even identities, all protected by a democratic state which legitimizes these choices, not least the choice of religion." Quoted by Gerardo Marti, "Religious Reflexivity: The Effect of Continual Novelty and Diversity on Individual Religiosity," *Sociology of Religion* 76, no. 1 (2015): 6.

11. The "cancerous growth" of individualism was already the subject of a study conducted in the mid-1980s by Robert Bellah and his team. See Robert N. Bellah et al., *Habits of the Heart: Individualism and Commitment in American Life* (Berkeley: University of California Press, 1985).

12. On the decline of civic participation, see Robert D. Putnam, *Bowling Alone: The Collapse and Revival of American Community* (New York: Simon & Schus-

ter, 2000). And on the parallel developments among Jews, see Arnold Eisen and Steven M. Cohen, *The Jew Within: Self, Family and Community in America* (Bloomington: Indiana University Press, 2000).

13. This is a common trope of writing within the Orthodox community about the religious detachment in the wider community. For an expression of this viewpoint by a non-Orthodox rabbi, see Shai Held, "Progressive Jews Need Torah in Intermarriage Fight," *Forward*, December 19, 2016, http://forward .com/opinion/national/357529/progressive-jews-need-torah-in-intermarriage -fight/?utm_content=opinion_Newsletter_MainList_Title_Position-1&utm _source=Sailthru&utm_medium=email&utm_campaign=Opinion%20Rede sign%202016-12-19&utm_term=Opinion.

14. Responding to the outcome of the 2016 presidential election, the editor in chief of the *New York Times* conceded that the mainstream media "don't get religion." Douglas Ernst, "NYT Executive Editor: "We Don't Get the Role of Religion in People's Lives," *Washington Times*, December 9, 2016, http://www.washingtontimes .com/news/2016/dec/9/dean-baquet-new-york-times-executive-editor-we-don/.

15. For an insightful discussion of how such views have infiltrated the Modern Orthodox sector, see Gil Perl, "Postmodern Orthodoxy: Giving Voice to a New Generation," *Lehrhaus*, November 6, 2017, http://www.thelehrhaus.com/com mentary-short-articles/2017/11/5/postmodern-orthodoxy-giving-voice-to-a -new-generation. A more rounded picture of the positive as well as negative consequences of the postmodern outlook on religion appears in Nikolai G. Wenzel, *Postmodernism and Religion: The Oxford Handbook of the Sociology of Religion* (Oxford: Oxford University Press, 2011).

16. Such a service was described to me by Rabbi Elaine Zecher of Boston's Temple Israel (interview of September 4, 2015). The congregation no longer treats "the great Aleinu" the same way but has introduced other innovations. For an example of a different Reform temple employing this practice, see http://www .rebjeff.com/blog/we-bow-we-prostrate-we-give-thanks (and the post by Reb Rachel). A Reconstructionist rabbi who engages in this custom has linked it to yoga exercises. See Brant Rosen, "Downward Facing Jews," *Yedid Nefesh Blog*, May 19, 2011, https://ynefesh.com/2011/05/19/downward-facing-jews/.

17. Renee Ghert-Zand, "The Mirror in the Mikveh," *Forward*, May 23, 2013, http://forward.com/articles/177195/the-mirror-in-the-mikveh/?p=all.

18. A particularly rich list of lectures and sessions was announced at the site in late December 2015. See http://adasisrael.org/jmcw/.

19. For a report on the largest gathering to celebrate the completion of the cycle, see Uriel Heilman, "90,000-Plus Crowd in N.J. Cheers Siyum HaShas," *Jewish Telegraphic Agency* (*JTA*), http://www.jta.org/2012/08/02/life-religion/90000 -plus-crowd-in-n-j-cheers-siyum-hashas.

20. These classes are advertised on synagogue websites. Even a relatively modest size congregation, such as Beth Shalom in Scranton, Pennsylvania, proudly announces its offerings: "We have daily minyanim and a wide array of classes on all levels including a daily Daf Yomi. We also have classes on Navi, Chumash for women, and a Chavrusah program customized to the needs of all individuals on all levels." http://jewishscranton.org/blog/orthodox-synagogue-in-scranton-pa/.

21. For an example, see Alan H. Feiler, "Associated Head On Willow Creek Lessons," *Baltimore Jewish Times*, May 16, 2008.

22. For an example of the latter, see Mel Gottlieb, "Mussar: A Jewish Psychoethical Model for Our Time," *Ideals, Institute for Jewish Ideas and Ideals*, https://www .jewishideas.org/article/mussar-jewish-psycho-ethical-model-our-time. The author is president of the Academy of Jewish Religion in California, a nondenominational rabbinical seminary.

23. Michelle Boorstein, "Passover Seders Move to Nights That Work for Busy Lives," *Washington Post*, April 13, 2014, https://www.washingtonpost.com/local/passover -seders-move-to-nights-that-work-for-busy-lives/2014/04/13/3eca9316-c106 -11e3-bcec-b71ee10e9bc3_story.html.

24. On Svara, see http://www.svara.org/about-svara/.

25. For an ethnographic portrait of a church where music, choreography, and art have become central, see Gerardo Marti, *A Mosaic of Believers: Diversity and Innovation in a Multi-ethnic Church* (Bloomington: Indiana University Press, 2005), especially chap. 4.

26. Robert Wuthnow, *After the Baby Boomers: How Twenty- and Thirty-Somethings Are Shaping the Future of Religion* (Princeton, NJ: Princeton University Press, 2007), 13–16.

27. See, for examples, Neil Cristopher, "Church in a Bar: Why Even the Darkest Spaces Can Be Sacred," *Huffington Post*, May 17, 2011, http://www.huffing tonpost.com/pastor-neil-christopher/is-nothing-sacred_1_b_861778.html;

Bryan Berghoef, "Pub Theology: Beer, Conversation, and God," *Huffington Post*, March 18, 2013, http://www.huffingtonpost.com/bryan-berghoef/beer-conver sation-and-god_b_2885329.html; and Gerardo Marti and Gladys Ganiel, *The Deconstructed Church: Understanding Emerging Christianity* (New York: Oxford University Press, 2014), 11–14.

28. Pew Research Center, "U.S. Public Becoming Less Religious."

29. An exemplary volume in this vein, which also attends to nondenominational developments, is Dana Evan Kaplan's *Contemporary American Judaism: Transformation and Renewal* (New York: Columbia University Press, 2009).

30. Jack Wertheimer, *A People Divided: Judaism in Contemporary America* (New York: Basic Books, 1993; repr., Lebanon, NH: Brandeis University Press, 1997).

31. See, for example, Samuel Heilman, "Holding Firmly with an Open Hand: Life in Two Conservative Synagogues," and Riv-Ellen Prell, "Communities of Choice and Memory: Conservative Synagogues in the Late Twentieth Century," both in *Jews in the Center: Conservative Synagogues and Their Members* (New Brunswick, NJ: Rutgers University Press, 2000); Frida Kerner Furman, *Beyond Yiddishkeit: The Struggle for Jewish Identity in a Reform Synagogue* (Albany: State University of New York Press, 1987); Bethamie Horowitz, "Connections and Journeys: Assessing Critical Opportunities for Enhancing Jewish Identity" (New York: UJA–Federation of New York, 2000; revised 2003), http://www.jewishdatabank.org/Studies/downloadFile.cfm?FileID=2631; Martin Laskin, *An Ethnographic Study of an American Conservative Synagogue* (Lewiston, NY: Edwin Mellen Press, 2002); Moshe Shokeid, *A Gay Synagogue in New York* (Philadelphia: University of Pennsylvania Press, 1995); Ido Tavory, *Summoned: Identification and Religious Life in a Jewish Neighborhood* (Chicago: University of Chicago Press, 2016); Phil Zuckerman, *Strife in the Sanctuary: Religious Schism in a Jewish Community* (Lanham, MD: AltaMira Press, 1999). A number of recent dissertations not yet in print are adding rich layers to the ethnographic literature on the religious practices of ordinary American Jews. Among them are studies by Mijal Bitton on Syrian Jews, Arielle Levites on Jewish spiritual communities, and Emily Sigalow on Jewish Buddhists. As more ethnographers study the lived Judaism of different kinds of American Jews, a more granular and complex picture surely will emerge.

32. For a pioneering effort to give voice to such "stories" told by ordinary people, see Nancy T. Ammerman, *Sacred Stories, Spiritual Tribes: Finding Religion in Everyday Life* (New York: Oxford University Press, 2013).

33. The distinction is discussed by Martin Reisebrodt in his *The Promise of Salvation: A Theory of Religion* (Chicago: University of Chicago Press, 2010), chap. 1.

34. Quoted by Elliott Jager, "Have Reform Jews Given Up on Israel?," *Jerusalem Post*, January 7, 2016, http://www.jpost.com/Jerusalem-Report/Have-Reform-Jews-given-up-on-Israel-435824. This parody appears, among other places, also in Norman Podhoretz, *Why Are Jews Liberals?* (New York: Doubleday, 2009), 287.

35. *Merriam-Webster* cites this as the "simple definition" of religion. http://www.merriam-webster.com/dictionary/religion.

36. Needless to say, rabbinic commentators disagree over the precise list, but the number has been enshrined as shorthand for the broad range of "thou shalts and thou shalt nots."

37. This literature and the related issues are discussed at length by Nancy Tatom Ammerman, *Sacred Stories, Spiritual Tribes*, chap., 2, esp. 42. Because this volume is about lived Judaism, not the spiritual lives of Jews, I do not cast my net as widely as does Ammerman.

38. The term "denomination" itself is taken from the Protestant context and does not do justice to the Jewish religious movements. Denominations of Protestantism tend to differ especially in their sacraments and liturgies. This is far less true in the Jewish case.

39. Wendy Cadge and Mary Ellen Konieczny, " 'Hidden in Plain Sight': The Significance of Religion and Spirituality in Secular Organizations," *Sociology of Religion* 75 (2014): 551–63.

40. This theme is developed by Gerardo Marti in "Present and Future Scholarship in the Sociology of Religion," *Sociology of Religion* 75, no. 4 (2014): 503–10.

41. Leora Batnitzky, *How Judaism Became a Religion: An Introduction to Modern Jewish Thought* (Princeton, NJ: Princeton University Press, 2011), 13.

42. On the history of this term and its evolution, see Noam Pianko, *Jewish Peoplehood: An American Innovation* (New Brunswick, NJ: Rutgers University Press, 2015).

43. Richard D. Alba, "The Twilight of Ethnicity among Americans of European Ancestry: The Case of Italians," *Ethnic and Racial Studies* 8, no. 1 (1985): 134–58.

44. Herbert Gans, "The Coming Darkness of Late-Generation European American Ethnicity," *Ethnic and Racial Studies Review* 37, no. 5 (2014): 757–65.

45. Asher Ginzberg wrote under the nom de plume Ahad Ha'Am. In the Hebrew original, the same verb is used to refer to Jews keeping the Sabbath and being guarded by the Sabbath. This appeared in his essay "Shabbat vetsiyonut" [The Sabbath and Zionism], *Hashiloah* 3, no. 6 (1898).

46. Over thirty-five years ago, my late friend, the sociologist Paul Ritterband, taught me the rule of "the more the more, the less the less" when describing the bipolar evolution of American Jewish life. His rule remains sound today. The more Jews are involved with Jewish religious life, the more they tend to be involved in many other aspects; and the less religiously involved tend to drop all their connections over time.

Chapter 1: Finding Meaning

1. Findings cited here appear in Pew Research Center, "A Portrait of Jewish Americans: Findings from a Pew Research Center of American Jews" (October 2013), 10, 72–77, http://assets.pewresearch.org/wp-content/uploads/sites/11/2013/10/jewish-american-full-report-for-web.pdf.

2. These data from the Pew study were run for me by Dr. Steven M. Cohen. Recent research has found that Americans tend to exaggerate the frequency with which they attend worship services when responding to surveys, probably because they feel attendance is a socially desirable behavior. See, for example, Cathy Lynn Grossman, "Poll: Americans Stretch the Truth on Attending Church," *Religion News Service*, May 17, 2014, http://www.religionnews.com/2014/05/17/christians-church-atheists-prri/.

3. The so-called *taryag mitzvot*, 613 commandments, serve as shorthand in traditional rabbinic parlance for the elaborate positive and negative rules of Judaism, the "thou shalts" and "thou shalt nots."

4. For an Orthodox rabbi's lament about the absence of God in synagogue and school discourse, see Aharon E. Wexler, "Just a Thought: About God,"

Jerusalem Post, November 10, 2016, http://www.jpost.com/Not-Just-News /Just-A-Thought-On-God-472259.

5. It deserves mentioning that some rabbis I interviewed have made clear they see it as part of their mission to help congregants connect to God and reflect on what God means in their lives. But this was not the priority of most rabbis with whom I spoke.

6. Gil Steinlauf, "Why Jews Should NOT Believe in God," Rosh Hashanah sermon 5774, http://adasisrael.org/wp-content/uploads/2013/06/Why-Jews -Should-NOT-Believe-in-God.pdf.

7. We note in this context that religious skepticism has deep historical roots in the American Jewish population. Gallup and Roper surveys conducted during the second half of the twentieth century found smaller proportions of Jews, as compared with Catholics and Protestants, expressing unquestioning belief in God. More recently, two sociologists compared survey data from 2008 to demonstrate that whereas between 72 and 90 percent of American Christian groups expressed "absolute certainty" about God's existence, only 41 percent of Jews made such a claim. Significantly, that study by Steven M. Cohen and Lauren Blitzer was titled *Belonging without Believing: Jews and Their Distinctive Patterns of Religiosity and Secularity* (New York: JCC Association, 2008), http://www.bjpa.org/Publications/details.cfm?PublicationID=795.

8. Mark Dov Shapiro, "The God Survey," *Reform Judaism*, Summer 2012, http:// www.reformjudaism.org/god-survey.

9. Data on the aggregate of American Jews and of synagogue members come from Pew Research Center, "Portrait of Jewish Americans," 114. Other data from the Pew study, as previously noted, were run for me by Steven M. Cohen.

10. For an example of such a Conservative synagogue and its attraction for members, see Riv-Ellen Prell's discussion of Beth El in "Communities of Choice and Memory," 269–358.

11. *Hesed* is spelled with a *chet* and is pronounced as a guttural like chutzpah.

12. This finding was noted in Paul Ritterband, "Public Worship: The Partnership between Families and Synagogues," in Wertheimer, *Jews in the Center*, 204–14.

13. Some Reform temples offer an alternative service for regular attenders.

14. Quoted in Abigail Pickus, "A Closer Look at Independent Bnei Mitzvah in the Chicagoland Area" (Jewish United Fund of Chicago, November 2, 2015), 13,

http://ejewishphilanthropy.com/wordpress/wp-content/uploads/2015/11
/CFJE-REPORTS-IND-BM.pdf.

15. The politicization of synagogues warrants treatment in a separate book. There is a long history of rabbis using the pulpit to explicate their views about public policy questions and implicitly endorse the positions of one party or another. Neither the left nor the right holds a monopoly over such talk. During the Donald Trump presidency, the era in which this book has been completed, these matters have reached fever pitch. Rabbis and their congregants have debated how explicitly they wish political matters to be addressed in synagogues. A study of this topic might ask whether the mixing of politics with religion is especially good for the latter—and whether it is even avoidable.

16. Nancy T. Ammerman, "Golden Rule Christianity: Lived Religion in the American Mainstream," in *Lived Religion in America: Toward a History of Practice*, ed. David Hall (Princeton, NJ: Princeton University Press, 1997). Ammerman distinguishes between two different types of Golden Rule Christians: those who wish to treat others well and those who are social justice warriors out of a sense of religious imperative. Both types exist among Jews too, though we lack information on the proportions.

17. Babylonian Talmud, tractate Shabbat 31a. By emphasizing the Golden Rule quality of today's non-Orthodox American Judaism, I build upon the pioneering work of others, most notably Marshall Sklare and Joseph Greenblum, who noted already in the post–World War II era the shift from what they called "sacramentalism to moralism." The current chapter, indeed, may be read as a revisiting, a half century later, of themes in their chapter on "The Lakeville Jew and Religion," in *Jewish Identity on the Suburban Frontier: A Study in Group Survival in the Open Society* (Chicago: University of Chicago Press, 1979), esp. 89–96.

18. Dahlia Schweitzer, "On Being Queer and Jewish—And Why Neither Should Matter," *Times of Israel*, August 22, 2014, http://blogs.timesofisrael.com/on -being-queer-and-jewish-and-why-neither-should-matter/.

19. Charles Liebman, "Concluding Reflections on the Condition of American Judaism," in *Cambridge Companion on American Judaism*, ed. Dana Evan Kaplan (Cambridge: Cambridge University Press, 2005), 133.

20. Jonathan Krasner, "The Place of Tikkun Olam in American Jewish Life" (Jerusalem: Jerusalem Center on Public Affairs, November 1, 2014), 1, http://jcpa

.org/article/place-tikkun-olam-american-jewish-life1/. Employing a Google search, Krasner was able to trace the rapid spread of this term to the 1980s.

21. For one such prominent voice, see Leonard Fein's 1988 volume *Where Are We? The Inner Lives of America's Jews* (New York: Harper & Row, 1988), quoted approvingly in Keren McGinity, *Still Jewish: A History of Women and Intermarriage in America* (New York: New York University Press, 2009), 159.

22. The facile use of Jewish slogans to justify predetermined social and political commitments has been exposed powerfully in Jeffrey K. Salkin, "Judaism Beyond Slogans," *Commentary*, January 17, 2018, https://www.commentarymaga zine.com/articles/judaism-beyond-slogans/.

Chapter 2: A Judaism for Peak Moments

1. For a preliminary ethnographic attempt to surface these broader trends, see Gila S. Silverman, "Multiple Judaisms and Mosaic Selves: An Ethnographic Exploration of Liberal American Jews," *Culture and Religion* 17 (2016).

2. See most prominently Sklare and Greenblum, *Jewish Identity on the Suburban Frontier*, 57ff.

3. The decline in Passover Seder attendance has been described by some professional observers of Jewish life as a "lagging indicator," a belatedly recognized indication of growing indifference to Jewish life in some quarters of the Jewish population that in the past would have participated in a Seder. See Steve Lipman, "Passover Seder Losing Steam as Key Marker of Affiliation," *Jewish Week* (New York), April 9, 2014, http://jewishweek.timesofisrael.com/pass over-seder-losing-steam-as-key-marker-of-affiliation/.

4. Pew Research Center, "Portrait of Jewish Americans," 77. It can be argued that families may have Friday night dinners together but not light candles, and undoubtedly some do, especially those who attend late Friday evening services where candles are lit in the synagogue. But only small minorities of members attend such services to begin with. Lighting candles is a reasonable proxy for learning about Friday night Shabbat dinners.

5. For a survey of *Haggadot* exploiting the holiday for such purposes, see Michael Medved, "The Preposterous Politics of Passover," *Commentary*, April 1,

2011, https://www.commentarymagazine.com/articles/the-preposterous-politics
-of-passover/.

6. Sephardi Jews traditionally have marked the day with a Tu Bishvat Seder fea-
    turing agricultural products of the land of Israel and poems explaining their
    symbolic significance.

7. On the commodification of Israeli products in the post-1948 era, see Emily
    Alice Katz, *Bringing Zion Home: Israel in American Jewish Culture, 1948–1967*
    (Albany: State University of New York Press, 2015), chap. 4.

8. On Tu Bishvat, see Tevi Troy, "I Think I Shall Never See a Jew as Lovely as a
    Tree," *Commentary*, February 2015, https://www.commentarymagazine.com
    /articles/i-think-that-i-shall-never-see-a-jew-as-lovely-as-a-tree/.

9. For a description of Simchat Torah eve on the Upper West Side of Manhattan,
    see Gary Rosenblatt, "On Simchat Torah, Holding Fast to 'The Tree of Life',"
    Jewish Week (New York), October 18, 2017, http://jewishweek.timesofisrael
    .com/holding-fast-to-the-tree-of-life/. Similar neighborhood gatherings are held
    in Riverdale, New York, and Prospect Park, Brooklyn—and in communities
    across the land.

10. On Dawn, see http://www.dawnfestival.org/about. The success of Dawn may
    have less to do with its offerings of Jewish content than its promise of enter-
    tainment, as in the following come-on: "Dawn 2010 will feature a packed,
    late-night evening of headlining performances and events including live bands,
    theatrical and spoken word performances, premiere film screenings, visual arts,
    dancing, DJs, lectures, comedy, readings and open-space discussion forums—
    AND the opportunity to explore the Academy's aquarium and exhibits after
    hours." It appears that Dawn is no longer sponsored, but as of 2016 a half
    dozen synagogues and other Jewish institutions joined together for a "travel-
    ing Tikkun Leil Shavuot"; its theme was "Sensual Torah." Sherith Israel bulle-
    tin, https://www.sherithisrael.org/event/traveling-tikkun-leil-shavuot.html. In
    Manhattan, the JCC of the Upper West Side organizes a "revelatory night of
    study, film, music, dance, yoga, cheesecake." https://www.jccmanhattan.org/jew
    ish-living/shabbat-and-holidays/tikkun/.

11. For a broad sampling of prayers and services to welcome a newborn girl, see
    Debra Nussbaum Cohen, *Celebrating Your New Jewish Daughter* (Woodstock,

VT: Jewish Lights, 2001). And for a wide-ranging historical and halakhic exploration making the case for a such ceremony, see Sharon R. Siegel, *A Jewish Ceremony for Newborn Girls: The Torah's Covenant Affirmed* (Lebanon, NH: Brandeis University Press, 2014).

12. The assault on *brit milah* has been analyzed by Jon D. Levenson, "The New Enemies of Circumcision," *Commentary*, March 2000.

13. The opposition of non-Jewish mothers to the rite is discussed below.

14. Marjorie Ingall, "To Cut or Not to Cut: Finding Alternatives to Circumcision," *Tablet*, July 9, 2014, http://www.tabletmag.com/jewish-life-and-religion/178356 /alternatives-to-circumcision.

15. Barry Kosmin, "The Coming of Age in the Conservative Synagogue: The Bar/ Bat Mitzvah Class of 5755," in Wertheimer, *Jews in the Center*, 232–68.

16. As with so many observances, we lack quantitative data, but reports indicate the trend to hold ceremonies independent of synagogues is spreading and threatening congregations. The increased incidence prompted the Jewish United Fund of Chicago to sponsor an extensive study documenting the growth, content, and reasons why more families are opting for these ceremonies. See Pickus, "Closer Look," 3–6. On developments in a different locale, see Sophia Hollander, "Bat Mitzvah, Brooklyn Style: Laid Back and Do-It-Yourself," *Wall Street Journal*, July 13, 2014, http://www.wsj.com/articles/bat -mitzvah-brooklyn-style-laid-back-and-do-it-yourself-1405304732.

17. For a sample of an interfaith ceremony, including a rabbi and a minister, see http://www.interfaithfamily.com/life_cycle/weddings/A_Sample_Interfaith _Wedding_Ceremony.shtml. The same website is replete with vignettes and advice about interfaith weddings and marriages.

18. I have examined the possible reasons why this prayer is now highlighted in synagogues of all denominations. See Jack Wertheimer, "Divine Intervention," *Wall Street Journal*, January 6, 2006, http://www.wsj.com/articles/SB1136518 46706839455.

19. Quoted by Rukhl Schaechter, "Shiva Shifts toward Shorter and Livelier Jewish Mourning for Dead," *Forward*, March 18, 2014, http://forward.com /news/194589/shiva-shifts-toward-shorter-and-livelier-jewish-mo/#ixzz3iRV Trj5o.

20. On one such outfit known as the Shiva Sisters, see Mitchell Landsberg, "Mourning, with L.A. Panache," *Los Angeles Times*, March 21, 2011, http://www.shiva sisters.com/press/LATimes_ShivaSisters.pdf.

21. Quoted by Schaechter, "Shiva Shifts."

22. On Jewish rates, see Josh Nathan-Kazis, "More Jews Opt for Cremation," *Forward*, June 27, 2012, http://forward.com/news/158218/more-jews-opt-for -cremation/. For recent nationwide figures for all Americans, see Susan Scutti, "Half in U.S. Choose Cremation as Views on Death Change," *CNN*, August 9, 2017, http://www.cnn.com/2017/08/09/health/cremation-tops-burials-in-us -study/index.html.

23. I described this characteristic of Reform congregants two decades ago in *A People Divided*, chap. 3.

24. Fern Chertok, "The Reform Tent: Half Full or Half Empty?," *eJewish Philanthropy*, August 18, 2014, http://ejewishphilanthropy.com/the-reform-tent-half -full-or-half-empty/.

25. Pew Research Center, "Portrait of Jewish Americans," 77.

26. This discussion of geography and culture is based on Steven M. Cohen and Samuel Abrams, "How Mountain and Pacific States Jews Differ," *Jewish Journal* (Los Angeles), January 28, 2016, http://jewishjournal.com/news/nation /181709/.

27. Still another variable for which we have only limited data is level of general education. In the aggregate, Jews who attain a higher level of education are less likely than those without an advanced education to believe in God and to consider religion to be an important part of their lives. For some suggestive data on this, see Pew Research Center, "In America, Does More Education Equal Less Religion?" (April 26, 2017), esp. 12, 22, http://assets.pewresearch.org/wp-content/uploads /sites/11/2017/04/25115302/Religion-and-education-FULL-REPORT.pdf.

28. Sylvia Barack Fishman and Daniel Parmer, *Matrilineal Ascent/Patrilineal Descent: The Gender Imbalance in American Jewish Life* (Waltham, MA: Hadassah Brandeis Institute and the Maurice and Marilyn Cohen Center for Modern Jewish Studies, 2008).

29. This was reported in Pew Research Center, "The Gender Gap in Religion around the World" (March 22, 2016), 40.

30. Pew Research Center, "Portrait of Jewish Americans," 40.

31. Shapiro, "God Survey."

32. Sylvia Barack Fishman, "Policy Implications of the Gender Imbalance among America's Jews" (Jerusalem: Jerusalem Center for Public Affairs, December 10, 2008), http://jcpa.org/article/policy-implications-of-the-gender-imbalance-among -americas-jews/.

33. Ibid.

34. Ibid.

35. Sylvia Barack Fishman, "American Jewishness Today: Identity and Transmissibility in an Open World," *Contemporary Jewry* 35 (2015): 119.

36. This quotation and the preceding discussion of families and intermarriage are based on Jack Wertheimer, *Linking the Silos: How to Accelerate the Momentum in Jewish Education Today* (New York: Avi Chai Foundation, 2005), 21–22.

37. The identification of children of intermarriage with Judaism is discussed in Steven M. Cohen in "Can Intermarriage Lead to an Increase in the Number of Jews in America?," *Mosaic*, November 9, 2015, http://mosaicmagazine.com/observation /2015/11/can-intermarriage-lead-to-an-increase-in-the-number-of-jews-in-america/.

38. This is the burden of two volumes by McGinity, *Still Jewish* and *Marrying Out: Jewish Men, Intermarriage and Fatherhood* (Bloomington: Indiana University Press, 2014). Online services to the intermarried, such as Interfaithfamily.com, are repositories of narratives written by spouses in interfaith marriages about their efforts to negotiate the different traditions threatening to drive a wedge in their relationships to each other and their children.

39. The precise demarcation of this group is hard to pin down. Some limit the group to those born between 1982 and 1997, and others include those born a few years earlier and also a few years later.

40. Pew's conclusions are quoted by Naomi Schaefer Riley, *Got Religion? How Churches, Mosques, and Synagogues Can Bring Young People Back?* (West Conshohocken, PA: Templeton Press, 2014), 13. In 2015, Pew issued an updated report containing more evidence of declining interest in religion and religious affiliation among millennials: Becka A. Alper, "Millennials Are Less Religious Than Older Americans, but Just as Spiritual" (Pew Research Center, November 23, 2015), http://www.pewresearch.org/fact-tank/2015/11/23 /millennials-are-less-religious-than-older-americans-but-just-as-spiritual/.

41. Pew Research Center, "Portrait of Jewish Americans," 8.

42. UJA-Federation of New York, "Stepping in to Engage Jewish Millennials: Understanding the New Generation of Young Adults" (March 2016), esp. 16–17, 23, 35, http://ejewishphilanthropy.com/wordpress/wp-content/uploads/2016/03/Insights-and-Strategies-for-Engaging-Jewish-Millennials.pdf. We should note this study was conducted with a sample of some 250 participants, virtually none of whom were Orthodox.

43. Neil Shah, "The End of the Suburbs and Four Other American Migration Myths," *Wall Street Journal*, January 23, 2015, http://blogs.wsj.com/economics/2015/01/23/the-end-of-the-suburbs-and-four-other-american-migration-myths/; and David Z. Morris, "Why Millennials Are about to Leave the Cities in Droves," *Fortune*, March 28, 2016, http://fortune.com/2016/03/28/millennials-leaving-cities/.

44. I have devoted little attention here to the religious lives of Jews who do not affiliate with a synagogue. They will appear in chapters 9 and 10. For one study that focuses on this population, see Lynn Davidman, "The New Voluntarism and the Case of Unsynagogued Jews," in *Everyday Religion: Observing Religious Lives*, ed. Nancy T. Ammerman (New York: Oxford University Press, 2007), 51–67.

Chapter 3: Diversity among the Orthodox

1. The shift of Orthodox groups to a self-conscious and deliberate educational enterprise in place of the mimetic folk culture of the past is traced in Haym Soloveitchik, "Rupture and Reconstruction: The Transformation of Contemporary Orthodoxy," *Tradition* 28, no. 4 (1994), reprinted by the Lookstein Center at Bar Ilan University, http://www.lookstein.org/links/orthodoxy.htm.

2. The popular rendering of this quotation likens reading Hebrew in translation to "kissing a bride through a veil," but that is an "improved" version of what the poet actually wrote. See Haim Nachman Bialik, "Nation and Language," in *Devarim shebe-'al peh* (Tel Aviv: Devir, 1935), 1:15–20.

3. Dara Horn, "My First Hebrew Test" (Stroum Center, University of Washington, March 7, 2016), https://jewishstudies.washington.edu/hebrew-humanities/dara-horn-my-first-hebrew-test/.

4. For a study of how Hebrew for the purposes of textual study and communication is treated differently in Orthodox as compared to non-Orthodox Jewish day schools, see Alex Pomson and Jack Wertheimer, "Hebrew for What? Hebrew at the Heart of Jewish Day Schools" (AVI CHAI Foundation, 2017), http://avichai.org/knowledge_base/hebrew-for-what-hebrew-at-the-heart-of-jewish-day-schools/.

5. Soloveitchik, "Rupture and Reconstruction," 99.

6. For more on this theme, see Jack Wertheimer, "The High Cost of Jewish Living," *Commentary*, March 2010, https://www.commentarymagazine.com/articles/the-high-cost-of-jewish-living/. A few Orthodox Jews have gone public to denounce the system and its onerous costs. See, for example, the anonymously written "I Can 'Do Jewish' on Just $40,000 a Year," *Times of Israel*, September 11, 2017, http://blogs.timesofisrael.com/i-can-do-jewish-for-40000/.

7. On the Orthodox contra-acculturative strategy, see Samuel C. Heilman, *Sliding to the Right: The Contest for the Future of American Jewish Orthodoxy* (Berkeley: University of California Press, 2006), 4. And for research pointing to the moderation of these tendencies, see Moshe Krakowski, "Moderate Ultra-Orthodoxy: Complexity and Nuance in American Ultra-Orthodox Judaism," *Religion and Education* 39, no. 3 (2012).

8. For a history of Orthodoxy in this country that mainly, but not exclusively, focuses on the Modern Orthodox, see Jeffrey S. Gurock, *Orthodox Jews in America* (Bloomington: Indiana University Press, 2009). Heilman adopts the terminology of "plural life worlds" from Peter Berger. See Heilman, *Sliding to the Right*, 3.

9. Sephardi Jews are probably the least studied population of Jews, and are usually neglected by journalists too. Due to the scant literature on Sephardim in America, this chapter's discussion of Sephardi Jews is heavily based upon interviews with insiders, especially with rabbis and informed professional observers.

10. The terms "Haredi(m)," "Hasid(im)," and "Hesed," which recur in this chapter, all begin with the Hebrew letter *chet*; in each case the letter is pronounced as a guttural consonant as in chutzpah and Hanukkah. "Haredim" and "Hasidim" are the plural forms of "Haredi" and "Hasid." In the rest of this chapter, I will eschew use of the term "ultra-Orthodox."

11. See, for example, the views cited by Yael Farzan, "Accepting Our Own: The Bias against Black Hatters," *Yeshiva University Observer*, April 29, 2013, http://

www.yuobserver.org/2013/04/accepting-our-own-the-bias-against-black-hat ters/; and Harry Maryles, "Deriding Black Hatters," *Emes Ve-Emunah*, April 30, 2013, http://haemtza.blogspot.co.il/2013/04/deriding-black-hatters.html.

12. Samuel C. Heilman, *Who Will Lead Us? The Story of Five Hasidic Dynasties in America* (Berkeley: University of California Press, 2017), chap. 5. And on the Satmar wars, see Michael Powell, "Hats On, Gloves Off: The Death of the Rebbe Frees His Sons Aaron and Zalmen to Go to War. But Is the Prize—All of Hasidic Williamsburg—a Poisoned Chalice?," *New York Magazine*, May 8, 2006, http://nymag.com/news/cityside/16864/.

13. On this population, see Heilman, *Who Will Lead Us?*, esp. chap. 3.

14. These trends were detailed by Moses Weinberger in his Hebrew volume, *Jews and Judaism in New York*, translated by Jonathan Sarna as *People Walk on Their Heads* (New York: Holmes and Meier, 1982).

15. Historians don't see things this way and tend to agree with an analysis put forward by the Israeli historian Jacob Katz, who understood Haredi culture as a response to and a form of modernization. For a particularly sharp analysis of how radical some of these traditionalists were, see Michael K. Silber, "The Emergence of Ultra Orthodoxy: The Invention of a Tradition," in *The Uses of Tradition: Jewish Continuity in the Modern Era*, ed. Jack Wertheimer (Cambridge, MA: Harvard University Press and JTS, 1992), 23–84.

16. The Lubavitchers are far outnumbered by several other sects and probably do not constitute more than one-seventh of all Hasidim in the United States. But their participation in the wider Jewish community and accessibility draws considerable attention. According to the sociologist Samuel Heilman (private communication, March 6, 2017), an authority on Orthodoxy in America, the Lubavitchers are probably the fifth largest Hasidic group in this country, outnumbered in rank order by Satmar, Bobov, Vishnitz, and Skvir.

17. Philip Roth, *Goodbye, Columbus: And Five Short Stories* (Boston: Houghton Mifflin, 1959).

18. It is stunning to read how few followers these Hasidic and Mitnagdic rabbis had upon their arrival in the United States. At early gatherings of Lubavitch Hasidim after their rebbe arrived in 1940, no more than fifty followers and students attended his Farbrengen. David Eliezrie, *The Secret of Chabad* (Jerusalem: Toby Press, 2015), 51. The Lakewood Yeshiva was started in 1941 with fourteen

students and a goal of growing to one hundred. David Landes, "How Lakewood, N.J., Is Redefining What It Means to Be Orthodox in America," *Tablet*, June 5, 2013. And as late as 1961, the Satmar community numbered no more than forty-five hundred people. Israel Rubin, *Satmar: Two Generations of an Urban Island*, 2nd ed. (New York: Peter Lang, 1997), 42.

19. See Emanuel Sivan, "The Enclave Culture," in *Fundamentalisms Comprehended*, ed. Martin Marty and R. Scott Appleby (Chicago: University of Chicago Press, 1995), 11–68; Heilman, *Sliding to the Right*, 4–5.

20. For an analysis of how Haredi communities developed in a section of Los Angeles in the last third of the twentieth century, see Tavory, *Summoned*, esp. 82–91.

21. The US census finding is cited by Marvin Schick, *A Census of Jewish Day Schools in the United States, 2013–14* (New York: Avi Chai Foundation, 2014), 29n27.

22. On the explosion of population in Lakewood, see Shannon Mullen, "Boomtown: Growth and Conflict in Lakewood," *app*, August 8, 2015, http://www.app .com/story/news/local/jackson-lakewood/2015/08/08/lakewood-growth-boom -changing-ocean-county/31318143/.

23. Schick, *Census of Jewish Day Schools*, 28.

24. Deborah Nussbaum Cohen, "New York Ultra-Orthodox Discover the Downside of Being Fruitful and Multiplying," *Ha'aretz*, September 24, 2012, http:// www.haaretz.com/israel-news/new-york-ultra-orthodox-discover-the-down side-of-being-fruitful-and-multiplying-1.466458.

25. Though most of this growth is attributable to large family size, the Haredi population has received a significant influx of recruits from other sectors of the Jewish community, most notably from Modern Orthodox families. As many as 20 percent of students at the Lakewood yeshiva were raised in non-Haredi homes. And Lubavitch too has attracted significant numbers to its brand of Hasidism.

26. UJA-Federation of New York, "Jewish Community Study of New York, 2011" (2011), 216.

27. Jacob Ukeles and Associates, "What Does the Future Hold? The 2010 Greater Baltimore Jewish Community Study" (Baltimore: The Associated, 2011), http:// www.jewishdatabank.org/studies/downloadFile.cfm?FileID=2721.

28. The emphasis on education does not necessarily include a strong commitment to high-quality general studies. To the contrary, most Haredi schools slight such

subject matter, especially in the education of males. This has become a source of scandal and outrage in some quarters. See Frimet Godberger, "When Hasidic Boys Grow Up without Real School," *Forward*, March 11, 2014, http://forward .com/sisterhood/194267/when-hasidic-boys-grow-up-without-real-school/.

29. For two accounts of the long journeys by former "reverse Marranos," see, for example, Leah Vincent, *Cut Me Loose: Sin and Salvation after My Ultra-Orthodox Girlhood* (New York: Doubleday, 2014), and Shulem Deen, *All Who Go Do Not Return: A Memoir* (Minneapolis: Greywood Press, 2015). See also Frimet Goldberger, "Ex-Hasidic Woman Marks Five Years since She Shaved Her Head," *Forward*, November 7, 2013, http://forward.com/articles/187128/ex -hasidic-woman-marks-five-years-since-she-shaved/.

30. "One in Ten Haredi Is Leaving the Orthodox World," a study conducted by Out for Change, an Israeli NGO for Haredi dropouts, February 4, 2016, https://vimeo.com/154174270?outro=1.

31. Mark Trencher, "Starting a Conversation: A Pioneering Survey of Those Who Have Left the Orthodox Community: An Exploration of Journeys, Practices, Beliefs, Identity, Community and Relationships—Across Chasidic, Yeshivish and Modern Orthodox Segments" (West Hartford, CT: Nishma Institute, June 19, 2016).

32. On Footsteps, see http://footstepsorg.org/. For one of the many articles on Off-the-Derech Jews, see Samuel Freedman, "Stepping Off the Path and Redefining Faith," *New York Times*, October 17, 2014, http://www.nytimes.com/2014/10/18 /us/stepping-off-the-path-and-redefining-faith.html?_r=0. See also Hella Winston, *Unchosen: The Hidden Lives of Hasidic Rebels* (Boston: Beacon, 2006), and Lynn Davidman, *Becoming Unorthodox: Stories of Ex-Hasidic Jews* (Oxford: Oxford University Press, 2015).

33. The Trencher survey estimates the number in the New York area alone as well over ten thousand. Trencher, "Starting a Conversation."

34. "An Exchange," *Rabbi Pruzansky's Blog*, March 17, 2014, http://rabbipruzan sky.com/2014/03/14/an-exchange/.

35. There are many religious reasons for praying in a quorum. Still, one wonders whether the function of attending public worship daily is to derive inspiration from fellow participants during a daily exercise that may otherwise become tedious.

36. UJA-Federation of New York, "Jewish Community Study of New York, 2011," 220.

37. This observation is true of Conservative and Reform synagogues too. Congregations and their members tend to reflect the cultures of their environments. Not surprisingly, Conservative synagogues in California, the so-called Left Coast, are far more liberal and experimental than their counterparts in the Midwest and East.

38. On this phenomenon, see Charles S. Liebman, "Extremism as a Religious Norm," *Journal for the Scientific Study of Religion* 22 (March 1983). The exclusionary practices tend less to be formalized than reinforced through social interactions and other forms of inhospitality.

39. The persistence of great religious laxity among members of Modern Orthodox synagogues in different parts of the country is the subject of a detailed portrait appended to Gurock's *Orthodox Jews in America*. See his "Epilogue: The Tentative Orthodox of the Twenty-First Century," 312–23.

40. Ibid., 314–15.

41. Jeffrey S. Gurock, "Checking Up on America's 'Tentative Orthodox' Jews," in *Black Fire on White Fire: Essays in Honor of Rabbi Avi Weiss*, ed. Daniel Goodman (New York: KTAV, 2017), 86.

42. Josh Nathan-Kazis, "Rabbis Declare War on Chit-Chat in Synagogue," *Forward*, September 3, 2013, http://forward.com/news/183217/rabbis-declare-war-on-chit-chat-in-synagogue/.

43. The dynamics in Haredi synagogues differ somewhat because women rarely attend at all. Certainly, in Hasidic services, loud cross-conversations are hard to miss. Nathan-Kazis, "Rabbis Declare War on Chit-Chat," quotes the dismay of a regular attender of a Hasidic synagogue who objects that "God really does not appreciate when [his fellow congregants] talk."

44. For a case study of such a conflict, albeit in a non-synagogue setting, see Ari L. Goldman, "Is Dancing Kosher? Jews Struggle to Define Orthodox," *New York Times*, November 28, 1990, http://www.nytimes.com/1990/11/28/nyregion/is-dancing-kosher-jews-struggle-to-define-orthodoxy.html?pagewanted=all.

45. With the massive growth of Passover escapes by Orthodox Jews, Modern Orthodox Jews are also staying at hotels with coed swimming pools. Here too the injunctions of rabbis seem to be losing out to the practices of their congregants, who

have no compunctions about mixed swimming. This point is briefly touched upon in Mark Oppenheimer, "Celebrating Passover, with All the Comforts of a Resort," *New York Times*, April 16, 2016, http://www.nytimes.com/2016/04/16 /us/celebrating-passoverwith-allthe-comforts-ofaresort.html?_r=0.

46. For a few examples, see Steve Lipman, "For Many Orthodox Teens, 'Half Shabbos' Is a Way of Life Texting on Saturdays Seen as Increasingly Common 'Addiction'," *Jewish Week* (New York), June 21, 2011, http://www.thejewishweek .com/news/national-news/many-orthodox-teens-half-shabbos-way-life; Aryeh Younger, "Texting and the Power of 'Half Shabbat,'" *Forward*, June 20, 2013, http://forward.com/opinion/178988/texting-and-the-power-of-half-shabbat/; Shira Telushkin, "Shabbat Is a Day of Rest—But Does That Mean I Can't Text My Friends?," *Tablet*, September 12, 2014, http://www.tabletmag.com/jewish -life-and-religion/184233/shabbat-phones.

47. Jay P. Lefkowitz, "The Rise of Social Orthodoxy: A Personal Account," *Commentary*, April 2014, https://www.commentarymagazine.com/articles/the-rise-of-so cial-orthodoxy-a-personal-account/. Though his analysis did not sit well with some rabbis in his movement, it was confirmed by at least one based in an area of dense Modern Orthodox concentration, who observed: "A lot of people really enjoy the intensity of commitment in the Orthodox community, but they would provide [*sic*] confidentially that they don't agree with the doctrines or dogmas. . . . They socially find meaning in that community. Every Orthodox rabbi knows such people exist, but there's an openness. We don't check to see who believes what." Rabbi Moshe Grussgott of Congregation Ramath Orah, an Orthodox synagogue in New York City, quoted in Ben Sales, "Jared and Ivanka Do Their Own Thing as Observant Jews—and That's Normal," *JTA*, June 15, 2017, http://www.jta.org/2017/06/15/news-opinion/politics/jared-and -ivanka-do-their-own-thing-as-observant-jews-and-thats-normal.

48. This leftward movement was suggested by Yehudah Turetsky and Chaim I. Waxman in "Sliding to the Left: Contemporary American Modern Orthodoxy," *Modern Judaism* 31, no. 2 (2011): 119–41.

49. Given the paucity of research on Sephardi Jews in the United States, this section relies heavily on ten interviews I conducted with rabbis serving those communities and a few lay observers. The observations here are of necessity impressionistic.

50. The "invisibility" of Sephardi Jews on the American scene is the driving theme of Aviva Ben-Ur, *Sephardic Jews in America: A Diasporic History* (New York: New York University Press, 2009). The author chronicles the "exclusion," "marginalization," and caricaturing of Sephardim in studies of American Jewish life.

51. UJA-Federation of New York, "Jewish Community Study of New York, 2011," 244n16.

52. We lack demographic data on this population because the Los Angeles Federation has failed to sponsor a study of its catchment area since 1997.

53. My thanks to Professor Steven M. Cohen for sharing data on different Sephardi groups in the New York Jewish population.

54. Zev Chafets, "The SY Empire," *New York Times*, October 14, 2007, http://www.nytimes.com/2007/10/14/magazine/14syrians-t.html?pagewanted=all.

55. For a history of one such congregation in Seattle, see Marc D. Angel, "The American Experience of a Sephardic Synagogue," in *The American Synagogue: A Sanctuary Transformed*, ed. Jack Wertheimer (Cambridge: Cambridge University Press, 1987), 153–69.

56. An estimated six thousand Iraqi-born Jews live in the New York area according to Rahel Musleah, who shared with me a manuscript article on the subject.

57. On the contours of this Central Asian community, see Alanna E. Cooper, *Bukharan Jews and the Dynamics of Global Judaism* (Bloomington: Indiana University Press, 2012).

58. Tara Isabela Burton, "Bukharan Jews Thrive in New York but Are Almost Gone in Central Asia," *National Geographic*, August 4, 2015, http://news.national geographic.com/2015/08/150804-jews-diaspora-bukhara-uzbekistan-asia -world/. The New York Jewish Population Study asked about Russian speakers and did not devote specific attention to Bukharan Jews. Another report on this community placed the number of Bukharan Jews in Forest Hills at thirty-five thousand and highlighted the difficulties in maintaining and transmitting its religio-cultural traditions. Gil Shefler, "Bukharan Jews Thrive in New York City," *Jerusalem Post*, July 12, 2011, http://www.jpost.com/Jewish-World /Jewish-News/Bukharan-Jewish-community-thrives-in-NYC.

59. Rahel Musleah, "Bukharian Jews: Preserving Identity," *Hadassah Magazine* 90, no. 1 (2008), http://www.hadassah.org/news/content/per_hadassah/ar-chive/2008 /08_sep/feature_1.asp.

60. The edict is discussed in detail by Chafets, "SY Empire." Syrian rabbis are expected to remind congregants at least once yearly of the edict.

61. Consisting of fairly recent immigrants, the Bukharans seem to differ in this regard: women have acculturated more quickly and entered the labor force, while their husbands have had a harder time making a living in the United States. See Rahel Musleah, "Bukharian Jews."

62. A study of Syrian Jews in New York found that 37 percent of women claimed to be homemakers versus 11 percent of Ashkenazi women, and only 20 percent of Syrian women had earned a degree beyond a bachelor's, compared to 34 percent of Ashkenazi women. Steven M. Cohen, Galia Avidar, and Marcie Yoselevsky, "The Syrian Jews of New York: Challenges to a Cohesive Community" (unpublished manuscript, October 2012), 15. My thanks to Cohen for sharing this manuscript with me. Rabbis also report on the reliance of these communities upon women volunteers and the lower proportions of women who work outside the home.

63. Elevating women to the role of keepers of the religious and family flame is commonplace in discourse about religious life. It is particularly difficult to gain access to hear firsthand from Sephardi women about their religious lives. For an account by a defector from that world, see Diane Cohler-Esses, "What the Hell Is a Syrian Jew?," *Journal of Feminist Studies in Religion* 19, no. 1 (2003): 111–18, http://www.jewishpinkelephant.com/2013/03/what-hell-is-syrian-jew-by-dianne.html.

64. These Iranian children are educated twice a week in supplementary programs offered by synagogues.

65. One observer contended the Persians have not yet experienced growing rates of intermarriage, and therefore regard day school education as less important.

66. The different relationship of Haredi versus Modern Orthodox Jews to Gedolim, authoritative rabbis whose judgments carry the weight of law, has been analyzed trenchantly by Chaim Saiman, "The Market for Gedolim: A Tale of Supply and Demand," *Lehrhaus*, October 13, 2016, http://www.thelehrhaus.com/scholarship/2016/10/12/the-market-for-gedolim.

67. Yitzchok Adlerstein, "In Praise of Diversity," *Klal Perspectives*, Fall 2011, 10–13. Similar concerns are raised by the erosion of rabbinic authority through the Internet by Heshie Billet, "Where We Are and Where We Are Heading," *Klal Perspectives* (Fall 2011): 22–25.

Chapter 4: Is Reform Judaism Ascendant?

1. Reconstructionism, once a school of thought within Conservative Judaism, also is organized as a denomination. Because of its minuscule size and currently negligible influence, it is not treated here as a fourth movement, but will be discussed in chapter 10 in the context of other unconventional groups.

2. Michael Lipka, "Mainline Protestants Make Up Shrinking Number of U.S. Adults," Pew Research Center, May 18, 2015, http://www.pewresearch.org /fact-tank/2015/05/18/mainline-protestants-make-up-shrinking-number-of-u -s-adults/. On the longer-term decline, see Joseph Bottum, "The Death of Protestant America: A Political Theory of the Protestant Mainline," *First Things*, August 2008, http://www.firstthings.com/article/2008/08/001-the-death-of-pro testant-america-a-political-theory-of-the-protestant-mainline.

3. On *Mishkan T'Filah*, see Laurie Goodstein, "In Reform Prayer Book, Signs of Broad Change," *New York Times*, September 3, 2007, http://www.nytimes .com/2007/09/03/us/03prayerbook.html; Stuart Kelman, "A Reform Prayer Book," *Jewish Book Council Review*, n.d., http://www.jewishbookcouncil.org /book/mishkan-tfilah. For a probing analysis of the new High Holiday *Mahzor*, see Clifford Librach, "A Revolution for Reform Judaism?," *Commentary*, December 14, 2015, https://www.commentarymagazine.com/articles/revolution -reform-judaism/.

4. On these developments, see Michael Meyer, *Response to Modernity: The History of the Reform Movement in Judaism* (New York: Oxford University Press, 1988), chaps. 6 and 7; Leon Jick, *The Americanization of the Synagogue, 1820– 1870* (Lebanon, NH: Brandeis University Press, 1992); and for a particularly interesting case study of this period, see Tobias Brinkman, *Sundays at Sinai: A Jewish Congregation in Chicago* (Chicago: University of Chicago Press, 2012).

5. For more on the background to this seminal document, see Jonathan D. Sarna, "New Light on the Pittsburgh Platform of 1885," *American Jewish History* (March 1987): 358–68.

6. On the early history of this organization, which continues today, see Thomas A. Kolsky, *Jews against Zionism: The American Council for Judaism, 1942–1948* (Philadelphia: Temple University Press, 1990).

7. I have discussed this shift in *A People Divided*, 10.

8. Marcus's address is quoted in Alan Tarshish, "How 'Central' Is the CCAR?," *CCAR Journal* 8 (January 1960): 32.

9. On these developments, see Dana Evan Kaplan, *American Reform Judaism: An Introduction* (New Brunswick, NJ: Rutgers University Press, 2003), chaps. 9 and 10.

10. Ibid., chap. 8.

11. In Conservative and Orthodox synagogues, by contrast, the respective figures were 12 percent and 5 percent.

12. Eric Yoffie, "Realizing God's Promise: A Reform Revolution" (sermon delivered at the Biennial Convention of the Union for Reform Judaism, December 18, 1999), https://ericyoffie.com/reform-worship-revolution/.

13. Kaplan, *American Reform Judaism*, chap. 5.

14. The aforementioned Zionist leaders, Rabbis Stephen S. Wise and Abba Hillel Silver, are a case in point. The former was close to Democrats and the latter to Republicans.

15. Congregational rabbis have a more jaundiced view of the proceedings because they see little broader impact or follow-up after the conventions.

16. Rukhl Schaechter, "Projected Prayers Grow in Popularity as Part of Jewish 'Visual Tefillah' Services," *Forward*, March 30, 2013, http://forward.com/culture/books/173515/projected-prayers-grow-in-popularity-as-part-of-je/#ixzz3hym9P344.

17. Visual T'fliah is promoted on the website of the Central Conference of American Rabbis, the Reform rabbinic arm. See https://www.ccarpress.org/shopping_product_list.asp?catID=3756.

18. From the temple bulletin, April 4, 2014.

19. The role of song leaders and composers of liturgical music for Reform congregations is discussed by Penny Schwartz, "The Reform Movement Is Alive with the Sound of Music," *JTA*, December 14, 2017. The article refers to a five-day annual retreat held by the Hava Nashira Institute where new compositions are shared.

20. It is hard to get a fix on the trajectory of temple memberships. These figures are closely held by the central offices of the movement. A good many Reform temples maintain robust levels of affiliation. But others are in severe decline, as is attested by the mergers and growing numbers of congregations shutting

their doors. Whether this is due to the normal geographic movement of Jewish populations or to a more systemic decline is presently unclear.

21. Eli Schaap, "URJ Portraits of Learning" (typescript, September 2007; summary by Jan Katzew, director, URJ, Department of Lifelong Jewish Learning), 2.

22. "Rabbi Yoffie Calls for Increased Shabbat Observance in Reform Movement" (URJ press release, December 14, 2007), http://www.urj.org/blog/2007/12/14/rabbi-eric-yoffie-calls-increased-shabbat-observance-reform-movement.

23. See Eric H. Yoffie, "Foreword," in *Reform Judaism: Challenges and Reflections*, ed. Dana Evan Kaplan (Philadelphia: Jewish Publication Society, 2013), ix; and "Commentary on the Principles for Reform Judaism" (Central Conference of American Rabbis, October 27, 2004), https://ccarnet.org/rabbis-speak/platforms/commentary-principles-reform-judaism/.

24. One of the first to call attention to the gender disparity has been Rabbi Jeffrey K. Salkin in his volumes *Searching for My Brothers* (New York: Putnam, 1999) and *The Modern Men's Torah Commentary* (Woodstock, VT: Jewish Lights, 2009). See also Sue Fishkoff, "Reform Trying to Lure Men Back," *JTA*, December 18, 2007.

25. The data are in a report published by the *Jewish Voice and Opinion* on June 16, 2007, in a section called "News Flash." It no longer seems to be online. One source cited by the article is Doug Barden, "Wrestling with Jacob and Essay: Fighting the Flight of Men—A Modern-Day Crisis of the Reform Movement" (National Federation of Temple Brotherhoods of the Reform Movement, 2005). Barden was then serving as the executive of the organization.

26. We have already noted her study *Matrilineal Ascent/Patrilineal Descent* in chapter 2. For an earlier discussion of these issues, see her paper "Growth and Challenges in the Contemporary Reform Movement," in *Hayehadut HaReforma: Hagut, Tarbut, Vehevra*, ed. Avinoam Rosenak (Jerusalem: Van Leer Institute, 2014).

27. It is hard to state this with precision because the Pew survey asked about only self-identification with a movement and synagogue membership, not the affiliation of the synagogue. Because 69 percent of intermarried families with a synagogue affiliation claimed to be Reform and we can assume that some of the 21 percent who chose the Conservative label are members of Reform tem-

ples, it appears that Reform congregations have cornered at least three-quarters of that market.

28. For a discussion about this slippery slope, see Michael A. Meyer, "On the Slope toward Syncretism and Sectarianism," *CCAR Journal* (Summer 1993): 41–44. I'm not aware of continuing public discussion of this issue.

29. The last survey conducted in 2007 found that 49 percent of children came from such homes. There is good reason to assume this figure has continued to rise, as ever higher percentages of Temple members are intermarried. On the 2007 data, see Schaap, "URJ Portraits of Learning."

30. Rabbi Janet Marder has been credited with creating this innovation; see "Not All Jewish Heroes Are Jewish," https://rabbibrad.wordpress.com/2010/03/14 /not-all-jewish-heroes-are-jewish-2/; and Eric Yoffie, "Recognizing Non-Jewish Heroes in Our Midst," *Reform Judaism*, Spring 2006, http://rjmag.org/Articles /index.cfm?id=1115.

31. "Reform Movement Leader Calls for Increased Effort to Convert Non-Jews to Judaism" (URJ press release, November 19, 2005), http://urj.org/pr/2005 /05119a/.

32. That policy is over thirty years old and hardly reflects current realities. More cynically inclined Reform rabbis have wondered aloud whether the policy has not been revisited because it would result in the elimination of any opposition to intermarriage. One policy that has been revisited in recent years is the ban on admitting intermarried Jews to the Reform movement's rabbinical school. For an overview of the debate, see Dana Evan Kaplan, "Reform Jewry Grapples with Intermarriage among Rabbinic Students," *Forward*, April 23, 2013, http://for ward.com/opinion/175093/reform-jewry-grapples-with-intermarriage-among -rab/. Thus far, the change in policy has been resisted, even as the Reconstruc- tionist Rabbinical College has removed the prohibition for its own students. J. Hersz, "Reconstructionist Movement Removes Ban on Intermarried Students," *Jewish Exponent*, October 9, 2015, http://jewishexponent.com/2015/10/09 /reconstructionist-rabbinical-college-removes-ban-on-intermarried-students/.

33. David Ellenson, "Michael A. Meyer and His Vision of Reform Judaism and the Reform Rabbinate: A Lifetime of Devotion," in *Mediating Modernity: Chal- lenges and Trends in the Jewish Encounter with the Modern World—Essays in*

Honor of Michael A. Meyer, ed. Lauren B. Strauss and Michael Brenner (Detroit: Wayne State University Press, 2008), 21.

34. This is the argument of Dana Evan Kaplan, a Reform rabbi, who has written extensively and critically about his movement's failure to define its approach to Jewish living. He writes: "The pluralistic theologies of Reform Judaism make it difficult to reach consensus on what we Reform Jews believe on any given issue. The liberal approach to observance makes it impossible to set and maintain high expectations in terms of communal participation. Without an omnipotent God who can compel believers to practice a prescribed pattern of behavior, religious consumerism becomes the movement's dominant ethos. As members focus on what they want rather than what they can contribute, it becomes increasingly difficult to build committed religious communities." Dana Evan Kaplan, "The Theological Roots of Reform Judaism's Woes," *Forward*, February 16, 2011, http://forward.com/opinion/135476/the-theological-roots-of-reform-judaism-s-woes/#ixzz47tCkDL9M.

Chapter 5: Conservative Judaism

1. Yair Ettinger, "Is Modern Orthodoxy Reaching Its Breaking Point?," *Forward*, August 31, 2015, http://forward.com/opinion/320073/is-modern-orthodoxy-reaching-its-breaking-point/?attribution=author-article-listing-2-headline.

2. Pew Research Center, "Portrait of Jewish Americans," 10. The rest identified either with no denomination (30 percent) or with a form of Judaism different from the major denominations (6 percent).

3. David Wolpe, "Conservative Judaism Seeks Its True Name," *Huffington Post*, November 23, 2015, http://www.huffingtonpost.com/rabbi-david-wolpe/conservative-judaism-seek_b_8612458.html; Wolpe addressed the political implications of the name more directly in Uriel Heilman, "Amid Identity Crisis, Conservative Jews Pay for Rebranding," *JTA*, November 20, 2015, http://www.jta.org/2015/11/20/news-opinion/united-states/amid-identity-crisis-conservative-jews-pay-for-rebranding.

4. This was the message of Prof. Neil Gillman of the Jewish Theological Seminary. See "Halakhic Divide May Push Conservative to the Right," *Jerusalem Post*, January 7, 2006, http://www.jpost.com/Jewish-World/Jewish-News/Halachic

-divide-may-push-Conservatives-to-the-Right. His remarks are published in Neil Gillman, "A New Aggadah for the Conservative Movement," *Conservative Judaism* (Winter–Spring 2006): 29–45.

5. David Wolpe described the slogan as an oxymoron, and former chancellor of JTS Ismar Schorsch called it "inane." Wolpe is quoted in Heilman, "Amid Identity Crisis," Schorsch in Samantha Shapiro, "One Mad Rabbi," *Slate*, August 28, 2006, http://www.slate.com/articles/life/faithbased/2006/08/one_mad_rabbi.html.

6. Leaders of Reform Judaism have not been bashful about labeling the Conservative movement as a laggard. Speaking to the *New York Times*, Rabbi Alexander Schindler, the head of the Reform congregational arm in the 1970s and 1980s, pronounced that when it comes to taking action, "it usually takes [the Conservative movement] about 10 years—like on the woman's issue." Quoted by Abraham Karp, "A Century of Conservative Judaism in the United States," *American Jewish Year Book* 86 (1986): 60.

7. An even longer debate wracked the movement over potential changes in the religious status of women in the synagogue and clergy. See Beth Wenger, "The Politics of Women's Ordination: Jewish Law, Institutional Power, and the Debate over Women in the Rabbinate," in *Tradition Renewed*, vol. 2, ed. Jack Wertheimer (New York: Jewish Theological Seminary, 2008), 483–524.

8. Elliott N. Dorff, Daniel Nevins, and Avram Reisner, "Homosexuality, Human Dignity, and Halakha;" Joel Roth, "Homosexuality Revisited;" Gordon Tucker, "Halakhic and Metahalakhic Arguments Concerning Judaism and Homosexuality;" Myron Geller, Robert Fine, and David Fine, "The Halakhah of Same Sex Relations in a New Context;" Leonard Levy, "Same-Sex Attraction and Halakhah;" and Baruch Frydman-Kohl, "Homosexuality and Halakhah." The Committee on Jewish Law and Standards, Rabbinical Assembly, December 6, 2006, http://www.rabbinicalassembly.org/jewish-law/committee-jewish-law-and-standards/even-haezer.

9. Rebecca Spence, "Conservative Panel Votes to Permit Gay Rabbis," *Forward*, December 6, 2006, http://forward.com/news/9576/conservative-panel-votes-to-permit-gay-rabbis/.

10. Steven M. Cohen, "Gays, Lesbians, and the Conservative Movement: The JTS Survey of Conservative Clergy, Students, Professionals, and Lay Leaders," Berman

Jewish Policy Archive, January 28, 2007, 36, http://www.jewishdatabank.org /Studies/details.cfm?StudyID=493.

11. Ben Harris, "JTS Move Sparks Pluralism Debate," *JTA*, July 1, 2007, http:// www.jta.org/2007/03/27/life-religion/jts-move-sparks-pluralism-debate. With openly LGBTQ students enrolled in the Conservative rabbinical seminaries, that position is now the only tenable one, and the two more restrictive opinions approved by the Law Committee are dead letters.

12. Lance Sussman, "The Myth of the Trefa Banquet: American Culinary Culture and the Radicalization of Food Policy in American Reform Judaism," *American Jewish Archives Journal* 57 (2005). A photograph of the menu appears in Jonathan Sarna, *American Judaism: A History* (New Haven, CT: Yale University Press, 2004), 146.

13. This thesis is put forward by Moshe Davis, *The Emergence of Conservative Judaism: The Historical School in Nineteenth Century America* (Philadelphia: Jewish Publication Society, 1963).

14. Marshall Sklare, *Conservative Judaism: An American Religious Movement* (Glencoe, IL: Free Press, 1955).

15. A third scenario has been advanced recently, which focuses sharply on the emergence of Conservative Judaism as a distinct movement and how leaders, especially rabbis, understood their relationship to Reform and Orthodoxy. See Michael R. Cohen, *The Birth of Conservative Judaism: Solomon Schechter's Disciples and the Creation of an American Religious Movement* (New York: Columbia University Press, 2012).

16. The unnamed rabbi was quoted in Howard Singer, "The Judaism Born in America," *Commentary*, December 1, 1986, https://www.commentarymagazine .com/articles/the-judaism-born-in-america/.

17. Charles S. Liebman, *The Ambivalent American Jew: Politics, Family and Religion in American Jewish Life* (Philadelphia: Jewish Publication Society, 1973), 46–47.

18. Sklare, *Conservative Judaism*, 37–40.

19. Morris Freedman, "New Jewish Community in Formation: A Conservative Center Catering to Present-Day Needs," *Commentary*, January 1955, https://www.unz .org/Pub/Commentary-1955jan-00036.

20. Louis Finkelstein, "The Things That Unite Us" (address to the Rabbinical Assembly, 1927), reprinted in Mordecai Waxman, ed., *Tradition and Change: The*

Development of Conservative Judaism (New York: Burning Bush Press, 1958), 323.

21. For a history of these achievements, primarily at the Jewish Theological Seminary, see my edited two-volume set, *Tradition Renewed*.

22. Steven M. Cohen, "Change in a Very Conservative Movement," *Sh'ma* (February 2006): 6.

23. Information about synagogue membership is not made public by any of the Jewish religious movements. The best we can do is estimate based upon national surveys, such as the most recent Pew study.

24. I base this on the number of children enrolled in Jewish supplementary schools under Conservative auspices, the number in Solomon Schechter schools, and the approximate number in community day schools. See my *A Census of Jewish Supplementary Schools in the United States, 2006–07* (New York: Avi Chai Foundation, 2007), 12, http://avichai.org/knowledge_base/a-census-of-jewish -supplementary-schools-in-the-united-states-2006-07-2008/.

25. To cite a few examples: the membership of Sinai Temple in Los Angeles is overwhelmingly drawn from the Iranian community; several Conservative congregations in South Florida have seen a resurgence thanks to the arrival of significant Latino populations from Venezuela and Argentina; and congregations in San Diego have received an influx of South African Jews.

26. These tensions tearing at the movement during the middle decades of the twentieth century are the subject of my essay "JTS and the Conservative Movement," in Wertheimer, *Tradition Renewed*, 2:403–42.

27. "Reform Leader's Swipe Sparks Angry Rebuttals from Conservatives," *JTA*, March 3, 2004, http://www.jta.org/2004/03/03/archive/reform-leaders-swipe -sparks-angry-rebuttals-from-conservatives.

28. Matthew Wagner, "YU Chancellor: Non-Orthodox Judaism on the Way Out," *JWeekly*, May 14, 2009, http://www.jweekly.com/article/full/38071/yu-chancellor -non-orthodox-judaism-on-the-way-out1/.

29. This comparison is based upon the Pew data and was first reported in an op-ed I coauthored with Steven M. Cohen and Steven Bayme, "On Conservative Judaism, Why All the Talk about Failure?," *JTA*, October 12, 2015, http://www .jta.org/2015/10/12/news-opinion/opinion/op-ed-on-conservative-judaism -why-all-the-talk-about-failure.

30. Alon Tal, "Conservative Judaism Rising: A Report from the Field," *Times of Israel*, October 11, 2015.

31. Michael Wasserman, "What We Talk about When We Talk about Synagogue Dues," *eJewish Philanthropy*, July 30, 2015, http://ejewishphilanthropy.com /what-we-talk-about-when-we-talk-about-voluntary-dues/.

32. Paul Drazin, "Survey: The Use of Musical Instruments on Shabbat/Yom Tov," United Synagogue of Conservative Judaism, February 2013, 3–6, https://can tors.org/sites/default/files/uploaded_files/site/Education/uscj_instrumentuse surveyresults_20130219.pdf.

33. An as yet unapproved responsum attempts to do precisely that. Submitted in 2011 by Rabbis Elie Kaplan Spitz and Elliot N. Dorff, it was still being debated five years later. My thanks to Elliot Dorff for sharing the responsum draft with me.

34. The *Shevut* issues are itemized and discussed in the responsa cited above.

35. Ibid., 8.

36. In the spring of 2017, a handful of Conservative rabbis publicly called for a change in policy that would permit them to officiate at intermarriages without being booted from the Rabbinical Assembly, their rabbinic organization. There was no way to know at the time whether these individuals represented a larger trend. For an overview on the debate, see Emma Green, " 'We're Headed toward One of the Greatest Divisions in the History of the Jewish People,' " *Atlantic*, July 16, 2017, https://www.theatlantic.com/politics/archive/2017/07 /intermarriage-conservative-judaism/533637/.

37. Live streaming of worship services is another decision taken in growing numbers of Conservative synagogues, despite the explicit ban on such recordings by the movement's Committee on Jewish Law and Standards. The rationale offered for contravening an explicit responsum forbidding live streaming because it violates the Sabbath is justified by noting that some members are shut-ins who cannot make it to the synagogue on the Sabbath or High Holidays. "At the end of the day," explained a rabbi who permits such streaming, "it is . . . our desire to be truly inclusive that takes precedence." Justin Katz, "Yom Kippur on Your Laptop?," *Washington Jewish Week*, October 19, 2016, http://washing tonjewishweek.com/34121/yom-kippur-on-your-laptop/news/local-news/.

38. Rabbi Jacob Agus quoted in Howard Singer, "The Judaism Born in America."

39. Data derived from the Pew study suggest that there may even be a reversal in the numerical decline of members. Looking at the distribution of synagogue members, Conservative-identified Jews lagged behind their Reform counterparts in the population over fifty-five, but among those between forty and fifty-four, Conservative and Reform Jews are roughly neck and neck, and among those between twenty-five and thirty-nine, the peak child-bearing years, more Conservative Jews are synagogue members.

Chapter 6: The Battle for the Soul of Modern Orthodoxy

1. Jeffrey S. Gurock, "Resisters and Accommodators: Varieties of Orthodox Rabbis in America, 1886–1983," *American Jewish Archives* 35 (1983): 100–187, http://americanjewisharchives.org/publications/journal/PDF/1983_35_02_00_gurock.pdf.
2. Daniel Bronstein, "Torah in the Trenches: The Rabbi Chaplains of World War II, 1940–1946" (PhD diss., Jewish Theological Seminary, 2009).
3. Quoted by Heilman, *Sliding to the Right*, 32.
4. A perusal of the *Jewish Observer*, the now-defunct house organ of the Yeshivish community led by Agudath Israel, will reveal dozens of articles with this theme between its founding in 1963 and its closure in 2010.
5. Yitzchak Blau itemizes the key areas of continuing differences between the Modern Orthodox and Haredi camps: beyond the question of secular education and attitudes toward the state of Israel, "other dividing lines include issues pertaining to women, attitudes toward gentiles and other Jewish denominations, . . . the role of the rabbi . . . , the credence given to ethical intuitions, . . . and the willingness to include communal and personal needs as a factor for halakhic leniency." "Contemporary Challenges for Modern Orthodoxy," in *The Next Generation of Modern Orthodoxy*, ed. Shmuel Hain (New York: Orthodox Forum, 2012), 299.
6. UJA-Federation of New York, "Jewish Community Study of New York, 2011," 216. Extracting the Modern Orthodox fertility figure from Pew data appears to be quite complicated. Even the "Jewish Community Study of New York, 2011" refrained from offering a fertility rate for the Modern Orthodox; it did allow that it "is firmly situated in the region of positive population growth," and estimated it as four times the rate of non-Orthodox Jews (214–15).

7. Schick, *Census of Jewish Day Schools*, 2.

8. Theodore Sasson claims that young Orthodox families have been overrepresented among *olim* for quite a while both because of their religious and ideological motivations as well as in response to the high costs of Jewish living in the United States. *The New American Zionism* (New York: New York University Press, 2014), 112. Heilman estimates the *Aliyah* figure for Modern Orthodox youth who spent a gap year in Israel at 20 percent. Heilman, *Sliding to the Right*, 120. I have not found comparable information on *Aliyah* by Haredi Jews. On the brain drain this emigration represents, Jonathan Sarna has written, "This may be terrific from an Israeli perspective, but can a movement that sends its most illustrious sons and daughters there truly expect to triumph here?" "The Future of American Orthodoxy," *Sh'ma*, February 1, 2001, http://shma.com/2001/02/the -future-of-american-orthodoxy/.

9. Alan Brill, "Is There a Post-Orthodox Judaism That Corresponds to Post-Evangelical?," *Book of Doctrines and Opinions*, November 19, 2009, https:// kavvanah.wordpress.com/2009/11/19/is-there-a-post-orthodox-judaism-that -corresponds-to-post-evangelical/.

10. On the emergence of these forces at YU in the period after the death of J. B. Soloveitchik, see Gurock, *Orthodox Jews in America*, 267–72.

11. There is some controversy over the incidence of "flipping out," with some contending it is overhyped. See Shalom Z. Berger, Daniel Jacobson, and Chaim I. Waxman, *Flipping Out? Myth or Fact: The Impact of the "Year in Israel"* (New York: Yashar Books, 2007) and the follow-up research conducted by David Pelcovitz and Steven Eisenberg, summarized in Michael Orbach, "Flipping Out in Israel Is Over-rated," *Jewish Star*, June 5, 2009.

12. A detailed accounting of this capitulation by Modern Orthodox institutions to Haredi personnel appears in Turetsky and Waxman, "Sliding to the Left?," 10. The admission of Haredi or neo-Haredi religious functionaries into the Rabbinical Council of America has been cited by some observers as the prime explanation for the hardening hostility of that organization toward more "open" versions of Modern Orthodoxy.

13. None of this is to suggest that the Haredi world has remained static or that it has not internalized some modern Orthodox perspectives. One of my informants has made the case for interpreting the embrace of college education by

Haredim and their entry into the labor force outside of the enclaves as a tacit acceptance of *Torah U'mada*, the slogan of Yeshiva University. I don't agree with that assessment, but it does open a conversation about mutual influence, rather than the one-way movement of ideas. We lack a comprehensive analysis of the current state of Haredi ideology and practice in the United States. Some pieces of this puzzle are provided by Adam S. Ferziger, *Beyond Sectarianism: The Realignment of American Orthodox Judaism* (Detroit: Wayne State University Press, 2015); Yoel Finkelman, *Strictly Kosher Reading: Popular Literature and the Condition of Contemporary Orthodoxy* (Boston: Academic Studies Press, 2011); Heilman, *Sliding to the Right*; Krakowski, "Moderate Ultra-Orthodoxy"; among other works.

14. Rabbi Greenberg elaborated on his views in a personal correspondence with me, dated May 15, 2014.

15. This is the theme of Turetsky and Waxman, "Sliding to the Left?"

16. The struggle to free agunot, women "chained" to recalcitrant husbands who refuse to divorce them or extort huge sums of money as the price of a *get*, a Jewish writ of divorce, has agitated Orthodox communities for many decades. It has led to the creation of special courts to free such women, which predictably have been denounced by prominent rabbis, including Joseph B. Soloveitchik in the past, and today sectors of the Rabbinical Council of America; and it has led to the approval of prenuptial agreements permitting courts to dissolve a marriage under certain circumstances. The literature on these controversies is immense. In the present context, what is more important is how damaging the failure of Orthodox rabbis to resolve these tragic circumstances has been to their own credibility and the respect accorded to them.

17. This issue came to a head when the congregational body of Modern Orthodoxy pronounced it impermissible for women to play such a role. On this controversy, see the statement issued by the Orthodox Union, https://www .ou.org/assets/OU-Statement.pdf; "Orthodox Union Bars Women from Serving as Clergy in Synagogue," *JTA*, February 2, 2017, http://www.jta.org /2017/02/02/top-headlines/ou-bars-women-from-serving-as-clergy-in-its-syn agogues. Numerous responses, both pro and con, appeared subsequently. Sixteen are collected on the *Lehrhaus* website, http://www.thelehrhaus.com/timely -thoughts/the-state-of-the-conversation.

18. For a consideration of some halakhic dimensions of this question, see Aryeh Frimer, "Women in Communal Leadership Positions: Shul Presidents," *Text & Texture*, June 2, 2010, http://text.rcarabbis.org/women-in-communal-leader ship-positions-shul-presidents-by-aryeh-frimer/. On the ways these questions have been resolved differently in Modern Orthodox synagogues, see "The First Women Shul Presidents in Orthodox White Plains," *JewFem*, February 15, 2013, http://www.jewfem.com/easyblog1/entry/from-the-jofa-blog-the-first -women-shul-presidents-in-orthodox-white-plains; Stuart Ain, "Young Israel Movement in Turmoil over Upstate Shul," *Jewish Week* (New York), June 29, 2010, http://www.thejewishweek.com/news/new_york/young_israel_movement _turmoil_over_upstate_shul; and Josh Nathan-Kazis and Shuly-Seidler Feller, "Rabbi of Historical Orthodox Synagogue Overturns Decision to Let Women Lead," *Forward*, June 30, 2010, http://forward.com/news/129105/rabbi-of -historic-orthodox-synagogue-overturns-dec/.

19. On controversies over girls donning tefilin, see Amanda Borschel-Dan, "Ortho- dox Girls Fight for the Right to Don Tefillin," *Times of Israel*, January 21, 2014, http://www.timesofisrael.com/modern-orthodox-girls-fight-for-the-right-to -don-tefillin/; Tully Harcsztark, "SAR Principal Explains Decision to Allow Girls to Wear Tefillin at School Minyanim," *Jewish Star*, January 26, 2014, http:// thejewishstar.com/stories/SAR-principal-explains-decision-to-allow-girls-to -wear-teffilin-at-school-minyanim,4665; and, for a scathing denunciation of the policy, *Rabbi Pruzansky's Blog*, January 26, 2014, https://rabbipruzansky.com /2014/01/26/the-real-story/.

20. Ari Segal, "The Biggest Challenge to 'Emunah' of Our Time," *Shalhevet Boiling Point*, September 14, 2016, http://www.shalhevetboilingpoint.com/opinion /2016/09/14/the-biggest-challenge-to-emunah-of-our-time/. In my own site visits to Orthodox day schools of different stripes, I encountered students deeply torn between religious teachings and their familiarity with gay relatives or friends.

21. As this book went to press, data from a new survey of Modern Orthodox Jews confirmed the divisions in that camp over the religious status of women and the homosexual population. Most noteworthy was the finding that 53 percent of those surveyed wished to see women assume a role as clergy and 78 percent were "ok" with synagogues accepting gay people as members. Hannah Dreyfus,

"53 Percent of Modern Orthodox Jews Believe Women Should Have Expanded Roles as Clergy," *Jewish Week* (New York), September 27, 2017, http://jewishweek.timesofisrael.com/53-of-modern-orthodox-jews-believe-women-should-have-expanded-roles-in-clergy/. The survey was not a random sample, but an opt-in, raising the question of how representative respondents were. Nevertheless, if nothing else, it illustrates the divisions in the Orthodox camp.

22. This estimate appears in Michelle Waldman Sarna, "An Emerging Approach to Emerging Adulthood and Modern Orthodoxy," in Hain, *Next Generation of Modern Orthodoxy*, 255.

23. Saul J. Berman, "Diverse Orthodox Attitudes" (Berkeley, CA: Edah, 2001). JOFA's mission statement appears on its website.

24. With the retirement of Rabbi Avi Weiss and the emergence of a new generation of leaders, these institutions have distanced themselves from the terminology of "Open Orthodoxy." This is especially true of YCT. Johanna Ginsberg, "Closing a Chapter on Open Orthodoxy," *Times of Israel*, August 16, 2017, http://jewishweek.timesofisrael.com/closing-a-chapter-on-open-orthodoxy/.

25. Gurock, *Orthodox Jews in America*, chap. 10, esp. 285–31, describes the emergence of these groups and some of the skirmishes of the 1990s and early twenty-first century.

26. On the controversies over so-called partnership minyanim, see Uriel Heilman, "'Partnership Minyan' Spreads among Orthodox—and Rabbis Fire Back," *Forward*, March 5, 2014, http://forward.com/news/193860/partnership-minyan-spreads-among-orthodox-and-ra/. On Women's Tefillah, see Batsheva Marcus and Ronnie Becher, "Women's Tefillah Movement," *Encyclopedia* (2009), http://jwa.org/encyclopedia/article/womens-tefillah-movement; and for the grounds for opposition as laid out by an Orthodox rabbi, see Michael J. Broyde, "Women Only Torah Reading," *Torah Musings*, October 15, 2012, http://www.torahmusings.com/2012/10/womens-only-torah-reading/.

27. The appearance of TheTorah.com, with its more questioning and open-minded approach to biblical criticism, has stirred new controversies. For a powerful critique of this new trend within Modern Orthodoxy by a one-time sympathizer with Open Orthodoxy, see Yoram Hazony, "Open Orthodoxy?," *Torah Musings*, May 27, 2014, http://www.torahmusings.com/2014/05/open-orthodoxy/. In his classic study of "Orthodoxy in American Jewish Life," Charles

Liebman already anticipated the revisiting of *Torah Min Hashamayim* (the belief that the Pentateuch in its entirety was dictated by God to Moses) by some Orthodox Jews who come into contact with biblical criticism. *American Jewish Year Book* 65 (1965): 46–47n40. (My thanks to Larry Grossman for drawing my attention to this source.)

28. For a more detailed description of how partnership minyanim work and the location of roughly thirty such groups, see the website of the Jewish Orthodox Feminist Alliance (JOFA), https://www.jofa.org/Resources/ritual/synagogue/partnershipm.

29. Rabbis Aryeh A. Frimer and Dov I. Frimer, "Women, Keri'at Hatorah, and Aliyyot," *Tradition* 46, no. 4 (2013), http://www.rcarabbis.org/pdf/frimer_article.pdf. This position paper was reaffirmed by two leading decisors on the website of the Rabbinical Council of America.

30. "RCA Passes Resolution Regarding Ordination of Women," *Rabbinical Council of America*, October 30, 2015, http://www.rabbis.org/news/article.cfm?id=105836. On the hiring of a graduate of Yeshivat Maharat by a Los Angeles congregation, see Esther D. Kustanowitz, "A Giant Step for Orthodox Women Clergy," *Jewish Journal* (Los Angeles), May 5, 2015, http://www.jewishjournal.com/los_angeles/article/a_giant_step_for_orthodox_women_clergy.

31. For personal reflections illustrating how little is done to welcome women to weekday services, see some of the essays in Michal Smart and Barbara Ashkenas, eds., *Kaddish: Women's Voices* (Jerusalem: Urim, 2013).

32. Hannah Dreyfus, "Leading Rabbi Deals Big Blow to Agunah Court," *Jewish Week* (New York), September 1, 2015, http://www.thejewishweek.com/news/new-york/leading-rabbi-deals-big-blow-agunot#LYuDu3xfbvBLWpVP.99.

33. The Internet and online journals have opened the door for laypeople to express their views in a public forum. For a layman's *cri de coeur* expressing dismay over the rightward lurch, see Joel Moscowitz, "Post-Orthodoxy," *Times of Israel*, December 27, 2015, http://blogs.timesofisrael.com/post-orthodoxy/. And for an attempt by another Modern Orthodox layman to articulate the basic characteristics of his movement, see David Zinberg, "Restating the Fundamentals of Modern Orthodoxy," *Times of Israel*, October 29, 2015, http://blogs.timesofisrael.com/restating-the-fundamentals-of-modern-orthodoxy/.

34. An exchange between a leading rabbinic resister and a lay accommodator highlights just how far apart the two sides are; see Avrohom Gordimer, "The Inevitable Moment of Truth for Modern Orthodoxy," *Yated Neʾeman*, January 6, 2016, https://yated.com/the-inevitable-moment-of-truth-for-modern -orthodoxy/; and Daniel B. Schwartz, "Modern Orthodoxy's Right: In Search of a Message," *Times of Israel*, January 10, 2016, http://blogs.timesofisrael.com /modern-orthodoxys-right-in-search-of-a-message/.

35. Blog postings have served as a major instrument for discrediting opponents on both sides of the Modern Orthodox divide, and as is the case with the Internet generally, these blogs often veer into vitriol. The main blogs employed by the resisters are *Cross-Currents* and *Torah Musings*, as well as the American newspaper *Yated Neʾeman*. Proponents of Open Orthodoxy tend to be more eclectic, publishing in newspapers and journals directed toward the larger American Jewish community.

36. For a few examples, see Ari Soffer, "'Open Orthodox' or 'Neo-Conservative'?," *Arutz Sheva*, April 1, 2014, www.israelnationalnews.com/News/News.aspx /179142; "Open and Closed," *Rabbi Pruzansky's Blog*, November 15, 2013, http:/rabbipruzansky.com/2013/11/15/open-and-closed/; and Avrohom Gordimer, "Open Orthodoxy and the Rebirth of the Conservative Movement," *Cross-Currents*, July 27, 2014, http://www.cross-currents.com/archives/2014/07/27 /open-orthodoxy-and-the-rebirth-of-the-conservative-movement.

37. Avi Weiss, "Defining 'Open Orthodoxy,'" *Tablet*, June 30, 2015, http://www .tabletmag.com/jewish-life-and-religion/191907/defining-open-orthodoxy. Nearly two decades earlier, Weiss formulated a different version of his creed, where the emphasis was first and foremost on the flexibility of halakhic decision making, albeit within Orthodox parameters. Avi Weiss, "Open Orthodoxy! A Modern Orthodox Rabbi's Creed," *Judaism* 46, no. 4 (1997): 409–21.

38. Yehuda Sarna, "The End of the Middle of the Road," in Hain, *Next Generation of Modern Orthodoxy*, 345.

39. This was Rabbi Avi Weiss's contention in "Open Orthodoxy!," 411.

40. Jay P. Lefkowitz, "The Rise of Social Orthodoxy," *Commentary*, April 2014, 37–42.

41. In focusing on the Modern Orthodox, I do not mean to suggest that all is tranquil and stable among the Haredim. In some Haredi sectors there is deep

dissatisfaction with the poor general education afforded to students, especially males, in Yeshivish and Hasidic day schools. A more insidious pressure is coming from the Internet, which is undermining the insularity the Haredi world has tried to maintain. But with the advent of smartphones and their social media apps, the larger world, its ideas and mores, intrudes. "There's nothing now of the outside world that doesn't find its way into these Haredi enclaves," sociologist Samuel Heilman observes. "And so this represents a real threat for their insularity." Amar Toor, "Ultra-Orthodox Jews Are Using Whatsapp to Defy Their Rabbis' Internet Ban," *Verge*, October 27, 2015, http://www.theverge .com/2015/10/27/9620752/whatsapp-hasidic-jewish-internet-ban. Direct challenges to the authority of Haredi leaders also appear on blogs. For an overview of the latter that looks at dissent in both the Haredi and Modern Orthodox sectors, see Shulem Deen, "Online and Unabashed: Orthodox Rabbis and Scholars Take to the Internet," *Tablet*, April 11, 2014, http://www.tabletmag.com /jewish-life-and-religion/168520/orthodox-rabbis-internet.

42. This first question is central to Rabbi Haskel Lookstein's response to "social Orthodoxy." "The Rise of 'Social Orthodoxy': Is It Good or Bad for the Jews?" (sermon, Kehillath Jeshurun, April 26, 2014). Lookstein asks whether the burdens of observance will be shouldered in the absence of belief in the divine origin of the mitzvot. But the reverse is also important for Modern Orthodoxy to address: if it does not find ways to accommodate some aspects of what passes for advanced Western culture, will it continue to be relevant to its adherents and will it heighten the cognitive dissonance they may feel?

Chapter 7: Who Needs Jewish Denominations?

1. *Journal News* (Westchester and Rockland counties, NY), September 14, 2003, 4B.
2. Protestant denominational structures have endured the same downward spiral. Mark Chaves, a sociologist of religion in America, has observed: "What is unambiguously a trend is lower amounts of money being given by churches to denominational offices, and that is causing financial turmoil at the denominational level. . . . Protestant churches are asking themselves . . . 'What do we get from the denomination?'" Quoted in Josh Nathan-Kazis, "Liberal Denominations

Face Crisis as Rabbis Rebel," *Forward*, February 9, 2011, http://forward.com /news/135323/liberal-denominations-face-crisis-as-rabbis-rebel/#ixzz3hyo6tjAX.

3. The small Reconstructionist movement was so hard-hit that it merged its congregational arm with the Reconstructionist Rabbinical College in 2012.

4. Congregational dues to those organizations are based on the number of affiliated family units.

5. I was present at a seminar in Oxford during the summer of 2014 when Rabbi Greenberg discussed what prompted that memorable remark.

6. See, for example, their joint statements on intermarriage and also President Trump's public recognition of Jerusalem as Israel's capital. Ben Sales, "Conservative Movement Doubles Down on Intermarriage Ban, but Urges Communities to Welcome Couples," *JTA*, October 18, 2017, https://www.jta.org/2017/10/18 /news-opinion/united-states/conservative-movement-keeps-intermarriage-ban; and Jeremy Sharon, "Conservative Movement Backs Trump's Recognition of Jerusalem as Capital of Israel," *Jerusalem Post*, December 10, 2017, http://www .jpost.com/Diaspora/Conservative-Movement-backs-Trump-recognition-of -Jerusalem-as-capital-of-Israel-517589.

7. Irving Greenberg, "Will There Be One Jewish People in the Year 2000?," *Perspectives*, n.d. The essay originally appeared in June 1985, a revised version in February 1986. See also Irving Greenberg, "The One in 2000 Controversy," *Moment*, March 1987, 17.

8. This encapsulation of his argument comes from a later essay. See also Greenberg, "One in 2000 Controversy," 17.

9. Quoted by Steven Bayme, *Conflict or Cooperation: Papers on Jewish Unity* (New York: CLAL and the American Jewish Committee, July 1989), v.

10. Samuel G. Freedman, *Jew vs. Jew: The Struggle for the Soul of American Jewry* (New York: Simon & Schuster, 2000).

11. Wertheimer, *A People Divided*, 196.

12. On Birthright Israel, see Shaul Kelner, *Tours That Bind: Diaspora, Pilgrimage, and Birthright Israel* (New York: New York University Press, 2010).

13. On the merger, see "Conservative, Orthodox, Pluralistic, Reform Day School Organizations to Merge," *JTA*, January 19, 2016, http://www.jta.org/2016/01/19 /news-opinion/united-states/conservative-onrthodox-pluralistic-and-reform

-day-school-organizations-to-merge. Orthodox day schools that do not identify as Modern still have separate organizations.

14. The Foundation for Jewish Camp was founded in 1998; PELIE, the Partnership for Effective Learning and Innovative Education, served congregational schools between 2008 and 2013 and then folded. Julie Wiener, "For Jewish Education Reform, A Messy Period," *Jewish Week* (New York), January 28, 2013, http://www.thejewishweek.com/news/new-york-news/jewish-education-reform-very-messy-period. JECEI, the Jewish Early Childhood Educational Initiative, was founded in 2004. http://www.jecei.org/history.php.

15. On T'ruah, see http://www.truah.org/who-we-are/what-we-do.html.

16. For an inventory of its offerings, see https://tikvahfund.org/about/.

17. For an endorsement of transdenominational Jewish day schools as superior to denominationally focused ones, see Jason Miller, "Judaism Is Increasingly Trans-denominational and That Is a Good Thing," *My Jewish Learning*, January 26, 2016, http://www.myjewishlearning.com/rabbis-without-borders/positive-implications-of-transdenominational-judaism/2/.

18. The New York Board of Rabbis issued a report in 1998 titled "Unity in Diversity: A Vision of Rabbinic Cooperation," which detailed such efforts. See Stewart Ain, "Rabbis Question Report on Movement's Harmony," *Jewish Week* (New York), October 9, 1998, 1.

19. A somewhat offbeat example of cross-denominational cooperation comes from a meeting of the North American Hevrah Kadisha, where seventy-five people met in Las Vegas to talk about Jewish burial customs. "Orthodox, Conservative and Reform participants had no inhibitions exchanging ideas, customs, and techniques. In death," observed the reporter, "there is no interdenominational tension." Ronnie Berman, *Jerusalem Report*, July 26, 2004, 9.

20. A coalition of eleven family foundations published a signed ad in thirty-five Jewish newspapers across the United States, urging "civil speech as a criterion for Jewish grant making." See Julia Goldman, "Ad Campaign Urges More Civil Discourse in Jewish Community," *Jewish News of Greater Phoenix*, November 5, 1999, and Tami Bickley, "Additional Groups Embrace Ad's Call for Civil Discourse," *Jewish News of Greater Phoenix*, November 5, 1999. The vice president of one of the lead foundations explicitly insisted "there should be economic consequences when people speak irresponsibly about other members

and groups in the Jewish community." Some organizations, such as the New
Israel Fund, and federations, such as the Jewish Federation Council of Greater
Los Angeles, are pumping money into Israeli institutions that promote reli-
gious pluralism. See "Funds Combat 'Who Is a Jew' Wars," *Jewish Journal* (Los
Angeles), January 5, 2003.

21. Felice Maranz, "Staying the Night," *Jerusalem Report*, July 26, 2004, 29.

22. Bethamie Horowitz, "Looking Beyond Labels," *Forward*, February 6, 2004, 11.

23. Michael Berenbaum and David N. Myers, "Imagine a Jewish World without
    Denominations," *Forward*, November 1, 2002.

24. Andrew Silow-Carroll, "Crossing Over," *Jewish Week* (New York), Decem-
    ber 15, 1999, 46–49.

25. For one version of this argument, see the remarks of Arthur Green, quoted in
    Eric Caplan, *From Ideology to Liturgy: Reconstructionist Worship and American
    Liberal Judaism* (Cincinnati: Hebrew Union College Press, 2002), 180n61.
    Green sees the divide as one between "the orthodox and the heterodox."

26. For an example of an article claiming that denominational "divisions no lon-
    ger serve the needs of a growing group of Jews," see Rebecca W. Sirbu, "7 Post-
    Denominational Opportunities: It's about Attitude, Not Structure," *eJewish Phi-
    lanthropy*, March 17, 2015, http://ejewishphilanthropy.com/7-post-denominational
    -opportunities-its-about-attitude-not-structure/.

27. Leon A. Morris, "Beyond, or Mixing, Denominations," *Jewish Week* (New
    York), March 7, 2003, 26.

28. The Jewish Renewal movement, which will be discussed in chapter 10, sees it-
    self as the embodiment of a post-denominational Judaism, but given how dif-
    fuse Renewal is and how many different views there are about how to do Re-
    newal, it is premature to determine whether it will play such a role successfully.
    For the self-description of a congregation that sees itself in the Renewal mode,
    see https://www.romemu.org/about/mission-history/. The same website car-
    ries the following description: "Renewal resembles Reform Judaism in some
    ways, Reconstructionism in other ways, and even Orthodoxy—especially Ha-
    sidism—in some ways. But it is not a denomination with a formal hierarchy
    or structure."

29. Freedman, *Jew vs. Jew*, 353. Olam was founded by an adherent of Chabad. A
    study of Aish Hatorah came to the same conclusion: "Aish Hatorah is more

open and candid about its ultra-Orthodox perspective in the environment of its yeshiva, whereas in other venues—such as in its outreach centres and the programmes offered there, Asih Hatorah advertises itself as a pluralistic, all-inclusive environment." Aaron Joshua Tapper, "The 'Cult' of Aish HaTorah: 'Baalei Teshuva' and the New Religious Movement Phenomenon," *Jewish Journal of Sociology* 44, nos. 1–2 (2002): 24n55.

30. For a strong defense of denominations against the dismissive post-denominationalists, see Dan Ehrenkrantz, "A Response to Post/Trans/Non-Denominational Critiques," *Reconstructionist* (Spring 2007): 16–25. Ehrenkrantz correctly notes that "'Post-denominational' and 'non-denominational' are negative definitions—they tell us what they are not, but fail to tell us what they are" (17).

31. The research was conducted by the Hartford Institute for Religion Research, http://hirr.hartsem.edu/cong/nondenom.html.

32. Among the studies documenting aspects of this shift are Bellah et al., *Habits of the Heart* and Putnam, *Bowling Alone*.

33. Yuval Levin, *The Fractured Society: Renewing America's Social Contract in an Age of Individualism* (New York: Basic Books, 2016), 79–80 and 149.

34. For a brief history of how thinking about Torah Mi'Sinai has undergone re-thinking among some Modern Orthodox scholars, see Lawrence Grossman, "In What Sense Did Orthodoxy Believe the Torah to Be Divine?," *The Torah*, n.d. (probably 2015), http://thetorah.com/in-what-sense-did-orthodoxy-believe-the-torah-to-be-divine/. A survey of Modern Orthodox Jews conducted in 2017 found that 36 percent of respondents either "tend" to believe this or do not believe it. Mark Trencher, "The Nishma Research Profile of American Modern Orthodox Jews" (West Hartford, CT: Nishma Institute, September 28, 2017), 19, http://nishmaresearch.com/assets/pdf/Report%20%20Nishma%20Research%20Profile%20of%20American%20Modern%20Orthodox%20Jews%2009-27-17.pdf. As noted, this was not a random sample, but it suggests that rabbinic assertions aside, beliefs among the laity vary.

35. For a related exploration of how irrelevant denominational pronouncements have become, see Jay Michaelson, "Do Endless Denominational Turf Wars Even Matter Anymore?," *Forward*, November 9, 2015, http://forward.com/opinion/324363/do-denominations-and-their-endless-turf-wars-even-matter-anymore/.

36. As with any generalizations, there are exceptions. Some remain members of synagogues out of a sense of family loyalty or inertia; and others may choose to join because they resonate to the clergy or because their friends belong.

37. Little wonder, then, that when congregants and their children see candle lighting in the synagogue on Friday night or partake of Havdala at the end of the Sabbath when they are in the synagogue, it rarely transfers to the home. For most Reform Jews, religion resides in the synagogue, not elsewhere.

38. A useful study might examine the Jewish language employed in synagogues of each denomination, and for that matter also the nondenominational ones. To what extent does the vocabulary employed in public settings differ from one type of congregation to the next? How often are Hebrew, Yiddish, or other Jewish words sprinkled into conversation? Are Jewish concepts rendered in English translation in order to be as inclusive as possible? And, of course, what role does the presence of non-Jews in synagogues play in shifting the language and the kind of discourse that can be conducted?

39. These observations are based upon my own conversations with rabbis of different stripes and visits to a range of synagogues. A systematic comparison of discourse in different denominational settings would yield rich insight into how distinctive rhetorical styles both reflect and shape the variety of American Judaisms, including nondenominational ones. For an exemplary analysis of how newcomers to Orthodox Judaism are initiated through language, see Sarah Bunin Benor, *Becoming Frum: How Newcomers Learn the Language and Culture of Orthodox Judaism* (New Brunswick, NJ: Rutgers University Press, 2012). Benor alludes to the necessity for other denominations of Judaism to initiate those who are ignorant of the insiders' Jewish language commonly employed (21).

40. Josh Nathan-Kazis, "Where Are All the Non-Orthodox Rabbis?," *Forward*, February 18, 2015. Some of this decline has been caused by financial retrenchment during the Great Recession. But as the economy has rebounded, enrollments at Jewish seminaries have remained low (outside the Orthodox sector). The reason has more to do with contracting synagogue membership than anything else. Of course, some rabbis in all of the movements have become entrepreneurial, founding their own congregations or religious start-ups, thereby creating demand—and taking a leaf from Orthodox outreach efforts.

41. Ehrenkrantz, "Response to Post/Trans/Non-Denominational Critiques," 19.

Chapter 8: Not Your Grandparents' Synagogue

1. The vignette appears in Amy Asin, "Innovate, Learn and Innovate Again," Strengthening Congregations: A Symposium, special issue of *Reform Judaism*, 2014, 7–10, http://www.reformjudaismmag.org/sites/default/files/Strengthening _Synagogues_FINAL.pdf. Several contributors to this symposium embrace the by-now standard trope about synagogue failings, even as others cite examples of positive developments in specific congregations. For another example of the conventional wisdom about synagogues as hidebound institutions, see, for example, Michael Knopf, "How Free Ice Water Can Save Your Synagogue," *Times of Israel*, November 10, 2015, http://blogs.timesofisrael.com/how-free-ice-water -can-save-your-synagogue/.

2. I have documented how widespread the critique of synagogues had become. See my essay, "The American Synagogue: Recent Trends and Issues," *American Jewish Year Book* 105 (2005): 3–5.

3. Quoted in Adam Stone, "Redefining Oheb," *Baltimore Jewish Times*, May 11, 2001, www.jewishtimes.com/1444.stm.

4. Ibid.

5. For a description of the seven services sponsored by Emanu-El of San Francisco, a Reform temple, see Kaplan, *American Reform Judaism*, 92–93. At the end of the past century, the STAR (Synagogue Transformation and Renewal) initiative urged congregations to adopt a Synaplex model, a play on synagogue and multiplex movie theaters, running concurrent services and other types of programs.

6. For a rundown of the half dozen services offered on Friday nights and an equal number on Saturday mornings at Adas Israel in Washington, DC, see http:// adasisrael.org/shabbat-and-daily-minyan/. This is hardly a unique example. The same multiplicity of options is offered at Beth Yeshurun in Houston (see https://bethyeshurun.org/family-worship-services), Sinai Temple in Los Angeles (http://www.sinaitemple.org/worship/), and the Germantown Jewish Center (https://germantownjewishcentre.org/Prayer/Saturday_Mornings).

7. The afternoon prayers are generally followed immediately, or after a short break, by the evening prayers, so that all three daily services can be recited in two visits to the synagogue.

8. Rabbi Hershel Billet quoted in Steve Lipman, "A Place for Everyone," *Jewish Week* (New York), April 7, 2000, 16. The congregation also attracts Sephardi Jews.

9. E. J. Kessler, "Rabbis Bucking for Friday Nights at the 'Synaplex': Trend Sees Practice of Holding Several Smaller Minyans within a Synagogue," *Forward*, June 5, 1998, 2.

10. See Kaplan, *Reform Judaism*, 151, where he quotes the complaint of Eric Yoffie: "the music of prayers has become what it was never meant to be: a spectator sport." Much effort has gone into converting that passivity into active participation since Yoffie uttered those words in 1999.

11. Rabbi Yosef Kanefsky, "Orthodoxy and Synagogue Renewal," *Contact* (Autumn 1999): 8–9.

12. Herb Keinon and Marilyn Henry, "Music to Their Ears," *Jerusalem Report* (October 29, 1999): 19.

13. For a description of such services in several Manhattan congregations during the first half of the twentieth century, see Jenna Weisman Joselit, *New York's Jewish Jews: The Orthodox Community in the Interwar Years* (Bloomington: Indiana University Press, 1990). Actually, there are a few synagogues in Manhattan and elsewhere that still adhere to this model.

14. It is not easy to ascertain how many synagogues offer healing services, but a network of some thirty healing centers, mostly based in Jewish family service agencies, is affiliated with the National Jewish Healing Center. See its website, http://www.ncjh.org/centers.php.

15. These questions are explored in Gila S. Silverman, "'I'll Say a Mi Sheberach for You': Prayer, Healing and Identity among Liberal American Jews," *Contemporary Jewry* 36 (2016).

16. Congregations do not confine themselves to this one prayer; some support the expressions of their congregants' Jewish needs "in health, spirituality, family relationships, education and social life." See, for example, the survey of synagogue initiatives in the Sun Valley (Phoenix, AZ): Barry Cohen, "Seeking Meaning: Synagogues Offer Cornucopia of Opportunities for Adults 35–55," *Jewish News of Greater Phoenix*, September 22, 2000, http://www.jewishaz.com/jewishnews/000922/seek.shtml.

17. The mixing of the two is evident in the growing movement of local congregations banding together to sponsor a night of study on Shavuot. Topics

discussed during study sessions range from the close reading of religious texts to geopolitics. For an example of a gathering that draws four hundred people from a variety of synagogues in Cleveland to a Tikkun Leil Shavuot, see Ed Wittenberg, "B'nai Jeshurun Congregation Tikkun Leil Shavuot Offers Many Programs," *Cleveland Jewish News*, June 1, 2016, http://www.clevelandjewish news.com/news/local_news/b-nai-jeshurun-congregation-tikkun-leil-shavuot -offers-many-programs/article_4fc1519c-282d-11e6-a630-7b3d104a1bab .html.

18. Steven M. Cohen and Aryeh Davidson, *Adult Jewish Learning in America: Current Patterns and Prospects for Growth* (New York: JCC Association, 2001), 27–28.

19. Noteworthy in this connection is the wide scope of PJ Library. Funded primarily by the Harold Grinspoon Foundation in partnership with some federations and local funders, this effort distributes books monthly to families with young children. One researcher outlined the goals of PJ: "The organization uses children's books to convince families that Judaism should be an important part of their lives and connect them to various networks that comprise American Jewish religion, one illustrated book at a time." Rachel Beth Gross, "To Have It in Their Hearts: PJ Library and American Jewish Religion" (paper, Association for Jewish Studies, 2016). PJ Library is not an effort by synagogues, but serves as a partner with various institutions seeking to reach families with young children.

20. For a description of these efforts at Prayer for Practice, see "Revitalizing Prayer," interview with Rabbi Nancy Flam, *Reform Judaism*, n.d., http://www.reform judaism.org/revitalizing-prayer.

21. One initiative in this direction is called the Bnai Mitzvah Revolution, which works with congregations to rethink how to prepare children and their families for their milestone in a way that is meaningful to them. See http://bnaim itzvahrevolution.org/about-us/bmr-in-the-news. For an example of efforts by one congregation in this program, see Stacy Eskovitz Rigler, "Transforming Our Temple through the Bnai Mitzvah Revolution," *eJewish Philanthropy*, February 3, 2015, http://ejewishphilanthropy.com/transforming-our-temple-through -the-bnai-mitzvah-revolution/.

22. Some of these are described in Jack Wertheimer, ed., *Learning and Community: Jewish Supplementary Schooling in the Twenty-First Century* (Lebanon, NH: Brandeis University Press, 2009), chaps. 4 and 5.

23. Isa Aron with Nachama Skolnik Moscowitz, "Beit Knesset Hazon: A Visionary Synagogue," in Wertheimer, *Learning and Community*, 269–70. The actual name of the synagogue in this case study is masked. For another example of an ambitious approach to family education in a synagogue, see, in the same volume, Harold Wechsler and Cyd Beth Weissman, "Belonging Before Belief," 123ff., about a Reconstructionist synagogue's family education efforts.

24. Eliezer Havivi, "Children Run Wild in the Sanctuary!," *Beth David Synagogue Bulletin*, May 20, 2012, http://www.bethdavidsynagogue.org/rabbis-message -may-20-2012/.

25. Menachem Creditor, "Children in the Sanctuary," *Huffington Post*, July 8, 2014, http://www.huffingtonpost.com/rabbi-menachem-creditor/children-in-the -sanctuary_b_5283826.html.

26. For a vivid account of this congregation's efforts to marshal its limited resources of personnel and finances toward extraordinary ends, see Susan L. Shevitz with Marion Gribetz, "The Power of Their Commitments: Lessons for the Jewish Community from a Small Synagogue School," in Wertheimer, *Learning and Community*, 47–78.

27. For a survey of such activities sponsored by synagogues in New York, see Steve Lipman, "The Multitasking Shul," *Jewish Week* (New York), June 24, 2005, 4–5. On the role of congregations in building social capital, see Putnam, *Bowling Alone*, chap. 4.

28. Riv-Ellen Prell, "Communities of Choice and Memory," 271.

29. Evyatar Friesel quoted in David Ellenson, "Envisioning Israel in the Liturgies of North American Liberal Judaism," in *Envisioning Israel: The Changing Ideals and Images of North American Jews*, ed. Allon Gal (Detroit: Wayne State University Press and Magnes Press, 1996), 147.

30. I have surveyed those efforts in some detail in "American Jews and Israel—A Sixty Year Retrospective," *American Jewish Year Book* 108 (2008): 2–78.

31. The front of the sanctuary in the synagogue I attend is faced in Jerusalem stone.

32. Joellyn Wallen Zollman, "Shopping for a Future: A History of the American Synagogue Gift Shop" (PhD diss., Brandeis University, 2002), 183–86, 201.

33. See Linda Motzkin, *Aleph Isn't Tough: An Introduction to Hebrew for Adults* (New York: Behrman House, 2003).

34. Lawrence Grossman, "Decline and Fall: Thoughts on Religious Zionism in America," in *Religious Zionism Post Disengagement: Future Directions*, ed. Chaim Waxman (New York: Orthodox Forum, 2008), 36–38, 34.

35. On the background to the composition of the prayer, see Ephraim Tabory, "The Piety of Politics: Jewish Prayers for the State of Israel," in *Liturgy in the Life of the Synagogue: Studies in the History of Jewish Prayer*, ed. Ruth Langer and Steve Fine (Winona Lake, IN: Eisenbrauns, 2005), 232–38.

36. The Art Scroll edition, the most widely sold Orthodox prayer book, omits the prayer. This prompted the Rabbinical Council of America, the largest Modern Orthodox rabbinical group, to commission its own edition of the Art Scroll prayer book, which includes it.

37. Ellenson, "Envisioning Israel in the Liturgies," 132–46; Caplan, *From Ideology to Liturgy*, 234–35; Ben Harris, "U.S. Jews Challenge Israel Prayer," *JTA*, April 3, 2008, http://www.jta.org/cgi-bin/iowa/news/print/2008040303022008Israel Prayer.html.

38. On the adoption of Israeli synagogue practices by American Orthodox congregations, see Chaim I. Waxman, "Israel in Orthodox Identity: The American Experience," in *Israel, the Diaspora, and Jewish Identity*, ed. Danny Ben-Moshe and Zohar Segev (Sussex: Sussex Academic Press, 2007), 58–59. Waxman attributes these borrowings to young Orthodox Jews' year or more of study in Israeli yeshivot.

39. Ellenson, "Envisioning Israel in the Liturgies," 148.

40. I have attended services on Tisha B'Av that conclude with the singing of Hatikvah, Israel's national anthem.

41. Historian Marc Lee Raphael has studied sermons focused on Israel during the first decades of statehood. He concluded that "even the most superficial inspection of synagogue bulletins in these years reveals that rabbis regularly delivered sermons on the subject of Israel. . . . In Conservative and Reform synagogues all over the country, and in numerous Orthodox congregations as

well, rabbis spoke about the War of Independence, the massive migration of Jews from Arab lands after this war, the Suez Crisis, and, regularly, the social, economic, political, and religious situation in Israel. In Baltimore, Chicago, Cleveland, Los Angeles, Miami, New York, Philadelphia, St. Louis, and Washington, DC, printed collections of High Holiday sermons and sermon titles listed in synagogue bulletins indicate that it was commonplace for one of the four or five Holy Day sermons rabbis delivered (some preached during the Memorial Service on Yom Kippur, some did not) to dwell on the topic of Israel." Marc Raphael, *Judaism in America* (New York: Columbia University Press, 2003), 129–30. All of these efforts intensified between 1967 and the 1990s, and though matters have become more complex, Israel remains a feature of public discussion in synagogues of all stripes to the present.

42. An extensive literature addresses the so-called "distancing" hypothesis. See the special issue of *Contemporary Jewry*, vol. 30, nos. 2–3 (October 2010). For a book-length discussion, see Dov Waxman, *Trouble in the Tribe: American Jewish Conflict over Israel* (Princeton, NJ: Princeton University Press, 2016).

43. Steven M. Cohen and Jason Gitlin, "Reluctant or Repressed: Aversion to Expressing Views on Israel among American Rabbis" (Jewish Council on Public Affairs, 2013), http://www.jewishdatabank.org/studies/downloadFile.cfm?FileID=3075. As an opt-in survey, the sample population for this study was not representative. Still, it points to concerns among a portion of rabbis about retribution for expressing their views about Israeli policies. Two widely reported incidents further highlighted the dangers faced by rabbis who incur the wrath of congregants over Israel. See Hank Sheinkopf, George Brinbaum, and Ronn Torossian, "Temple Israel of White Plains Support of Israel Boycott," *Jerusalem Post*, November 12, 2015, http://www.jpost.com/Opinion/Temple-Israel-of-White-Plains-support-of-an-Israel-boycott-432886; and Gary Rosenblatt, "Anatomy of a Takedown: Community Builder and Lover of Israel, or Glorifier of Arab Terrorism: Could This Be the Same Texas Conservative Rabbi?," *Jewish Week* (New York), August 30, 2016, www.thejewishweek.com/editorial-opinion/gary-rosenblatt/anatomy-takedown#KfVOSxiJppHH7ChG.99.

44. For an overview of some of these flash points, see Etta Prince-Gibson, "Religious Rift Deepens between Israel and Diaspora," *Forward*, August 2, 2016,

http://forward.com/news/israel/346706/religious-rift-deepens-between-israel
-and-diaspora/?utm_content=daily_Newsletter_MainList_Title_Position-1&utm
_source=Sailthru&utm_medium=email&utm_campaign=New%20Daily
%202016-08-09&utm_term=The%20Forward%20Today%20Monday-Friday.
Matters deteriorated still further during the summer of 2017 when the Israeli
government, under pressure from Orthodox coalition partners, reneged on a
commitment to expand egalitarian religious worship at a section of the Hero-
dian Wall. Judging from the harsh rhetoric at the time, this was the last straw
in a long-simmering battle. But as this struggle has been a feature of Israel-
Diaspora relations for decades, it is unlikely that it will be resolved anytime
soon. For an overview of the confrontation and competing antagonists, see
Allison Kaplan Sommer, "Israel's Western Wall Crisis: Why Jews Are Fighting
with Each Other over the Jewish Holy Site, Explained," *Ha'aretz*, June 27, 2017,
http://www.haaretz.com/israel-news/1.797925.

45. Recent moves by the Chief Rabbinate to disqualify conversions by Modern Orthodox rabbis in the United States now have placed the shoe on the other foot, so
that what has long irritated non-Orthodox rabbis and congregants is now a cause
of dismay even in some Modern Orthodox circles. On these developments, see
Michelle Chabin, "Top U.S. Rabbis Not Kosher Enough for Israel's Chief Rabbinate," *Jewish Week* (New York), September 23, 2016, http://www.thejewishweek
.com/news/israel-news/top-us-rabbis-not-kosher-enough-israels-chief-rabbinate.

46. For an example, see Elliot Cosgrove, "New Light on Zion" (sermon delivered
on Rosh Hashanah, [Conservative] Park Avenue Synagogue, New York, October 3, 2016), https://pasyn.org/resources/sermons/new-light-zion.

47. In fact, synagogues continue to sponsor trips to Israel. A survey of Reform educators found that 80 percent claimed their congregation had run such a trip in
recent years. See Lisa Grant and Michael Marmur, "The Place of Israel in the
Identity of Reform Jews: Israel/Diaspora Joint Commentators," in Ben-Moshe
and Segev, *Israel, the Diaspora, and Jewish Identity*, 131.

48. The Young Israel movement of some 140 congregations in the United States,
alone, banned its constituents from elevating women to the rank of president.
This caused a good deal of controversy. See, on this, Stewart Ain, "Young Israel
Movement in Turmoil over Upstate Shul," *Jewish Week* (New York), June 29,
2010, http://www.thejewishweek.com/news/new_york/young_israel_movement

_turmoil_over_upstate_shuland; Uriel Heilman, "National Council of Young Israel Changes Rule to Let Shuls Quit," *JTA*, January 31, 2013, http://www.jta .org/2013/01/31/news-opinion/united-states/national-council-of-young-israel -changes-rule-to-let-shuls-quit.

49. As evidence of a new engagement with the ramifications of having openly LGBTQ individuals in their congregations, the Rabbinical Council of America devoted a day of study and discussion to this issue in 2016. See Efrem Goldberg, "Seeing the Rainbow in Grey Rather Than Black and White: LGBT and the Orthodox Community," *Times of Israel*, June 29, 2016, http://blogs.time sofisrael.com/seeing-the-rainbow-in-grey-rather-than-black-and-white-lgbt -the-orthodox-community/. The fault lines in the Orthodox camp were exposed again when Eshel, an organization for Orthodox parents of gay children, held its retreat at an Orthodox synagogue on the Lower East Side of Manhattan, which was promptly denounced by several neighboring Orthodox congregations. See Hannah Dreyfus, "Orthodox Shuls Host LGBT Event amidst Row," *Jewish Week* (New York), June 7, 2016, http://www.thejewishweek.com /news/new-york/orthodox-shuls-host-lgbt-event-amid-row.

50. For reports about two synagogues in the Phoenix area actively working to create an inviting environment for the unmarried or no longer married, see Deborah Muller, "Synagogues Often Overlook Singles, Childless," *Beth Ami Temple Bulletin*, August 26, 2015, http://www.bethamitemple.org/2015/11 /jewish-news-article-synagogues-often-overlook-singles-childless/.

51. Anthony Weiss, "Boston Initiatives Reach for Young Jews Where They Are," *Times of Israel*, August 13, 2014, http://www.timesofisrael.com/boston-initiatives-reach -for-young-jews-where-they-are/.

52. Abigail Pickus, "Creating a Millennial Access Point in Dallas," *eJewish Philanthropy*, February 4, 2014, http://ejewishphilanthropy.com/creating-a-millennial -access-point-in-dallas/.

53. Ryan Torok, "Sinai Temple's Friday Night Live to Undergo Change," *Jewish Journal* (Los Angeles), April 23, 2014, http://www.jewishjournal.com/los_angeles /article/sinai_temples_friday_night_live_to_undergo_change. For accounts of this service when it was attracting its largest number of attendees, see Michael Aushenker, "Will Friday Nights Ever Be the Same?," *Jewish Journal* (Los Angeles), May 6, 1999, http://jewishjournal.com/old_stories/1670/; Angela Aleiss,

"Greeting Shabbat with Song, Dance," *Cleveland Plain Dealer*, June 10, 2000. For a scholarly analysis of the phenomenon, see J. Liora Gubkin, "Friday Night Live: It's Not Your Parents' Shabbat," in *GenX Religion*, ed. Richard W. Flory and Donald E. Miller (New York: Routledge, 2000), 199–210. Though Sinai continues to sponsor the service, attendance has declined in recent years.

54. Advertising its Rooftop High Holiday Services for Young Professionals, the synagogue appeals to millennials by promising the worship will hit "the highlights of the High Holiday Services while you mingle, learn, pray, and get in touch with your inner Judaism." Synagogue membership is not required and the fees are a pittance.

55. See Adam Chandler, "As the Jewish Community Goes Gray, Synagogues Adapt to Serve Older Congregants," *Tablet*, January 6, 2016, http://www.tabletmag .com/jewish-life-and-religion/155916/synagogues-older-congregants.

56. Ron Wolfson captured the zeitgeist with his widely read book, *Relational Judaism: Using the Power of Relationships to Transform the Jewish Community* (Woodstock, VT: Jewish Lights, 2013).

57. For an example of one such congregation, see Don Cohen, "Sacred Space," *Detroit Jewish News*, October 1, 2004, http://detroit.jewish.com/modules.php?na me=News&file=print&sid=1693.

58. Warren G. Stone, "A Place of Jewish Personal Revelation," *Reform Judaism*, Winter 1996, 70–71.

59. The importance of such connectivity is examined by Robert Evans and Bryan Schwartzman, "Where Everybody Knows Your Name: Small Groups, Connectivity and a Path Forward for Synagogues," *eJewish Philanthropy*, July 31, 2014, http://ejewishphilanthropy.com/where-everybody-knows-your-name-small -groups-connectivity-and-a-path-forward-for-synagogues/.

60. Some Orthodox congregations have innovated unofficial "kiddush clubs" that make available high-quality liquor after the Shabbat Torah reading. The Orthodox Union grew so concerned about the serving of hard drinks at these clubs, which can lead to embarrassing disruptions of the service, and at the "official" synagogue kiddush afterward that it tried to ban them. See Gabriel Sanders, "Orthodox Union Sets Ban on Clubs for Scotch Tipplers," *Forward*, January 28, 2005, http://www.forward.com/main/printer-friendly.php?ref=sanders200; and Steve Lipman, "Whiskey Rebellion," *Jewish Week* (New York), February 18,

2005, http://www.thejewishweek.com/news/newscontent.php3?artid=10519&offset=&B1=1&author=Steve%20Lipman&issuedates=&month=05&day=13&year=2005&issuedate=20041112&keyword=Kiddush%20clubs.

61. Daniel Sack, *Whitebread Protestants: Food and Religion in American Culture* (New York: Palgrave Macmillan, 2000), 62.

62. Robert Wuthnow, *All in Sync: How Music and Art Are Revitalizing American Religion* (Berkeley: University of California Press, 2003), 151.

63. Inclusiveness also has very different connotations in churches than in synagogues. The former are far more preoccupied with ensuring racial and multi-ethnic diversity. For a fascinating ethnographic study of how one church has achieved such diversity, see Marti, *Mosaic of Believers*.

64. Penny Edgell Becker, *Congregations in Conflict: Cultural Models of Local Religious Life* (Cambridge: Cambridge University Press, 1999), 104–5.

65. Ibid., 104.

66. The sociologist Nancy T. Ammerman has commented on the divergent emphases of synagogues and churches in their approaches to learning. The types of subject matter differ, as does the purpose of study. There are also significant variations in the focus of Bible study in Catholic and Orthodox churches, as compared with Protestant ones of the mainline and evangelical varieties. See Nancy Tatom Ammerman, *Pillars of Faith: American Congregations and Their Partners* (Berkeley: University of California Press, 2005), 30–34, 47–49.

67. My thanks, once again, to Steven M. Cohen for running the data that made it possible to draw this comparison. The complication in doing so is that the 1990 data refer to households while the Pew data refer to individuals. This should have resulted in somewhat higher rates of frequent attendance in 2013. Yet even with that built-in bias, there were no significant increases in synagogue attendance rates over the twenty-three-year period.

68. Eisen and Cohen, *Jew Within*, 155–56.

69. This is true for a portion of the Modern Orthodox population too, especially younger ones. A survey conducted in 2017 found that roughly one-fifth of respondents over age fifty-five agreed only a little or not at all with the statement "the prayer experience is meaningful to me," a figure that rose to one one-quarter among those eighteen to thirty-four. Trencher, "Nishma Research," 38–40.

70. Robert Wuthnow, *After Heaven: Spirituality in America since the 1950s* (Berkeley: University of California Press, 1998), 3.

71. Perhaps for this reason, the STAR initiative, seeking to transform congregations, suggested alternatives to worship services to bring in members who cannot relate to public prayer.

72. Families also must consider where to spend their discretionary dollars, but this affects decisions to join and maintain memberships, not attendance. I have written about the stratified dues structures created by synagogues to address the varied ability of people to pay. See Wertheimer, "American Synagogue," 24–28. For more recent discussions, see Michael Paulson, "The 'Pay What You Want' Experiment at Synagogues," *New York Times*, February 2, 2015, http://www.nytimes.com/2015/02/02/us/the-pay-what-you-want-experiment-at-synagogues.html?_r=0; and Lianna Levine Reisner and Dan Judson, "Connection, Cultivation and Commitment: New Insight on Voluntary Dues" (UJA Federation of Greater New York, 2017). Based on data collected from several dozen synagogues that switched to a system of voluntary dues, the authors saw much merit in moving away from compulsory membership dues.

73. Steve Lipman, "Timing Is Everything," *Jewish Week* (New York), June 2, 2000, 12.

74. Sharon Brous, "Synagogues Reimagined," in Schwarz, *Jewish Megatrends*, 58–59.

Chapter 9: Orthodox Outreach

1. The chapter title is a variation on a prescient prediction put forth by Charles Liebman in his pioneering study, "Orthodoxy in American Jewish Life," 92. Liebman anticipated that Orthodoxy by virtue of its "strength and will to live . . . may yet nourish all the Jewish world." His observations are cited by Ferziger, *Beyond Sectarianism*, 223. In the writing of this chapter, I have benefited from Prof. Ferziger's work and his generous sharing of information.

2. Photographs of the study sessions may be found at https://partnersdetroit.org/about/.

3. Lori Palatnik, "If We Do Not Change, We Will Lose," *Klal Perspectives* (Fall 2012): 32–36, 33. For the data, see the Annual Report for 2015 of the JWRP, http://www.jwrp.org/sites/default/themes/bricktheme/pdfs/JWRP_Annual_Report_2015.pdf.

4. A fuller description appeared in my article, "Vital Signs: Adult Education, Chabad-Style," *Jewish Ideas Daily*, March 22, 2010, www.Jewishideasdaily.com /content/detail/continue-reading-vital-signs-adult-education-chabad-style. My thanks to Rabbi Efraim Mintz for furnishing me with these data and educating me about the remarkable JLI he has created, and Rabbi David Eliezrie, who has been my guide to the world of Chabad for over a decade.

5. "2020: A Strategic Plan to Impact the Jewish Future," https://ncsy.org/assets /NCSY-2020-Vision1.pdf.

6. Sharon Otterman, "A SoHo Synagogue Exports Its Own Brand of Jewish Out-reach," *New York Times*, January 31, 2013, http://www.nytimes.com/2013/02/01 /nyregion/soho-synagogue-exports-its-own-brand-of-jewish-outreach.html?_r=0.

7. The grammatically correct Hebrew pronunciation of *kiruv* would be *kayruv*, but in Orthodox circles *keyruv* is preferred. Its proper pronunciation aside, the term is now regarded by some in the field as arrogant because it presumes that Orthodox people possess the formula for attaining closeness to God. Equally important, the goals of these efforts have shifted considerably from "making" Orthodox Jews to "building bridges" between all Jews.

8. Zev Eleff, *Living from Convention to Convention: A History of the NCSY, 1954–1989* (New York: KTAV, 2009).

9. Eliezrie, *Secret of Chabad*, 71ff. Rabbi Joseph I. Schneerson, the penultimate Lubavitcher rabbi, already sent out two campus emissaries, but the mass ef-fort took off under his successor—and even more so after the death of the last Rebbe. See Sarna, *American Judaism*, 346, on the first foray.

10. As there is only a limited amount of reporting about Orthodox outreach pro-grams, I have relied heavily in this chapter on interviews with some thirty-six outreach professionals and close observers of their work.

11. Faygie Levy, "In Just Five Years, CTeen Movement Attracts Tens of Thousands of Young Jews," *eJewish Philanthropy*, May 28, 2015, http://ejewishphilan thropy.com/?s=In+Just+Five+Years%2C+CTeen+Movement+Attracts+Tens +of+Thousands+of+Young+Jews.

12. Jeffrey F. Barken, "In 2016, Chabad's Personal Touch Might Make Largest Strides on College Campuses," *eJewish Philanthropy*, January 3, 2016, http://ejewish philanthropy.com/in-2016-chabads-personal-touch-might-make-largest-strides -on-college-campuses/.

13. On the network of friendship circles created by Chabad centers to offer support to families raising developmentally disabled children and the large cadre of volunteers who visit such families to offer them much-needed aid, see http://www.friendshipcircle.com/friendship_circle_mission.asp.

14. In some parts of the country, as many as half the members of Orthodox synagogues are members of Chabad Centers. See "2014 Great Miami Jewish Federation Population Study: A Portrait of the Miami Jewish Community," 4, http://www.jewishdatabank.org/studies/downloadFile.cfm?FileID=3224.

15. Adam Bell, "Miami Jewish Life and Chabad Are Sizzling," *Chabad.org*, November 2014, http://www.chabad.org/news/article_cdo/aid/2768594/jewish/Miami-Jewish-Life-and-Chabad-Engagement-Are-Booming.htm.

16. My thanks to Rabbi Motti Seligson for gathering this information in response to my query.

17. On the role of Rabbi Noach Weinberg and the philosophy of Aish, see Ferziger, *Beyond Sectarianism*, 159–61. Ferziger then goes on to describe the outreach approaches of other yeshivas.

18. Adam Ferziger offers a historical survey of how the community Kollels were established. See "From Lubavitch to Lakewood: The Chabadization of American Orthodoxy," *Modern Judaism* 33, no. 2 (May 2013).

19. For articles on three different Kollelim, each following a somewhat different model, see Esther Perkal, "The Columbus Kollel: Planting Rootes, Cultivating Community, Tending to Torah," *Inyan Magazine*, 27 Sivan 5771 (June 29, 2011): 26–29; Pauline Dubkin Yearwood, "Rabbis without Borders," *Chicago Jewish News*, May 14, 2010, cover story; Bentzi Epstein, "There's a Makom Torah in Dallas: How Community Kollels Are Raising Communities," *Klal Perspectives* (Winter 2012): 26–31.

20. Hasidic Jews, aside from Chabad adherents, are less likely to engage in Kiruv. An exception is the Traveling Chasidim belonging to the Belz sect who spend a Shabbat in different communities and infuse the Sabbath with spirited song and dance. They see themselves as adjuncts to outreach organizations, such as Aish HaTorah. See http://www.thetravelingchassidim.com/#!faq/cirw.

21. This is the contention too of Adam Ferziger in *Beyond Sectarianism*, 211–17.

22. The other economic circumstance stems from the big donors who dominate the field. Should they decide the jig is up, it is not at all certain that many of the outreach organizations would continue their operations.

23. One of the most scathing critiques of Modern Orthodox rabbis was presented in an interview I conducted with a leader of that movement who castigated those of his colleagues who take pulpit positions solely because it affords them more time to study, even as they show no interest in touching the lives of their congregants and other Jews.

24. This is the argument of Rabbi Ilan Feldman: "The more confident Orthodoxy is the more likely it is going to be interested in sharing with others its values and, indeed, its love of God and Torah. Alas, the corollary is also true. When Orthodoxy feels it is fighting for survival, beset by internal social, economic and spiritual problems, it will begin to see the unaffiliated as important but distant cousins who cannot now be invited to the 'Shabbos table,' at least not while the parents or the kids, or both, are still working out their problems." "Why the Giant Sleeps," *Klal Perspectives* (Fall 2012): 12.

25. The number was given to me by Rabbi Yitzchok Lowenbraun, head of AJOP, interview of July 5, 2016. According to him, 60 percent of these members engage in outreach full time.

26. Olami aims to coordinate the work of non-Chabad outreach activities worldwide. It is heavily funded by the Wolfson family and several partners to the tune of $100 million annually in the United States alone. On the central role played by Zev Wolfson in the global outreach movement, see the obituary by Elliott Mathias, August 26, 2012, http://www.aish.com/jw/s/Zev-Wolfson-A-Modest -Visionary.html?s=rab.

27. This view was quoted by Avraham Edelstein, "The Global Teshuva Movement Continues," *Klal Perspectives* (Fall 2012): 4.

28. This dismissive description of Chabad is widely held in some Kiruv circles.

29. See http://www.aish.com/ai/96244754.html.

30. See Ferziger, *Beyond Sectarianism*, chap. 8, 175–94. Ferziger writes of the Chabadization of Haredi Orthodoxy, but he also describes the impact of Chabad on Haredi outreach.

31. "Response of Rabbi Ephraim Buchwald," *Klal Perspectives* (Fall 2012): 23.

32. This is the contention of Edelstein, "Global Teshuva Movement Continues," 9–10.

33. That said, a study of Chabad campus outreach has found that those with the least prior Jewish education who are drawn to Chabad are also most likely to make the greatest strides toward observance and belief. These tend to be small minorities, but the payoff when they are reached is greatest. See Mark Rosen et al., "Chabad on Campus: The Hertog Study" (Cohen Center, Brandeis University, September 2016), 101–3, http://www.bjpa.org/Publications/download File.cfm?FileID=22304.

34. Edelstein, "Global Teshuva Movement Continues," 7, refers to Haredi leaders who have made an eschatological case for Kiruv.

35. There is an important study to be done on how Orthodox outreach is funded. Several of the biggest givers to Chabad and Yeshivish outreach are well-known names within the Orthodox sector. But it also appears that a good deal of funding for outreach efforts comes from Jews who are not Orthodox. Why they give to those causes and how they are recruited is a story worth pursuing to gain insight into how donors think about ensuring the Jewish future.

36. We have enough accounts about individuals who are drawn into an Orthodox lifestyle to know that quite a few have been influenced at various times in their lives by different outreach workers. For two accounts illustrating how "it takes a village" of outreach workers, see Devora Lakein, "Former Choir Boy Turns Chabad Campus Rabbi," *Lubavitch International News*, May 12, 2016, http://lubavitch.com/news/article/2057441/Former-Choir-Boy-Turns-Chabad-Campus-Rabbi.html Lubavitch.com; and for another on the way the Chabad emissary network operates, see R. C. Berman, "How Elena Met Rami, or the Chabad-Lubavitch Network, a Model of Causality," *Lubavitch International News*, November 3, 2008, http://lubavitch.com/news/article/2024360/How-Elena-Met-Rami-or-The-Chabad-Lubavitch-Network-A-Model-of-Causality.html.

37. The wild card here is Chabad's increasing attractiveness to younger families who might have joined Conservative and possibly even Reform temples in the past. If large numbers of younger people raised in the non-Orthodox movements come to regard Chabad centers as their synagogues, Chabad may become the new middle ground between Orthodoxy and liberal Judaism. The

greatest loser will be the Conservative movement, which had occupied that territory in the past. For an analysis contending that this has already come to pass, see David Eliezrie, "The Realigning of American Jewry," *Jerusalem Post*, July 11, 2016, http://www.jpost.com/Opinion/The-realigning-of-American -Jewry-460116. In some parts of the country, such as Florida and California, this process is well under way. It remains to be seen whether Chabad will make similar inroads in other regions.

38. The figures include only the professionals engaged in outreach. Some kiruv groups are trying to mobilize laypeople to serve as part-time volunteers. This is already happening through Partners in Torah, where volunteers engage non-Orthodox Jews in study, and in the efforts of the NCSY. Some in the outreach movement see a vastly expanded corps of lay volunteers as the greatest need of the field.

39. Ferziger, *Beyond Sectarianism*, 145.

40. Quoted in Sue Fishkoff, *The Rebbe's Army: Inside the World of Chabad Lubavitch* (New York: Schocken, 2003), 121.

41. Ibid., 20.

42. Edelstein, "Global Teshuva Movement Continues," 10.

43. "Torah Codes Explained," http://www.aish.com/atr/Torah_Codes_Explained .html.

44. I have addressed this topic in my essay "Between 'West Point Standards' and Life in the Trenches: The Halakhic Dilemmas of Orthodox Outreach Workers," in *Between Jewish Tradition and Modernity: Essays in Honor of David H. Ellenson*, ed. Michael A. Meyer and David Myers (Detroit: Wayne State University Press, 2014), 67–79.

45. Given the many difficulties likely to arise in a synagogue setting, some *kiruv* workers try to avoid conducting religious services, confining their work to education and social programming.

46. The operative category of Jewish law is *lifnei ivair* (i.e., do not place an obstacle in the way of the blind).

47. A similar dilemma arises on fast days: does the *kiruv* worker inform a group with which he is meeting that it is a fast day—and thereby transform their inadvertent nonobservance into a deliberate act—or keep them ignorant?

48. Moshe Neuman and Mordechai Becher, *Avotot Ahava: inyenei kiruv rechokim behalkha* (Jerusalem: Feldheim, 2002) and more recently Chaim Avraham

Zakutinsky, *Umekarev Beyemin: iyunim besheelot shmitorrerot etzel eleh sheoskim bekiruv rechokim* (Flushing, NY: Hasheveinu, 2011).

49. "An Interview with HaRav Sholom Kamentsky, Shlita," *Klal Perspectives* (Fall 2012): 1. It is not entirely clear from the text where the words of the two rabbis Kamenetsky, father and son, begin and end.

50. Ibid.

51. Chabad claims forty-four million unique visitors to its website in 2015, while an Aish representative referred to three million monthly visitors to its website. These figures refer to people all over the globe who find their way to these sites; many obviously are not Jewish, given there are fourteen million Jews in the entire world. On Chabad's figures, see Rosen et al., "Chabad on Campus," 19.

52. Outreach organizations tend to be trailblazers in creating means—both low and high tech—for reaching Jews. Aside from their growing online presence, they also were the first to go to pubs and supermarkets to buttonhole Jews and engage them in conversations. Viewed in this context, the observation I heard from an outreach professional that "*kiruv* is the R & D of the Orthodox community" is probably too modest. Outreach professionals are pioneers for the entire American Jewish community.

53. Feldman, "Why the Giant Sleeps," 14.

Chapter 10: Looking for Judaism in Unconventional Places

1. The description comes from Janice Williams, "What Is Burning Man? Inside the History of the 2017 Arts Festival," *Newsweek*, August 30, 2017, http://www.newsweek.com/burning-man-festival-2017-nevada-657868. Burning Man actually began in 1986 near San Francisco and then moved four years later to Nevada. See too the master's thesis of Becca Grumet, "Doing Jewish at Burning Man: A Scholarly Personal Narrative on Identity, Community and Spirituality" (Hebrew Union College, 2016), which surveys the evolution of organized Jewish activities at the festival.

2. Alessandra Wollner, "Ritual Principles of Milk + Honey, Purveyors of Radical Shabbat since 2008," *Burning Man Journal*, May 24, 2017, https://journal.burningman.org/2017/05/philosophical-center/spirituality/ritual-principles

-of-milk-honey-purveyors-of-radical-shabbat-since-2008/. It is evident that non-Jews also attend.

3. Johanna Ginsberg, "Marathon Minyan Sets Record," *New Jersey Jewish News*, November 10, 2010, http://njjewishnews.com/article/2437/marathon-minyan -sets-record?source=njjnrelated#.WbLx69Hnra8. On the logistics, "FAQs," November 2013, https://www.jrunnersclub.org/the-jrunners-international-marathon -minyan-faq/.

4. For an overview of programs offered by Rabbi Jamie Kornsgold, whose moniker is Adventure Rabbi, see http://www.adventurerabbi.org/.

5. "Shabbat Tent: History," http://shabbattent.org/about-us/history/; Ben Kaye, "Jewish Attendees Celebrated Passover at Coachella with Matzahchella Seders," April 24, 2016, https://consequenceofsound.net/2016/04/jewish-attendees-cele brated-passover-at-coachella-with-matzahchella-seders/.

6. Shawn Landres, "Emergence Unbound," *Sh'ma*, October 2, 2012, http://shma .com/2012/10/emergence-unbound/.

7. Hannah Dreyfus, "High Holidays for Millennials, but Far from Shul," *Jewish Week* (New York), September 16, 2016, http://www.thejewishweek.com /news/new-york/high-holidays-millennials-far-shul.

8. Pickus, "Creating a Millennial Access Point in Dallas."

9. Nancy T. Ammerman, *Congregation and Community* (New Brunswick, NJ: Rutgers University Press, 1996), 130–31.

10. This theme has been central to the writing of Rabbi Sid Schwarz. See, for example, his "The Rabbi as Spiritual Leader," *Reconstructionist* (Fall 1999): 30–31.

11. See the description of the Shir Hadash Reconstructionist havurah, with its emphasis on the pride and self-reliance of the members, in Susie Davidson, "Shir Hadash Includes Jews of All Types," *Boston Jewish Advocate*, September 5–11, 2003, 2.

12. See http://www.chavurah.com/directory/index.html.

13. For the directory of Reconstructionist congregations, see https://jewishrecon .org/directory.

14. On the history of the merger that resulted in the formation of the Jewish Reconstructionist Communities, see http://www.rrc.edu/About/Movement%20 Restructuring/Timeline%3A%202/11%20-%206/12.

15. See http://www.dorhadash.org/welcome-to-dor-hadash.html.

16. See http://aarecon.org/who-we-are/values-and-vision/.

17. See http://www.rsns.org/worship.

18. Julie Wiener, "Are the Reconstructionists Becoming More Mainstream?," *JTA*, November 7, 2000, www.jta.org/index.exe?0011075.

19. Gaby Wenig, "Standup, Sit-down, See the Light," *Jewish Journal* (Los Angeles), September 14, 2002, www.jewishjournal.com/hom/preview.php?id=9229.

20. Anne Cohen, "How David Ingber Got God Intoxicated," *Forward*, September 20, 2013, http://forward.com/opinion/184217/how-david-ingber-got-god-intoxicated.

21. For a discussion of leadership, see Rachel Delia Berman and Yithak Bronstein, "Can Jewish Renewal Keep Its Groove On?," *Tablet*, January 22, 2016, http://www.tabletmag.com/jewish-life-and-religion/196518/renewal-after-reb-zalman.

22. On the Aleph seminary of Renewal, see Sue Fishkoff, "Renewal Wants to Keep the Same Spirit while Standardizing Rabbis' Training," *JTA*, January 16, 2007, http://www.jta.org/2007/01/16/archive/renewal-wants-to-keep-same-spirit-while-standardizing-rabbis-training.

23. For a thoughtful overview, which sees Renewal "as an extension of Reconstructionism" and places it in a broader historical context, see Shaul Magid, "A Perspective on Jewish Renewal," *Network of Spiritual Progressives*, n.d., http://spiritualprogressives.org/newsite/?p=655. The author overreaches when he suggests that Jewish Renewal may "provide the beginnings of a new American Judaism that will change the face of Judaism in the twenty-first century." Renewal may influence that Judaism, but at this point its success at attracting followers is negligible.

24. Because most Havurot do not have their own buildings but usually meet either in members' homes or in rented facilities, they struggle to gain visibility. See the letter to the editor from Mark Frydenberg, incoming chair of the National Havurah Committee, *Boston Jewish Advocate*, August 29–September 4, 2003, 15.

25. "Four Worlds, Eighteen Affirmations, One Covenant: Aleph Statement of Principles," http://www.aleph.org/principles.html. They include a commitment "to consult with other spiritual traditions, sharing with them what we have found

in our concerned research and trying out what we have learned from them, to see whether it enhances the special truths of the Jewish path."

26. That is, Jewish Buddhists, Jewish Sufis, and Hindu Jews. See Rami Shapiro, "Jewish Renewal Makes It to Film," *Tikkun*, November/December 2001.

27. *Ohr Hadash* is discussed by Caplan, *From Ideology to Liturgy*, 350–64.

28. Given the far-flung and unaffiliated status of many Havurot, it is hard to generalize about their ideologies. Quite a few are defined less by their social and political outlook than by their goal of creating an intimate community; others are serving small groups of Jews in remote places that have no synagogues. But the leadership of the National Havurah Committee is heavily drawn from the so-called progressive community.

29. Melissa Minkin, "Celebration of 'Life': The First Lesbian and Gay Synagogue Marks Its 30th Anniversary," *Jewish Journal* (Los Angeles), July 1, 2002, www .jewishjournal.com/hom/preview.php?id=8708.

30. Jim Schwartz, Jeffrey Scheckner, and Laurence Kotler-Berkowitz, "Census of U.S. Synagogues, 2001," *American Jewish Year Book* 102 (2002): 129.

31. Debra Nussbaum Cohen, "Rabbis Explore Uniqueness of Gay Shuls," *Jewish Week* (New York), June 9, 2000, 49.

32. The most detailed study of one such synagogue, Congregation Beth Simchat Torah in Manhattan, is Shokeid's *Gay Synagogue in New York*. Its discussion of a new prayer book for the congregation is on 100–117.

33. Cohen, "Rabbis Explore Uniqueness," 10.

34. It is thought that only 16 percent of gay Jews affiliate with any kind of synagogue. See Steven M. Cohen, Caryn Aviv, and Ari Kelman, "Gay, Jewish, or Both?," *Journal of Jewish Communal Service* (Winter/Spring 2009), which claims the proportion of gay and lesbian Jews affiliated with a synagogue is 23 percent less than membership among straight Jews; much of the difference is due to the paucity of children in the homes of the former (163).

35. For a good discussion of the various factors at work, see Michal Lemberger, "Gay Synagogues' Uncertain Future," *Tablet*, March 11, 2013, http://www.tabletmag .com/jewish-life-and-religion/126512/gay-synagogues-uncertain-future. The views of leaders in a number of synagogues established for LGBTQ Jews are surveyed by Rob Gloster, "Iconic San Francisco Synagogue Is No Longer Just for

LGBT Jews," *Times of Israel*, August 26, 2017, https://www.timesofisrael.com /iconic-san-francisco-synagogue-is-no-longer-just-for-lgbt-jews/.

36. Its website is http://www.shj.org/communities/find-a-community/.

37. "What Do Humanistic Jews Do?," www.shj.org/do.htm.

38. "Beth Chair Leaves National Movement," *Washington Jewish Week*, January 19, 2003, http://washingtonjewishweek.com/localstory.html?/wjw/27968739677 5336.bsp. This congregation is now a member of the National Havurah Committee.

39. We lack definitive numbers for these groups. The Pew survey identified twenty thousand adults who identify as Reconstructionists and are members of synagogues. And though a few gay and lesbian synagogues attract a thousand worshippers on the High Holidays, most niche synagogues have a few hundred members, at most. Hence, the estimated figure given here.

40. Quoted in Sharyn Jackson, "Jews in Middle America Fret about Attracting Millennials," *USA Today*, November 3, 2014, http://www.usatoday.com/story /news/nation/2014/11/01/jewish-millennials/18140137/.

41. Justin Korda, "Following the Breadcrumbs: Three Insights on Jewish Millennials," *eJewish Philanthropy*, March 23, 2015, http://ejewishphilanthropy.com/follow ing-the-breadcrumbs-three-insights-on-jewish-millennials/. ROI, of course, stands for return on investment.

42. Alan Shavit-Lonstein, "Dear Jewish Millennials, It's Not Your Fault," *eJewish Philanthropy*, March 16, 2016, http://tcjewfolk.com/dear-jewish-millennials-fault/.

43. The term "Emergent Congregations" is taken from the Christian context. Christian Emergents are united by a common theology and liturgy that has no analogue in Jewish spiritual communities. I therefore do not employ this term. On Emergent churches, see Scot McKnight, "Five Streams of the Emerging Church," *Christianity Today* 51, no. 2 (January 19, 2007). On the few "superficial similarities" between the so-called Emergent Jewish communities and emergent churches—and the even greater theological dissimilarities, see "Emerging Synagogues?," *Christianity Today*, May 9, 2008, http://www.christianitytoday .com/le/2008/may-online-only/emerging-synagogue.html. For a different view of the "Emergent Synagogues," see Landres, "Emergence Unbound."

44. Ben Harris, "7 Fast-Growing Independent Congregations Join Forces in New Group," *Forward*, February 8, 2016, http://forward.com/news/breaking-news

/333063/7-fast-growing-independent-congregations-join-forces-in-new-group/?utm_content=opinion_Newsletter_BreakingNews_Position-3&utm_source=Sailthru&utm_medium=email&utm_campaign=Opinion%20Redesign%202016-02-08&utm_term=Opinion.

45. Peter Beinart, "San Francisco and the New Jewish Frontier: The Struggle to Keep Judaism Alive in the Most Secular City in America," *Ha'aretz*, April 21, 2015, http://www.haaretz.com/beta/.premium-1.652856.

46. Harris, "7 Fast-Growing Independent Congregations."

47. Mishkan website, http://www.mishkanchicago.org/who-we-are/concept/.

48. Hannah Dreyfus, "High Holidays for Millennials, Far from Shul," *Jewish Week* (New York), September 16, 2015, http://www.thejewishweek.com/news/new-york/high-holidays-millennials-far-shul.

49. Lauren Markoe, "Women Rabbis Are Forging a Path outside Denominational Judaism," *Religion News Service*, April 8, 2015, http://religionnews.com/2015/04/08/women-rabbis-forging-path-outside-denominational-judaism/.

50. The Kitchen's approach is discussed in Beinart, "San Francisco and the New Jewish Frontier."

51. See http://www.mishkanchicago.org/who-we-are/concept/.

52. The political expectations of the Kitchen and Ikar are discussed in Beinart, "San Francisco and the New Jewish Frontier."

53. Needless to say, communities approach these matters in different ways and at different paces. Romemu, for example, announces its commitment to "climate justice" and promises new partnerships for other causes (https://www.romemu.org/community/social-action/). Sixth and I in Washington does not list specific political causes.

54. We lack a good study of the politicization of the contemporary American synagogue that might shed light on the interplay between religious ideology and political preferences in synagogue life. A thoughtful analysis of how Jewish communal life in general is being torn asunder by the seemingly unbridgeable partisan divide over politics appears in Yehuda Kurtzer, "The Biggest Threat to the Jews? The Partisan Divide," *Forward*, January 22, 2018, https://forward.com/opinion/392116/the-biggest-threat-to-the-jews-the-partisan-divide/?attribution=home-hero-item-text-2.

55. Some observers regard these communities as "the nucleus of an American Jewish renaissance." No doubt the political slant will be congenial for certain

Jews; others may find it off-putting. For the perspective of a cheer leader, see Sid Schwarz, "The New Paradigm Spiritual Communities Initiative," *eJewish Philanthropy*, March 31, 2016, http://ejewishphilanthropy.com/the-new-para digm-spiritual-communities-initiative/.

56. The organizer of Ohel Ayala is Rabbi Judith Hauptman, a retired professor of Talmud and Rabbinics at the Jewish Theological Seminary. See Dreyfus, "High Holidays for Millennials, Far from Shul." Ohel Ayala has sponsored Passover Seders and in the past offered Friday night dinners on occasion. On the intentional effort to provide a High Holiday experience to all comers, especially millennials, see Jonathan Mark, "Walk Right in, Sit Right Down," *Times of Israel*, September 13, 2017, http://jewishweek.timesofisrael.com /walk-right-in-sit-right-down/. The precedent for Ohel Ayala were the so-called mushroom synagogues in the middle decades of the twentieth century, which provided a place to worship for Jews who had no synagogue affiliation but wanted to attend High Holiday services. These mushroom synagogues, though, were money-making propositions, which is not the goal of Ohel Ayala. On the mushroom synagogues, see "New York Rabbis Start War on Mushroom Synagogues," *JTA*, August 17, 1930, http://www.jta.org/1930/08/17 /archive/n-y-rabbis-start-war-on-mushroom-synagogues.

57. Madison Margolin, "Experimental NY Rabbi Engages by Keeping Judaism Honest," *Times of Israel*, March 13, 2016. In contrast to other congregational settings for millennials, politics is kept out of Because Jewish.

58. Danielle Berrin, "East Side Jews Enact Do-It-Yourself Judaism," *Jewish Journal* (Los Angeles), October 19, 2011, http://www.jewishjournal.com/hollywood jew/item/do-it-yourself_judaism_20111019/.

59. Daniel S. Horwitz, "The Well Flows in Metro Detroit with Lessons for Us All," *eJewish Philanthropy*, January 3, 2016, http://ejewishphilanthropy.com /the-well-flows-in-metro-detroit-with-lessons-for-us-all/. It appears that something similar is now available in the Washington, DC, area that goes under the name Gather the Jews. See http://www.gatherthejews.com/local-information /organizations/.

60. On the location of these houses, see https://www.moishehouse.org/houselist. Moishe Houses have now spread abroad, including to South America and Israel.

61. See "Theory of Change," http://www.moishehouse.org/data/MoisheHouse EvaluationOutline.pdf.

62. Daniel Aaron Tarle, "Community Built upon Relationships: How Moishe House Engages the Millennial Generation" (master's thesis, USC and Hebrew Union College, December 2013), 46. The Moishe House organization claimed to have reached six hundred thousand young Jews throughout the world during its first decade. "Moishe House Marks a Decade with Global Shabbat Celebration," *eJewish Philanthropy*, September 21, 2016, http://ejewishphilanthropy.com /moishe-house-marks-a-decade-with-global-shabbat-celebration/#more-97004.

63. For a directory, see the website of Mechon Hadar, https://docs.google.com /spreadsheets/d/1Gu_NsVaQDqU83N9H3lslpeNXucghBqomTSJmlFiQZKQ /edit#gid=0.

64. On the demographic profile of participants in Independent Minyanim, see Steven M. Cohen, Shawn J. Landress, Elie Kaunfer, and Michelle Shain, *Emergent Jewish Communities and Their Participants: Preliminary Findings from the 2007 National Spiritual Communities Study* (New York: Mechon Hadar, Synagogue 3000, November 2007), http://www.bjpa.org/Publications/details.cfm ?PublicationID=2828.

65. For the advice offered to minyanim and examples of how some go about ensuring quality control, see the section on "Being Inclusive in Davening without Sacrificing Quality," https://www.mechonhadar.org/prayer-policy-and-practice/#Guidelines.

66. These New York minyanim for the post-baby-boom generation are surveyed in Debra Nussbaum Cohen, "The New Gen-X Judaism," *Jewish Week* (New York), August 2, 2002, www.thejewishweek.com/news/newscontent.php3?artid=6503& print=yes.

67. On this debate and for an insightful comparison of the Independent Minyanim and the Havurot, see Riv-Ellen Prell, "Independent Minyanim and Prayer Groups of the 1970s: Historical and Sociological Perspectives," *Zeek*, January 2008, http://www.zeek.net/801prell/.

68. An exception to the urban-centric character of these groups is Makom, "a new model for an intentional Jewish community on Long Island." Rabbi Deborah Bravo, Sherry Gutes, and Michelle Schneider, "Just What IS a New Model for Jewish Community? Reflections on the First Year of Makom NY, a New Kind

of Jewish Community," *eJewish Philanthropy*, July 10, 2016, http://ejewish philanthropy.com/just-what-is-a-new-model-for-jewish-community.

69. Regardless of how expansive programming is in the various groups, the question of membership dues is a contentious issue. When we recall that one of the criticisms leveled against synagogues was that membership dues are unreasonable, it may be jarring to learn that financial arrangements are a source of much discussion in all of the unconventional settings. Some, in fact, are more stringent than synagogues in denying entry to nonmembers; others charge fees for services.

70. Initially, the institute was designed to help rabbis reconnect to their own spiritual lives through guided meditation practices and exposure to Hasidic literature. The guiding assumption was that "leaders who engage in Jewish spiritual practices that are grounded in mindfulness are better equipped to contribute to building Jewish communities that are vibrant, resilient, and wise; they are able to meaningfully addressing the brokenness of our world." In recent years, the institute has developed approaches to help clergy going through its program translate what they have experienced into the congregational setting.

71. We note in this connection, the proliferation of study groups aimed cross-denominationally and/or at younger Jews. One of the success stories in this regard is SVARA: A Traditionally Radical Yeshiva. Based in the Chicago area, SVARA exposes learners to the Talmud unmediated by translations. Students use dictionaries and guides prepared by the teachers of SVARA to delve into the Talmud. Texts are chosen deliberately to engage with controversial issues and to demonstrate how the rabbis were radically innovative "change agents." On SVARA's approach to study, see http://www.svara.org/about-svara/ and also Rachel Cort, " 'Traditionally Radical' Jewish Learning," *eJewish Philanthropy*, March 17, 2014, http://ejewishphilanthropy.com/traditionally-radical-jewish -learning/. Kevah offers a less radical approach to Talmud study that addresses a range of classical Jewish texts and also is geared toward millennials. See "Keva Offers a DIY Approach to Jewish Learning," *Faith and Leadership*, April 21, 2015, https://www.faithandleadership.com/kevah-offers-diy-approach-jewish -millennials. Kevah began on the West Coast but has spread to other parts of the country.

Notes to Conclusion

1. For a description of the project, see https://www.letmypeoplesing.org/#mission -section. My description of what occurs at the retreats is based upon interviews with a few participants.

2. Its initial foray beyond the retreat center was held in Philadelphia. See https://www.letmypeoplesing.org/philadelphia/.

3. An inclusive orientation is built into the DNA of Let My People Sing in part because its founders were rabbinical students at the nondenominational Boston Hebrew College.

4. Elisa Kreisinger, "What Is a Remix, Exactly?," September 23, 2011, https://elisakreisinger.wordpress.com/2011/09/23/what-is-a-remix-exactly/.

5. These were already noted at the end of the past century by Charles S. Liebman, "Ritual, Ceremony and the Reconstruction of Judaism," *Contemporary Jewry* 6 (1990): 272–83. All of these categories appear in that essay and several of his additional publications.

6. This last term is used by Eisen and Cohen, *Jew Within*, chap. 2.

7. The terminology employed here probably originated with Harold Rosenberg, "The Herd of Independent Minds: Has the Avant-Garde Its Own Mass Culture?," *Commentary*, September 1948, https://www.commentarymagazine.com/articles/the-herd-of-independent-mindshas-the-avant-garde-its-own-mass-culture/.

8. For some of the sociological literature linking behavior to peer influences, see, on smoking, David R. Schaefer, Jimi Adams, and Steven A. Haas, "Social Networks and Smoking: Exploring the Effects of Peer Influence and Smoker Popularity through Simulations," *Health Education and Behavior*, October 1, 2013, http://journals.sagepub.com/doi/abs/10.1177/1090198113493091. On obesity, see Katherine Harmon, "How Obesity Spreads in Social Networks," *Scientific American*, May 5, 2011, https://www.scientificamerican.com/article/social-spread -obesity/. And on voting behavior, see Betsy Sinclair, *The Social Citizen: Peer Networks and Political Influence* (Chicago: University of Chicago Press, 2012).

9. Jacob J. Schacter, "Halakhic Authority in a World of Personal Autonomy," in *Radical Responsibility: Celebrating the Thought of Chief Rabbi Lord Jonathan Sacks*, ed. Michael J. Harris, Daniel Rhynold, and Tamra Wright (London:

Maggid Books, 2013), 168. My thanks to Neal Kozodoy for drawing my attention to this essay.

10. Marti, "Religious Reflexivity."

11. One of the rabbis interviewed put this colloquially when he observed: "Culture eats vision for breakfast." By this he meant to underscore how difficult it is for Jewish institutions to resist the allure of the worldviews, values, assumptions, and mores of the wider culture, especially because so many Jews have internalized them.

12. The concept of plausibility structures refers to the conditions in a society that make certain beliefs seem reasonable or unreasonable. On this concept, see Peter L. Berger, *The Sacred Canopy: Elements of a Sociological Theory of Religion* (New York: Random House, 1967), esp. chap. 6.

13. James Davison Hunter, *American Evangelicalism: Conservative Religion and the Quandary of Modernity* (New Brunswick, NJ: Rutgers University Press, 1983), 15.

14. For an example of how the focus on the needs of a couple trumps communal considerations, see Adina Lewittes, "Intermarriage, I Do," *Tablet*, February 4, 2015, http://www.tabletmag.com/jewish-life-and-religion/188465/inter marriage-i-do.

15. This is not the way intermarriage is understood in many quarters of the Jewish community, where it is seen solely as an effect of poor Jewish education and/or indifference. I have argued that intermarriage is also a cause, driving well-educated and once-committed Jews away from Jewish life because religion becomes a third-rail issue in the homes of many intermarried people. See my essay, "Intermarriage: Can Anything Be Done," *Mosaic*, September 2013, http://mosaicmagazine.com/essay/2013/09/intermarriage/.

16. "Creating an Open, Remixable, Meaningful, and Connected Jewish Life" was the theme of Limmud Atlanta's 2011 gathering.

17. This notion has now taken hold even in Silicon Valley, where some speak of the virtues of an Internet or Tech Sabbath, a day of being "unplugged." See, for example, Pico Iyer, *The Art of Stillness: Adventures in Going Nowhere* (New York: TED Books, 2014), excerpted at http://ideas.ted.com/why-we-need-a-secular -sabbath/.

18. Sklare and Greenblum, *Jewish Identity on the Suburban Frontier*, 57.

19. The universalization of Passover was already noted by Sklare and Greenblum, ibid.

20. For some discussion about these trends and their limitations, see Amy L. Sales, "Future of the Synagogue," *CCAR Journal* (Winter 2009): 116–24, and Nanette Fridman, "Is Your Synagogue Being Proactive," *eJewish Philanthropy*, August 12, 2015, http://ejewishphilanthropy.com/is-your-synagogue-being-proactive/.

21. Conceiving of the synagogue as a business also can lead to treating congregants as consumers. To counter this, Rob Weinberg, an educational consultant, usefully contends that "successful synagogues regard 'members' as parties to a covenant (b'rit), not as consumers of a set of services." Rob Weinberg, "Six Faces of Synagogue Success," *Reform Judaism*, Special Issue on Strengthening Congregations (2014): 16, http://www.urj.org/sites/default/files/Strengthening_Syna gogues_FINAL_0.pdf. I have discussed the specific demands made by some synagogue boards of their rabbis to conform to corporate expectations in "The Rabbi Crisis," *Commentary*, May 2003, https://www.commentarymagazine.com /articles/the-rabbi-crisis/.

22. Robert Isaacs, "Netflix, Blockbuster, and Disruptive Change in Synagogues," *eJewish Philanthropy*, November 24, 2015, http://ejewishphilanthropy.com/net flix-blockbuster-and-disruptive-change-in-synagogues/.

23. Liel Leibovitz, "To See Those Pews Full Again, Synagogues Should Learn from Best Buy," *Tablet*, September 4, 2015, http://www.tabletmag.com/jewish-life -and-religion/193316/learn-from-best-buy.

24. For a good overview and also a case for synagogues to make room for more spirituality, see Steven M. Cohen and Lawrence Hoffman, "How Spiritual Are America's Jews? Narrowing the Spirituality Gap between Jews and Other Americans," *SK3000 Report*, no. 4 (March 2009), http://www.bjpa.org/Publi cations/downloadFile.cfm?FileID=1998.

25. A survey of Americans conducted in 2017 found that 27 percent of adults surveyed self-identified as spiritual but not religious. See Michael Lipka and Claire Gecewicz, "More Americans Now Say They Are Spiritual but Not Religious" (Pew Research Center, September 6, 2017), http://www.pewresearch.org/fact -tank/2017/09/06/more-americans-now-say-theyre-spiritual-but-not-religious/.

26. For a sympathetic analysis of Jewish spiritual groups in America, see Arielle Levites, "Raising Jewish Spirits: American Jews, Religious Emotion and the

Culture of Contemporary American Spirituality" (PhD diss., New York University, 2016).

27. Nancy T. Ammerman, "The Reality behind 'Spiritual but Not Religious,'" *Studying Congregations*, July 23, 2014, http://studyingcongregations.org/blog/ask-the-expert-the-reality-behind-spiritual-but-not-religious. See also her study *Sacred Stories, Spiritual Tribes*, 288–304.

28. Sid Schwarz, "The New Spiritual Paradigm Communities Initiative," *eJewish Philanthropy*, March 31, 2016, http://ejewishphilanthropy.com/the-new-paradigm-spiritual-communities-initiative/.

29. Marvin Glassman, "Hollywood's Beth El Introduces Shabbat Lite Service," *Sun Sentinel*, August 10, 2016, http://www.sun-sentinel.com/local/broward/hollywood/fl-jjbs-shabbat-0810-20160809-story.html?utm_content=daily_Newsletter_Florida_Title_Position-1&utm_source=Sailthru&utm_medium=email&utm_campaign=New%20Daily%202016-08-20&utm_term=The%20Forward%20Today%20Monday-Friday.

30. Daniel S. Horwitz, "The Well Flows in Metro Detroit," *eJewish Philanthropy*, January 3, 2016, http://ejewishphilanthropy.com/the-well-flows-in-metro-detroit-with-lessons-for-us-all/.

31. Franz Kafka, "Letter to My Father," excerpted in Paul Mendes-Flohr and Jehuda Reinharz, *The Jew in the Modern World: A Documentary History* (New York: Oxford University Press, 1980), 219.

32. For a particularly egregious example, see Jay Michaelson, "Why You Should Not Go to the Synagogue on Rosh Hashanah This Year," *Forward*, September 15, 2016, http://forward.com/opinion/349500/why-you-shouldnt-go-to-synagogue-on-rosh-hashanah-this-year/.

33. On the indispensable role of community in reinforcing Jewish ritual behavior, see Charles S. Liebman, "Orthodox Judaism Today," *Midstream* (August/September 1979): 25.

34. Yossi Klein Halevi, "The Tragedy of the Western Wall," *Times of Israel*, June 26, 2017, http://blogs.timesofisrael.com/the-tragedy-of-the-western-wall/.

35. For an example of this educational approach, which unfortunately comes at the expense of literacy, note the contention of David Bryfman: "We need to pivot away from content mastery—like does the child know the Bible stories or can s/he navigate a siddur—and focus on how the student can apply the lesson

learned back to their actual life." Hannah Dreyfus, "Forget Continuity, Keep Teens Happy," *Jewish Week* (New York), January 11, 2017, http://jewishweek .timesofisrael.com/forget-continuity-keep-teens-happy/. On the movement away from Hebrew literacy and Judaic knowledge as a precursor to Bar/Bat Mitzvah and the elevation of social action in their stead, see Laurie Goodstein, "Bar Mitzvah Gets New Look to Build Faith," *New York Times*, September 3, 2013, http:// www.nytimes.com/2013/09/04/us/bar-mitzvahs-get-new-look-to-build-faith .html?pagewanted=all&_r=0.

36. Michael S. Berger, "Israel and the 'Intentional Judaism' of American Jews" (paper, Leffell Foundation Seminar on the Impact of Israel on American Jewish Life, August 2016), 4.

37. Michael S. Berger, "Religious Purposefulness in Jewish Day Schools," *Ha-Yidion* (September 2008): 6–13, https://prizmah.org/religious-purposefulness -jewish-day-schools.

Bibliography

Newspapers and Journals

American Jewish Yearbook
Arutz Sheva
Atlanta Jewish Times
Atlantic
Baltimore Jewish Times
Boston Jewish Advocate
CCAR Journal
Chicago Jewish News
Christianity Today
Cleveland Jewish News
Cleveland Plains Dealer
Commentary
Conservative Judaism
Contact
Daily Mail
Detroit Jewish News
Fortune
Forward
Ha'aretz
Inyan Magazine
Jerusalem Post
Jerusalem Report
Jewish Arizona
Jewish Exponent
Jewish Journal (Los Angeles)

Jewish News of Greater Phoenix
Jewish Star
Jewish Times (Baltimore)
Jewish Week (New York)
JWeekly
Los Angeles Times
Modern Judaism
New Jersey Jewish News
Newsweek
New York Magazine
New York Times
Reconstructionist
Reform Judaism
Sh'ma
Slate
Tikkun
Times of Israel
Verge
Wall Street Journal
Washington Jewish Week
Washington Post
Washington Times
Yated Ne'eman

Blogs and Online Journals

Book of Doctrines and Opinions
CCAR Press
Cross-Currents
eJewish Philanthropy
Emes Ve-Emunah
Faith and Leadership
Huffington Post
Ideals, Institute for Jewish Ideas and Ideals
Inside Leadership
InterfaithFamily
Jerusalem Center for Public Affairs
JewFem
Jewish Ideas Daily
Jewish Telegraphic Agency
Klal Perspectives
Lehrhaus

Lubavitch International News
Mosaic
My Jewish Learning
Rabbi Brad
Rabbi Pruzansky's Blog
Rabbinical Council of America
Reb Jeff
Religion News Service
Shalhevet Boiling Point
Studying Congregations
Tablet
Text & Texture
The Torah
Torah Musings
Yedid Nefesh Blog
Yeshiva University Observer

Books and Articles

Ahad Ha'Am, "Shabbat vetsiyonut" [The Sabbath and Zionism]. *Hashiloah* 3, no. 6 (1898).

Alba, Richard D. "The Twilight of Ethnicity among Americans of European Ancestry: The Case of Italians." *Ethnic and Racial Studies* 8, no. 1 (1985): 134–58.

Alper, Becka A. "Millennials Are Less Religious Than Older Americans, but Just as Spiritual." Pew Research Center, November 23, 2015. http://www.pew research.org/fact-tank/2015/11/23/millennials-are-less-religious-than-older -americans-but-just-as-spiritual/.

Ammerman, Nancy T. *Congregation and Community.* New Brunswick, NJ: Rutgers University Press, 1996.

———, ed. *Everyday Religion: Observing Religious Lives.* New York: Oxford University Press, 2007.

———. "Golden Rule Christianity: Lived Religion in the American Mainstream," in Hall, *Lived Religion in America.*

———. *Pillars of Faith: American Congregations and Their Partners*. Berkeley: University of California Press, 2005.

———. *Sacred Stories, Spiritual Tribes: Finding Religion in Everyday Life*. New York: Oxford University Press, 2013.

Angel, Marc D. "The American Experience of a Sephardic Synagogue." In Wertheimer, *American Synagogue*.

Aron, Isa, and Nachama Skolnik Moscowitz. "Beit Knesset Hazon: A Visionary Synagogue." In Wertheimer, *Learning and Community*.

Batnitzky, Leora. *How Judaism Became a Religion: An Introduction to Modern Jewish Thought*. Princeton, NJ: Princeton University Press, 2011.

Bayme, Steven. *Conflict or Cooperation: Papers on Jewish Unity*. New York: CLAL and the American Jewish Committee, July 1989.

Becker, Penny Edgell. *Congregations in Conflict: Cultural Models of Local Religious Life*. Cambridge: Cambridge University Press, 1999.

Bellah, Robert N., et al. *Habits of the Heart: Individualism and Commitment in American Life*. Berkeley: University of California Press, 1985.

Ben-Moshe, Danny, and Zohar Segev, eds. *Israel, the Diaspora, and Jewish Identity*. Sussex: Sussex Academic Press, 2007.

Benor, Sarah Bunin. *Becoming Frum: How Newcomers Learn the Language and Culture of Orthodox Judaism*. New Brunswick, NJ: Rutgers University Press, 2012.

Ben-Ur, Aviva. *Sephardic Jews in America: A Diasporic History*. New York: New York University Press, 2009.

Berger, Michael S. "Israel and the 'Intentional Judaism' of American Jews." Paper presented at the Leffell Foundation Seminar on the Impact of Israel on American Jewish Life, August 2016.

———. "Religious Purposefulness in Jewish Day Schools." *HaYidion*, September 2008, 6–13. https://prizmah.org/religious-purposefulness-jewish-day-schools.

Berger, Peter L. *The Sacred Canopy: Elements of a Sociological Theory of Religion*. New York: Random House, 1967.

Berger, Shalom Z., Daniel Jacobson, and Chaim I. Waxman. *Flipping Out? Myth or Fact: The Impact of the "Year in Israel."* New York: Yashar Books, 2007.

Berman, Saul J. "Diverse Orthodox Attitudes." Berkeley, CA: Edah, 2001.

Bialik, Haim Nachman. *Devarim shebe-'al peh*. Tel Aviv: Devir, 1935.

Blau, Yitzchak. "Contemporary Challenges for Modern Orthodoxy." In Hain, *Next Generation of Modern Orthodoxy*.

Bottum, Joseph. "The Death of Protestant America: A Political Theory of the Protestant Mainline." *First Things*, August 2008. http://www.firstthings.com/article /2008/08/001-the-death-of-protestant-america-a-political-theory-of-the-protestant-mainline.

Brill, Alan. "Is There a Post-Orthodox Judaism That Corresponds to Post-Evangelical?" *Book of Doctrines and Opinions*, November 19, 2009, https://kavvanah.wordpress.com/2009/11/19/is-there-a-post-orthodox-judaism-that -corresponds-to-post-evangelical/.

Brinkman, Tobias. *Sundays at Sinai: A Jewish Congregation in Chicago*. Chicago: University of Chicago Press, 2012.

Bronstein, Daniel. "Torah in the Trenches: The Rabbi Chaplains of World War II, 1940–1946." PhD dissertation, Jewish Theological Seminary, 2009.

Brous, Sharon. "Synagogues Reimagined." In Schwarz, *Jewish Megatrends*.

Burton, Tara Isabela. "Bukharan Jews Thrive in New York but Are Almost Gone in Central Asia." *National Geographic*, August 4, 2015. http://news.nationalgeographic.com/2015/08/150804-jews-diaspora-bukhara-uzbekistan-asia-world/.

Cadge, Wendy, and Mary Ellen Konieczny. "'Hidden in Plain Sight': The Significance of Religion and Spirituality in Secular Organizations." *Sociology of Religion* 75 (2014): 551–63.

Caplan, Eric. *From Ideology to Liturgy: Reconstructionist Worship and American Liberal Judaism*. Cincinnati: Hebrew Union College Press, 2002.

Chaves, Mark. *American Religion: Contemporary Trends*. Princeton, NJ: Princeton University Press, 2011.

Cohen, Debra Nussbaum. *Celebrating Your New Jewish Daughter*. Woodstock, VT: Jewish Lights, 2001.

Cohen, Michael R. *The Birth of Conservative Judaism: Solomon Schechter's Disciples and the Creation of an American Religious Movement*. New York: Columbia University Press, 2012.

Cohen, Steven M. "Can Intermarriage Lead to an Increase in the Number of Jews in America?" *Mosaic*, November 9, 2015. http://mosaicmagazine.com/observation/2015/11/can-intermarriage-lead-to-an-increase-in-the-number-of-jews-in -america/.

———. "Gays, Lesbians, and the Conservative Movement: The JTS Survey of Conservative Clergy, Students, Professionals, and Lay Leaders." Berman Jewish Policy Archive, January 28, 2007. http://www.jewishdatabank.org/Studies /details.cfm?StudyID=493.

Cohen, Steven M., and Samuel Abrams. "How Mountain and Pacific States Jews Differ." *Jewish Journal* (Los Angeles), January 28, 2016. http://jewishjournal .com/news/nation/181709/.

Cohen, Steven M., Galia Avidar, and Marcie Yoselevsky. "The Syrian Jews of New York: Challenges to a Cohesive Community." Unpublished manuscript, October 2012.

Cohen, Steven M., Caryn Aviv, and Ari Kelman. "Gay, Jewish, or Both?" *Journal of Jewish Communal Service*, Winter/Spring 2009.

Cohen, Steven M., and Lauren Blitzer. *Belonging without Believing: Jews and Their Distinctive Patterns of Religiosity and Secularity.* New York: JCC Association, 2008. http://www.bjpa.org/Publications/details.cfm?PublicationID=795.

Cohen, Steven M., and Aryeh Davidson. *Adult Jewish Learning in America: Current Patterns and Prospects for Growth.* New York: JCC Association, 2001.

Cohen, Steven M., and Jason Gitlin. "Reluctant or Repressed? Aversion to Expressing Views on Israel among American Rabbis." Jewish Council on Public Affairs, 2013. http://www.jewishdatabank.org/studies/downloadFile.cfm?FileID=3075.

Cohen, Steven M., Shawn J. Landress, Elie Kaunfer, and Michelle Shain. *Emergent Jewish Communities and Their Participants: Preliminary Findings from the 2007 National Spiritual Communities Study.* New York: Mechon Hadar, Synagogue 3000, November 2007.

Cohler-Esses, Diane. "What the Hell Is a Syrian Jew?" *Journal of Feminist Studies in Religion* 19, no. 1 (2003). http://www.jewishpinkelephant.com/2013/03 /what-hell-is-syrian-jew-by-dianne.html.

Cooper, Alanna E. *Bukharan Jews and the Dynamics of Global Judaism.* Bloomington: Indiana University Press, 2012.

Davidman, Lynn. *Becoming Unorthodox: Stories of Ex-Hasidic Jews.* Oxford: Oxford University Press, 2015.

———. "The New Voluntarism and the Case of Unsynagogued Jews." In Ammerman, *Everyday Religion.*

Davis, Moshe. *The Emergence of Conservative Judaism: The Historical School in Nineteenth Century America.* Philadelphia: Jewish Publication Society, 1963.

Deen, Shulem. *All Who Go Do Not Return: A Memoir.* Minneapolis: Greywood Press, 2015.

Drazin, Paul. "Survey: The Use of Musical Instruments on Shabbat/Yom Tov." United Synagogue of Conservative Judaism, February 2013. https://cantors.org /sites/default/files/uploaded_files/site/Education/uscj_instrumentusesurveyre sults_20130219.pdf.

Ehrenkrantz, Dan. "A Response to Post/Trans/Non-Denominational Critiques." *Reconstructionist*, Spring 2007.

Eisen, Arnold, and Steven M. Cohen. *The Jew Within: Self, Family and Community in America*. Bloomington: Indiana University Press, 2000.

Eleff, Zev. *Living from Convention to Convention: A History of the NCSY, 1954–1989*. New York: KTAV, 2009.

Eliezrie, David. *The Secret of Chabad*. Jerusalem: Toby Press, 2015.

Ellenson, David. "Envisioning Israel in the Liturgies of North American Liberal Judaism." In *Envisioning Israel: The Changing Ideals and Images of North American Jews*, edited by Allon Gal. Detroit: Wayne State University Press and Magnes Press, 1996.

———. "Michael A. Meyer and His Vision of Reform Judaism and the Reform Rabbinate: A Lifetime of Devotion." In *Mediating Modernity: Challenges and Trends in the Jewish Encounter with the Modern World—Essays in Honor of Michael A. Meyer*, edited by Lauren B. Strauss and Michael Brenner. Detroit: Wayne State University Press, 2008.

Fein, Leonard. *Where Are We? The Inner Lives of America's Jews*. New York: Harper & Row, 1988.

Ferziger, Adam S. *Beyond Sectarianism: The Realignment of American Orthodox Judaism*. Detroit: Wayne State University Press, 2015.

———. "From Lubavitch to Lakewood: The Chabadization of American Orthodoxy." *Modern Judaism* 33, no. 2 (May 2013).

Finkelman, Yoel. *Strictly Kosher Reading: Popular Literature and the Condition of Contemporary Orthodoxy*. Boston: Academic Studies Press, 2011.

Finkelstein, Louis. "The Things That Unite Us." In Waxman, *Tradition and Change*.

Fishkoff, Sue. *The Rebbe's Army: Inside the World of Chabad Lubavitch*. New York: Schocken, 2003.

Fishman, Sylvia Barack. "American Jewishness Today: Identity and Transmissibility in an Open World." *Contemporary Jewry* 35 (2015).

———. "Growth and Challenges in the Contemporary Reform Movement." In Rosenak, *Hayehadut HaReforma*.

———. "Policy Implications of the Gender Imbalance among America's Jews." Jerusalem: Jerusalem Center for Public Affairs, December 10, 2008. http://jcpa .org/article/policy-implications-of-the-gender-imbalance-among-americas-jews/.

Fishman, Sylvia Barack, and Daniel Parmer. "Matrilineal Ascent/Patrilineal Descent: The Gender Imbalance in American Jewish Life." Waltham, MA: Hadassah Brandeis Institute and the Maurice and Marilyn Cohen Center for Modern Jewish Studies, 2008.

Flory, Richard W., and Donald E. Miller, eds. *GenX Religion*. New York: Routledge, 2000.

Freedman, Samuel G. *Jew vs. Jew: The Struggle for the Soul of American Jewry*. New York: Simon & Schuster, 2000.

Frimer, Aryeh A., and Dov I. Frimer. "Women, Keri'at Hatorah, and Aliyyot." *Tradition* 46, no. 4 (2013). http://www.rcarabbis.org/pdf/frimer_article.pdf.

Furman, Frida Kerner. *Beyond Yiddishkeit: The Struggle for Jewish Identity in a Reform Synagogue*. Albany: State University of New York Press, 1987.

Gans, Herbert. "The Coming Darkness of Late-Generation European American Ethnicity." *Ethnic and Racial Studies Review* 37, no. 5 (2014): 757– 65.

Grant, Lisa, and Michael Marmur. "The Place of Israel in the Identity of Reform Jews: Israel/Diaspora Joint Commentators." In Ben-Moshe and Segev, *Israel, the Diaspora, and Jewish Identity*.

Green, Arthur. *Radical Judaism: Rethinking God and Tradition*. New Haven, CT: Yale University Press, 2010.

Greenberg, Irving. "The One in 2000 Controversy." *Moment*, March 1987.

———. "Will There Be One Jewish People in the Year 2000?" *Perspectives*, n.d.

Grossman, Lawrence. "Decline and Fall: Thoughts on Religious Zionism in America." In Waxman, *Religious Zionism Post Disengagement*.

———. "In What Sense Did Orthodoxy Believe the Torah to Be Divine?" *The Torah*, n.d. http://thetorah.com/in-what-sense-did-orthodoxy-believe-the-torah-to-be-divine/.

Grumet, Becca. "Doing Jewish at Burning Man: A Scholarly Personal Narrative on Identity, Community and Spirituality." Master's thesis, Hebrew Union College, 2016.

Gubkin, J. Liora. "Friday Night Live: It's Not Your Parents' Shabbat." In Flory and Miller, *GenX Religion*.

Gurock, Jeffrey S. "Checking Up on America's 'Tentative Orthodox' Jews." In *Black Fire on White Fire: Essays in Honor of Rabbi Avi Weiss*, edited by Daniel R. Goodman. New York: KTAV, 2017.

———. *Orthodox Jews in America*. Bloomington: Indiana University Press, 2009.

———. "Resisters and Accommodators: Varieties of Orthodox Rabbis in America, 1886–1983." *American Jewish Archives* 35 (1983). http://americanjewisharchives.org/publications/journal/PDF/1983_35_02_00_gurock.pdf.

Hain, Shmuel, ed. *The Next Generation of Modern Orthodoxy*. New York: Orthodox Forum, 2012.

Hall, David, ed. *Lived Religion in America: Toward a History of Practice*. Princeton, NJ: Princeton University Press, 1997.

Heilman, Samuel. "Holding Firmly with an Open Hand: Life in Two Conservative Synagogues." In Wertheimer, *Jews in the Center*.

———. *Sliding to the Right: The Contest for the Future of American Jewish Orthodoxy*. Berkeley: University of California Press, 2006.

———. *Who Will Lead Us? The Story of Five Hasidic Dynasties in America*. Berkeley: University of California Press, 2017.

Henry, Patrick. "'And I Don't Care What It Is': The Tradition-History of a Civil Religion Proof-Text." *Journal of the American Academy of Religion* 49, no. 1 (March 1981): 35–49.

Horn, Dara. "My First Hebrew Test." Stroum Center, University of Washington, March 7, 2016. https://jewishstudies.washington.edu/hebrew-humanities/dara -horn-my-first-hebrew-test/.

Horowitz, Bethamie. "Connections and Journeys: Assessing Critical Opportunities for Enhancing Jewish Identity." New York: UJA-Federation of New York, 2000. Revised 2003. http://www.jewishdatabank.org/Studies/downloadFile.cfm ?FileID=2631.

Hunter, James Davison. *American Evangelicalism: Conservative Religion and the Quandary of Modernity*. New Brunswick, NJ: Rutgers University Press, 1983.

———. *The Death of Character: Moral Education in an Age without Good or Evil*. New York: Basic Books, 2001.

Iyer, Pico. *The Art of Stillness: Adventures in Going Nowhere*. New York: TED Books, 2014.

Jick, Leon. *The Americanization of the Synagogue, 1820–1870*. Lebanon, NH: Brandeis University Press, 1992.

Jones, Jeffrey M. "Sept. 11 Effects, Though Largely Faded, Persist." Gallup, September 9, 2003. http://www.gallup.com/poll/9208/sept-effects-though-largely -faded-persist.aspx.

Joselit, Jenna Weisman. *New York's Jewish Jews: The Orthodox Community in the Interwar Years*. Bloomington: Indiana University Press, 1990.

Kafka, Franz. "Letter to My Father." Excerpted in Paul Mendes-Flohr and Jehuda Reinharz, *The Jew in the Modern World: A Documentary History*. New York: Oxford University Press, 1980.

Kaplan, Dana Evan. *American Reform Judaism: An Introduction*. New Brunswick, NJ: Rutgers University Press, 2003.

―――, ed. *Cambridge Companion on American Judaism*. Cambridge: Cambridge University Press, 2005.

―――. *Contemporary American Judaism: Transformation and Renewal*. New York: Columbia University Press, 2009.

―――, ed. *Reform Judaism: Challenges and Reflections*. Philadelphia: Jewish Publication Society, 2013.

Karp, Abraham. "A Century of Conservative Judaism in the United States." *American Jewish Year Book* 86 (1986).

Katz, Emily Alice. *Bringing Zion Home: Israel in American Jewish Culture, 1948–1967*. Albany: State University of New York Press, 2015.

Kelman, Ari. "Traditional Judaism: The Conceptualization of Jewishness in the Lives of American Jewish Post-Boomers." Unpublished manuscript, 2016.

Kelman, Stuart. "A Reform Prayer Book." *Jewish Book Council Review*, n.d. http://www.jewishbookcouncil.org/book/mishkan-tfilah.

Kelner, Shaul. *Tours That Bind: Diaspora, Pilgrimage, and Birthright Israel*. New York: New York University Press, 2010.

Kolsky, Thomas A. *Jews against Zionism: The American Council for Judaism, 1942–1948*. Philadelphia: Temple University Press, 1990.

Kosmin, Barry. "The Coming of Age in the Conservative Synagogue: The Bar/Bat Mitzvah Class of 5755." In Wertheimer, *Jews in the Center*.

Krakowski, Moshe. "Moderate Ultra-Orthodoxy: Complexity and Nuance in American Ultra-Orthodox Judaism." *Religion and Education* 39, no. 3 (2012).

Krasner, Jonathan. "The Place of Tikkun Olam in American Jewish Life." Jerusalem: Jerusalem Center for Public Affairs, November 1, 2014. http://jcpa.org/article/place-tikkun-olam-american-jewish-life1/.

Laskin, Martin. *An Ethnographic Study of an American Conservative Synagogue*. Lewiston, NY: Edwin Mellen Press, 2002.

Lefkowitz, Jay P. "The Rise of Social Orthodoxy: A Personal Account." *Commentary*, April 2014. https://www.commentarymagazine.com/articles/the-rise-of-social-orthodoxy-a-personal-account/.

Levenson, Jon D. "The New Enemies of Circumcision." *Commentary*, March 2000.

Levin, Yuval. *The Fractured Society: Renewing America's Social Contract in an Age of Individualism*. New York: Basic Books, 2016.

Levites, Arielle. "Raising Jewish Spirits: American Jews, Religious Emotion and the Culture of Contemporary American Spirituality." PhD dissertation, New York University, 2016.

Librach, Clifford. "A Revolution for Reform Judaism?" *Commentary*, December 14, 2015. https://www.commentarymagazine.com/articles/revolution-reform-judaism/.

Liebman, Charles S. *The Ambivalent American Jew: Politics, Family and Religion in American Jewish Life.* Philadelphia: Jewish Publication Society, 1973.

———. "Concluding Reflections on the Condition of American Judaism." In Kaplan, *Cambridge Companion on American Judaism.*

———. "Extremism as a Religious Norm." *Journal for the Scientific Study of Religion* 22 (March 1983).

———. "Orthodox Judaism Today." *Midstream*, August/September 1979.

———. "Orthodoxy in American Jewish Life." *American Jewish Year Book* 65 (1965).

———. "Ritual, Ceremony and the Reconstruction of Judaism." *Contemporary Jewry* 6 (1990).

Lipka, Michael. "Mainline Protestants Make Up Shrinking Number of U.S. Adults." Pew Research Center, May 18, 2015. http://www.pewresearch.org/fact-tank/2015 /05/18/mainline-protestants-make-up-shrinking-number-of-u-s-adults/.

Lipka, Michael, and Claire Gecewicz. "More Americans Now Say They Are Spiritual but Not Religious." Pew Research Center, September 6, 2017. http://www .pewresearch.org/fact-tank/2017/09/06/more-americans-now-say-theyre-spir itual-but-not-religious/.

Magid, Shaul. *American Post-Judaism: Identity and Renewal in a Postethnic Society.* Religion in North America. Bloomington: Indiana University Press, 2013.

Marcus, Batsheva, and Ronnie Becher. "Women's Tefillah Movement." *Encyclopedia*, 2009. http://jwa.org/encyclopedia/article/womens-tefillah-movement.

Marti, Gerardo. *A Mosaic of Believers: Diversity and Innovation in a Multi-ethnic Church.* Bloomington: Indiana University Press, 2005.

———. "Present and Future Scholarship in the Sociology of Religion." *Sociology of Religion* 75, no. 4 (2014).

———. "Religious Reflexivity: The Effect of Continual Novelty and Diversity on Individual Religiosity." *Sociology of Religion* 76, no. 1 (2015).

Marti, Gerardo, and Gladys Ganiel. *The Deconstructed Church: Understanding Emerging Christianity.* New York: Oxford University Press, 2014.

Marty, Martin, and R. Scott Appleby, eds. *Fundamentalisms Comprehended.* Chicago: University of Chicago Press, 1995.

McGinity, Keren. *Marrying Out: Jewish Men, Intermarriage and Fatherhood.* Bloomington: Indiana University Press, 2014.

———. *Still Jewish: A History of Women and Intermarriage in America.* New York: New York University Press, 2009.

Medved, Michael. "The Preposterous Politics of Passover." *Commentary*, April 1, 2011. https://www.commentarymagazine.com/articles/the-preposterous -politics-of-passover/.

Meyer, Michael A. "On the Slope toward Syncretism and Sectarianism." *CCAR Journal*, Summer 1993.

———. *Response to Modernity: The History of the Reform Movement in Judaism.* New York: Oxford University Press, 1988.

Meyer, Michael A., and David Myers, eds. *Between Jewish Tradition and Modernity: Essays in Honor of David H. Ellenson.* Detroit: Wayne State University Press, 2014.

Motzkin, Linda. *Aleph Isn't Tough: An Introduction to Hebrew for Adults.* New York: Behrman House, 2003.

Musleah, Rahel. "Bukharian Jews: Preserving Identity." *Hadassah Magazine* 90, no. 1 (2008), http://www.hadassah.org/news/content/per_hadassah/ar-chive /2008/08_sep/feature_1.asp.

Neuman, Moshe, and Mordechai Becher. *Avotot Ahava: inyenei kiruv rechokim behalkha.* Jerusalem: Feldheim, 2002.

Perl, Gil. "Postmodern Orthodoxy: Giving Voice to a New Generation." *Lehrhaus*, November 6, 2017. http://www.thelehrhaus.com/commentary-short-articles/2017 /11/5/postmodern-orthodoxy-giving-voice-to-a-new-generation.

Pew Research Center. "The Gender Gap in Religion around the World." March 22, 2016.

———. "In America, Does More Education Equal Less Religion?" April 26, 2017. http://assets.pewresearch.org/wp-content/uploads/sites/11/2017/04/251 15302/Religion-and-education-FULL-REPORT.pdf.

———. "A Portrait of American Orthodox Jews: A Further Analysis of a 2013 Survey of U.S. Jews." August 2015. http://assets.pewresearch.org/wp-content /uploads/sites/11/2015/08/Orthodox-Jews-08-24-PDF-for-web.pdf.

———. "A Portrait of Jewish Americans: Findings from a Pew Research Center of American Jews." October 2013. http://assets.pewresearch.org/wp-content /uploads/sites/11/2013/10/jewish-american-full-report-for-web.pdf.

———. "U.S. Public Becoming Less Religious." November 3, 2015. http://www .pewforum.org/2015/11/03/u-s-public-becoming-less-religious/.

Pianko, Noam. *Jewish Peoplehood: An American Innovation.* New Brunswick, NJ: Rutgers University Press, 2015.

Pickus, Abigail. "A Closer Look at Independent Bnei Mitzvah in the Chicagoland Area." Jewish United Fund of Chicago, November 2, 2015. http://ejewish philanthropy.com/wordpress/wp-content/uploads/2015/11/CFJE-REPORTS -IND-BM.pdf.

Podhoretz, Norman. *Why Are Jews Liberals?* New York: Doubleday, 2009.

Pomson, Alex, and Jack Wertheimer. "Hebrew for What? Hebrew at the Heart of Jewish Day Schools." AVI CHAI Foundation, 2017. http://avichai.org/knowl edge_base/hebrew-for-what-hebrew-at-the-heart-of-jewish-day-schools/.

Prell, Riv-Ellen. "Communities of Choice and Memory: Conservative Synagogues in the Late Twentieth Century." In Wertheimer, *Jews in the Center.*

———. "Independent Minyanim and Prayer Groups of the 1970s: Historical and Sociological Perspectives." *Zeek*, January 2008.

Putnam, Robert D. *Bowling Alone: The Collapse and Revival of American Community.* New York: Simon & Schuster, 2000.

Raphael, Marc. *Judaism in America.* New York: Columbia University Press, 2003.

Reisebrodt, Martin. *The Promise of Salvation: A Theory of Religion.* Chicago: University of Chicago Press, 2010.

Riley, Naomi Schaefer. *Got Religion? How Churches, Mosques, and Synagogues Can Bring Young People Back.* West Conshohocken, PA: Templeton Press, 2014.

Ritterband, Paul. "Public Worship: The Partnership between Families and Synagogues." In Wertheimer, *Jews in the Center.*

Rosen, Mark, et al. "Chabad on Campus: The Hertog Study." Cohen Center, Brandeis University, September 2016. http://www.bjpa.org/Publications/down loadFile.cfm?FileID=22304.

Rosenak, Avinoam, ed. *Hayehadut HaReforma: Hagut, Tarbut, Vehevra.* Jerusalem: Van Leer Institute, 2014.

Roth, Philip. *Goodbye, Columbus: And Five Short Stories.* Boston: Houghton Mifflin, 1959.

Rubin, Israel. *Satmar: Two Generations of an Urban Island.* 2nd ed. New York: Peter Lang, 1997.

Sack, Daniel. *Whitebread Protestants: Food and Religion in American Culture.* New York: Palgrave Macmillan, 2000.

Saiman, Chaim. "The Market for Gedolim: A Tale of Supply and Demand." *Lehrhaus*, October 13, 2016. http://www.thelehrhaus.com/scholarship/2016/10/12/the-market-for-gedolim.

Sales, Amy L. "Future of the Synagogue." *CCAR Journal*, Winter 2009.

Salkin, Jeffrey K. "Judaism Beyond Slogans," Commentary, January 17, 2018. https://www.commentarymagazine.com/articles/judaism-beyond-slogans/.

———. *The Modern Men's Torah Commentary*. Woodstock, VT: Jewish Lights, 2009.

———. *Searching for My Brothers*. New York: Putnam, 1999.

Sarna, Jonathan D. *American Judaism: A History.* New Haven, CT: Yale University Press, 2004.

———. "New Light on the Pittsburgh Platform of 1885." *American Jewish History*, March 1987.

Sarna, Michelle Waldman. "An Emerging Approach to Emerging Adulthood and Modern Orthodoxy." In Hain, *Next Generation of Modern Orthodoxy.*

Sarna, Yehuda. "The End of the Middle of the Road." In Hain, *Next Generation of Modern Orthodoxy.*

Sasson, Theodore. *The New American Zionism*. New York: New York University Press, 2014.

Schacter, Jacob J. "Halakhic Authority in a World of Personal Autonomy." In *Radical Responsibility: Celebrating the Thought of Chief Rabbi Lord Jonathan Sacks*, edited by Michael J. Harris, Daniel Rhynold, and Tamra Wright. London: Maggid Books, 2013.

Schick, Marvin. *A Census of Jewish Day Schools in the United States, 2013–14.* New York: Avi Chai Foundation, 2014.

Schwartz, Jim, Jeffrey Scheckner, and Laurence Kotler-Berkowitz. "Census of U.S. Synagogues, 2001." *American Jewish Year Book* 102 (2002).

Schwarz, Sidney. *Finding a Spiritual Home: How a New Generation of Jews Can Transform the American Synagogue*. Woodstock, VT: Jewish Lights, 2000.

———, ed. *Jewish Megatrends: Charting the Trends of the American Jewish Future.* Woodstock, VT: Jewish Lights, 2013.

Shapiro, Mark Dov. "The God Survey." *Reform Judaism*, Summer 2012. http://www.reformjudaism.org/god-survey.

Sheskin, Ira M. "2014 Greater Miami Jewish Federation Population Study: A Portrait of the Miami Jewish Community." Greater Miami Jewish Federation, 2014. http://www.jewishdatabank.org/Studies/downloadFile.cfm?FileID=3225.

Shevitz, Susan L., and Marion Gribetz. "The Power of Their Commitments: Lessons for the Jewish Community from a Small Synagogue School." In Wertheimer, *Learning and Community*.

Shokeid, Moshe. *A Gay Synagogue in New York*. Philadelphia: University of Pennsylvania Press, 1995.

Siegel, Sharon R. *A Jewish Ceremony for Newborn Girls: The Torah's Covenant Affirmed*. Lebanon, NH: Brandeis University Press, 2014.

Silber, Michael K. "The Emergence of Ultra Orthodoxy: The Invention of a Tradition." In *The Uses of Tradition: Jewish Continuity in the Modern Era*, edited by Jack Wertheimer. Cambridge, MA: Harvard University Press and JTS, 1992.

Silverman, Gila S. "'I'll Say a Mi Sheberach for You': Prayer, Healing and Identity among Liberal American Jews." *Contemporary Jewry* 36 (2016).

———. "Multiple Judaisms and Mosaic Selves: An Ethnographic Exploration of Liberal American Jews." *Culture and Religion* 17 (2016).

Sinclair, Betsy. *The Social Citizen: Peer Networks and Political Influence*. Chicago: University of Chicago Press, 2012.

Singer, Howard. "The Judaism Born in America." *Commentary*, December 1, 1986. https://www.commentarymagazine.com/articles/the-judaism-born-in-america/.

Sivan, Emanuel. "The Enclave Culture." In Marty and Appleby, *Fundamentalisms Comprehended*.

Sklare, Marshall. *Conservative Judaism: An American Religious Movement*. Glencoe, IL: Free Press, 1955.

Sklare, Marshall, and Joseph Greenblum. *Jewish Identity on the Suburban Frontier: A Study in Group Survival in the Open Society*. Chicago: University of Chicago Press, 1979.

Smart, Michal, and Barbara Ashkenas, eds. *Kaddish: Women's Voices*. Jerusalem: Urim, 2013.

Soloveitchik, Haym. "Rupture and Reconstruction: The Transformation of Contemporary Orthodoxy." *Tradition* 28, no. 4 (1994).

Sussman, Lance. "The Myth of the Trefa Banquet: American Culinary Culture and the Radicalization of Food Policy in American Reform Judaism." *American Jewish Archives Journal* 57 (2005).

Tabory, Ephraim. "The Piety of Politics: Jewish Prayers for the State of Israel." In *Liturgy in the Life of the Synagogue: Studies in the History of Jewish Prayer*, edited by Ruth Langer and Steve Fine. Winona Lake, IN: Eisenbrauns, 2005.

Tapper, Aaron Joshua. "The 'Cult' of Aish HaTorah: 'Baalei Teshuva' and the New Religious Movement Phenomenon." *Jewish Journal of Sociology* 44, nos. 1–2 (2002).

Tarle, Daniel Aaron. "Community Built upon Relationships: How Moishe House Engages the Millennial Generation." Master's thesis, USC and Hebrew Union College, December 2013.

Tarshish, Alan. "How 'Central' Is the CCAR?" *CCAR Journal* 8 (January 1960).

Tavory, Ido. *Summoned: Identification and Religious Life in a Jewish Neighborhood.* Chicago: University of Chicago Press, 2016.

Trencher, Mark. "The Nishma Research Profile of American Modern Orthodox Jews." West Hartford, CT: Nishma Institute, September 28, 2017.

———. "Starting a Conversation: A Pioneering Survey of Those Who Have Left the Orthodox Community: An Exploration of Journeys, Practices, Beliefs, Identity, Community and Relationships—Across Chasidic, Yeshivish and Modern Orthodox Segments." West Hartford, CT: Nishma Institute, June 19, 2016.

Troy, Tevi. "I Think I Shall Never See a Jew as Lovely as a Tree." *Commentary,* February 2015. https://www.commentarymagazine.com/articles/i-think-that-i-shall-never-see-a-jew-as-lovely-as-a-tree/.

Turetsky, Yehudah, and Chaim I. Waxman. "Sliding to the Left: Contemporary American Modern Orthodoxy." *Modern Judaism* 31, no. 2 (2011).

UJA-Federation of New York. "Jewish Community Study of New York, 2011." 2011.

———. "Stepping in to Engage Jewish Millennials: Understanding the New Generation of Young Adults." March 2016. http://ejewishphilanthropy.com/wordpress/wp-content/uploads/2016/03/Insights-and-Strategies-for-Engaging-Jewish-Millennials.pdf.

Ukeles, Jacob, and Associates. "What Does the Future Hold? The 2010 Greater Baltimore Jewish Community Study." The Associated, 2011. http://www.jewishdatabank.org/studies/downloadFile.cfm?FileID=2721.

Vincent, Leah. *Cut Me Loose: Sin and Salvation after My Ultra-Orthodox Girlhood.* New York: Doubleday, 2014.

Waxman, Chaim I. "Israel in Orthodox Identity: The American Experience." In Ben-Moshe and Segev, *Israel, the Diaspora, and Jewish Identity.*

———, ed. *Religious Zionism Post Disengagement: Future Directions.* New York: Orthodox Forum, 2008.

Waxman, Dov. *Trouble in the Tribe: American Jewish Conflict over Israel.* Princeton, NJ: Princeton University Press, 2016.

Waxman, Mordecai, ed. *Tradition and Change: The Development of Conservative Judaism.* New York: Burning Bush Press, 1958.

Wechsler, Harold, and Cyd Beth Weissman. "Belonging Before Belief." In Wertheimer, *Learning and Community.*

Weinberg, Rob. "Six Faces of Synagogue Success." *Reform Judaism*, Special Issue on Strengthening Congregations, 2014. http://www.urj.org/sites/default/files/Strengthening_Synagogues_FINAL_0.pdf.

Weinberger, Moses. *Jews and Judaism in New York.* Translated by Jonathan Sarna as *People Walk on Their Heads.* New York: Holmes and Meier, 1982.

Weiss, Avi. "Open Orthodoxy! A Modern Orthodox Rabbi's Creed." *Judaism* 46, no. 4 (1997).

Wenger, Beth. "The Politics of Women's Ordination: Jewish Law, Institutional Power, and the Debate over Women in the Rabbinate." In *Tradition Renewed,* vol. 2, edited by Jack Wertheimer. New York: Jewish Theological Seminary, 2008.

Wenzel, Nikolai G. *Postmodernism and Religion: The Oxford Handbook of the Sociology of Religion.* Oxford: Oxford University Press, 2011.

Wertheimer, Jack. "American Jews and Israel—A Sixty Year Retrospective." *American Jewish Year Book* 108 (2008).

———. "The American Synagogue: Recent Trends and Issues." *American Jewish Year Book* 105 (2005).

———, ed. *The American Synagogue: A Sanctuary Transformed.* Cambridge: Cambridge University Press, 1987.

———. "Between 'West Point Standards' and Life in the Trenches: The Halakhic Dilemmas of Orthodox Outreach Workers." In Meyer and Myers, *Between Jewish Tradition and Modernity.*

———. *A Census of Jewish Supplementary Schools in the United States, 2006–07.* New York: Avi Chai Foundation, 2007.

———, ed. *Learning and Community: Jewish Supplementary Schooling in the Twenty-First Century.* Lebanon, NH: Brandeis University Press, 2009.

———. *Linking the Silos: How to Accelerate the Momentum in Jewish Education Today.* New York: Avi Chai Foundation, 2005.

———, ed. *Jews in the Center: Conservative Synagogues and Their Members.* New Brunswick, NJ: Rutgers University Press, 2000.

———. *A People Divided: Judaism in Contemporary America.* New York: Basic Books, 1993. Reprint, Lebanon, NH: Brandeis University Press, 1997.

Wertheimer, Jack, and Steven M. Cohen. "The Pew Survey Reanalyzed—More Gloomy News but a Glimmer of Hope." *Mosaic*, November 2015. http://mosaicmagazine.com/essay/2014/11/the-pew-survey-reanalyzed/.

Winston, Hella. *Unchosen: The Hidden Lives of Hasidic Rebels*. Boston: Beacon, 2006.

Wolfson, Ron. *Relational Judaism: Using the Power of Relationships to Transform the Jewish Community*. Woodstock, VT: Jewish Lights, 2013.

Wuthnow, Robert. *After the Baby Boomers: How Twenty- and Thirty-Somethings Are Shaping the Future of Religion*. Princeton, NJ: Princeton University Press, 2007.

———. *After Heaven: Spirituality in America since the 1950s*. Berkeley: University of California Press, 1998.

———. *All in Sync: How Music and Art Are Revitalizing American Religion*. Berkeley: University of California Press, 2003.

Yoffie, Eric H. "Commentary on the Principles for Reform Judaism." Presented at the Central Conference of American Rabbis, October 27, 2004. https://ccarnet.org/rabbis-speak/platforms/commentary-principles-reform-judaism/.

———. "Foreword." In Kaplan, *Reform Judaism*.

Zakutinsky, Chaim Avraham. *Umekarev Beyemin: iyunim besheelot shmitorrerot etzel eleh sheoskim bekiruv rechokim*. Flushing, NY: Hasheveinu, 2011.

Zollman, Joellyn Wallen. "Shopping for a Future: A History of the American Synagogue Gift Shop." PhD dissertation, Brandeis University, 2002.

Zuckerman, Phil. *Strife in the Sanctuary: Religious Schism in a Jewish Community*. Lanham, MD: AltaMira Press, 1999.

Index